PUBLIC RIGHTS, PRIVATE RELATIONS

Public Rights, Private Relations

JEAN THOMAS

OXFORD
UNIVERSITY PRESS

OXFORD
UNIVERSITY PRESS

Great Clarendon Street, Oxford, OX2 6DP,
United Kingdom

Oxford University Press is a department of the University of Oxford.
It furthers the University's objective of excellence in research, scholarship,
and education by publishing worldwide. Oxford is a registered trade mark of
Oxford University Press in the UK and in certain other countries

First Edition published in 2015

Published in the United States of America by Oxford University Press
198 Madison Avenue, New York, NY 10016, United States of America

British Library Cataloguing in Publication Data
Data available

Library of Congress Control Number: 2015933892

ISBN 978–0–19–967773–3

Jacket image: © Shutterstock

To my beloved father,
Brian Thomas (1939–2014)

Acknowledgements

I have benefited from the insights and support of many people in writing this book. Foremost among these were my teachers and mentors at New York University School of Law, where I developed the initial ideas. Jeremy Waldron, Liam Murphy, and Samuel Scheffler were each immensely generous with their time and comments, and I am deeply grateful to each of them. I am enormously indebted to the late Ronald Dworkin, whose Colloquium Seminar in Legal, Political, and Moral Philosophy was my introduction to graduate study in law, and whose dedication to teaching, scholarship, and justice continue to inspire me. The JSD program at NYU, directed by Joseph Weiler, was a wonderful home for me, and my thinking was enriched by all my peers and colleagues over many weeks of workshops, coffees, and colloquia.

I developed the ideas in the book thanks to a post-doctoral fellowship at Stanford University's McCoy Family Center for Ethics in Society. Thanks to everyone at the Center, especially Debra Satz and Rob Reich, and to the participants in the weekly workshop in Political Theory, especially to Joshua Cohen. I also benefited from the opportunity to engage with my fellow Max Weber Fellows at the European University Institute.

Many thanks to Les Green, for introducing me to legal philosophy and for his friendship and support. I owe the greatest debt to Denise Réaume, for encouraging, challenging, teaching, and supporting me from the first day of law school, and of course for teaching me torts.

I am immensely grateful to my family, for believing in me, and for their generous support, and to Nicolas, for everything.

Contents

Table of Cases

Table of Legislation

List of Abbreviations

CAT	Convention against Torture and Other Cruel, Inhuman or Degrading Treatment or Punishment
CED	International Convention for the Protection of All Persons from Enforced Disappearance
CEDAW	Convention on the Elimination of All Forms of Discrimination against Women
CMW	International Convention on the Protection of the Rights of All Migrant Workers and Members of Their Families
CPD	Convention on the Rights of Persons with Disabilities
CRC	Convention on the Rights of the Child
ECHR	European Court of Human Rights
ICCPR	International Covenant on Civil and Political Rights
ICERD	International Convention on the Elimination of All Forms of Racial Discrimination
ICESCR	International Covenant on Economic, Social and Cultural Rights
UDHR	Universal Declaration of Human Rights

Introduction to the Argument

> *Betwixt subject and subject, they will grant there must be measures, laws and judges, for their mutual peace and security: but as for the* ruler *he ought to be* absolute, *and is above all such circumstances; because he has power to do more hurt and wrong, it is right when he does it. To ask how you may be guarded from harm, or injury, on that side where the strongest hand is to do it, is presently the voice of faction and rebellion: as if when men quitting the state of nature entered into society, they agreed that all of them but one, should be under the restraint of laws, but that he should still retain all the liberty of the state of nature, increased with power, and made licentious by impunity. This is to think, that men are so foolish, that they take care to avoid what mischiefs may be done them by* pole-cats, *or* foxes; *but are content, nay, think it safety, to be devoured by* lions.
>
> Locke[1]

There are two ways of looking at Locke's idea in section 93 of his *Second Treatise of Government*. The first is the conventional interpretation, and, to be fair, the meaning he intended. There is a difference between subjects and ruler: the ruler has the power of law and is therefore a lion among foxes. To allow for unrestrained government, therefore, is to allow the subjects to be devoured. This is the idea taken up by political philosophy since Locke, and, until fairly recently, there has been little reason to take another meaning from the passage. But if we leave aside the dominant interpretive context of governor and governed, we can observe that the concern about the ruler is *because* of the concern 'to ask how you may be guarded from harm, or injury, *on that side where the strongest hand is to do it*'.[2] The first interpretation views the zoological simile as naturally mapping onto the ruler/ruled relationship, while the second focuses on the simile itself: lions are to be constrained not because they are lions, but because they are, relative to pole-cats and foxes, *un*restrained in their ability to 'harm, or injure'. And the simile is misleading in another way as well: lions are *naturally* more powerful than foxes or polecats; the state is *made* powerful, at least in part, by the acquiescence of the

[1] John Locke, *Second Treatise of Government (1690)*, ed C. B. Macpherson (Indianapolis: Hackett Publishing Company, Inc, 1980).

[2] Locke, *Second Treatise of Government (1690)*, 50.

governed in the renunciation of their force-right to defend their interests. The state *becomes* the lion through its increase in power and because it is 'made licentious by impunity'. This means that if we leave aside the formal designation of political stations and look at the situation in which individuals in the modern world find themselves, we might identify the lions among us slightly differently: we might say that those who have the 'power to do more hurt and wrong' are the modern lions and that the kinds of constraints Locke had in mind to restrain the government ought to apply to them too so that people continue to be 'guarded from harm, or injury, on that side where the strongest hand is to do it'.

States are powerful because they are made powerful by social forces and practices, including laws and the acquiescence of citizens in being governed by them. But law, and especially private law, has created another kind of modern lion. These lions become powerful by the acquisition of property, and their power is reinforced by private laws that protect property rights. Modern lions are also made powerful by international social practices: trade practices, corporate practices, and international institutions all contribute to creating private agents who have the kind of capacity to hurt and injure that Locke thought ought to be restrained. If, in order to keep her job, for example, a woman is forced to prove she is menstruating every month to her factory supervisor; if she sleeps in a small room with twelve other women on the floor, all of whom work eleven-hour days six or seven days a week; if these women are effectively unprotected in these conditions by the regulations of her state's government against the web of contracts through which profit flows up to giant multinational corporations; under such circumstances even Locke might agree that the state may more aptly be described as the fox, and the corporate giant as the lion.

This kind of interpretation of the modern world has led many advocates, lawyers, scholars, and concerned individuals to the conclusion that there ought to be constraints against the modern lions just as there are against the state. The constraints we have against the state, in our modern world, are constitutional and human rights—I will use the phrase 'public law rights' to denote this class of rights against the state.[3] In order to fully take notice of the changed situation in which individuals find themselves in this century, therefore, the rights individuals hold against states must, in order to provide meaningful protection of individuals from harm and injury, be *directly* imposed on the modern lions to constrain their conduct and the way it affects us. It is this basic normative position that I assume in what follows: our most fundamental rights ought to protect us against violations by powerful actors no matter whether those actors are states or not. Having made that assumption, this book takes up the question of *how* such fundamental rights might justifiably be applied to non-state actors, and develops a theoretical framework for such application.

[3] I will use this phrase, 'public law rights', a great deal in what follows, at varying levels of technicality. I mean simply to denote our rights against the state that are considered most fundamental; although this group could include rights in more particular areas of public law such as administrative law, constitutional and human rights are the most pertinent class of these fundamental rights.

I. Why (Public Law) Rights?

One initial question we might ask about this assumption is: why *rights*? Rights, after all, seem to have become problematic: they have proliferated to the point where they are becoming less and less meaningful, they are difficult to enforce at the international level, and their claim to universality has become shaky.[4] Some suggest that the problem of modern lions might be better handled by regulation with reference to the *values* of constitutional and human rights.[5] But rights have certain advantages that other approaches lack. Rights—at least, the public law rights that I will be focusing on here—protect individuals against a powerful agent, namely, the state. Rights thus have a function that is structurally distinct from values: values are pursued *by* the state, whereas rights constrain the kinds of actions the state can take in pursuit of those values. Rights protect vulnerable individuals at the precise point where the state *cannot* or *will not* protect them. So the protection of individuals associated with the importance of public law rights ought not to be left to ordinary political processes such as regulation, even regulation in the name of important values. It is the very nature of constitutional and human rights, after all, to set a standard by which such regulations are to be judged. To say that states can or should regulate to protect individuals in workplaces, prisons, or in their ability to survive in the modern state can mean to put the fox in charge of the henhouse. Constitutional and human rights are not always strictly enforced, to be sure, but that does not render them meaningless: they are, by virtue of being above ordinary political and regulatory processes, the moral standards that we use to judge conduct, and the means to shame those treating people in the worst possible ways. They offer a normative vocabulary for holding the powerful to account and for the articulation of the most minimal standards of decency in the treatment of others.

Furthermore, private actors operate in an arena that is itself already defined by rights, namely, private law rights: corporations, property owners, and contractual powers are all created and sustained by rights. To create effective tools for the protection of individuals within that environment, those tools must be the kind of thing that the private law context can work with and recognize. They must, in other words, be *cognizable* within the private law environment. Moreover, introducing rights into a context that is already suffused with rights means that the reasonably well understood—albeit difficult—process of rights balancing is possible for guarding the interests of those who will be affected by the new protections.

This discussion of applying public law rights to private actors against the background of Locke's concern about the danger of the 'lions' among us could inspire

[4] Carl Wellman, *The Proliferation of Rights: Moral Progress or Empty Rhetoric?* (Boulder, Colorado: Westview Press, 1999); Mark Tushnet, 'An Essay on Rights', *Texas Law Review* 62 (1984): 1363.

[5] See, for an extensive elucidation of the shared values between 'public' and 'private', Dawn Oliver, *Common Values and the Public–Private Divide* (London: Butterworths, 1999).

another way of thinking about the problem that I wish to address before proceeding. I have so far discussed the application of *public* law rights to private actors, and I will, in the course of the book, develop an extrapolative approach to 'reconstructing' core public law rights in the private sphere. But from a Lockean standpoint, we might naturally think about rights the other way round, as it were: that is, we might think that rights are fundamentally 'private' ones individuals have in virtue of their personhood, their capacity for self-ownership, and thus held primarily against one another. Locke's argument for restraining and constraining the state follows this structure, where private rights come first. On his view, we have certain moral rights pre-politically that we cannot renounce on our entry to civil and political society. A person cannot give up what he does not have, and no one, so Locke argues, has the right to give away or otherwise alienate his natural rights.[6] The state, therefore, in order for people to be able to consent to it, must be limited, even at its inception, on the basis of these rights.

So Locke makes an extrapolative kind of argument about rights, as do I but its structure is the reverse of the one I will suggest. And to the extent that we have had any theory of where rights against the state come from, it has predominantly had this Lockean structure, where the state is constrained because individuals have natural or pre-political rights. Public law rights are built up out of these fundamental moral rights, on this reasoning, and so we might wonder why we would need an extrapolative argument of the kind I am suggesting, that goes *through* public law rights to create new private ones. Why not just bypass public law rights altogether, and follow Locke's argument where it might seem to lead naturally: that is, to assert that the moral rights we have in the state of nature against other private actors simply ought to be applied more thoroughly and extensively, following that Lockean insight to its conclusion.

There are several reasons why this apparently attractive approach is unworkable, but the central problem is that the picture Locke presents is essentially a mythical one, based on the heuristic device of the state of nature. In that imagined setting, Locke has to simply assert the content of the rights he thinks exist, based on the moral importance of the person. This way of thinking seems attractive precisely because our contemporary rights discourse still thinks of rights largely in terms of the moral importance of the individual person, either through his or her moral status or through the importance of his or her interests and ultimate intrinsic value. But our contemporary way of thinking about rights is in fact based on a much more complex, nuanced, and ultimately realistic picture of the person and what is important to, and about, him or her, than Locke's myth can explain. We have developed public law rights through a long process of social practice that has evolved incrementally, identifying and enumerating human interests that are important to protect, and, in particular, to protect in the context of modern social life. The content of public law rights has evolved with the nature of the world in which the person finds him or herself; that evolved content is now part of what

[6] Locke, *Second Treatise of Government (1690)*, Chapter. XI, section 135, 70.

we take our human and constitutional rights to be and to mean, and the mythical nature of the structurally Lockean approach to better protecting private actors against one another is thus fatal to it.

II. The Waning of the Modern State

Before I proceed to spell out my approach in more detail, a few illustrations of the problem may help to contextualize the discussion. Why do we need new private law rights? Why are the interests protected by human rights under threat in new ways? It is often said that the reason is privatization or globalization or both—but what does that actually mean? How does that translate into infringements of people's interests that are in some way not accounted for by existing public law rights? We can think of the factory fires and collapses in Bangladesh for one recent example of the situation. Another problematic situation arises more systematically. Many developing countries seek foreign investment by creating incentives for corporations to operate within their borders. These incentives often consist of tax benefits and sometimes of infrastructure and even police and military support to make their operation possible. One common tool used by states is to create what is called an export-processing zone, which is an area of preferential tax conditions within the borders of the state. Manufacturers contract with multinational corporations and then operate within these zones to avoid certain kinds of liability and regulation. Since the countries involved are often so impoverished, it is not difficult for the contracting factories to find people—often the rural poor—who are desperate enough to be willing to work under any conditions whatsoever and to bring them into the zones. This means that the corporations get the benefit not only of tax and trade preferences but of cheap labour, so that they can focus their expenditures on brand development and market competitiveness. As Naomi Klein pointed out in an early and seminal description of the problem, 'Fear pervades the zones. The governments are afraid of losing their foreign factories; the factories are afraid of losing their brand-name buyers; and the workers are afraid of losing their unstable jobs.'[7]

Although they certainly need the wages, however minimal and insufficient, the workers in these zones face manifold obstacles to decent treatment. The conditions there are well documented and described, but because the workers are there voluntarily, the right way to think about protecting them against abusive and degrading conditions has been problematic. For one thing, these people have human rights to decent treatment of various kinds both generally and in respect of employment that are clearly violated in such situations. But there is no accepted theory of corporate liability for these violations.[8] Even human rights advocates

[7] Naomi Klein, *No Logo* (New York: Picador, 2000), 206.

[8] For some discussion of human rights and the duties they ought to impose, see: Philip Alston and Katarina Tomasevski, *The Right to Food* (Netherlands: Martinus Nijhoff Publishers, 1984); Elizabeth Ashford, 'The Inadequacy of our Traditional Conception of the Duties Imposed by Human Rights', *Canadian Journal of Law and Jurisprudence* 19, no. 2 (2009): 217; Baez et al.,

have a difficult time conceptualizing *duties* for corporations in respect of these conditions; rather they resort to talking about the 'human rights impact' that corporate actors have.[9] In the absence of recognized duties in respect of those basic rights, advocates for the abused must refer to violations of corporations' *own* codes of conduct, accepted voluntarily by them and ignored at will.

To be sure, employment regulations exist in these countries, but they are routinely left unenforced, partly because of the desperation of governments for foreign investment, partly because of corruption, and partly because of the difficulty of attributing responsibility to those with real power. Corporations such as Nike, Gap, and Walmart deliberately structure their corporate operations so that they have as distant a legal relationship from the impact they have on the local

'Multinational Enterprises and Human Rights', U. Miami Int'l & Comp. L. Rev. 8 (1999–2000): 183; Ilias Bantekas, 'Corporate Social Responsibility in International Law', *Boston University International Law Journal* 22, no. 2 (2004): 309–47; Adolf A. Berle, 'Constitutional Limitations on Corporate Activity—Protection of Personal Rights from Invasion Through Economic Power', *University of Pennsylvania Law Review* 100, no. 7 (1952); Erwin Chemerinsky, 'Rethinking State Action', *Northwestern University Law Review* 80, no. 3 (1985): 503–57; Barbara Cochrane Alexander, 'Lack of Access to HIV/AIDS Drugs in Developing Countries: Is there a Violation of the International Human Rights to Health?', *Human Rights Brief* 8 (2001): 12; Dawn Oliver and Fedtke, *Human Rights and the Private Sphere: A Comparative Study* (New York: Routledge-Cavendish, 2007); Stephen Gardbaum, 'The "Horizontal Effect" of Constitutional Rights', *Michigan Law Review* 102 (2003): 1–91; Saby Ghoshray, 'Searching for Human Rights to Water Amidst Corporate Privatization in India: Hindustan Coca-Cola Pvt. Ltd. v. Perumatty Grama Panchayat', *Georgetown International Law Review* 19 (2006): 643; Peter H. Gleick, 'The Human Right to Water', *Water Policy* 1 (1998): 487; Abigail Gosselin, 'Global Poverty and Responsibility: Identifying the Duty-Bearers of Human Rights', *Human Rights Review* October–December (2006): 35–52; Ivar Kolstad, 'Human Rights and Assigned Duties: Implications for Corporations', *Human Rights Review* 10 (2009): 569–82; Andrew Kuper (ed), *Global Responsibilities: Who Must Deliver On Human Rights?* (New York: Routledge, 2005); Adam McBeth, 'Crushed by an Anvil: A Case Study on Responsibility for Human Rights in the Extractive Sector', *Yale Human Rights & Development Law Journal* 11 (2008): 127; Stephen C. McCaffrey, 'A Human Right to Water: Domestic and International Implications', *Georgetown Environmental Law Review* 5 (1992): 1; Julio Montero, 'Global Poverty, Human Rights and Correlative Duties', *Canadian Journal of Law and Jurisprudence* 22, no. 1 (2009); Aoife Nolan, 'Addressing Economic and Social Rights Violations by Non-State Actors through the Role of the State: A Comparison of Regional Approaches to the Obligation to Protect', *Human Rights Law Review* 9 (2009): 2; Steven R. Ratner, 'Corporations and Human Rights: A Theory of Legal Responsibility', *The Yale Law Journal* 111, no. 3 (2001): 443–545; Andras Sajo and Renata Uitz, *The Constitution in Private Relations: Expanding Constitutionalism* (Utrecht, The Netherlands: Eleven International Publishing, 2005); John Scalon, Angela Cassar, and Naomi Nemes, 'Water as a Human Right', *IUCN Envtl. Policy & Law Paper* 51 (2004); Amartya Sen, 'The Right Not to Be Hungry', in *The Right to Food*, International Studies in Human Rights (Netherlands: Martinus Nijhoff Publishers, 1984); Thomas Pogge, *Freedom from Poverty as a Human Right: Who Owes What to the Very Poor?* (Oxford: Oxford University Press, 2007); G. G. A. Tzeutschler, 'Corporate Violator: The Alien Tort Liability of Transnational Corporations for Human Rights Abuses Abroad', *Colum. Human Rights L. Rev.* 30 (1998): 359; Stephen G. Wood and Brett G. Scharffs, 'Applicability of Human Rights Standards to Private Corporations: An American Perspective', *The American Journal of Comparative Law* 50 (2002): 531–66; Florian Wettstein, *Multinational Corporations and Global Justice: Human Rights Obligations of a Quasi-Governmental Institution* (Stanford: Stanford University Press, 2009); George Andreopolous, Zehra F. Kabasakal Arat, and Peter Juviler (eds), *Non-State Actors in the Human Rights Universe* (Connecticut: Kumarian Press, Inc, 2006).

9 Human Rights Watch, 'On the Margins of Profit', February 18, 2008, <http://www.hrw.org/en/reports/2008/02/18/margins-profit-0>; Ashford, 'The Inadequacy of our Traditional Conception of the Duties Imposed by Human Rights'.

workforce and populations as possible.[10] They do not own the factories; they do not even contract with them directly. They exist in fact at many levels of contractual remove from conditions and conduct in the actual places where the goods they profit from are produced. Klein points to Disney spokesman Ken Green's frustration that Disney was being 'taken to task for the desperate conditions in a Haitian factory that produces Disney clothes. "We don't employ anyone in Haiti," he said, referring to the fact that the factory is owned by a contractor.'[11] Yet, in the web of manufacturing contracts and factories, it is the multinationals who have the power of choice among contractors and governments desperate for their investment, and who therefore have the greatest control over the whole chain of operation. This means that the zones are effectively non-state areas themselves, and yet no particular private actor owns them, so they cannot be construed as privately owned towns. They are, as Klein illustrates,

> a tax-free economy, sealed off from the local government of both town and province—a miniature military state inside a democracy... The EPZs... exist within a kind of legal and economic brackets, apart from the rest of their countries—[one such zone], for example, is under the sole jurisdiction of the Philippines' federal Department of Trade and Industry; the local police and municipal government have no right even to cross the threshold. The layers of blockades serve a dual purpose: to keep the hordes away from the costly goods being manufactured inside the zone, but also, and perhaps more important, to shield the country from what is going on inside the zone.[12]

But the problem is not only one of a lack of regulation and enforcement: even leaving these practical difficulties aside, there is a moral argument for establishing direct rights and obligations among private actors in respect of fundamental rights. Human and constitutional rights express a distinct level of concern; a standard against which institutions are measured. Currently, human rights complaints can only be made against states. But in the context of a woman working in an export-processing zone in Guatemala, for example, where her privacy and dignity are violated almost constantly, it seems wrong even at a moral level to say that the problematic relationship—the one in which she faces the real lion—is only and exclusively between her and the state of Guatemala. As Saskia Sassen points out, the state becomes an irrelevance in the face of corporate power; the zones are places where 'an actual piece of land becomes denationalized'.[13]

Relying on existing institutions and regulations to solve the problems created by the 'modern lions' thus not only faces practical difficulties in light of the power structures at work in the modern world of globalization—it also fails to recognize that the fact that these problems 'should' be governed by workplace regulation does not mean that those conditions are not *also* violations of human rights.

[10] Klein, *No Logo*, 197. [11] Klein, *No Logo*, 198. [12] Klein, *No Logo*, 206–7.

[13] Saskia Sassen, *Losing Control? Sovereignty in an Age of Globalization* (New York: Columbia University Press, 1996), 8–9.

III. The Problem of the Modern Lion

So far, I have referred to the problem I am concerned with only obliquely: I have pointed to Locke's attribution of rights to individuals against those to whom they are vulnerable; and I have described one context in which governments are less powerful than corporations. So the problem arises due to the increasing importance and power of non-state actors in many contexts of modern life. In the West, for example, our right to privacy is jeopardized not only by the NSA and other intelligence services, but also by Google and Facebook. Domestically as well as internationally, corporations have taken on an increasingly powerful role in social life; they have a growing impact on the lives of individuals, and their power has made them capable of threatening the very interests that, through the use of public law, we have been trying so hard to protect.[14] So, in other words, the interests protected by constitutional and human rights are becoming just as vulnerable to private agents as to states, and yet, as against these private agents, these interests are not understood to be rights and are often left unprotected. What follows is a small set of circumstances in which the problem of private impact on the interests protected by human and constitutional rights becomes dramatically clear. Human Rights Watch research provides numerous, though not exhaustive, examples of what it calls 'direct abuses carried out in a business context'.[15] Employers and transnational labour recruitment agents in Malaysia, Saudi Arabia, Singapore, the United Arab Emirates, and the United States have denied workers' freedom of movement by forcibly confining them and confiscating their passports or other identity papers.[16]

A company security force in Indonesia has used intimidation tactics, beat several people, destroyed and stolen property, and detained villagers in an effort to silence opposition to the company's logging activities; such abuses have impeded, among other rights, the villagers' rights to property, to be free from arbitrary detention, and to exercise their freedoms of expression, association, and peaceful assembly.[17]

[14] For an institutional assessment of the reach of transnational corporations, see UNCTAD, *World Investment Report 2007: Transnational Corporations, Extractive Industries and Development* (New York: United Nations, 2007), online: UNCTAD <http://www.unctad.org/en/docs/wir2007_en.pdf>. For a discussion of the growing awareness of the problem from the standpoint of Corporate Social Responsibility, see Chip Pitts, 'The Drivers of CSR' in *Corporate Social Responsibility: A Legal Analysis* (Lexisnexis, 2009) 33–52.

[15] 'On the Margins of Profit'.

[16] Human Rights Watch, 'Swept Under the Rug', vol. 18, no. 7(C), July 2006, 73–6; Human Rights Watch, 'Help Wanted', vol. 16, no. 9(B), July 2004, 5, 26, 32–3, 40–2; Human Rights Watch, 'Bad Dreams', July 2004 Vol. 16, No. 5(E), 48–53, 58, 62, 76, 78; Human Rights Watch, 'Maid to Order: Ending Abuses against Migrant Domestic Workers in Singapore', vol. 17, no. 10(C), December 2005, 42–8, <http://hrw.org/reports/2005/singapore1205/singapore1205wcover.pdf>; Human Rights Watch, 'Building Towers, Cheating Workers', vol. 18, no. 8(E), November 2006, 38–9; Human Rights Watch, 'Hidden in the Home', vol. 13, no. 2(G), June 2001, 12–15,<http://www.hrw.org/reports/2001/usadom/usadom0501.pdf>.

[17] Human Rights Watch, 'Without Remedy', vol. 15, no. 1(C), January 2003, 33–46, <http://www.hrw.org/reports/2003/01/06/without-remedy>.

Businesses that run or partially staff detention facilities have been implicated in abuses of the right to freedom from ill treatment, for example, when private United States contractors at Abu Ghraib prison in Iraq were alleged to have engaged in acts of torture, rape, intimidation, and humiliation of detainees.[18] Private security guards in Burundi routinely have held hospital patients against their will in state hospitals until they have provided payment.[19] Supervisors of female agricultural workers in the United States, and of beauticians and domestic workers in Saudi Arabia, have allegedly raped and sexually assaulted workers.[20] Supervisors have beaten children working on Egypt's cotton plantations and in a multitude of industries in India.[21] Employers have made employees work in conditions that are degrading or life threatening in United States meat and poultry processing plants.[22] Employers have physically abused, psychologically tormented, sexually assaulted, and threatened bodily harm against women and child domestic workers in many counties, including Morocco, Singapore, and the United States.[23]

Transnational labour recruitment agencies based in Indonesia have confined prospective domestic workers at training facilities for months in overcrowded and unsanitary facilities where women have little or no access to health care, are deprived of adequate food and rest, and at times suffer physical and sexual abuse as well as anxiety and depression associated with their ill treatment.[24]

A United States energy company's diversion of large quantities of water left villagers in India with barely enough water to sustain themselves, sparking protests that were then systematically suppressed.[25] United States agricultural employers

18 Center for Human Rights and Global Justice, Human Rights First and Human Rights Watch, 'By the Numbers: Findings of the Detainee Abuse and Accountability Project', vol. 18, no. 2(G), April 2006, 6, 19–20, <http://hrw.org/reports/2006/ct0406/>.

19 Human Rights Watch, 'A High Price to Pay: Detention of Poor Patient's in Burundian Hospitals', vol. 18, no. 8(A), September 2006, 31–4, <http://hrw.org/reports/2006/burundi0906/burundi0906webwcover.pdf>.

20 Human Rights Watch, 'Fingers to the Bone: United States Failure to Protect Child Farmworkers' (New York: Human Rights Watch, 2000), 52, <http://www.hrw.org/reports/2000/frmwrkr/>; 'Bad Dreams: Exploitation and Abuse of Migrant Workers in Saudi Arabia', 57–63.

21 Human Rights Watch Children's Rights Project and Human Rights Watch/Asia, 'The Small Hands of Slavery: Bonded Child Labor in India' (New York: Human Rights Watch, 1996), 28–9, <http://hrw.org/reports/1996/India3.htm>, and testimonials in Chapter V, 'Children in Bondage', 65–161; Human Rights Watch, 'Underage and Unprotected: Child Labor in Egypt's Cotton Fields', vol. 13, no. 1(E), January 2001, 14–15, <http://www.hrw.org/reports/2001/egypt>/; 'Small Change: Bonded Child Labor in India's Silk Industry', vol. 15, no. 2(C), January 2003, 27–8, 34–5, <http://www.hrw.org/reports/2003/india/>.

22 Human Rights Watch, 'Blood, Sweat, and Fear: Workers' Rights in U.S. Meat and Poultry Plants' (New York: Human Rights Watch, 2005), <http://www.hrw.org/reports/2005/usa0105/>, see especially, Chapter IV, 'Worker Health and Safety in the Meat and Poultry Industry', 24–56.

23 Human Rights Watch, 'Swept Under the Rug: Abuses Against Domestic Workers Around the World', July 2006, 10–13, 16–20, <http://hrw.org/reports/2006/wrd0706/>; 'Hidden in the Home: Abuse of Domestic Workers with Special Visas in the United States', vol. 13, no. 2(G), June 2001, 12, 18–19, 21–2, <http://www.hrw.org/reports/2001/usadom/>.

24 Human Rights Watch, 'Help Wanted: Abuses against Female Migrant Domestic Workers in Indonesia and Malaysia', vol. 16, no. 9(C), July 2004, 33, 78, <http://hrw.org/reports/2004/indonesia0704/>.

25 Human Rights Watch, 'The Enron Corporation', 45–6, <http://www.hrw.org/reports/1999/enron/>.

have not provided child workers with adequate drinking water and sanitation facilities, with serious negative effects on the children's health.[26] Pollution from Nigeria's oil industry has severely affected the livelihood of local communities, ruining crops, destroying fishing grounds, and damaging drinking water supplies.[27]

Human Rights Watch, along with the many others who are trying to do something about these kinds of situations, describe 'corporate abuses' as failures of corporate social responsibility, and, more specifically, as failures of corporations to attend to the human rights *impact* of their business activities. The reason these advocates use such vague and weak language is that the well-developed rights norms of public law do not, as a legal matter, apply in relation to non-state actors; therefore no direct violations of human or constitutional rights by corporate actors can be established. Yet it is clear that *something* is wrong, as is evidenced by the determined use of human rights language to condemn non-state conduct that is degrading, abusive, humiliating, threatening, and even deadly.

There are a number of *diagnoses* of the problem I have been describing as that of the 'modern lion', each of which leads to a different kind of remedy. It seems to me that the problem itself, as well as the shortcomings of the existing remedies, is most clearly brought to light by the various different diagnoses, so I am going to proceed by first laying these out.

IV. Diagnosing the Problem

One aspect of the problem is that states are performing 'intrinsically' public or state-like functions by delegation—through contract or outright privatization—to corporations, leaving quintessentially state functions improperly constrained and supervised. Call this the *inadequate constraint of actors exercising public functions* diagnosis.

Another type of diagnosis takes the problem to be one of constitutional theory. The problems arising in the public consciousness, on this view, are only pointing out an oversight: the provisions of private law rules and the enforcement of those rules by the courts *are* actions of the state in a way we may so far have failed to notice. This diagnosis leads to the following remedy: all law, or all court orders, or both, should be brought under constitutional scrutiny. Call this the *failure of constitutional scrutiny* diagnosis.

A third important way of describing the situation is that crucial interests are going unprotected. This way of thinking says that people's interest in freedom from summary execution and torture, for instance, is radically under-protected when Shell, for example, can participate in the violation of those interests and have claims brought against it in the United States under the *Alien Tort Claims Act*

[26] Human Rights Watch, 'Fingers to the Bone', 2, 26–30.

[27] Human Rights Watch, 'The Price of Oil', HRW Index No. 1-56432-225-4 January 1999, 7, 53–74.

thrown out partly on the basis that its actions are insufficiently connected to a government to be eligible for accountability. Call this the *vulnerable valuable interest* diagnosis.

Now as I said, each diagnosis suggests a different remedy. Inadequate state constraint seems to be the main general diagnosis of the problem in North America. Arguments for reform there are directed at the doctrines that delineate the possible targets of constitutional scrutiny: 'governmental action' doctrine in Canada[28] and the 'state action' doctrine in the United States. In general, the idea behind the latter doctrine is that if a private actor does something that, if done by the state, would amount to a constitutional violation, then we ask whether, by some agreement or some fact (the offending action was taken by an individual acting in his or her capacity as an agent of the state) the action in question can be attributed *to* the state. One important variation on this approach goes one step beyond the requirement to find a sufficiently close nexus between the action and the state itself, and imputes certain types of actions with the categorical attribution of 'public function'. This has been the approach taken in the United Kingdom.

The second diagnosis and remedy of the problem, which we called *failure of constitutional scrutiny*, has been largely predominant in Europe, following the example of Germany. The German doctrine is known as *Drittwirkung*, which translates roughly as 'third-party effects', and stands for *Drittwirkung der Grundrechte*, or third party effects of fundamental rights. This doctrine was expressed by the German constitutional court in the 1958 *Lüth* case.[29] The case

[28] For some views of the Canadian 'governmental action' doctrine see Edward P. Belobaba, 'The Charter of Rights and Private Litigation: the Dilemma of Dolphin Delivery', in N. R. Finkelstein and B. M. Rogers (eds), *Charter Issues in Civil Cases* (Toronto: Carswell, 1988); Gordon P. Crann, 'How far does the Charter reach? A theoretical review of the section 32(1) debate and Canada's emerging "governmental action" doctrine', *U.T. Fac. L. Rev.* 47 (1988): 56; R. Eliot and R. Grant, 'The *Charter's* Application in Private Litigation', *University of British Columbia Law Review* 23 (1989): 459; Brian Etherington, 'Constitutional law—Charter of Rights and Freedoms, sections 2(b) and 1—Application of the Charter to the common law in private litigation—Freedom of expression—Picketing in labour disputes', (Case comm.) *Canadian Bar Review* 66 (1987): 818; Peter W. Hogg, 'The *Dolphin Delivery* Case: The Application of the *Charter* to Private Action', 51 *Saskatchewan Law Review* (1987): 273; Robert Howse, 'Dolphin Delivery: the Supreme Court and the public/private distinction in Canadian constitutional law', (Case comm.) 46 *University of Toronto Faculty of Law Review* (1988): 248–58; Allan C. Hutchinson and Andrew Petter, 'Private rights/public wrongs: the liberal lie of the Charter', 38 *University of Toronto Law Journal* (1988): 278; Michael Kanter, 'The Government action doctrine and the public/private distinction: searching for private action', 15 *Queen's Law Journal* (1990): 33; W. R. Lederman, 'Democratic Parliaments, Independent Courts, and the Canadian Charter of Rights and Freedoms', 11 *Queen's Law Journal* (1985–6): 1; Kate Sutherland, 'The New Equality Paradigm: The Impact of Charter Equality Rights on Private Law Decisions' in D. Schneiderman and K. Sutherland (eds), *Charting the Consequences: The Impact of Charter Rights on Law and Politics in Canada* (Toronto: University of Toronto Press, 1997), 245–70.

[29] BVerfG 15 January 1958, *BVerfGE* 7, 198 (*Lüth*). For more on the German context see for example Donald P. Kommers, *The Constitutional Jurisprudence of the Federal Republic of Germany*, 3rd ed, (Durham: Duke University Press, 2012); Kenneth M. Lewan, 'The Significance of Constitutional Rights for Private Law: Theory and Practice in West Germany', 17 *International & Comparative Law Quarterly* (1968): 571; Christian Starck, 'Human Rights and Private Law in German Constitutional Development and in the Jurisdiction of the Federal Constitutional Court' in Daniel Friemann and Daphne Barak-Erez (eds), *Human Rights in Private Law* (Portland, Oregon: Hart Publishing, 2001), as well as Olha Cherednychenko, 'The Constitutionalization of

involved a prominent film director of the Nazi era, Veit Harlan, who produced an anti-semitic propaganda film in 1940. Harlan produced another film in 1950, at which time Erich Lüth, a high-ranking public official, criticized Harlan for his involvement in the Nazi regime. Lüth wrote an open letter calling for a boycott of Harlan's new film. The producer and distributor of the film applied for an injunction to prevent Lüth from repeating his criticism, on the basis that Harlan had been acquitted of criminal charges in relation to the propaganda film. In response to the injunction, Lüth filed a constitutional complaint against the court order on the basis of Article 5(1), the free speech provision of the Basic Law. The court there distinguished between two possible positions. Under the first, it would accept the idea that the public and private legal spheres are completely separate and must develop independently of one another, so that constitutional law would have no bearing on private law.[30] Under the second, it would accept the idea that fundamental rights apply *directly* to private individuals, so that rights and obligations flowing from the protections for individuals constitutionally enumerated would obtain as between private parties. The court rejected both positions and instead articulated what has been considered a kind of middle ground.

Fundamental rights, on this view, protect all private persons but obligate only the state. This obligation, however, will find expression not only in legislative acts but in adjudicative ones, where civil court judges are balancing competing private interests. In those cases, where the civil law is not exclusively determinative—where it contains clauses of general interpretation or open-textured norms such as 'reasonability', 'good faith', 'legitimate interests', and 'good morals'—the court must turn to the constitution to give content to those clauses. The constitution, on this view, is considered to be a sphere of objective value such that its provisions ought to inform the spaces in private law left open to judicial interpretation. So, on this view, the fundamental rights expressed in the constitution do not apply directly to private litigation but must be taken account of by civil courts because the constitution is understood to be an overarching value system that must permeate all areas of the law. In the *Lüth* case, the injunction was found to be contrary to the private law principle of good faith.

Two important related points stand out in this approach to the application of public law rights. First, fundamental rights do not, on this model, bind private parties directly. They do not create relations of obligation directly between individuals or between private entities that are not the state. Second, these rights find their way into the private sphere because their *effects* are felt there when courts intervene in private disputes. Public law norms radiate into private law, in this model, not because public law rights are understood to bind private individuals but because *law*, as a creation of the state, is understood to be controlled by

Contract Law: Something New Under the Sun?', vol. 8.1 *Electronic Journal of Comparative Law*, (March 2004), <http://www.ejcl.org/81/art81-3.html>.

[30] See, for example, Amnon Reichman, 'A Charter-free domain: in defence of Dolphin Delivery', 35 *University of British Columbia Law Review* (2002): 329 and 'Property Rights, Public Policy and the Limits of the Legal Power to Discriminate' in *Human Rights in Private Law*.

constitutional values. This is why this kind of approach to the factual problem is sometimes referred to as the 'constitutionalization' of private law. On this view, wherever law is, there rights are too in some sense, since the constitution informs all law.

In the United States, something like this second diagnosis of the problem and its attendant remedy has been used to argue for the *reform* of the state action doctrine. One such proposed remedy of the problem would understand courts as agents of the state whenever they enforce legal rules. In other words, a court order is effectively an action of the state that ought to be subject to constitutional scrutiny, and this is no less true when such an order is made in a private law context. In one way, this is similar to the German approach, insofar as the latter takes constitutional norms to be given effect in civil law through the actions of courts. But whereas the German model seems to emphasize the idea that the constitution supervises all *law* as such, the American model takes the aim of the constitutional norms to be the state itself. In the American model constitutional rights could, in theory, apply to court orders because courts represent one branch of the state itself.

An example of the way this logic is used to argue for the extension of the state action doctrine is Seana Shiffrin's argument concerning the application of due process requirements to contract law.[31] Shiffrin argues that credit card late fees could be considered unconstitutional if we view their enforcement as an action taken by the state. So, for example, she has maintained—compellingly, I would add—that credit card late fee penalties should be brought under constitutional scrutiny because, after all, the contractual and statutory schemes that support the structure of the credit card industry are ultimately approved and passed by the government.

Shiffrin presses the argument a step further, highlighting the active role of the state in enabling these fees: 'the state', she says, 'does not merely allow these private arrangements but takes an active role in enforcing them'.[32] Late fees, she argues, are a form of punitive damages imposed on credit card customers for violating the terms of the borrowing agreement. Punitive damages are normally prohibited in the contract context, but are statutorily enabled for this purpose: 'State and federal legislatures enacted statutes and regulations to overcome the standard ban against punitive damages and punitive damage agreements for contractual breach in order to facilitate the business of banks, to attract their business to particular states, and in the case of the [National Bank Act,] to promote nationally-chartered banks.'[33] If the enforcement of such fees against customers by courts is considered state action then it would be subject to constitutional scrutiny. Shiffrin makes the substantive argument that such enforcement is not constitutional by referring to the line of cases finding that punitive damages in

[31] Seana Valentine Shiffrin, 'Are Credit Card Late Fees Unconstitutional?', 15 *William & Mary Bill of Rights Journal.* (2006): 457.

[32] Shiffrin, 'Are Credit Card Late Fees Unconstitutional?', 470.

[33] Shiffrin, 'Are Credit Card Late Fees Unconstitutional?', 471.

the tort context must satisfy a proportionality requirement in order to pass due process muster.[34]

Notice that in the kind of case in which Shiffrin diagnoses a failure of appropriate constitutional scrutiny we have two uncontroversially private parties—unlike on the *inadequate state constraint* diagnosis. Neither party, in other words, *is* the state, and it is not argued that the choices made by the credit card companies can be directly attributed *to* the state. This type of reformist argument is not so much about the state itself as it is about good and bad rules—this kind of argument says that these are bad—meaning unconstitutional—*rules* that are facilitated and enforced by the state. In my view, there are several problems with this approach.

First, notice that this 'hitherto unnoticed' call for constitutional scrutiny of certain kinds of rules won't be able to capture and describe the initial intuition I began with, involving the wrongness of what appear to be human rights violations occurring across borders by multinational corporations. The 'indirect effect' solution to the problem relies heavily on there being a constitutional order whose values can be shared by all the participants and expressed by the constitution. And at the very least, trying to apply this kind of solution to the human rights problem presents a whole variety of conflicts of laws problems—whose constitution is being misunderstood? Whose private law rules will be interpreted to give indirect effect to the relevant constitutional norms, assuming we can identify them?

But, for the sake of argument, assume we could construct solutions to those difficulties. We would be left with the 'bad rules' diagnosis of the problem. *This* outcome has two important shortcomings. First, rules—especially in the complex international arena—can be worked around. Remember the case of Disney's disavowal of any legal relation with employees making products bearing its brand in an export processing zone in Haiti. The whole *point* of these manufacturing areas is that they come as close as possible to legal black holes: *no one* is responsible for what goes on inside them. So it will be very difficult to pinpoint the 'bad rule' that make the abuses possible.

But this is an instrumental argument. The second problem with this type of 'bad rules' approach is that it does not fully describe the problem. It seems to me that what produces the moral intuition that something is going very wrong, in this context, is precisely that something *is* going wrong and that that thing is much simpler than a failure of constitutional theory: one party is wronging another. One party is, at a minimum, failing to treat another with the requisite regard. Fundamental rights, on this view of the problem—either expressed in constitutions or human rights declarations and instruments—are fleshing out *how*, in *what way*, in respect of *which aspects of well-being or dignity*, one party is mistreating the other.

[34] *State Farm Mutual Automobile Insurance Co. v. Campbell* 538 US 408 (2003) (finding that a punitive damage award of $ 145 million for a harm worth $ 1 million violated the due process clause of the Fourteenth Amendment); *Cooper Indus., Inc. v. Leatherman Tool Group, Inc.*, 532 US 424 (2001); *BMW of N. Am., Inc. v. Gore*, 517 US 559 (1996); *Honda Motor Co. v. Oberg*, 512 US 415 (1994); *Pac. Mut. Life Ins. Co. v. Haslip*, 499 US 1 (1991).

Just as we have state-based modes of prosecuting wrongs criminally that are appropriately parallel to a system of private claims that allow those same acts to be identified as being wrongs between two private parties as well as between the criminal and the state, it is simply inadequate to say in cases of degrading and abusive treatment that the problem is exhaustively described by reference to a failure of regulation alone.

This brings me to the final remedy: remember that the third type of diagnosis on the list was that important interests are going unprotected by new social and economic realities. The *vulnerable valuable interest* diagnosis of the problem seems to underlie arguments for corporate responsibility in relation to human rights in a legal environment in which *legal* responsibility, legal liability under international human rights law, for human rights violations, is still the near exclusive domain of states.[35] The report of the Special Representative of the Secretary-General of the United Nations for business and human rights, John Ruggie, on transnational corporations and their 'impact' on human rights,[36] emphasizes the role of states, since the participation of corporations themselves in policing the effects of their conduct is voluntary. The international interest in the problem seems to be a clear illustration of the idea that the interests articulated by human rights agreements and enumerations are extremely important. The remedy offered by these approaches is to try to articulate a space apart from direct legal liability that encourages corporations to behave better where their activities impact the interests articulated by human rights.

Now this diagnosis, at least, satisfies two features of the problem that I've just been arguing are central. It is, first, a moral diagnosis, describing a problem of human suffering and well-being—so far that makes it seem like it is getting to the heart of the matter. Second, because it's describing a moral state of affairs, instead of an institutional one, it works to describe human rights problems, international problems, problems that are so far not the subject of legal claims because there are so few existing legal mechanisms to address them. So those make it seem like a promising diagnosis.

The United Kingdom, fairly uniquely, has addressed this diagnosis perhaps most directly, by passing the *Human Rights Act 1998*, which came into effect in 2000, and made common law rules subject to judicial scrutiny on the basis of human rights articulated in the European Convention. Now since I said that human rights problems are captured by the 'unprotected interests' diagnosis of

[35] Arguments for legal mechanisms for protecting the interests articulated as rights against non-state actors in general, and against corporations in particular, is the subject of a vast literature. See, for two excellent examples, Philip Alston (ed), *Non-State Actors and Human Rights* (Oxford: Oxford University Press, 2005); Andrew Clapham, *Human Rights Obligations of Non-state Actors* (Oxford: Oxford University Press, 2006).

[36] See the 2011 report to the Human Rights Council of the United Nations: United Nations, Human Rights Council, Seventeenth Session, 21 March 2011, A/HRC/17/31, online at <http://www.business-humanrights.org/media/documents/ruggie/ruggie-guiding-principles-21-mar-2011.pdf>; see also the 2011 report on the implementation of the 'Promote, Respect and Remedy' Framework at <http://www.business-humanrights.org/media/documents/applications-of-framework-jun-2011.pdf>.

the problem, and since I said that that diagnosis seems in some ways closest to the truth, this approach might seem promising.

But of course opening up the range of interests that can be protected among private actors in this way is itself problematic: it is widely acknowledged as creating a vast raft of unmanageable new duties. So the United Kingdom combines *two* diagnoses of the problem in response. It says, first, that human rights ought to be somehow protected even under common law, addressing the vulnerability of the interests set out in the European Convention on Human Rights to violation by private actors. Manifesting the unconstrained state diagnosis, judges responded to this mandate with the intuition that the problem is the unconstrained state—except it is a more expansive variant—the 'public function'.[37] But even this combined diagnosis and remedy—that human rights obligations are justified only against actors performing public functions—doesn't solve the problem. Here is an explanation for this failure once offered by Steven Sedley. Sedley has been a Lord Justice of appeal for England and Wales and president of the British Institute for Human Rights. He considers that it might be necessary to 'start a family...of new duties to go with [the new rights]'.[38] This is because, as he says, the transition from vertical to horizontal application of rights involves a shift 'from restrictions on the power of the state to positive standards of human conduct'. And when we envisage 'rights as inhering between individual and individual', then 'responsibilities can begin to move in the same plane'.

But imposing this potentially vast new array of 'positive standards of conduct' on all individuals in virtue of one another's rights has left the British judiciary in the position of deciding what these standards are, and to whom they apply: the *HRA* uses what seems to be a functional and purposive formula for deciding this question, which 'places responsibilities on public authorities, leaving it to courts to enforce them'.[39] Sedley points out that this idea of responsibility bypasses a central area of human rights—'the institutional treatment of the vulnerable: old people, ill people, mentally and physically disabled people'.[40] If this test of 'public function' is the only principle for delineating the new duties associated with the horizontal application of constitutional and human rights, the judiciary is left, it seems, with vast discretion and what amounts to an exercise in line-drawing. In one instance cited by Sedley, the House of Lords held that 'the private care homes in which local authorities place elderly people are not fulfilling public functions and thus have no obligation to respect their patients' human rights'. In response to the problem he describes as the possible degradation of 'the protection afforded by law to vulnerable people', Sedley considers the possible merit of a charter of responsibilities, 'making it the duty of private as well as public care providers to respect...elementary rights'.[41] A charter setting out the duties

[37] Dawn Oliver describes the relevant section of the HRA, s. 6, as 'primarily concerned to give the Convention rights effect against "public authorities" and private bodies exercising function of a public nature' at 69, 'Chapter 2: England and Wales: The Human Rights Act and the Private Sphere' in Oliver and Fedtke (eds), *Human Rights and the Private Sphere*, 63–98.

[38] Stephen Sedley, 'No Ordinary Law' in the *London Review of Books*, vol. 30, June 2008.

[39] Sedley, 'No Ordinary Law', 20.

[40] Sedley, 'No Ordinary Law', 21.

[41] Sedley, 'No Ordinary Law', 21.

of care providers would be one improvement, but which other institutions would bear the same obligations, and who would decide this question?

The major problem with the 'unprotected interests' diagnosis, then, and the remedy of simply applying public law rights on the horizontal plane is this: if we accept that constitutional and human rights cannot apply only 'vertically' against the state, then the potential applicative scope of those rights expands exponentially. Even when we restrict the application of rights to the state, as has been the convention, each right generates a number of duties, such as non-interference, protection against violation by third parties, and possibly also positive measures to diminish the likelihood that rights will be violated.[42] If we now accept the horizontality principle, then each right will potentially generate all those duties on all other agents all the time. There is, in other words, no principled limitation for the applicative scope of these rights once we make the move from vertical to horizontal application.

And the public function limitation is not much help, partly because many functions will, as Sedley said, simply fall through the cracks. The idea of 'publicness', on this approach, seems to be either a substitute for functions we associate with the state because the state once performed them (hardly a principled distinction), or ones that the state somehow *ought* to perform.[43] The latter criterion might be taken to be a proxy for the importance of the interest perhaps. But as Sedley said, what about the interests of the vulnerable in particular?

V. A New Diagnosis, A New Remedy

In Chapter 1 I lay out in more detail the drawbacks of existing methods of applying public law rights to private interactions, and I try to show that in the end,

[42] This implication was given seminal philosophical justification in Henry Shue, *Basic Rights: Subsistence, Affluence, and U.S. Foreign Policy* (Princeton, New Jersey: Princeton University Press, 1980); it has been given contemporary institutional support by the Special Rapporteur for the Human Rights Council of the United Nations, John Ruggie, as discussed above, at note 38,

[43] In the German context, for instance, the idea of public function relates to the constitutional role of the welfare state. Individuals are understood to have certain social and economic needs in a modern state because they are unable to provide certain necessary goods for themselves. There is considerable debate about precisely which of such goods constitute public functions, but broadly speaking the state is required to make 'public provision for existence' (*Daseinsvorsorge*) including water supply, taking care of waste water and rubbish, building and cleaning streets, public transportation for short distances (subways, etc.), planning of geographic space and its real estate use, regulating the housing market, public banks, culture, schools and pre-schools, and security. These functions are considered to be *imposed* on the state constitutionally, so that it is not only limited in the way it can carry out these tasks but it is also largely prevented from wholly privatizing these services. So even if a private entity is carrying out some portion of such a service, its obligation in respect of fundamental rights flows from the fact that its activity is mandated by the positive requirements of the constitution. This idea brings us back to the first point I made about the German model, which is that all fundamental rights are understood to be imposed on the state. But in this context, those rights have both negative and positive implications and can thus have effects that radiate more substantially into the private sphere where the state's functions have been partially delegated to private entities.

the problem—however one diagnoses it—cannot be adequately solved without a direct confrontation of the underlying moral issue.

The problem is that one party is doing something wrong to another—in the case of fundamental rights, something badly wrong. But, one may ask, if the problem is cast in terms of the *moral* equities, what role is left for fundamental rights as positive law? In Chapter 2 I develop a method of argument that treats theory—moral theory in this case—and practice—namely, the practice of rights protection embodied in constitutional and human rights taken as positive law—as mutually informative and answerable to one another. Public law rights, on this view, have normative status even in moral theory—even when addressing the question of what exactly non-state actors owe one another as a moral matter. However, I argue that the best way to bring the practical achievements of rights discourse and rights consciousness to bear on the problems associated with privatization and globalization is not to apply public law rights to private relations directly. Rather, I use what I take to be the moral importance of public law rights to argue for a legal reform of *private* law doctrine that would recognize new *private* law rights. The content of these new rights would be derived through an extrapolative analysis from the set of fundamental public law rights.

My method is to look to the constitutional and human rights most widely accepted as an indication of certain moral commitments we have made in respect of rights. This set of public law rights I argue, represents our best understanding of what rights are and what is important about them. The set of public law rights can, therefore, be the basis for an extrapolative analysis in both a conceptual and a substantive sense: it gives us an indication about our best understanding of what *kind of thing* rights are, and also suggests the *range of interests* that we understand to be most important, to most clearly warrant the special protections associated with rights.

In developing my argument, however, I do not rely exclusively on the social practice of rights protection. Rather, in Chapters 3 and 4 I consider moral theory as well, drawing on the various attempts at conceptualizing what rights are. I treat theory and practice as operating in a reflective equilibrium, each informing and to some extent constraining the other. It is through an overall extrapolative analysis of both theory and practice that, in the following chapters, I develop a model of public law rights. I then use this model as a tool to abstract the moral structure of public law rights from the institutional context of public law, and to derive from it the content of new private legal obligations. One advantage of this approach is that it allows us to recognize public law rights in conceptual terms as basically similar to private law rights and to see how the moral structure of public law plays out in the private law context.

This now brings us to my own diagnosis of the problem and the remedy that will flow from it. One implicit feature of the three conventional diagnoses of the problem I laid out above—important interests being inadequately protected, appropriate constraints on state behaviour being evaded through delegation and privatization, and the significance of rights in the development and assessment of rules and policies being evaded—is that each one has a certain plausibility, a certain compellingness as a way of diagnosing the problem.

This point is suggestive of these different approaches: each takes the problem to be the inadequate protection of public law rights beyond the public sphere, but each conceptualizes public law rights in a way that overemphasizes only one element of what they are. One views public rights as being, and as justified by, a set of highly important interests that warrant special protection. Another takes them to be agreed-upon constraints on the pursuit of social goals, and the third takes them as setting out important constraints on the exercise of the power the state has over its citizens.

My own diagnosis is—*with* these others—that public law rights have been institutionally marginalized by social conditions. And I take those rights to represent the best existing moral practice expressing what each of us is entitled to by way of basic respectful treatment. But I diverge from conventional approaches—and from conventional theories of rights—in my conceptualization of public law rights. My approach is to construct a model of core public law rights that is three-dimensional. I point out the one-dimensionality of conventional accounts of rights in Chapter 3, and identify the drawbacks of focusing on a single feature of them in Chapter 4. In Chapter 5 I argue that it is conventional one-dimensional conceptualizations of *public law rights* in particular that create the problems of indeterminacy or overbreadth associated with conventional methods of applying public rights to private relations. The way we conceptualize a public law righ t is important, I argue, because extrapolating what is morally salient about it can answer further questions about what we owe one another in the private law context. Thus the concept of rights we use will determine our ability to translate public rights into the context of private relations. In Chapter 6 I argue that the problem of indeterminacy in public law rights is a manifestation of a conceptual problem of the same kind that plagues theories of rights more generally.

I go on in Chapter 7 to argue that every right consists of *three* elements: the interest it protects, the constraint it establishes to effect that protection even in the face of other important social goals, and the relational context in which it arises. So on my account, what public rights *are* involves values or interests deemed to be highly important, the constraint associated with the form of rights, and the moral features of the relational context of individual and state. And it is public rights, taken in *all* these three dimensions that are being inadequately protected in the private sphere.

The remedy that flows from this diagnosis and approach is to conclude that the special scrutiny of action associated with fundamental rights ought to obtain among private actors where, and only where, one of these core enumerated interests is at stake *and* where the relational context in which it is at stake has the same structure as the one between individual and state.

In Chapter 8 I lay out the particular relation—a conception of interpersonal dependency—that I claim is the relational context of public law rights. Dependency, in my analysis, has both a descriptive and a normative dimension.

It is both an accurate *characterization* of the individual's relation with the state, and its constitutive features are ones that appropriately attract moral scrutiny. In other words, dependency is what the relational context of public law rights *is*, and it also serves to justify the imposition of the duties associated with those rights on private actors as well as on the state.

Interpersonal dependency as I extrapolate it from the moral context of public law rights has several features. First, it is closely related to power and vulnerability, which are already widely taken to warrant special moral scrutiny in general. Interpersonal dependency isn't fundamentally different from the power-and-vulnerability way of thinking, in particular, of the relationship between individual and state; it is rather a more specific instantiation of that form that is more descriptive of relationality than is reference to power in general. So one can think of the dependency relation as a kind of species of the genus of power and vulnerability.

Dependency articulates a particular relation between parties rather than being, as power and vulnerability each are, simply an abstract description of a relational concept. In order to amount to a relation of dependency, both the parties to it—the controlling and the depending party—must be involved in the relation in a particular way. Dependency thus links parties specifically to one another in a way that is especially important for constructing a moral framework for interpersonal obligations.

Dependency consists of, first, agency and control over, second, the depending party's enjoyment of some good or interest. It obtains or occurs, third, within the context of an undertaking by the controlling party—an undertaking that includes the good or interest of the depending party in its scope. The undertaking is not a legal category, and dependency is not tied to a legal relation. The concept of the undertaking allows us to connect the interest of some party where that interest is threatened—say, the health of a nursing home patient—to the party whose undertaking both includes that interest reasonably within its scope and which allows the more powerful party to control the individual's ability to enjoy that good or interest. This means that the moral obligation will finally only obtain between the party whose enjoyment of the interest is threatened—the nursing home patient—and the party who in fact exercises the greatest agency over that patient's enjoyment of her health within the scope of the controlling party's undertaking. The connection between right-holder and duty-bearer can in this way be made no matter what the legal relation between them is or, as in the case of multinationals like Disney, is not. If the doctor or nurse making a given decision about transfer to a lower level of care has immediate decision-making power but does not make directing policies for the institution, that counts against the duty falling on the doctor. Moreover, the undertaking that makes the patient vulnerable in this particular way *to* the control of someone else is not the doctor's. The undertaking is more aptly attributed to the nursing home director or the board of directors (depending on the circumstances), who have the greatest agency over what goes on in the home.

Notice that these conditions for imposing rights scrutiny on private actors are ones that normally attract moral scrutiny: the restriction of the possible range of interests to the scope of the undertaking reflects the moral scrutiny that a) attaches to the exercise of agency or freedom in a given domain, and that b) is appropriate given that the existence of the undertaking itself indicates that some benefit is flowing to the party who is exercising their freedom by undertaking the activity in question.

This kind of analysis, connecting the elements of agency, control over a good or interest within a given scope as defined with reference to the more powerful party's activity, allows us to limit the range of duties that could arise simply in respect of the naked importance of interests. Take the human rights context, for example. If the only analytical framework we have is simple power and vulnerability, then, confronted with an interest—take health again—the right and obligation would have to fall, respectively, on the weakest and the most powerful parties in respect of that interest. The sickest, then, and those with the greatest power to improve those people's enjoyment of the good of health, would be the relevant candidates for right and obligation. But where do we begin with this as a moral limiting framework? Power tends to reside with the wealthy and with the politically powerful. So are ultra-rich individuals to bear the human rights obligations associated with the very sickest people around the world? It seems to me that this very utilitarian analysis might be a good way of structuring *some* institutions, *some* solutions to problems, but it does not, as a remedy for the problem of increased threat to fundamental rights, even capture the problem all that well.

It misses, crucially, two of the elements of public law rights I identified earlier and that are widely—and rightly, in my view—taken to justify them. Part of what rights *are* involves special constraints on conduct; a framework of power and vulnerability in respect of interests doesn't begin with *conduct*, as does the undertaking analysis within the dependency framework, so it misses this aspect of constraint. Fundamental rights, both constitutional and human rights, are widely and rightly taken to restrict two kinds of especially bad behaviour, whether associated with negative or positive duties—they are supposed to protect us against the very worst kinds of treatment and especially in the context of the abuse of power.

This is reflected in the dependency analysis in a way that it is not reflected in a power/vulnerability framework because, on my approach, simply *being powerful* is not enough to generate rights scrutiny of one's actions. Threats to important interests are scrutinized when they are generated by an exercise of power. It is to that extent that public law rights are *relational* in a strong sense.

The method I develop does not envision that constitutional rights apply, as a legal matter, to the private sphere either through application to private law itself or to the action of courts. Rather I advocate articulating new legal rights that are specifically *private* in nature. That is, the rights that would be created in private law on my model are ones that would be held by private individuals against other private individuals. To contrast the application of this model with that of Shiffrin in this respect, the credit card company would, on my account, be obligated directly by the rights of the customer rather than simply being constrained with respect to the manner in which it can enforce its rules against that customer through court action.

The second major difference between the approaches I outlined and my own is that the content of the new private law rights I advocate for would be morally derived from the set of public law rights—constitutional and human ones—that are most widely accepted, taken as a whole. In one sense, then, I adopt the logic of the German model that views the public law sphere as manifesting a set of values that must be viewed as morally paramount. But because my argument is a moral rather than a legal one, I draw on the practice of rights protection as a global matter. The model I develop, therefore, is not limited to the charter or particular values of any one polity. Rather, I argue that the global practice of rights protection informs our best moral understanding of what rights are, and thus the model can be relevant anywhere rights are applied.

Why does this difference matter? How will the difference affect the way the model I advance cashes out in practice from the other types I outlined? The third significance of the distinct model I develop has both theoretical and practical repercussions. The moral model for reform I advocate actually *preserves* the traditional importance of state action and also, to some extent, the philosophical rationale on which it is based. This is in contrast to those models for the expansion of public law rights protection that see that expansion as flowing through the law from the constitution to the civil or private sphere. Those models seem to adhere to the logic of state action because their arguments are made under the rubric of the state action doctrine, or through the action of the courts. But, when they are considered more closely, it becomes clear that they annihilate the vertical/horizontal distinction rather than conserving it to a certain extent.

A model that says that constitutional scrutiny is engaged whenever a court makes a legal order is one that effectively eradicates the special moral significance traditionally attributed to the state where rights are concerned. That eradication reflects the facts: the state is no longer the only significant threat to rights. But the *reason* the state was, and is, a threat to rights—though no longer the only one—is obscured by the 'state action' or 'constitutionalization' analysis. This is because that analysis distinguishes between the state and private actors only on a formal basis—a party either is the state or it is not—or on a functional basis that flows through the positive mandate on the state imposed by certain constitutions. The normative concern about privatization and globalization is that there *is* a reason why the state has traditionally been of special concern, namely, its superior power by virtue of its monopoly on the use of coercive force. But the power to violate rights seems to be emanating outward from the state to include some, but not all, other private actors.

The 'state action' and 'constitutionalization' models, in short, try to have it both ways: they want to apply public law rights more broadly because these rights afford *special* protections to individuals; but at the same time, because of the argument that these rights will apply anywhere the law is enforced, the specialness of these rights—their special stringency of protections—actually becomes diffuse or diluted. The state, in other words, cannot at the same time be both special, from a rights standpoint, and also not special. If there is a moral reason to think that rights held against it *should* be more stringent than those in the private sphere—and I argue that there is—then that reason, too, must be taken into consideration in the broader application of public law rights. In applying public law rights more broadly, we cannot, in other words, have it both ways, thinking these rights are really morally important for some reason (that they are exceptional) and then argue that they can be applied to everyone as though there were nothing exceptional about them.

The 'state action' approach treats the 'horizontal' axis as though it were horizontal in the literal sense—flat, where all 'horizontal' instances of application are in principle the same. The problem is that, in fact, the 'horizontal' plane—the private sphere—is actually rocky and bumpy: in some places, such as among myself and my neighbours, it is quite flat; in other places, though, such as between individuals and huge corporate entities that employ them, sell to them, or harm them, the flat 'horizontal' plane seems more uneven and vertical. Relational contexts within the private sphere, in other words, vary enormously, and these models of application do not address that variability. The model I argue for, by contrast, extrapolates from the public law context for precisely this reason. Part of what is extrapolated to form the model of rights is the moral context of the vertical relationship between individual and state. This means that the special protection associated with that relationship can be replicated on a principled basis within the private sphere so that not all relational contexts within that sphere are treated as though they were the same.

The major problem, in other words, is this: if we accept that constitutional and human rights cannot apply only 'vertically' against the state, then the potential applicative scope of those rights begins to proliferate exponentially. Even when we restrict the application of rights to the state, as has been our convention, each right generates a number of duties, such as non-interference, protection against violation by third parties, and possibly also positive measures to diminish the likelihood that rights will be violated. If we now accept the horizontality principle, then each right will potentially generate all those duties on all other agents all the time. There is, in other words, no principled limitation for the applicative scope of these rights once we make the move from vertical to horizontal application.

Some version of the argument for horizontality has been, both theoretically and practically, the main response to the problem of rights violations by powerful private agents I described at the outset. But the horizontality principle, while indicating the right normative direction, has itself no mechanism for determining *which* private law interactions will be subject to rights scrutiny, and it therefore effectively undermines its own purpose by creating a crucial question without answering it: Which private actors will bear the responsibilities attached to horizontal rights? It is my argument that this problem of applicability makes horizontality—either on the 'state action' model or on some version of the 'constitutionalization' one—an insufficient principle on its own to address the problem at issue; what is required, in addition, is a distinct model of rights. This model must capture the content of the constitutional and human rights that we want to see applied at the horizontal level, but it must also articulate a principled mechanism for discerning which private law actions can be considered rights violations. In Chapter 9, I show how the application of the three-dimensional model of rights I develop functions in precisely this way, to focus and limit the obligations associated with the new rights I propose.

To summarize briefly, the method of argument I advocate for applying public law rights to private law is, in fact, not a method for the *application* of those rights as a legal matter. Rather, it is an extrapolative argument: it draws on public law rights both conceptually and substantively but it is also based in moral theory about rights. This approach has the distinct advantage of bringing the moral protection of individuals that has been achieved through public law into the private law setting, in which such protection is becoming increasingly necessary, while at the same time addressing the important problems connected to recognizing and enforcing the duties associated with public law rights against private individuals.

The kind of model of rights I offer can operate within the existing doctrine of private law and be balanced against private law rights. I will argue that public law rights are not conceptually distinct from private law ones—they are not, in other words, a different kind of thing, and thus conceptually difficult to reconcile with private law rights. Rather they manifest special protections for a certain range of important human interests. They are understood as differing from private law rights essentially as a matter of degree, in short, rather than of kind. The special protections they offer, I will suggest, reflect the moral significance of the nature of the relationship between individual and state, and that moral context ought therefore to be understood to be part of what those rights are. What I argue for, then, is the development of a new set of private law rights, the content of which reflects the core public law rights on which there is greatest global convergence. Because these new rights will be private ones, enforced through private law, but will be reconstructed from an extrapolative analysis of public law ones, it will be helpful at this point to stipulate how I will refer to them for the sake of clarity. These new private rights, then, I will henceforth call 'rights of personal independence'.

1

Setting the Scene

In the United States, the argument that private actors ought sometimes to be held responsible in respect of one another's public law rights has been made since the earliest rights adjudication.[1] In the main, it has failed. The reason for this failure—and for the problems associated with applying public law rights more broadly in other jurisdictions as well—can be understood as partly owing to the method of argument used to achieve the goal of broader public rights application.

For the most part, arguments made for this proposition are made in institutional terms; and because they are institutional arguments, they lead to institutional solutions. The problem with these kinds of solutions is that they cannot transcend the institutional features of public and private law. That is, institutional arguments for applying public law rights to private actors usually envision this application within existing institutional structures. As I argue, however, these institutional structures are themselves barriers to the central project of applying public law rights more broadly. Arguments from within constitutional law and theory, for instance, lead to the proposed application of constitutional rights to private actors on the basis of constitutional law and theory. They cannot, therefore, conceive of rights that are mutually cognizable—meaning that they make structural, analytical, and moral sense—to both public *and* private institutions. Institutional approaches thus consistently encounter difficulties at the stage at which public and private institutions collide. The institutions of private law, after all, are widely understood in light of a different theory than the one animating constitutional law. Private law theory, doctrine, and adjudication have all proved stubbornly resistant to the application of rights derived from public law. The problem thus requires an approach that is not normatively or analytically specific to one institution or the other.

The institutional solutions grounded in constitutional law and theory, I will argue, continue to fall short because the institution of private law—the way it conceptualizes rights and duties—is structurally different from that of constitutional or public law. Constitutional modes of reasoning thus fail to make sense to judges in private litigation, and to provide the kind of guidance necessary in private adjudication about what is to be protected and against whom. The method I will advance for the application of public law rights to private actors will therefore

[1] See *The Civil Rights Cases*, 109 US 3, 15 October 1883.

be based on a moral argument for the construction of new, *private* legal rights, and will provide an analytical mechanism for identifying the appropriate duty-bearers of these new rights.

The basic commitment to protecting individual rights against all potential violators—state or non-state—I will henceforth simply call 'the normative mandate'. In this chapter I describe the current state of affairs in respect of this mandate and identify the most important problems with existing mechanisms for its implementation. Identifying these problems will give us a clearer sense of the kind of method that would, ultimately, be necessary in order for the mandate of broader rights application to be successfully implemented.

It is helpful to isolate this core normative commitment from the particular arguments made for the 'constitutionalization of private law' or for the 'horizontalization' of constitutional rights. But if we abandon institutional methods for implementing the normative mandate, we are left with the mandate by itself. And surely the idea that people's core public law rights ought to apply against private actors as well as against the state is simply too vague to be effectively applicable. After all, once we unhinge the normative insight from the institutional structure of public law, then a morass of difficult questions appears: we don't know, for example, if we are talking about constitutional or human rights, or even moral or legal ones.

Consider, for instance, the argument that everyone ought to have his or her freedom of religion protected against everyone else and not only against the state. One case in which the extrapolation of freedom of religion from the public sphere to the private has been suggested involves tenants who are orthodox Jews.[2] Their landlord installs an electronic lock on the front of their apartment building in place of the mechanical one. They claim on the basis of their religion that because of their religious duty not to use electricity on the Sabbath they are unduly burdened by this change. They bring a court action against the landlord, asking that he be required to change the lock back to a mechanical one in respect of their right. If we think that the tenants ought to succeed, does the principle of extrapolation extend to requiring restaurants in nearby areas to serve kosher food, for example? Would it require the adoption by other businesses of Sabbath-compatible technology of the kind observant Jews use in many of their homes? Where, in other words, does the scope of the extrapolated right end?

Next, take the right to privacy. Privacy, we might think, is not a problematic extrapolation to make in this context, because, in many places and in many ways, privacy is already protected within the 'purely' private sphere through laws of tort, breach of confidence, etc. But consider a scenario in which none of these particular rules applies (where, for instance, there is no general tort of invasion of privacy): an employee is fired for keeping personal material on his office computer.[3] The employer's rules state clearly that such personal use of office computers is forbidden and will be met with dismissal. The employee admits that he had such

[2] Chambre Civile 3, 18 December 2002, *Bulletin Civile* III, no. 262.

[3] See *Societe Nikon France SA v. M Onof*, D.2001, 3148.

material on his computer but argues that the employer found out about it in a manner that was invasive of his right to privacy, which—as extrapolated from the public sphere context—entitled him to a reasonable expectation to be free from searches of the kind the employer conducted. Even if we accept that the right to privacy as it is interpreted and enforced in the public context ought to be extrapolated to this private one, how do we account for the role that the employer's property and contractual rights ought to play in the analysis? Does the right to privacy even make sense if applied against an employer as compared to the state? Is losing one's job sufficiently analogous, in terms of its detrimental effect, to having the police or the tax authorities seize one's property? Even if so, do we revert, in the analysis, to the kind of publically oriented justification of the employer's purpose and the proportionality of his methods? Or does his business interest itself constitute such a justification? The right to privacy as extrapolated in that simple way from the public sphere, in other words, cannot begin to address the more difficult questions that arise in the context of the private rights involved.

A third example: a woman in a privately owned and operated nursing home is moved to a lower level of care. This move has a significant impact on her health, her well-being, and perhaps even her life expectancy. She claims, say, on the basis of her fourteenth-amendment right not to be deprived of life, liberty, or property without due process, that the decision regarding her level of care ought to have been made according to certain procedural constraints such as notice, hearing, and transparency in the giving of reasons. Leaving aside the question of whether the fourteenth amendment ought to apply to the nursing home, does the deprivation of a particular standard of care constitute a violation of the woman's right in this context?

Fourth, consider the right to vote. How can this be extrapolated to the private sphere? Would it support an argument requiring that workplaces operate according to some kind of democratic principles, for example? Or consider the right to a fair trial: can it be extrapolated from the context of public law to require that employees be given certain procedural protections if they are to be disciplined or dismissed?

Finally, consider one of the positive rights that find expression in human rights instruments as well as in many of the newer constitutions, the right to some very minimal level of subsistence or welfare. How would this kind of right find expression in the private sphere? One way in which such an extrapolation has been suggested pertains to the argument for a human right to water: a corporation producing beverages has a bottling plant in a developing country, where the plant uses water on its property to produce soft drinks. The local residents complain that the taking of the water is endangering the sustainability of the resource in the long term and jeopardizing their sustenance in the short one.[4] They assert that although they have no proprietary interest in the water, and although the corporation is acting wholly in accordance with its property and licensing entitlements,

[4] See, for example, *Hindustan Coca-Cola Beverages (P) Ltd. v. Perumatty Grama Panchayat* 2005 (2) KLT 554.

the right to sustenance in general, and to water in particular, ought to impose an obligation on the corporation to use the water in a way that does not entail negative effects on the local population.

In all these cases, the normative mandate seems to open the possibility of enforcing rights against a wide variety of private actors; it does not imply any limitation on their scope. Also, they all seem to entail the protection of a number of possible interests, whose precise scope is undefined by the normative mandate itself. On both fronts, then—what, exactly, such public law rights protect and against whom—the normative mandate appears to offer no guidance. Some of these extrapolations seem more problematic than others, and, within each example, the imposition of some new duties seems more justifiable than that of others. To sort out the plausible from the implausible, the justifiable from the unjustifiable, we need a principled limiting mechanism by which to establish both the appropriate contours of the rights in question and those of the duties they can give rise to.

I want to suggest that the institutional solutions that have been developed in response to the normative mandate offer no real guidance of the kind we seek. Indeed, the institutional methods for implementing the mandate seem themselves to exacerbate some of the problems involved in extrapolating rules from one institutional context and applying them to another. In this respect, then, a brief consideration of these various institutional arguments and the methods for implementation of the mandate they give rise to will give us a clearer sense of the features a successful method for applying public law rights to private law would need to have.

I. An Introduction to 'Horizontality'—The Centrality of the State as Duty-Bearer

The first thing to notice about all the jurisdictions that have tried some form of 'horizontalization' is that the public law rights they seek to apply more broadly are not viewed as addressing private actors directly. The move from constitutional or human rights to their implication of private responsibility is always made, in one way or another, by moving, analytically, through the state and *its* responsibilities. This is true despite the fact that there are two main methods (though of course with substantial variations) for horizontalization, which are called 'direct' and 'indirect'. The direct method means that private actors would bear constitutional or human rights duties in respect of those rights; the indirect method means that courts must, in one way or another, take the protection of those rights into account in the course of private litigation. Despite this apparent distinction, the analytical and theoretical focus of both methods remains on the state. This is because the argument for applying public rights to private actors is virtually everywhere a legal one. The authority for such application must therefore either be directly given by a constitutional document or inferred from it. So, for example, one common way of inferring some constitutional application to private litigation is to treat the state's obligation to protect fundamental rights as requiring not only that *it* respect those rights in its own actions, but that it protect individuals against the rights violating conduct of other private actors.

This theory, and the legal method of its application, is currently widely employed, partly following its inception in Germany beginning in the 1950s, in its *Drittwirkung* doctrine.[5] According to this view, fundamental rights are not *addressed* to private actors, only to the state. They *protect* all private actors, though, in all potential situations. This means that rights are identified within private interactions, but the duties corresponding to those rights are not; those duties are borne only by the state. This approach leads to the indirect method of application, whose implication is that fundamental rights[6] do not create new causes of action against private actors but require that courts, in their adjudication of private disputes, take fundamental rights into account. This is the model of application followed by many other constitutional jurisdictions, such as Greece, India, and, to a lesser extent, Israel, Canada, and South Africa.

While in all those states the method is understood as generating only indirect obligations on private actors, this analytically state-oriented approach to the authorization for horizontality is also the one taken by Ireland, a state that uses a direct method of such application. The authority for the 'constitutional tort', as it is known, is found in the Irish constitution's Article 40.3.1, which states that 'the State guarantees in its laws to respect, and, as far as practicable, by its laws to defend and vindicate the personal rights of the citizen'. Beginning with *Ryan v. Attorney General*[7] in 1965, Irish courts have 'recognized this provision as a source of unenumerated but fully enforceable constitutional rights, whose content is to be derived by judicial reasoning from the nature of the Irish state and the relationship between the citizen and the state as envisaged by the text of the Constitution taken as a whole'.[8]

The idea that the state must be the duty-bearer of public law rights, of course, also animates the state action doctrine in the United States, which is the current mechanism there for delineating the sphere in which constitutional scrutiny will apply.[9] This similarity between the United States and other jurisdictions is obscured by the fact that most commentators consider the United States to be the primary example of a 'vertical' system of rights protection, meaning that public law rights apply only against the state. This is contrasted with what is called the 'horizontal' application of public law rights in most of the European countries,

[5] BVerfGE 7, 198.

[6] I use the term 'fundamental'—as it is often used in the context of the application of public law rights—because it can in principle refer to basic rights that are given legal protection either through constitutional or human rights law.

[7] [1965] IR 294.

[8] Colm O'Cinneide, 'Ireland: Irish Constitutional law and Direct Horizontal Effect—A Successful Experiment?', in Dawn Oliver and Jorg Fedtke (eds), *Human Rights and the Private Sphere: A Comparative Study* (New York: Routledge-Cavendish, 2007), 216.

[9] See *Civil Rights Cases,* at note 1 in this chapter, *Shelley v. Kramer*, 334 US 1 1948.

including the United Kingdom, as well as Israel, South Africa, and Canada, and several constitutional jurisdictions in South America as well. A principled difference does exist between the United States' system and the jurisdictions that adopt some form of 'horizontality', but that difference, in practice, is not as considerable as one might expect.

The main difference, at least in principle, between the two systems, lies not in the fact that the United States views the government as the exclusive duty-bearer of constitutional rights—many, if not most, of the other jurisdictions that employ horizontalization take a similar fundamental view of constitutions. Rather, the difference lies in the structure of the duties the constitution is viewed as imposing on the state. In Germany, and most of the jurisdictions that follow a 'horizontal' theory of constitutional rights, the constitution is understood to impose duties on the state in respect of the interests it articulates. Those duties are taken to include both the forbearance of the state itself from violating those interests unjustifiably *and* the requirement that the state protect individuals against unjustified violations by third parties (the doctrine of *Drittwirkung*, establishing horizontality, actually means 'third-party effect'). But this latter requirement is seen as signifying that the state's obligations in respect of constitutional rights are not exclusively negative ones of forbearance: this doctrine is the source of duties on the state that are structurally positive.

In the United States, there was a similar sequence of events in the development of the theory of the structure of constitutional rights that led to a contrasting conclusion. The 'state action' doctrine that controls the scope of public law rights was conceived in close connection with the view taken of the structure of the rights imposed by the constitution on the state. In *The Civil Rights Cases*,[10] widely considered to be the origin of the state action doctrine, the court declared that federal legislation that set out to regulate civil rights was unconstitutional to the extent that it purported to regulate the interactions between private actors. The federal government, the court reasoned, simply did not have the authority to impose any penal sanctions for the relations between individuals, since penal power is reserved, under United States federalism, to the States. The individuals seeking to have their civil rights vindicated against private actors argued that the federal government had the authority to regulate the conduct in question through civil rights legislation on the basis of the fourteenth amendment. The petitioners argued that the constitutional right to equal protection created a legal right to equal treatment that the federal government could—and in fact had a duty to—enforce, whether the treatment in question was an action of a state or of an individual. This analytical move, from the negative duty on the state to forbear from itself violating rights to the effectively positive duty to enforce those rights against private actors, is the one taken by the 'horizontality' jurisdictions, but it is one the United States court refused to take. The United States court reasoned that the structure of the constitutional rights set out in the fourteenth

[10] At note 1 in this chapter.

amendment is negative—those rights impose only duties of forbearance on the federal and state governments, so that the federal government's power to protect those rights is limited to actions taken by states. This reasoning about the significance of the structure of constitutional rights in the United States then precluded courts from later concluding that the constitution imposed legal duties on individuals directly in respect of the rights it set out.[11] This doctrine of the structure of constitutional rights in the United States has meant that the duties associated with them are understood to fall exclusively on the state. Constitutional scrutiny, therefore, only applies to those private agents who act, effectively, 'like' or 'with' the state in such a way that the state can be said to be effectively responsible for their actions.

Now it might be sensibly reasoned that constitutional rights operate against lawmaking, because lawmaking is an exclusive function of the state. Much of the action in the debate about the state action doctrine, therefore, is about what exactly constitutes the relevant law, making it subject to constitutional scrutiny. Constitutional and civil rights claims can be brought only against private agents acting 'under colour of law' because those actions are, through the law that authorizes them, attributable *to* the state. One central way of arguing for the broader protection of constitutional rights under the state action doctrine, then, is to suggest that private law—rules of property, contract and tort—are themselves laws of the state, and that private agents acting on the basis of those laws are effectively, therefore, acting 'under colour of law'. On this view, individuals' control over their property through testamentary and trespass rules would be subject to constitutional scrutiny. The idea that the 'background rules' of a society—its private law—should be as much subject to direct constitutional scrutiny as are its statutory acts remains highly controversial in United States scholarship and is virtually rejected as a matter of United States law. If private law were, even as a product of the state, viewed as subject to rights scrutiny, then private actors could be held to bear constitutional duties when acting in accordance with private law.[12]

The idea of this application of constitutional rights to private actors, mediated through the lawmaking function of the state is, in fact, too much even for the jurisdictions that *do* adopt horizontal application to accept. Those jurisdictions take the view—one a United States court took in one controversial United States state action case, *Shelley v. Kramer*—that is not so much about the legal scrutiny of private law itself as about courts, as state actors, who enforce those laws. Courts, on this less extreme theory of horizontality, wield the power of the state, and thus must be subject to constitutional scrutiny. When a court makes an order, on this view, and especially when an individual relies on that order and a court enforces it, it is acting as part of the executive branch of government. When it does so, it

[11] The thirteenth amendment, of course, is the exception to this, but its direct effect was very early construed as limited entirely to actions taken that were directly linked with the history and institution of slavery.

[12] This is the general argument made by Stephen Gardbaum, 'The "Horizontal Effect" of Constitutional Rights', *Michigan Law Review* 102 (2003): 388, at 412–28.

must respect the constitutional rights of those on whom that executive force will fall. This mode of horizontality is the way that, in many places, constitutional or human rights find their way into 'purely private' litigation: not by viewing one individual as owing duties in respect of those rights to another, but by viewing courts as constrained by those rights either because they are state actors or because they are making law.

The idea that courts are state actors and that their actions should therefore not go unsupervised by constitutions even in common law cases pertaining to private rights seems to manifest itself mainly in the view that court *orders* are state acts, and therefore should be subject to rights scrutiny. This means, though, that it is the *remedies* associated with private law actions, rather than the primary rules of tort, contract, and property, that must conform to constitutional standards. Conceiving of courts as state actors and conceiving of them as lawmakers are, of course, closely connected, but in the latter case private law itself—even before it is enforced by court order—must be subjected to rights scrutiny because the constitution is the supreme *law* of the land, one with which *all* other law, including private law, must conform.[13] Even on this view, though, private actors are generally not said to hold constitutional duties directly but only to attract them when they rely on the law in their interactions with others.[14]

Another version of this approach to courts as lawmakers is the theory that underpins the German position, which is that the constitution represents a sphere of objective *value* for the polity, and that as such it must inform all the value judgments made by judges as interpreters of the law. Once again, this view does not generally imply that private actors must conform their conduct to constitutional values, but rather that judges must, when interpreting the law, take those values into account. In some jurisdictions that adopt this view, though, such as Canada and South Africa, litigation under the common law is explicitly excluded from this scrutiny.

The value-based constitutional argument can have implications for private actors in another way as well, as it does in Germany and in those jurisdictions that follow the German model. Constitutional rights, as I indicated above, can positively require the state to perform certain functions—those which are necessary for life in a modern welfare state, for example, such as waste removal and water treatment—that become 'public functions' not because the state performs them but because they are *required* of the state. This means that if the state privatizes one of those functions it is seen as delegating its constitutional responsibilities, and those responsibilities then fall on the private actors that take them up.

This brief tour of various conceptualizations of constitutional rights in private litigation is meant only to illustrate the simple point that, as currently constructed, institutional methods for implementing the normative mandate do not actually impose duties associated with public law rights on private actors directly. The importance of this point is not so much that it signifies a failure to implement

[13] Gardbaum, 'The "Horizontal Effect" of Constitutional Rights', 412–28.
[14] Gardbaum, 'The "Horizontal Effect" of Constitutional Rights', 412–28.

the normative mandate at all, but rather that it leads to other problems in application that undermine the achievement of the mandate, and it is to some of those challenges that I now turn.

II. Horizontalization: Problems with Existing Institutional Methods

In the literature on 'horizonalization' or 'constitutionalization of private law', much has been made of the variety of methods used to implement the normative mandate. Some jurisdictions apply human rights (Denmark, the United Kingdom, France), some apply constitutional rights (Germany, Italy, Greece, India); some apply constitutional 'values' *and* constitutional rights, depending on circumstances (Canada); some apply one or the other set of rights to all law, statutory and judge-made (Germany); while others specifically insulate the common law from public law rights scrutiny (Canada, South Africa). The major methodological difference is widely considered to be manifested by the place countries occupy on the spectrum of directness or indirectness of application. A few jurisdictions hold that private actors bear human rights or constitutional duties (at least in theory), such as Ireland and France, while most adopt some form of indirect application.

As Mattias Kumm has argued, however, this so-called 'major divergence' between directness and indirectness of application has almost no implication in practice,[15] at least in the way both of these methods conceptualize public law rights and the theory of their application to private law. This indistinguishability of two apparently distinct methods of implementing the normative mandate is likely due to the fact that, as I pointed out at the outset, the justification for applying public law rights to private law is almost universally taken to be a matter of constitutional theory, wherein the duties associated even with implications of rights for private actors are primarily understood to be morally borne by the state.

When I isolated the normative mandate from its institutional implementation, I pointed out the natural assumption that institutional solutions to the problem of public rights in the private sphere make sense because the normative mandate by itself simply seems too vague to be applicable. But, in fact, the existing institutional methods for implementing the normative mandate are fundamentally flawed because they do not perform the clarifying function we want from them. The constitutionally oriented or state-oriented institutional solutions to the problem fail because despite offering some theorizing about the implementation of the normative mandate based on the role of the state, these institutional solutions simply pass the buck on the difficult normative questions down the line to judges. The *mandate* of protecting these rights more broadly, in other words,

15 Mattias Kumm, 'Who is Afraid of the Total Constitution? Constitutional Rights as Principles and the Constitutionalization of Private Law', *German Law Journal* 7, no. 4 (2006): 341.

has been very widely taken up; but the *method* of implementing that mandate has proved so problematic, conceptually vague, and undertheorized, that it has faltered nearly everywhere it has been tried. The legal mandate for applying public law rights more broadly—the answer to the question of *why* apply public law rights to private actors, in other words, does not include much guidance in the way of answering the question of *how* it ought to come about. In some cases, legislatures require that some set of public law rights be protected by judges in private litigation—either through the process of constitutionalization itself[16] or through a more particular legislative act—[17] and in other cases judges take on that mandate themselves.[18] In both instances, though, judges are left to *develop* the method of application on their own. But the argument for applying public law rights more broadly—saying it should be done—does not address the theory or conceptualization of rights necessary to address the kinds of problems that arise when one tries to extrapolate rights from one sphere—the public—and to apply them to another sphere—the private.

The various modes of applying public law rights more broadly are therefore plagued by two problems that severely undermine the willingness of judges and lawmakers to apply these rights to private actors. First, judges are faced with one of the most difficult questions in rights theory—how do we decide, given a particular right, who ought to bear duties associated with that right? Second, in the absence of a clear mechanism for delineating the duties associated with public law rights in the private sphere, judges are, in taking on this mandate, given a vast *discretion* to answer the question of which private actors ought to bear duties associated with public law rights. These two facts together—the complexity of the problem and the judicial application of rights—make that discretion both very broad and enormously consequential. It is perhaps for this reason that, despite the nominal legal commitment to protecting public law rights in the private sphere or in private litigation in many places, the actual protection is weak and heavily circumscribed.

Many of what appear to be objections to the normative mandate itself are, in fact, objections to this institutional feature of the existing judicial implementation of rights, and, more fundamentally, to the imposition of the institutional features of public law rights and their adjudication on the different institution of private law. One commonly cited objection, for example, is grounded in the need for a separation of public and private 'spheres'.[19] There must be, it is sometimes said, a sphere of private action that is not hindered or supervised by the state in

[16] As, for example, in South Africa: see Jorg Fedtke, 'South Africa: From Indirect to Direct Effect in South Africa—A System in Transition', in *Human Rights and the Private Sphere: A Comparative Study*, 351.

[17] e.g. *The Human Rights Act 1998* in the United Kingdom.

[18] e.g. Germany and others, see BVerfG 15 January 1958, *BVerfGE* 7, 198 (*Lüth*).

[19] This can be a formal assertion about the independence of private law, see for example Amnon Reichman, 'Property Rights, Public Policy, and the Limits of the Legal Power to Discriminate', in Daniel Friedmann and Daphne Barak-Erez (eds), *Human Rights in Private Law* (Portland, Oregon: Hart Publishing, 2001), 245–83, or a more political one about the social role of the private sphere of life.

the form of constitutional control. At the level of substantive reasoning, though, this objection simply overlooks the fact that the private sphere is already regulated by a set of laws, namely, those 'background rules' of tort, contract, and property that are also ultimately determined by the state and the courts.[20] Even if one takes the primary rules of private law to be quintessentially self-justifying as protecting extra-political moral rights, one must recognize that courts intervene in private interactions as a matter of course: the involuntary obligations of tort; doctrines of unconscionability and public policy in contract; and the limitation of property rights through various necessity and use restrictions—all these are ways in which courts determine the scope of individual rights in the private sphere. The objection is therefore perhaps more aptly grounded in a normative prioritization of one set of rights (those of property and contract) over another—the set of public ones. What is the justification for this normative position? At one level, there is none except legal convention. We might say, though, that the first set protects primary negative rights of individuals to go about their business undisturbed by others. If this is the essence of the objection, then it will be addressed by a method of implementing the normative mandate that allows for the consideration, preservation, and perhaps even prioritization of individual autonomy. In fact, the protection and preservation of dignity and autonomy—the very values often cited as supplying the reason for maintaining the institutional separateness of private law—also represent two of the primary reasons given *for* the mandate: autonomy and dignity, it is said, are the chief concern of human rights, and their protection in the private sphere can therefore only enhance those values.[21]

To take this central objection to the normative mandate seriously, though, we must recognize that its concern is not with the human rights of those it would protect, but with the negative, private rights of those whom such new rights would protect *against*. Many of the models of implementation address this objection concerning the autonomy of private actors by some form of interest-balancing. Kumm addresses the objection to the normative mandate grounded in concern about individual autonomy, for example, in the following way. He first argues that where there is a 'total' constitution, as in the case of Germany, 'private law is in effect a form of applied constitutional law'.[22] Assuming a highly interest-based view of rights, he goes on to argue that private autonomy is not threatened by constitutionalization, since *all* rights can, in effect, be seen as incarnations of constitutional ones. Private autonomy, on this kind of approach, will be respected as long as the constitutional analysis takes the defendant's constitutional rights into account as well, and asks the question of whether the rule or the legislature

20 See, for example, Cass Sunstein, 'The Partial Constitution' (Cambridge, Mass: Harvard University Press, 1993), and Mark Tushnet, 'The Issue of State Action/Horizontal Effect in Comparative Constitutional Law', *International Journal of Constitutional Law*. 1 (2003): 79.

21 See, for example Dawn Oliver's introduction in Dawn Oliver and Fedtke, *Human Rights and the Private Sphere: A Comparative Study*.

22 Kumm, 'Who is Afraid of the Total Constitution? Constitutional Rights as Principles and the Constitutionalization of Private Law', 359.

has appropriately balanced the two interests.[23] But this reduction of rights to the interests they represent leaves judges entirely responsible for reconstructing rights out of those interests and contributes to the judicial discretion and uncertainty involved in this type of method. As Dawn Oliver points out, 'achieving this balancing would, in the absence of specific regulations, create enormous judicial discretion'.[24] So what seems like a normative objection to the general idea of applying public law rights in the private sphere—that they will infringe private autonomy—is, in practice, transformed into an institutional concern about the role of courts. These objections, then, asserting the need to maintain the separateness of a private sphere, are not responding to the *mandate* of applying public law rights to private actors, but to the moral downstream effects of doing so when the method for applying them is of the general kinds currently used. This is evidenced by the fact that these objections tend to surface in jurisdictions that are already trying to apply public law rights to private law, not in response to the mandate for doing so but within the *process* of that application.

In France, for example, human rights articulated in the European Convention on Human Rights are in some cases applied directly in private litigation. The case I referred to earlier of the Jewish tenants taking legal action against their landlord on the basis of their freedom of religion, for instance, was upheld by the court of appeal, but then denied by the Cour de Cassation. The higher court reasoned that requiring the landlord to install a different system would be a positive duty; how, under future circumstances, would one draw the line of foreseeability for such a duty? How many of the tenants' requirements would the landlord have to investigate?[25] Myriam Hunter-Henin describes the difficulty in the French context in the following way:[26]

> The distinction between positive and negative duties is a fine one and, ultimately, it will be up to judges to strike the right balance between human rights and freedom of contract, as they do when they confront conflicting human rights. The horizontal application of human rights in France has therefore released huge powers for the judiciary and French private law is now largely a creation of judges, even in very codified areas, such as labour law.[27]

The reluctance of judges in the United States to expand the state action doctrine has also been explained in terms of an unwillingness to expand the scope of constitutional rights scrutiny to an undetermined class of potential litigants. In *Flagg Bros*,[28] Justice Rehnquist stated an unwillingness to 'broaden' the state

[23] Kumm, 'Who is Afraid of the Total Constitution? Constitutional Rights as Principles and the Constitutionalization of Private Law', 364.

[24] See Oliver's Introduction in Dawn Oliver and Fedtke, *Human Rights and the Private Sphere: A Comparative Study*, 20.

[25] (Court of appeal decision) Civ. 3eme 18 December 2002, *Bulletin Civile* III, no. 262.

[26] Myriam Hunter-Henin, 'France: Horizontal Application and the Triumph of the European Convention on Human Rights', in *Human Rights and the Private Sphere: A Comparative Study*, 98–125.

[27] Hunter-Henin, 'France: Horizontal Application and the Triumph of the European Convention on Human Rights', 124.

[28] *Flagg Brothers v. Brooks*, 436 US 149.

action doctrine 'beyond the scope of our previous cases', to take 'the notion of state action under the Fourteenth Amendment to hold that the mere existence of a body of property law in a state, whether decisional or statutory, itself amounted to "state action" even though no state process or state officials were ever involved in enforcing that body of law'. Such an expansion he described as 'intolerable'.[29]

Ireland is one of the few jurisdictions that nominally protect constitutional rights against private actors directly, and thus we might expect that there the conceptual cloudiness of the indirect approach might be mitigated; in fact, though, the result has been perhaps even more problematic. The existence of a constitutional tort began with the *Meskell* decision in 1973.[30] Colm O'Cinneide argues that 'the circumstances where the constitutional tort should be applied remain unclear and unsettled. There is a serious lack of conceptual clarity as to when and how horizontal effect should be given to fundamental rights.'[31] O'Cinneide articulates the questions associated with the doctrine as follows:

> How is the sweeping principle to be applied to the wide range of circumstances where it might potentially 'bite'? Can it fit into the more incremental common law approach now favoured by the Supreme Court, or will its scope have to be clipped or contained? Is the Irish 'direct horizontal effect' doctrine capable of being applied in a society with greater levels of social and economic complexity, but perhaps less consensus or core values?[32]

In the *Meskell* case itself, and the ones following it, he points out, there was

> no real discussion of the types of alleged violations, justifications and methods of balancing competing rights claims that could be pleaded in support of defence of a constitutional tort claim. In other words, there was no real blueprint laid down as to how the constitutional tort action would be applied to non-state bodies.[33]

This has led, he argues, to a state of affairs where 'considerable uncertainty still shrouds the scope and extent of the Meskell doctrine',[34] so that there is some question about 'whether direct horizontal approach has actually been established as a fixed constitutional doctrine in Irish constitutional law'.[35]

Indeed, in the *Irish Law of Torts*, McMahon and Binchy suggest that it is extremely uncertain what the circumstances are in which a constitutional right will give rise to a cause of action. The lack of legal clarity on this matter involves the type of private action that will generate a constitutional cause of action, the proof of fault that will have to be shown for such an action, and whether or not

[29] *Flagg Brothers v. Brooks*, 436 US 149 at 160, fn 10. [30] [1973] IR 121.

[31] O'Cinneide, 'Ireland: Irish Constitutional Law and Direct Horizontal Effect—A Successful Experiment?'.

[32] O'Cinneide, 'Ireland: Irish Constitutional Law and Direct Horizontal Effect—A Successful Experiment?', 223.

[33] O'Cinneide, 'Ireland: Irish Constitutional Law and Direct Horizontal Effect—A Successful Experiment?', 227.

[34] O'Cinneide, 'Ireland: Irish Constitutional Law and Direct Horizontal Effect—A Successful Experiment?', 223.

[35] O'Cinneide, 'Ireland: Irish Constitutional Law and Direct Horizontal Effect—A Successful Experiment?', 224.

proof of damage will be required or whether constitutional actions against private actors will be actionable per se, as is the case in intentional torts of interference with the person. McMahon and Binchy summarize the legal uncertainty produced by this judicial mechanism for implementing the normative mandate as follows:

> Completely undeveloped in Irish judicial analysis of the action for infringement of constitutional rights is the investigation of whether *all* constitutionally protected rights are enforceable against the state and against individuals without discrimination. The case-by-case basis on which the Supreme Court has adjudicated constitutional tort claims has meant that no overarching test has been established to determine whether a constitutional right will be given horizontal effect, and if so, to what degree and extent.[36]

O'Cinneide suggests that this legal uncertainty is the real problem for individual autonomy in the private sphere: 'private bodies and individuals', he points out, 'may be unsure or unaware of the constitutional obligations that may be imposed on them'.[37] Its lack of clarity, he goes on to argue, 'can also deter lawyers, judges and litigants from making use of the constitutional tort action'; he writes that

> the direct horizontal effect of the Irish Constitution has been notably under-utilized by judges and practitioners. Its prominent status in comparative constitutional commentary on the horizontal effect of human rights instruments is not matched by a similar profile internally within the Irish legal system.[38]

The reaction to this problem of legal uncertainty associated with the conceptual murkiness of implementing the normative mandate has in many cases been for judges to maintain the existing institutional division between public and private law by simply deferring to private law rules and regulations where they exist. In the Irish context, O'Cinneide says that

> the impact of the direct horizontal effect doctrine has often been muted and even nullified by the adoption of a cautious approach by the judiciary towards developing private law remedies to reflect rights norms, in particular where existing private law rules clearly apply to the matter at issue.[39]

This approach is based on the reasoning that as long as the public law interests are adequately balanced against the private ones by the lawmaker (judicial or legislative), there is no need to disturb that balance. Rather than embarking on a fresh application of the public law rights, therefore, judges look to whatever existing balancing mechanism is in place and then apply some form of scrutiny to it, in which they are often highly deferential. In the German context, for example, Kumm argues that private autonomy will be respected as long as the

[36] Bryan McMahon and Binchy, *Law of Torts*, 3rd ed (Dublin: Butterworths, 2000).

[37] O'Cinneide, 'Ireland: Irish Constitutional Law and Direct Horizontal Effect—A Successful Experiment?', 230.

[38] O'Cinneide, 'Ireland: Irish Constitutional Law and Direct Horizontal Effect—A Successful Experiment?', 247.

[39] O'Cinneide, 'Ireland: Irish Constitutional Law and Direct Horizontal Effect—A Successful Experiment?', 215.

constitutional analysis takes the defendant's constitutional rights into account as well as those of the plaintiff and asks the question of whether the rule in question or the legislature has appropriately balanced the two interests.[40]

In his argument for the application of the constitution as supreme *law* under its supremacy clause, in relation to private law, Stephen Gardbaum makes a similar point about the status of existing rules. He argues that the application of constitutional scrutiny to private law is only a threshold matter, and that the question of whether some private law rule actually violates the constitution will be subject to the same kind of moderate scrutiny as in the current constitutional context. This means, of course, that for many constitutional rights, only a rationality test would apply, and as long as the rule of contract or property made some attempt to balance the private interests, then the constitutional requirement would be satisfied.[41] This reinforces the point that institutional methods of implementing the normative mandate combine the conceptual lack of clarity and legal uncertainty involved in that mandate itself with the judicial application of rights generally, meaning that judges are for one reason or another deferential to existing private law rules, thus defeating the implementation of the mandate.

Existing institutional modes of implementation exacerbate the lack of clarity in another way as well: in moving from the 'vertical' to the 'horizontal', they effectively make the legal presumption that non-state actors are all the same, so far as rights are concerned. The method of 'indirect' application, for example, generally requires judges to consider constitutional values or constitutional rights when they are interpreting private law norms such as 'reasonability', 'good morals', 'good faith', etc. This method therefore inserts constitutional rights norms into any private law rule where such interpretation is called for—that is to say, in nearly all of them. The idea of public law rights on which this method of application is based, therefore, does not in principle distinguish between one potential rights violator and another. The question of which private actors ought to bear the duties associated with these public law rights, therefore, is again left to the judicial interpreter.

There are only two existing methods for solving this problem of judicial discretion. The indirect models of application restrict the possible set of state actors to courts. In enforcing laws, on that view, courts are agents of the state and thus their orders must be supervised constitutionally. But of course this leads to the very problem it seems aimed at solving: in trying to prevent the spectre of floodgates of litigation and infringement of autonomy associated with holding private actors responsible for violations of public law rights, all the responsibility is put at the feet of courts. And, of course, the court is an actor in *all* litigation; this

40 Kumm, 'If existing private law strikes the right balance between the relevant concerns, then existing private law rules can be justified within the constitutional rights paradigm', 'Who is Afraid of the Total Constitution? Constitutional Rights as Principles and the Constitutionalization of Private Law', 363.

41 See Gardbaum, 'The "Horizontal Effect" of Constitutional Rights'.

method, then, again puts all private actors equally under the scrutiny of constitutional examination, with the task of limiting that application being left entirely to judges.

The second existing way of addressing this problem of judicial latitude in deciding which private actors should bear the duties associated with public law rights is to restrict the application of constitutional scrutiny to private actors who perform a 'public function', or whose conduct is sufficiently closely associated with the state that they can be deemed a state actor. This way of determining potential duty-bearers takes a step in the direction of limiting the scope of public law rights in the private sphere in advance of their application, but it is, as applied, a highly contingent and semantic approach, and it therefore fails to effectively address the problem.

One way of defining a public function is highly formal: it says that public functions are ones that the state has historically performed. This also makes this solution fairly arbitrary and contingent: in some states, the operation of hospitals is a public function; in others it is a private one. Moreover, this approach does not adequately explain *why* functions formally associated with the state are to remain 'public' when performed by private actors. If the function of running prisons or building roads is performed by the state and is therefore public simply based on that historical social practice, then when the practice shifts and these functions are widely privatized, why should we continue to defer to the former practice and consider them to be public ones?

In the United States, the state action doctrine alternatively requires there to be a nexus between the act or function in question and the state such that the conduct can be attributed *to* the state. How, on this approach, would we reform the doctrine based on the normative mandate of protecting individual rights against private as well as public power? One possibility[42] is to consider the conduct of entities facilitated or enabled by the state, such as corporations, as attributable to the state. But this is also a kind of semantic solution: not all private corporations are even remotely the same in terms of their capacity to violate rights. It seems unclear why they should all bear the duties associated with those rights without any more principled limitation. A small mom-and-pop operation can be a private corporation, and can be an employer, and yet it is far from clear that simply for those reasons it should bear duties in respect of constitutional or human rights identical with those of Walmart or Unocal. This public function or state action test, then, leaves that decision entirely up to the discretion of judges.

What kind of alternative methodology would avoid or solve these problems of overbreadth and legal and conceptual uncertainty? To address both the institutional problems and the normative one concerned with maintaining respect for private autonomy, we would need an analytical framework that reconstructs

[42] For some such arguments, see, for example, Adolf A. Berle, 'Constitutional Limitations on Corporate Activity—Protection of Personal Rights from Invasion Through Economic Power', *University of Pennsylvania Law Review* 100, no. 7 (1952): 933; Shiffrin, 'Are Credit Card Late Fees Unconstitutional?' 15 *William and Mary Bill of Rights Journal* (2006): 457.

public law rights *in advance* of their application in particular cases. Their scope should, in other words, be delineated before judges are called on to apply them.

The analysis I will offer is in part a response to this difficulty of judicial discretion in the face of such a conceptually nuanced problem. This challenge must be addressed, I will argue, by the development of an analytical framework for taking up the normative mandate that confronts the various difficulties with, and objections to, its implementation. The existing methods adopted for applying public law rights in the private sphere, I contend, fail to recognize the problems associated with extrapolating rights from one sphere and applying it to another. We need a framework that addresses the complex conceptual structure of the rights in question; such a framework would also allow for the differentiation of, and assignment of duties among, private actors in a principled way that does not simply relate to the function they are performing and their formal association with the state.

III. The Structure of Rights and the Allocation of Duties

Despite the widespread centrality of the state as primary duty-bearer of public law rights, the question of how to decide whom rights should be held against has become central to the discussion of both types of public law rights from which the normative mandate is drawn—human and constitutional ones. In the constitutional context, the question of applying public law rights against private actors is recognized as both urgent and difficult in most constitutional states. The difficulties associated with this matter are generated by the problem that constitutional theory cannot itself answer the question of who—aside from the state—ought to bear the duties associated with constitutional rights, for the simple reasons that constitutional theory is, by and large, a theory *of* the state, or *for* the state.

But even leaving that difficulty aside, the general problem cannot be solved by constitutional theory alone: part of the normative mandate, after all, involves holding non-state actors, multinational corporations acting in particular according to international private law, responsible for *human rights* violations. Human rights, so the argument goes, are deontological ethical commitments[43]—because they are widely understood to be universal in some broad sense—and it makes little sense then to protect them against only certain kinds of actors. But the theory of corporate responsibility for such duties is by no means clear.[44] Moreover, human rights law and theory are troubled, more generally, by the question of who ought to bear the vast array of duties associated with those rights.[45] Holding non-state actors to bear duties associated with human rights is but one part of that

[43] Ivar Kolstad, 'Human Rights and Assigned Duties: Implications for Corporations', *Human Rights Review* 10 (2009): 569–82.

[44] See discussion referred to at note 9.

[45] See note 9 in this chapter, and Onora O'Neill, 'The Dark Side of Human Rights', *International Affairs* 81, no. 2 (2005): 427–39.

larger question, albeit an important one from the perspective of the normative mandate of protecting individual rights against non-state actors.

It is perhaps easier to understand why theorists and practitioners of both constitutional and human rights law are struggling to conceptualize the broader application of the relevant rights to new, non-state antagonists when we consider that the question of how we know who ought to bear the duties associated with rights is one of the most contentious and unresolved ones within rights theory itself. The question involves the relationship between rights and duties, and it lies at the heart of the central fault line of disagreement between the two major branches of rights theory. Broadly deontologically based theories, on one hand—such as the will theory[46] and the Nozickean one,[47] and formalist ones such as the Hohfeldian scheme[48]—view rights and their associated obligations in terms of entailment relations, or logically necessary correlatives. A right just *is*, on this kind of view, the logical correlate of the existence of a duty, and so if we can identify a right, then there is, somewhere, someone who must bear the duty associated with it not as a matter of moral judgment, but of logical or moral correlation. On this account, identifying duty-bearers in respect of rights is not a matter of *deciding* who should bear them, but of answering the question of whom the rights normatively implicate.

On the other hand, interest-based theories, of which Raz's is the best known,[49] view rights as logically prior to the identification of duties. Rights, on this view, are 'the way interests generate duties'.[50] But that process of 'generating' duties involves a judgment about who, given the moral importance of the right, is the most appropriate person to bear the duty associated with it—a judgment about which the right itself, on this view, has nothing to say. A right just is an interest, in other words, that is sufficiently morally important to warrant holding *someone* to bear an obligation in respect of it. But the right itself does not tell us who that someone should be.

Given the vast literature within rights theory itself that attempts to answer this question about the right way to think about the relationship between rights and duties, it is perhaps unsurprising that many people concerned with the legal enforcement of constitutional and human rights find the matter of assigning *new*

[46] See, for more on the will theory, Hillel Steiner, 'Working Rights', in *A Debate Over Rights: Philosophical Enquires* (Oxford: Clarendon Press, 1999); *An Essay on Rights* (Oxford: Blackwell Publishing, 1994); Carl Wellman, *Real Rights* (New York: Oxford University Press, 1995). Other broadly non-consequentialist theories of rights would also include Judith Jarvis Thomson, *The Realm of Rights* (Cambridge, Massachusetts: Harvard University Press, 1990) and F. M. Kamm, *Intricate Ethics: Rights, Responsibilities and Permissible Harm* (Oxford: Oxford University Press, 2007).

[47] Robert Nozick, *Anarchy, State, and Utopia* (New York: Basic Books, 1974); Jeffrey Paul (ed), *Reading Nozick: Essays on Anarchy, State, and Utopia* (Totowa, New Jersey: Rowman & Littlefield, 1981); Jeremy Waldron, 'Nozick and Locke: Filling the Space of Rights', 22 *Social Philosophy and Policy* (2005): 81–111.

[48] Wesley Newcomb Hohfeld, *Fundamental Legal Conceptions as Applied in Judicial Reasoning* (Westport, Connecticut: Greenwood Press, 1978).

[49] J. Raz, *The Morality of Freedom* (Oxford: Clarendon Press, 1986).

[50] I borrow this phrase from Jeremy Waldron, 'Rights in Conflict', in *Liberal Rights: Collected Papers, 1981–1991* (Cambridge: Cambridge University Press, 1993), 214.

duties somewhat vexing. It would be one thing if constitutional or human rights theorists could at least reach some clear consensus about whether the relevant rights ought to be understood in deontological or interest-based terms—that way, at least, they would be able to ignore the theoretical complexities of rights theory and limit themselves to one view or the other. But neither theorists of constitutional rights nor of human rights can agree on one clear interpretation or justification for the rights in question,[51] and so, when attempting to broaden the application of those rights to new potential duty-bearers, they are forced to grapple with the most difficult problem of rights theory afresh.

We have seen that an exclusively legal method for implementing the normative mandate, such as the ones animating the institutional approaches I described above, ultimately lead to a semantic argument of one kind or another that leaves the serious moral analysis to judges. The best approach, therefore, to an extrapolative argument from the public sphere to the private one must be an explicitly moral method that addresses the role of relational context in the conceptual structure of rights rather than simply glossing over the differing contexts of public and private rights. It is for this reason that the method I advocate is neither a constitutional one nor one based in human rights law, but an argument for the construction of *new, private law* rights whose content is based on an extrapolation of the set of constitutional and human rights that are the basis of the normative mandate. The method of extrapolative analysis I advocate will be effective where others fail, I will argue, because it directly confronts the problem of *how* interests generate duties, or who ought to bear the duties associated with rights—the problem at the heart of the difficulties associated with applying public law rights to private law.

The claim here is that the moral importance of their form is what distinguishes rights from interests (even if we qualify the term 'interest' by saying 'very important interest' or 'interest deemed sufficiently important to warrant imposing duties'). Interest theory and, perhaps consequently, interest-based extrapolations of public rights into the private sphere treat the identification of a highly important interest as sufficient to say that a given right exists. I will argue, though, that when it comes to figuring out what rights are, there is a lot of action, so to speak, *in-between* the identification of an important interest and the imposition of the obligation it warrants. This in-between space—mediating interest and duty—is not, as many theorists of rights seem to suggest, simply an intermediary temporal stage in the imposition of a right;[52] rather it represents the relational structure of any given right, and is morally integral to it. This means that identifying any

[51] See, for example, the discussion of human rights referred to at note 8 and of constitutional rights in Chapters 3 and 5.

[52] For some discussions of the stages of abstract, meta, and basic rights, see, for example, Kramer, 'Rights Without Trimmings' in *A Debate Over Rights: Philosophical Enquiries*; Amartya Sen, 'Elements of a Theory of Human Rights', *Philosophy and Public Affairs* 32, no. 4 (2004): 315–51; Henry Shue, *Basic Rights: Subsistence, Affluence, and U.S. Foreign Policy*, (Princeton, New Jersey: Princeton University Press, 1980); Henry Shue, 'Mediating Duties', *Ethics* 98, no. 4 (1988): 687–704; Onora O'Neill, 'Review: In a Starving World, What's the Moral Minimum?', *The Hastings Center Report* 11, no. 6 (December 1981): 42–4.

public law right for the purpose of extrapolating it to the private law context requires that we treat its relational dimension as necessary to it and thus also as necessary to apply, along with the given interest, in the private sphere.

Treating this relational, structural dimension of rights as necessary to understanding what they are, and thus to how they are to be applied, offers an insight into rights that can help to make sense of how they mediate interest and duty. But, for the purpose of fulfilling the normative mandate of applying public law rights to private law, it will serve another function as well: it addresses the problem of judicial latitude and discretion in extrapolating and applying public law rights to private actors by providing a principled way of delineating rights' applicative scope in advance of their adjudication.

2

Moral Argument and Positive Law

A Method for Constructing A Model of Rights

In this chapter I will describe my method of argument in more detail. Although it is a moral argument, it will remain deferential to the practice of rights protection in the public sphere, treating that practice as a social, moral one as well as a legal one. My method will refer to both moral theory and legal practice, and will treat theory and practice as operating in a kind of reflective equilibrium, each informing the other. I will refer to this particular method of drawing on both theory and practice to make a moral argument for legal reform as an *extrapolative* analysis, in contrast to a purely legal, theoretical, or conceptual one. The model of rights I will develop, based in both rights theory and rights practice, will be extrapolative in that sense.

I. Laying the Methodological Foundations

Suppose someone claims that everyone has a right to freedom of religion, and that that right ought to be respected not just by the state but by everyone. Protecting such a right would entail much more than prohibiting legislation in abridgement of it. It would have potential implications for every interaction in which the right-holder is involved. This is roughly the proposition I am arguing for in taking up the normative mandate, and, as we have seen, it is an idea that seems fraught with problems. But if we accept it in a basic way and set out to implement it, dealing with the problems it involves as we proceed, there remains a central question: what is the appropriate method of argument for the change we advocate? This chapter will address some of the methodological questions raised by an attempt to reconstruct a set of core public law rights that can be applied among private individuals.

The animating thesis of this book is that a certain set of norms, the *source set*, that applies in context A—public law—ought to apply in context B—private law. Two immediate objections to the thesis present themselves and both relate to the differences between contexts A and B. First, we might object that there is no reason for the 'source rights' in context A to apply to context B, since although we find rights norms in both public and private law, they are in fact two different kinds of things; public law rights, in other words, are conceptually inextricable from the public law context.

The second objection goes as follows: even if we accept the thesis that there appear to be some situations in which it seems intuitively morally appropriate to apply rights from the public law source set to private interactions, there are a vast number of other private interactions for which that intuition does not hold. Simply asserting that the source rights ought to apply in the private law context would seem to suggest that they all ought to apply there in any given situation. Public law rights, in short, do not seem to offer a sufficiently determinate scope of application.

These are the two basic objections to our central thesis that must be addressed by our methodological approach. I will call the first the objection from *institutional provenance*; I will call the second the objection from *indeterminate applicability*. In response to the first, I will argue that we must abstract from the legal institutional context of public law rights and that in order to do so we must reject a purely legal argument in favour of a moral one. I will maintain, though, that the argument must remain grounded in the source set of public *law* rights; we must continue, in other words, to view those legal rights as the normative source of our moral argument.

In response to the second objection, I will contend that we cannot argue for the application of public law rights to private interactions without a principled way of delineating which interactions will and won't be subject to those rights. That kind of principled delineation, I will argue, requires a theory of rights that can both account for the set of source rights and at the same time explain why certain private interactions count as rights violations while others do not. A purely theoretical or conceptual analysis of those public law rights, it might seem, would accomplish this second task; I will suggest, however, that a concept capable of fulfilling this second condition would better be termed an extrapolative model.

We are considering an argument for the recognition of new legal rights. There are two conventional methods for making such arguments: legal ones, based in the practice of law, and moral ones, based in theory and conceptual analysis. These two methods differ most centrally in the way they treat practice, and there exists a widespread assumption that they are mutually exclusive and that practice, therefore, must either be authoritative or negated as a moral matter.

In *The Concept of Law*, Hart described his project as both 'descriptive sociology' and 'analytic jurisprudence'—a conjunction that has seemed endlessly puzzling to legal scholars ever since;[1] this puzzlement is perhaps the result of a pervasive understanding of the methodology of jurisprudence as dichotomous. The central claim of this chapter is that, as applied to the question of how to argue for the contents of new legal rights, this dichotomy is a false one: the method I advocate for

[1] For one example summarizing the debate and surrounding confusion, see Veronica Rodriguez Blanco, 'The Methodological Problem in Legal Theory: Normative and Descriptive Jurisprudence Revisited', 19 *Ratio Juris* (2006): 26–54.

the application of public law rights to private law is both normative and descriptive, involving both positive law and moral argument. This claim is based on the view of law, described by Simmonds, as 'not simply a sphere for the application of moral insights derived from elsewhere, but a significant focus for philosophical reflection and a source of self-understanding'.[2] My extrapolative method will therefore involve the interweaving of a *moral* argument and an analysis of a practice grounded in positive law. On one hand, I argue on moral grounds for the recognition of a new set of private legal rights. This aspect of the argument, in effect, is of the 'there ought to be a law' variety. On the other hand, I do not base that argument on a purely conceptual analysis of rights, private law principles, nor any other first principles, morally speaking. Rather, I base it on an existing, remarkably widespread moral practice: rights protection in the sphere of public law. In this chapter I will elucidate and advocate for this method of argument as the one best suited to the project at hand.

A. The case for a moral argument

The rights norms that we are concerned with originate in public law; this would seem to suggest that they are, or that we should treat them as, exclusively legal ones. I argue, however, that the public law rights that we want to see applied in the private sphere are better conceived as hybrids of legal and moral rights. Insofar as many of these are constitutional rights against the state, they rest on the idea of an extra-political normativity: they therefore also seem to be moral rights. The first question, therefore, is whether, when we seek to extend the protections we find in public law rights to private law, we are concerned with applying moral or legal rights. If the answer were strictly legal rights, then the argument would be positivistic—internal to the law. If the answer were strictly moral rights, then the argument would be essentially censorial or critical. In this section, I will argue that despite the fact that the normative source for our argument is a set of (at least partly) legal rights, the best method for making the argument is in fact a moral one: to argue, on moral grounds, that a new set of private legal rights ought to have a particular content, and that that content will reflect a model of the source set of positive public law rights.

Since in the case of both public and private law we are dealing with legal rights, it seems that some kind of strictly legal argument would be the most straightforward. There are two major modes of legal argument, which we can view as operating on successive levels of increasing abstraction. Those who approach the problem of rights protection among private actors through some version of the 'horizontality' principle are arguing for the application of certain legal rights to a new context. A more abstract approach would be a Dworkinian interpretive one. It would be, or it would claim to be, an argument about legal principles rather

[2] N. E. Simmonds, 'Rights at the Cutting Edge', in *A Debate Over Rights: Philosophical Enquires* (Oxford: Clarendon Press, 2000), 120.

than legal rules. On this approach, we would argue for the application of certain moral principles on the basis that they have become inculcated in the law and are now legal principles; we would claim that it is upon these *legal* principles that we base our argument.[3] Both the applicative and the interpretive legal methods suffer from serious weaknesses.

There are two problems of what we might call institutional authority with respect to *applying* public law rights to private law. The first is the problem of jurisdictional diversity: the set of public law rights that represents the moral commitments animating our normative mandate extends across many legal jurisdictions.[4] The problem is that legal norms are binding only where they have been made binding legally. Jurisdictional diversity creates a lack of institutional authority in any given private law context to apply rights from the public law of a different jurisdiction; this means that extra-jurisdictional public law rights cannot be binding within private law, and thus cannot, legally speaking, *apply* there. In order to take account of this objection we must acknowledge that our argument is not that the jurisdictionally diverse set of public law rights are, as a legal matter, *already binding* in private law. Public law norms from a variety of states, in other words, cannot be taken to apply, directly, to the private interactions of any single state.

Even if the problem jurisdictional diversity poses for institutional authority could be somehow overcome, however—if perhaps we argued for the application of the public law rights of each state to its own private law rules—the straightforwardly applicative legal method seems doomed for a second reason. Public law rights, after all, do not already apply, as a matter of existing legal doctrine, to private actors—that is the reason for our reform argument. There is therefore a lack of institutional authority to apply public law rights to private law in many jurisdictions, and even in those jurisdictions where there is some horizontality, the application is indirect, as rights are applied not to private individuals but to the legal rules themselves. Our argument cannot therefore use the applicative legal method.

The second possibility for a legal argument would be a more *interpretive* method: we would apply public law rights to private settings only in light of their point or purpose in the public context. Although this approach abstracts somewhat from the institutional setting of the source rights, thus perhaps responding

[3] For a discussion of how moral principles become inculcated into the law such that they can properly be called legal principles, see Stephen Perry, 'Two Models of Legal Principles', 82 *Iowa Law Review* (1996–7): 801.

[4] Some of the international and regional documents that have raised public consciousness about rights include: *Universal Declaration of Human Rights; International Covenant on Civil and Political Rights; International Covenant on Economic, Social and Cultural Rights; Convention on the Elimination of All Forms of Discrimination Against Women; International Convention on the Elimination of All Forms of Racial Discrimination; African [Banjul] Charter on Human and Peoples' Rights; American Convention on Human Rights; American Declaration of the Rights and Duties of Man; European Convention for the Prevention of Torture and Inhuman or Degrading Treatment or Punishment; European Convention on Human Rights; European Social Charter; Declaration of the Rights of Man and of the Citizen; Optional Protocol to the Covenant on Civil and Political Rights; Convention Against Genocide; The Geneva Conventions; Convention on the Rights of the Child.*

to the problem of institutional authority and the objection from institutional provenance, it falls foul of the objection from indeterminate applicability. This is because the point or purpose of public law rights will be susceptible to differing interpretations depending on one's moral point of view. Deontologists, for instance, will view public law rights as valuable and justified as manifestations of real moral rights; consequentialists will understand their value in instrumental terms. The application of extrapolated public law rights to private law will therefore differ according to which moral standpoint one takes. If, as a legal matter, I have a right to freedom from sex discrimination, then it is unclear why, as a matter of principle, my right should apply against some private actors—employers or health insurers, for example—but not against others—such as family members, friends, neighbours, or people I pass on the street. Yet these distinctions between different potential rights respondents in the private sphere are crucial to overcoming the central problems of extrapolating public law norms to the private setting. When our method is a legal one, even an interpretive legal one, we have scant moral resources to decide between the different ways in which various moral understandings of public law rights will cash out in the private sphere.

As a problem for legal argument, this deep disagreement about moral justification might not be such an important one where we are dealing with the extension of a law from one area—say insurance law and family law—to another—say estate law—within a single polity. Within one jurisdiction, justificatory integrity comes either as a result of the legislative process or because of the coherence and consistency of precedent that binds adjudication. So if a law has been passed by the legislature of some state, then the moral reasons for its justification have been debated and somehow sufficiently resolved so that the law was enacted. In the context of its development through judicial interpretation, its content has been similarly constrained by a particular kind of reasoning, so that the reasons for which it is valuable—its purpose—remain faithful to the context in which it was initially adopted and accepted. But in the case of a set of international and inter-jurisdictional norms, we cannot find a unified coherent purpose because of the lack of a single enacting body; we have no reason to assume, despite convergent acceptance of a set of rights, that those rights can be understood to be justified by a unified moral standpoint, since they were enacted in different contexts.

Given the disagreement about the justification and value of rights protection, we must explain why and how the justifications for rights in the public context retain their validity when those rights are applied in the private sphere. The only way to make such an argument for legal reform convincing at the level of moral theory is to accept that it is a moral argument and that, as such, it must be at some level compatible with the competing moral views underlying rights theory. In taking this step outside the law, methodologically speaking, we are no longer arguing, from a legal standpoint, that we can extrapolate legal principles from one area of law into another. Rather we must take a normative position that is, insofar as it is a moral argument, external to the law. Our method, then, will involve making a moral argument for recognizing new legal rights in the private sphere.

B. Theory and practice: possible sources for a concept of rights

If the argument for new private law rights is to be a moral one, the question remains: what should the *content* of these new legal rights be? It is one thing, after all, to recognize that private law is lagging behind public law rights protection in fulfilling the moral commitments manifested in the public sphere. Finding the solution to that problem is a different matter. We may accept, as a partial solution, that new private law rights ought to be recognized. But if that position is a moral rather than a legal one, then we have detached ourselves, methodologically speaking, from the public law context that animated our recognition of the problem. This detachment means that we are at liberty to argue for new legal rights from a purely moral standpoint. But there are a number of possible answers to the question of what the content of the new rights should be.

One thing is certain: an argument for any new legal rights has to draw in some way on the kind of thing a right is. In looking for a conceptual basis for our argument for new rights, two avenues present themselves. The first consists of the theoretical attempts that have been made to define the concept of rights. There have been a number of such attempts, which have generated a range of significant theories of rights, each of which views them as involving some essential quality, namely, human welfare or 'interests'; 'basic rights'; will or choice; 'side-constraints'; or 'trumps'. One possible methodological approach, therefore, would be to engage with one of these theories and proceed to argue for the content of the new private legal rights on its terms.

The second category from which we could construct a conceptual framework for rights is the social practice of rights protection. Given its centrality to our normative mandate, rights protection in the public sphere would seem to be the obvious practice on which to base a conceptualization of what rights are. Rights are, of course, legally protected in a wide variety of ways: virtually all forms and categories of law protect rights of some sort. So, in theory, there is a social practice of rights protection everywhere there is law. What justifies, then, the conceptual focus on the social practice of rights protection in *public* law? The answer to this question points to the special moral significance of this set of rights, and I will argue for that significance later in the chapter.

I will argue that taking only one of these two methodological approaches to a moral argument for a new set of private law rights is misconceived. The approach I will defend here is one that draws freely but not uncritically on both theory and practice. On the one hand, I will suggest that we should be wary of abstract theorizing that has the consequence of rejecting whole swathes of rights that have come to be considered important and are widely accepted and enforced. Practice, I will suggest, raises considerations that theory alone can easily overlook.

On the other hand, the argument is ultimately for a change in practice—the recognition of new legal rights—so practice cannot be treated as sacrosanct. If a theory we have good reason to accept calls some dimension of practice into question, we ought to pay attention to its challenge. I will assume, therefore, that neither theory nor practice has absolute priority over the other, but that, rather, each can correct for the limitations of the other. The method will therefore combine theory and practice, looking back and forth between the two and treating them as mutually supportive, in a kind of reflective equilibrium.

II. Reflective Equilibrium of Theory and Practice

Rawls introduced the concept of reflective equilibrium as a method for moral reasoning. The idea is that we begin with principles of right and wrong, and test them against our intuitions about what morality requires in particular cases. Where our intuitions conflict with the requirements of the principles, we can revise our principles in light of our intuitions.[5] But, similarly, we can use our considered judgments to reflect on and challenge our intuitions. The process, then, involves moving back and forth between moral judgments in the abstract and as applied, allowing each to inform the other so that we eventually arrive at a set of considered judgments that reflects both our principles and the intuitions that arise with the exigencies of particular circumstances.

Reflective equilibrium was designed and is generally used as a method for moral reasoning that tests moral principles and considered judgments against intuitions in particular cases. This method would clearly seem to apply in the realm of theorizing about what rights are, but, we might wonder, what does it have to do with practice? And how can theory and practice themselves be understood to operate in reflective equilibrium?

Theory and practice correct for the defects of one another in much the same way that considered judgments and intuitions do in a process of reflective equilibrium. If I teach my son the principle that he should never hit people, for example, I reflect the principle that people ought not to harm others. But if I see him being attacked by older boys, I might have the intuition that it is acceptable for him to hit back in that particular case. In response to that intuition I might revise my principle, and teach him, perhaps, that it is never acceptable to hit people in aggression. In this case, we can see that a particular practical experience raises a consideration that the original theory did not adequately account for, namely that other people sometimes attack us. The intuition in that circumstance allowed for the refinement and improvement of the principle. But, conversely, we would not want simply to extrapolate from my intuition in that situation that it is acceptable to hit others; that intuition must be tempered by the principled background prohibiting harm to others that I started out with.

Considered on their own, both theory and intuitive responses to particular circumstances have defects, which are corrected for through the reflective process, and this process functions at the larger scale of theory and practice as well as at the individual level. Theoretical attempts to define the concept of rights correspond

[5] John Rawls, *Justice as Fairness: A Restatement* (Cambridge, Massachusetts: The Belknap Press of Harvard University Press, 2001); *The Law of Peoples, with 'The Idea of Public Reason Revisited'* (Cambridge, Massachusetts: Harvard University Press, 1999).

to principles and considered judgments in the reflective process, while the body of practice purporting to identify rights corresponds to the intuitive responses to particular cases, because the legal recognition of rights can be understood as particular responses to the facts of specific circumstances. Both theory and practice have their advantages and defects, and the two categories are mutually informative and supportive.

A. The presumptive advantage of theory: a summary of the case against practice

Consider, first, the case of practice. From the standpoint of moral argument, this is the more counter-intuitive category from which to draw conceptual and moral guidance. In making a moral argument, we may well ask: why look to practice at all? There is one glaring defect in basing one's decisions on past practice: as a general rule, we take it as given that the fact that we do something does not make it something we ought to do. This follows straightforwardly from the classical distinction between 'is' and 'ought'. Just because we do things in a certain way does not mean that we *should* do them in that way.

There are two ways in which this defect of practice as a moral signpost is often manifested in ordinary discourse, which we can think of as the suspicion of culture and the suspicion of law. One of the reasons the normativity of culture—as distinct from religion or conscious conviction—is so contentious is that cultural normativity seems to rely in part on the moral status of tradition. We do things in a certain way, in other words, because we have always done them that way. It takes more than the merely long-standing quality of a practice to lend it the status of tradition. We do not say, for example, that we have a tradition of mistreating the homeless and that we therefore value that practice. But even where a practice does attract the deference associated with 'tradition' it does not also attract clear normative status. Some traditional practices, such as polygamy and *sati* (the practice of the suicide of wives by self-immolation on their husbands' funeral pyres), are inherently inimical to liberal or even modern societies. So practice cannot be normatively significant simply because it is traditional, or because it has a long history.

If culture is viewed with suspicion as moral source material, as it were, law does not fare much better. There are those who view law as necessarily connected with morality, but even such non-positivists would agree that not everything that purports to be law is morally justified. Nazi and apartheid legal regimes are the classic examples of this way of thinking about law as a social practice that can be independent of morality.

Practice cannot, therefore, have independent moral status merely because it has a long history or because it enjoys the prestige of legality. And if these defects alone were not enough, the moral significance of practice must be tempered in the case of our present argument for the application of public law norms to private law precisely because we are arguing for a change in the practice of rights protection on a large scale. Our argument advocates a change in practice not only because it demands the recognition of new rights in the private sphere but also because it will, at least to some degree, call for the abolition of the long-accepted conceptual *and* practice-based division between public and private rights. So practice cannot be viewed as sacrosanct and given total priority; we must retain and recognize the relevance of theory in developing a conceptual framework for rights.

These arguments in favour of a theoretical approach seem straightforward and persuasive; but a closer examination of the practice of rights protection, and its advantages for the argument at issue, will reveal that drawing on practice as a moral and conceptual source has significant advantages for the kind of moral argument at issue here. There are two major arguments for including the practice of public law rights protection as a source of information about rights. The first reflects the defects of an exclusively theoretical approach in the context of our argument. The second involves the independent moral significance of the practice in question; and, in particular, the way in which its strength can temper the weakness of a theoretical method.

B. Defects of an exclusively theoretical approach: conceptual difference and disagreement among theories of rights

The very idea of applying public law rights to private law seems implicitly to endorse a practice-based method. It suggests, in other words, that the content of new private legal rights will derive entirely and exclusively from public law—so much so, in fact, that people who advocate or practice 'horizontality' can reasonably consider their practice to be one of application. This approach, we will recall, suffers from the two objections I called *institutional provenance* and *indeterminate applicability*. The latter objection in particular seems to strike directly against a method that draws on practice because public law rights simply do not seem themselves to delineate their own new scope in the private sphere. But in fact, I will argue, this is not a problem that a purely theoretical approach can solve.

The objection from indeterminate applicability pointed to a crucial problem with applying public law norms to private law: surely *all* public law rights ought not to apply to *all* private law interactions? That idea would seem to fly in the face of our guiding intuition about the wrongness of certain private interactions that seem like rights violations, since other such interactions do not seem, intuitively, to give rise to violations. Surely, for example, a parishioner ought not to have a right to freedom of religion against her Church even if she ought to have such a right against her employer—particularly if that employer is a large corporation. Similarly, it might make sense to say that a person has a human right to health care—or to respect for a minimal level of good health—against his health insurer, while it would make less sense to assert that right on his behalf against, say, his Church. But why is this? What is the nature of the difference between these cases?

The objection from indeterminate applicability tells us that we need a principled way of distinguishing those private law circumstances in which the public law norms seem properly applicable. A plausible solution to this problem might lie in a conceptual analysis that would allow us to abstract public law rights from their institutional context. Once removed from that context, we would make sense of the set of rights and make them applicable to the private sphere by describing them in different terms. We need to find a way of describing them, in other words, that does not refer to them only as 'public law rights', since that is the legal context from which we seek to extricate them. Conceptual analysis would allow us to describe the set of public law rights as manifestations of an *idea* of rights—one that does not rest on the fact that these norms were created as legal ones. So in addition to extricating the source rights from their institutional context, we would extrapolate a concept of rights from that set.

An exclusively theoretical method, then, seems to address the objection from institutional provenance because it would allow us to develop a concept of rights that is independent of their institutional context. Such a concept could also address the objection from indeterminate applicability if it turned out to describe the necessary and sufficient conditions that would limit the situations in which private law interactions can properly be called rights violations. The method, then, ought not only to describe a set of legal data (namely public law rights) in terms of a concept, it ought to be able to predict which future cases will be instances of that concept and which will not be. The objection from indeterminate applicability would be addressed by this method because the concept of rights would itself delineate and explain which private law contexts implicate rights and which do not, so the enterprise of developing such a concept seems methodologically promising. But here we find that the theoretical method suffers from the problem of disagreement or dissensus. There are many theories about the concept of rights, and they differ substantially from one another. Each one claims to offer the best explanation of what rights *are*, thus limiting the class of future cases to which the concept can be applied. This poses a problem for our argument that undermines the advantage of conceptual analysis in its potential ability to limit the scope of applicability.

The problem is this: theories of rights are so different from one another that they identify very different subsets of rights from our larger source set of public ones as valid. And these differing sets of rights, when applied to the private law context, would pick out substantially different kinds of situations in which the source rights would apply. Rights theory, in other words, taken as a whole, has a kind of prismatic effect: it sheds light on what rights are in widely varying ways. This is an obstacle for our argument in two ways. First, these differing schemes of rights isolate criteria so different from one another that they become, as the major critic of conceptual analysis suggests, untranslatable.[6] This is a problem because if we argue for the application of public law rights on the basis of one particular concept, then while those who share that conceptual view of rights will accept our

[6] See Donald Davidson, *Inquiries into Truth and Interpretation* (Oxford: Clarendon Press, 1984).

argument, others will not. They will not, in fact, even accept that the things we are proposing to apply to private law contexts are rights at all.

The second problem with the prismatic nature of rights theory for our purpose is this: if each concept can only identify some of the members of that set as rights, and if the ones it leaves out are not viewed by the theory as borderline cases but as categorically different kinds of things, then the theory does not even capture our subject—public law rights. Each of the concepts of rights described below is itself the subject of a vast literature and debate.[7] The scope of my discussion will aim to describe each of the main theories only in sufficient detail to make its claims and contours clear enough that we can see how it would identify rights from the source set and how it would delineate the scope of application to the private law context.

Consider, first, the interest theory. The basic definition Raz gives of rights is:

> 'X has a right' if and only if X can have rights, and, other things being equal, an aspect of X's well-being (his interest) is a sufficient reason for holding some other person(s) to be under a duty.[8]

The interest theory of rights thus offers a concept that says that important interests ground duties. The interest theory, it seems, would succeed admirably at identifying rights in the source set as rights. The public law rights we are interested in, such as widespread constitutional and human ones, can virtually all be described as interests that have been deemed sufficiently important to warrant the imposition of duties on others—that is how they become legal rights.

The theory would fail, however, at delineating in advance a principled scope for their application to private law. When we consider the facts of several private law circumstances, such as the one involving a person's rights against her health insurer and against her Church, the interest theory cannot explain our differing intuitions about the two situations. Its likely and plausible explanation would be that while the person's interest in health care in both cases is equally important, in the case of the health insurer there is a moral reason why that interest ought to ground some kind of duty, while in the case of the Church, the latter's own interests, as well as the interests of others more generally, create reasons why the Church ought not to have to bear the burden of the duty correlative to the right to health care. This may be a plausible explanation, but on this theory such distinctions can only be made on a case-by-case basis, and they must be made according to a potentially different set of values than the one embedded in the

[7] Many theories of rights are cited in this part of the chapter; for a sample of some that are not, see: Jeremy Waldron, *The Right to Private Property*, (Oxford: Clarendon Press, 1988); George W. Rainbolt, *The Concept of Rights* (The Netherlands: Springer, 2006); H. L. A. Hart, 'Legal Rights' in *Essays on Bentham* (Oxford: Oxford University Press, 1982); Joel Feinberg, 'Duties, Rights and Claims', 3 *American Philosophical Quarterly* 137 (1966); John Finnis, 'Some Professorial Fallacies About Rights', 4 *Adelaide Law Review* (1972): 377; Joseph Singer, 'The Legal Rights Debate in Analytic Jurisprudence from Bentham to Hohfeld', *Wisconsin Law Review* 975 (1983): 988; Shelley Kagan, *Normative Ethics* (Colorado: Westview Press, 1998).

[8] Joseph Raz, *The Morality of Freedom*, (Oxford: Clarendon Press, 1986), 166.

source set of rights. If such decisions are left to a judge, for instance, rather than delineated by the theory, then two significant problems arise: first, if the judge will apply the rights from the source set to *any* private law circumstances, once undertaken, this project will create an almost unlimited judicial discretion. A judge could decide that a Church *does* have moral reasons to protect a person's health care, for instance, because of the assertions of its holy book. Whatever we think of that reasoning, it demonstrates that a case can be made for the imposition of duties correlative to very important rights for many different particular kinds of reasons, even if all of them are moral ones. Partly this problem arises because the interest theory does not emphasize or describe a mechanism for limiting the scope of rights. As Waldron says, while the theory is an attractive one in certain important ways, on its way of conceiving of them 'conflicts of rights must be regarded as more or less inevitable'.[9]

The second major problem is that a judge, left with the kind of discretion I have just described—even given the prescription to, for instance 'develop the common law in accordance with [whatever source set we identify associated with public law rights]', as is currently done in certain places—could easily conclude that *all* private law circumstances are ones that, precisely because both parties are private ones, generate moral reasons *against* the imposition of new private law duties on the basis of the interests protected by the source set.

A more deontologically oriented view of rights is the will theory. According to the will theory rights consist of duties where a right-holder has the power to enforce or waive the exercise of those duties. It therefore confers on individuals spheres of practical choice or 'discretionary domains'. The delineation of the sphere is made without reference to the content of the choices that will be made within it. One prominent claim about the modern will theory, in fact, is that it protects only choices, and that it is thus an entirely formal normative system; that is, there is no 'justice test' to determine whether or not a right exists.[10]

It seems reasonably clear how the will theory would select 'real' rights from the source set of public ones, since most of those are taken to be inalienable and *no one* can actually *waive* them—that is their very point. Constitutional rights seem to include the more important and abstract ones which seem morally inalienable, like the right to free speech or freedom of conscience, and others, like the right against self-incrimination or the right to a jury trial, which can be legally waived. This seems consonant with the idea that the will theory does not take rights to necessarily protect any substantive interests: in the private law context, procedural rights could be applied following the logic of the will theory, but it would still have difficulty responding to the problem of indeterminate applicability—of limiting the situations within which those procedural rights would apply. There seems no principle within the theory, in other words, to tell us whether I have different procedural rights against my Church than I do against the restaurant where

[9] Jeremy Waldron, *Liberal Right: Collected Papers, 1981–1991*, (Cambridge: Cambridge University Press,1993), 203–24.

[10] Steiner, 'Working Rights' in *A Debate Over Rights: Philosophical Enquiries.*

I eat dinner. But the will theory seems to be an unhelpful concept of rights on which to base the application of public rights to private law in any event, since it recognizes so few of the public law rights *as* rights. It is much more at home in the private law context, but therefore could not achieve the normative purpose of our project, which is to argue for the creation of new private law rights that recognize the moral content of public law ones.

Robert Nozick's interpretation of rights is relatively straightforward and has become influential. He distinguishes goals (which are the domain of value) from rights, which 'determine the constraints upon your actions'.[11] He says that rights are spheres of moral inviolability, defined by a 'line (or hyper-plane)' that 'circumscribes an area in moral space around an individual'. This view describes rights violations as 'encroachments' upon this 'circumscribed area' or 'transgressions' of 'the boundary'.[12] Nozick's view, therefore, is that all duties are duties of forbearance, or non-interference.

Which rights from our source set would Nozick's concept recognize as rights, properly understood? Since rights, on his view, are negative duties of forbearance, socio-economic rights would not be taken to constitute rights at all. This division between negative and positive rights would apply to both constitutional and human rights. This means that, when applied to private law, this concept suffers from the same problem as the others we have seen: although it selects a subset of public law rights on a principled basis, it cannot limit the application of the rights it selects in a similar way.

Nozick's concept of rights as constraints on the pursuit of goals is an agent-relative theory of limitations on individual action; Dworkin's theory also views rights as constraints on the pursuit of goals, but, on his account, they are constraints on legal and political decision-making. Dworkin's view of rights is famous for his description of rights as 'trumps'. According to Dworkin, 'if someone has a right to something, then it is wrong for the government to deny it to him even though it would be in the general interest to do so'. This idea he calls 'the anti-utilitarian concept of a right'.[13] This might suggest that rights, by their very nature, protect individual freedoms against decisions made in pursuit of welfare. Dworkin's later, more nuanced concept, though, concerns a particular kind of reason that is excluded from political decision-making. Rights are trumps not over the general good, but 'over some background *justification* for political decisions that states a goal for the community as a whole'[14] (emphasis mine). In other words, rights do not trump goods, in the substantive sense, but rather trump a purely utilitarian calculus of that good that could include people's preferences *about* other people's preferences—to prefer, for instance, that the preference of some person or persons, however defined, not count in the calculus.

[11] Robert Nozick, *Anarchy, State, and Utopia* (New York: Basic Books, 1974), 29.

[12] Nozick, *Anarchy, State, and Utopia*, 57.

[13] Ronald Dworkin, *Taking Rights Seriously* (Cambridge: Cambridge University Press, 1977).

[14] Ronald Dworkin, 'Rights as Trumps' in Jeremy Waldron (ed), *Theories of Rights* (Oxford: Oxford University Press, 1984), 153.

This is a concept of rights that operates within the confines of a political decision-making body and thus cannot make sense of any rights from within the subset that do not originate in a single political community. Unlike Nozick's theory, it is not about constraining individual actions; it is about limiting the basis on which actions can be taken by a group. What effect does this have on the concept's ability to identify public law rights? It will identify as rights those that have the effect of limiting the basis on which political decisions can be made. If freedom of religion is entrenched as a constitutional right, then governments constrained by that right cannot legislate on the basis of a majority's preference about the value of any particular religion. The concept could thus recognize constitutional rights that limit government's decision-making processes by reference to features of human life such as religion, conscience, and expression, that are related to, and tend to affect, people's values. It could not, however, recognize positive socio-economic rights that do not constrain decision-making formally but rather do so entirely substantively, requiring that governments do certain specified things. Nor would the concept allow for the transposition of rights from the public context to the private one, since in the latter context it is arguable that there is no communal political decision-making going on, even if decisions are being made on the basis of policy.

Different conceptions of rights recognize different sets of rights as real ones because they use different criteria for identifying rights. The interest theory recognizes all the rights in the source set. The will theory recognizes only those rights over which the right-holder has powers of waiver and enforcement, thus capturing only a small number out of the set, mainly procedural rights. Non-consequentialist theories vary in the ones they recognize—the Nozickean concept is very limited, while theories such as Thomson's and Kamm's[15] are more expansive; but in either case, these theories make a principled distinction between negative and positive rights because of the important distinction within ethical theory of doing and allowing. Within rights theory, therefore, we find very deep disagreement about what rights are.

C. A role for practice: convergence on rights and the moral importance of overlapping consensus

In the context of public law rights protection we find considerable variation among various jurisdictions regarding the specific contents of rights. Nevertheless, the practice of public law rights protection offers a significantly convergent view about rights. This convergence within rights practice, I will suggest, provides a useful starting point for the development of a model of rights. The reason to think of this convergence as normatively important involves the consensus around rights protection as a social moral practice; a practice, in other words, that seems quite

[15] Judith Jarvis Thomson, *The Realm of Rights* (Cambridge, Massachusetts: Harvard University Press, 1990); F. M. Kamm, *Intricate Ethics: Rights, Responsibilities and Permissible Harm* (Oxford: Oxford University Press, 2007).

explicitly to be one of the central social vehicles for implementing moral commitments. A social practice such as that of rights protection involves remarkable convergence of moral judgments on the validity of the practice of rights protection as well as an important convergence on the content of many of those rights.[16]

We might think of this convergence in terms of an overlapping consensus. Rawls introduced the idea of the overlapping consensus to describe a situation in which people agree at a political level about certain social practices for different reasons.[17] This kind of consensus eliminates the necessity for wholesale agreement among people with differing views of the good—different religious, philosophical, and moral views. Rather, it allows for agreement on a kind of second-tier level about a social practice that can be justified according to the terms of any of those views. The important thing about the idea of the overlapping consensus for our purposes is that it is not understood to be a political bargain: the ideas that are the subject of the consensus are morally accepted as valid by all parties, although for different reasons.[18] If we view a social or political moral practice as the subject of an overlapping consensus, then it retains its moral importance while accommodating the variety of views that support it.

[16] In the face of social convergence around a moral practice, we are faced with the problem of differing moral views. International human rights treaties in particular are drafted in such a way that they do not make the rights they declare depend on any normative first principles. For more on the development of such international instruments see: Mary Ann Glendon, 'Knowing the Universal Declaration of Human Rights', 73 *The Notre Dame Law Review* (1998); Mary Ann Glendon and E. Abrams, 'Reflections on the UDHR', *First Things* (1998): 18; Oona A. Hathaway, 'Why Do Countries Commit to Human Rights Treaties?', 51 *The Journal of Conflict Resolution* (2007); Oona Hathaway, 'Making Human Rights Treaties Work: Global Legal Information & Human Rights in the 21st Century', 31 *International Journal of Legal Information* (2003); Oona Hathaway 'Do human rights treaties make a difference?', 111 *The Yale Law Journal* (2002); Andrew Moravcsik, 'The origins of human rights regimes: democratic delegation in postwar Europe', 54 *International Organization* (2000).

People may accept and advocate the practice of rights enforcement, for example, because they view the rights as direct reflections of real 'natural' individual moral rights; they may also, however, view those rights as instrumentally necessary to promote one or another view of the good. Or the practice of rights protection may emerge as a result of a political agreement between various factions, as well as others who may advocate for rights protection for other reasons. We might be inclined to think that these different reasons for accepting rights undermines the role of consensus in the social practice of rights protection, rendering it a purely legal product of political compromise. If this were the case, though, we might not expect to see such widespread continuity of the protection of individual rights through constitutionalization and entrenchment. The widespread and historically dominant aspect of rights protection suggests, more plausibly, that it is in fact more accurate to describe the support for rights protection, even where it is animated by diverging first-order moral views, as indicating moral judgments as well, albeit second-order ones. The convergence on rights protection for a number of different moral reasons, then, suggests that the legal enforcement of these interests is a social moral practice that exists at a different level from first-order moral views, but which, at that level, represents a kind of independent moral convergence of its own.

[17] John Rawls, 'The Idea of an Overlapping Consensus', *Oxford Journal of Legal Studies* 7 (1987): 1; *Justice as Fairness*, 32.

[18] For other views on human rights in terms of overlapping consensus see: Talbott, *Which Rights Should be Universal?* (Oxford: Oxford University Press, 2005),8; also Charles Taylor, 'The Conditions of an Unforced Consensus on Human Rights', in *The Politics of Human Rights* (London: Verso, 1999), and Beitz, *The Idea of Human Rights* (Oxford: Oxford University Press, 2009).

Thinking of the practice of rights protection in terms of an overlapping consensus suggests that it might temper or diminish the defect of conceptual disagreement in a purely theoretical approach. But Rawls's overlapping consensus was on a set of moral principles rather than a practice—what, then, justifies treating a *practice* as an overlapping consensus and thus giving it a certain amount of normative weight?

One approach to theorizing about the nature of rights treats existing positive law ones as essentially irrelevant. This is the position implied in one moral strategy for arguing for the contents of legal rights. In exploring what rights private individuals might have in relation to one another outside the purview of the state, some political philosophers use the heuristic of the state of nature to prove or disprove the existence of some 'natural' rights. This approach seems to be intended to help clarify our moral intuitions about rights outside the influence of the state and the rights it tells us we already have. Contractarian arguments for certain political arrangements, too, presuppose a domain external to existing positive law in which it is possible to decide whether some proposition is reasonable or not. Rawls's methodology of the original position might be said to be a kind of intermediary approach, in which those elements of existing social life he deems morally irrelevant (such as social status, wealth, and particular personal commitments) are removed from the discussion, but in which others (such as the awareness of particular conceptions of the good, together with facts such as moderate scarcity and reasonable pluralism) are not.[19]

The idea behind these kinds of heuristic devices seems to be that reliance on moral ideas drawn from existing positive rights is in some sense anachronistic, muddying our deliberation about individual moral judgments. But this is to make two assumptions that seem questionable. The first is that such an absolutely hypothetical, ahistorical deliberation is possible. It presumes that we can determine what a 'reasonable' person, free from the constraining awareness of existing legal rights, would agree to. This deliberation would require an awareness of personal moral intuitions that is dissociated from the moral practice of one's society—such a 'pure' deliberation seems impossible. There are a number of ways of arguing against such an ahistorical, non-social approach. Simmonds argues that the debate over rights ought not to be seen as a 'controversy… concerning the setting forth of a concept's contour's by means of careful excavation' but rather 'as an attempt to construct a coherent concept from the ragged materials of gradually evolving doctrinal forms'.[20] Raz makes a much stronger claim for such an idea. In *The Practice of Value* he defends the thesis that the greater part of value is at least partly dependent on social practice. His claims are:

(1) *The special social dependence thesis:* Some values exist only if there are (or were) social practices sustaining them.

[19] Rawls, *Justice as Fairness: A Restatement*, 80.
[20] Simmonds, 'Rights at the Cutting Edge', 134.

(2) *The (general) social dependence thesis:* With some exceptions, all values depend on social practices either by being subject to the special thesis or through their dependence on values that are subject to the special thesis.[21]

William Talbott takes a slightly different approach, describing a process of moral discovery involving a kind of feedback between 'bottom up' application of moral intuitions to social rules and the impact of those social rules on moral intuitions in later situations that he calls the '*Historical–Social Process of Moral Discovery paradigm*'. The proposition, he says, that 'human beings *should have* certain legally protected basic rights is a partly moral, partly empirical discovery based on thousands of years of accumulated experience of human social existence'.[22]

Other writers have offered other considerations in favour of giving normative weight to a consensus on social practice. Waldron, for example, presents the normative role of convergent positive law in terms of a cumulative process of reflective moral judgment. In his discussion of the 'modern natural law' argument *ius gentium,*[23] he analogizes consensus on legal norms to the importance of scientific norms: when faced with a controversial legal question, he says, we ought to 'treat it as a problem to be solved in part by attending to the established deliverances of legal science'. This is characterized by 'the enterprise... of grappling with, untangling, and resolving the rival rights and claims that come together in issues of this kind'.[24]

On this view, the consensus itself is significant both because of the element of agreement and because of the importance of the reasons behind it. Judicial decisions and legislative acts both reflect processes whose epistemic value we have confidence in. But also, as in the case of science, the element of consensus is itself important: Waldron refers to this kind of legal consensus as 'the accumulated wisdom of the world on justice and right' from 'the decisions of judges and lawmakers grappling with real problems'.[25] A body of scientific evidence, which he compares to the law of nations, is significant *as a body.* This significance, too, is not because of the mere fact of 'accumulated' results in the crude sense of 'one thing being added to another, but in the sense of overlap, duplication, mutual elaboration, and the checking and rechecking of others' conclusions which is characteristic of true science'.[26]

Waldron thus suggests the possibility that positive law can play a role in our normative deliberation that straddles any distinction between the value of strictly

[21] Joseph Raz, *The Practice of Value* (Oxford: Clarendon Press, 2003), 19.

[22] Talbott, *Which Rights Should be Universal?,* 34–5.

[23] Jeremy Waldron, 'Foreign Law and the Modern *Ius Gentium*', 119 *Harvard Law Review* 129 (2005). There have been several attempts to describe the role that a *legal* consensus among foreign norms ought to play in our legal and moral reasoning. Lee, for example, uses the analogy of aesthetic consensus to suggest that the importance of consensus lies in the reasons that underlie it (Youngjae Lee, 'International Consensus as Persuasive Authority in the Eighth Amendment', *University of Pennsylvania Law Review* 156 (2007): 67). The existence of foreign norms themselves per se, he argues, is not important, but it is significant if the reasons behind them are in accord with our own.

[24] Waldron, 'Foreign Law and the Modern *Ius Gentium*', 138.

[25] Waldron, 'Foreign Law and the Modern *Ius Gentium*', 139.

[26] Waldron, 'Foreign Law and the Modern *Ius Gentium*'. 142.

legal reasons and that of moral agreement. The importance of legal consensus in this context is actually threefold: first, the fact of legality is important in itself—it is significant, in other words, that these moral norms have become legal ones; second, it is important that there are persuasive reasons and morally desirable epistemic processes *behind* the consensus; and, third, there is the importance of the fact of consensus. The most important insight in Waldron's analysis of a consensus on legal norms for our purposes concerns the role of positive law (or social practice) in moral analysis:

> it is not necessary that *ius gentium* be understood positivistically: what is necessary is that it be seen as a source of *normative insight grounded in the positive law* of various countries and relevant to the solution of legal problems (emphasis mine).[27]

These arguments also counter the second assumption implicit in state-of-nature arguments about natural rights, namely that such a dissociated deliberation is desirable, even if it were possible. This assumption, too, seems questionable, particularly if we are seeking to identify the moral intuitions that would be relevant to contemporary political and legal questions, rather than a set of entirely pre-political natural rights.

A more plausible interpretation of the relationship between individual moral intuition and social moral practice is that each informs the other. On this view, individuals are understood to reason about, intuit, or feel, moral approbation or disapprobation in certain circumstances, and those approvals and disapprovals—especially in any kind of political system based on representation—then influence social moral practice, and thereby also the content of the law. But at the same time, the social mores that form the context of those individual reasonings, intuitions, and sentiments also affect the moral appraisals and the moral judgments that flow from them. Simmonds points to the importance of positive law that reflects political communities, such as public law, in the process of moral argument or discovery: 'Our moral identities', he says, 'must be bound up with constitutive forms of association, and reflection upon such forms of association must be an integral part of moral philosophy.'[28]

The development of rights consciousness seems to be a paradigmatic example of such a phenomenon. For surely the entrenchment and enumeration of rights that began to occur in the eighteenth century and that gained momentum following the widely known brutalities and atrocities that marked the early twentieth century can be said to have sprung from the intuitive moral responses of many individuals. And yet at the same time, the way in which people perceive and morally evaluate what is going on around them—whether events are viewed as inevitable facts of social life or as unjustifiable atrocities—is partly shaped by their sense of what they and their fellow humans are entitled to expect from one another and from their social and political environment. But how do we know what we are entitled to expect from one another? One source of such standards is

[27] Waldron, 'Foreign Law and the Modern *Ius Gentium*', 142.
[28] See Simmonds, 120, n. 20.

the conventions of social moral practice; in this case those conventions are articulated in the form of our practice of rights protection. If we accept that the content of social moral conventions impact people's first-order moral judgments, and we also accept that first-order judgments impact the development of moral practices, then we are left with a picture of a feedback loop between what we might think our 'natural' rights are and what we understand our 'conventional' rights to be.

If we accept this view of the relationship between dominant social moral practice and individual moral judgment, then existing positive rights have a threefold moral significance. First, as we have seen, the social practice of rights protection indicates a strong acceptance of the moral importance of the interests protected by those rights, since they are seen as justifying the use of coercion for their enforcement. Moreover, where they will be applied primarily against the state, they are accepted as sufficiently morally important to limit the ability of the social group to pursue its collective goals.

This justificatory integrity is even weightier where the rights in question are recognized by public or representative bodies—their public pedigree suggests that they reflect the moral judgments of deliberative bodies, rather than—as in the case of private law—the moral and legal judgments of adjudicators. This reflection of moral judgment is the second feature of the moral weight of positive rights: their public pedigree and widespread acceptance indicates not only their moral legitimacy, justifying legal enforcement, but also suggests that they reflect the views and judgments of many individuals.

The third reason to attribute moral weight to these existing rights is related to the fact that, as I suggested earlier, once they have begun to be entrenched, that very entrenchment produces a trend toward further recognition of rights of the same kind. This suggests that the intuitions reflected in people's acceptance of the legal protection and enforcement of certain interests have been sufficiently pervasive and powerful as to contribute to people's views about what humans are entitled to expect from one another in subsequent situations that call for fresh moral judgments.

If we accept the idea of giving normative weight to a social practice like legal rights protection, and if we accept, in particular, the moral significance of public law rights protection because of the convergence which that practice exhibits, a question remains concerning what, exactly, is the subject of the convergence at issue. Two major possibilities seem to present themselves. The first is convergence on the desirability of rights protection itself. That is, the widespread entrenchment of rights might be considered to evidence a moral commitment to rights frameworks as a moral practice distinct from, say, a purely utilitarian or otherwise consequentialist mode of moral practice.

The second possibility puts emphasis not on the rights entrenchment itself as a subject of convergence but on the substantive content protected by those rights. As I said earlier, there is considerable variety among jurisdictions with respect to this content, but, even in this more contentious aspect of rights protection, certain trends of convergence can be identified. Some very general norms, such as anti-slavery, anti-trafficking, and anti-torture norms have emerged both through the development of *jus cogens* and through the overlap between rights treaties and constitutions. But even with respect to more diverse and specific rights content, some trends of convergence can be identified. Among the many conventions on human rights, as well as the many basic laws and constitutions of more than a hundred states, there is a great deal of convergence on which human interests are most important to protect. Although we are presented with the apparent choice between focusing on rights entrenchment itself and on rights content, the extrapolative method indicates that what ought to attract the most normative weight is whatever is most widely agreed upon. This would suggest that we ought to take seriously *both* the fact of rights protection as a form of moral practice *and* the fact that there seems to be widespread agreement on a kind of hierarchy of values that are the subject of widespread rights protection. It is therefore partly the fact that the practice of public law rights protection seems to clearly embody both types of convergence that will lead me to argue for a composite or three-dimensional model of rights that takes into account the form of rights protection, the hierarchy of value expressed by entrenched rights, *and* the moral context of rights held by individuals against the state, namely the relational context of individual and state.

Conclusion

The moral significance of the practice of public law rights protection implies that we must treat rights theory as tempered and informed by practice. Yet the argument is for a change in practice overall, and so practice cannot be over-prioritized. The extrapolative analysis of the practice in question will itself be grounded in the normative principles found in rights theory. The reflective method I propose, therefore, will draw on both practice and on theory.

3

Duelling Concepts in Rights Theory

I. Introduction

In Chapter 2 I touched briefly on a few of the most important theories of rights only to show that they take very diverse views on that question. In this chapter I want to argue that despite this apparently prismatic character, the various theories of rights are in fact dominated by a central conceptual dichotomy: rights have been consistently viewed in terms of either *constraint* or *value*. Discussions about rights have tended to cling to the idea that rights naturally fall into one conceptual category or the other and have viewed the two categories as conceptually incompatible—that is, we have in general been presented with two views of rights and exhorted to choose between them. My central claim in this chapter and in Chapter 4 is that despite its pervasiveness, the idea that the two conceptual views are mutually exclusive is consistently undermined: in almost every case where it seems as though there is only one appropriate way of seeing rights, we can, in fact, also see them in the other way. The two views of rights are, on the view I will advance, not so much competing, accurate conceptual explanations of what rights are but rather represent two conceptual lenses that draw attention to different *aspects* of what rights are. Neither of these two main types of concept exhaustively captures any right such that the other way of making sense of it is excluded.

I will introduce the conceptual dichotomy of value and constraint by showing how it operates within several strands of rights theory. Along the way, I will also begin to undermine the idea that the two conceptual views are mutually exclusive. I will introduce the idea, which I will pursue fully in Chapter 4, that the two aspects of rights that are highlighted by the two views are jointly necessary to the concept of a right.

II. The Dichotomy

There is a nearly universal division of rights theory into two conceptual camps. The first espouses what I will call the primacy of *value*; the second adopts the primacy of *constraint*. The normative importance of constraint, on the one hand, implies a presumptive priority for rights over other considerations and is thus oriented to some notion of individual inviolability. Theories that emphasize value in the concept of rights, on the other hand, articulate another element, namely, that of the particular interest protected by any given right. I will contend that although rights tend to be viewed through one of these two conceptual lenses, each view is insufficient on its own to either capture the panoply of rights found in the source set of constitutional and human rights or even to bear up as a complete theory of what rights are. *Both* aspects, rather—constraint and value—are integral to what rights are. I will later develop the argument that despite being insufficient in itself as a concept of rights, each of the two elements I identify is a necessary component of rights; the model of rights I ultimately reconstruct from the source set of public law rights, therefore, will consist of both of these two conceptual features, as well as an additional one.

The division of the terrain of rights theory into constraint-based and value-based views encompasses both the primarily conceptual accounts of rights, such as the interest theory and the will theory, and the more morally substantive ones, broadly divisible into the deontological and the consequentialist. In order to illustrate the pervasiveness of these two lenses through which the vast majority of theories variously views rights, I will trace the dichotomous division within several different realms of theory. Some will be mainly conceptual, others mainly normative.

A. Value and constraint in rights theory

The central dispute within rights theory involves the debate about which aspect of rights has conceptual and normative primacy—value or constraint. The best-known argument about rights is between what is known as the interest theory and the will or choice theory. These two theories are so caught up in the dichotomy of value and constraint that they will themselves serve as introductions to it.

The interest theory delineates the concept of rights by insisting that we cannot identify a right without reference to the value of what the right is *to*, and also perhaps to the competing interests of those on whom the right would impose obligations. It therefore makes the comparative value of things, of interests, paramount in answering the questions that determine the scope of rights. Joseph Raz says that X has a right if some aspect of his or her well-being is of sufficient importance to hold others to be under a duty with respect to it.[1] Duties, on this view, flow from valuable or important interests. This is not to say that the interest theory views *all* duties as flowing from rights, but simply that it does not view rights as themselves simply correlative to duties, or derivative from them. One prominent feature of this theory, therefore, is that before interests can become rights they must be viewed in the context of other interests: so my interest in smoking in

[1] Joseph Raz, *The Morality of Freedom* (Oxford: Clarendon Press, 1986), 166. See also Matthew Kramer, 'Rights Without Trimmings' in Matthew Kramer, Nigel Simmonds, and Hillel Steiner (eds), *A Debate Over Rights: Philosophical Enquiries* (Oxford: Clarendon Press, 1999); D. N. MacCormick, 'Rights in Legislation', in P. M. S. Hacker and J. Raz (eds), *Law, Morality and Society: Essays in Honour of H. L. A. Hart* (Oxford: Oxford University Press, 1977), 99–202; Jeremy Waldron, 'Rights in Conflict' in *Liberal Rights: Collected Papers, 1981–1991* (Cambridge: Cambridge University Press, 1993).

the subway might be important because it is an expression of my freedom, but because smoking in the subway is harmful to the health of others we do not view my interest in smoking in the subway to be, on balance, of sufficient importance to hold others to be under a duty to respect it. I can, therefore, be prevented from doing so without violation of my rights. The theory therefore can be said to track the value of various interests, elevating to rights status only those that are of truly paramount importance.

Another important feature of Raz's theory is that rights are conceptually prior to the duties that would correspond to them. This is a feature of theories of rights that has been described as rights' dynamism,[2] but that I will henceforth refer to as the idea of rights being in some sense prior to the duties which they generate. It is a way of thinking about rights that is unique to the interest theory, and it is partly this feature of the interest theory that many people find compelling: it means that we can say that every child in the world has the right to subsistence, to education, and to health care even without being able to specify on whom the duty to provide those things can be justifiably imposed. It means that we can say that the right to racial equality was a right even before it was ever enforced as such. Duties *ought* to have been imposed on the ground of that important interest, in other words, even if they were not. This is perhaps the clearest manifestation of the fact that the interest theory conceptualizes rights as protecting things of value—important interests—rather than being primarily about constraint, since the theory can identify rights even in the absence of any constraint at all. The interest theory is all about things that *warrant* constraint, rather than viewing rights as the constraints that structure normative interactions.

The will or choice theory, by contrast, purports to present a concept of rights that is essentially devoid of substantive value. It emphasizes choice, and, to the extent that we can see choice as a valuable thing, that is the value it embraces. According to the will theory, rights just *are* the constraint involved in an enforceable duty. The person who *has* the right is the person who has effective control over the exercise of the constraint associated with it. This right-holder is not necessarily the same person as the one whose interests are protected by the constraint.[3] So if a person has a property right, it is because she has control over whether, if someone trespasses on her land, for example, he will be held liable for breaching her duty not to trespass. The choice theory requires several aspects of control over the exercise of a duty to be present before it identifies a right, but the important thing about the theory is that while it views the *duty* as protecting whatever, substantively speaking, the right involves—person, property, speech, etc.—the right is the *constraint* that the right-holder can choose to impose on the duty-bearer when he or she chooses to enforce it. On this view, rights protect a

[2] See Waldron's discussion of 'waves of duties' in 'Rights in Conflict' in *Liberal Rights: Collected Papers 1981–1991*, 212.

[3] Hillel Steiner, 'Working Rights' in *A Debate Over Rights: Philosophical Enquiries*; Carl Wellman, *Real Rights* (New York: Oxford University Press, 1995); see also H. L. A. Hart, *Essays on Bentham* (Oxford: Oxford University Press, 1982), 183–4.

sphere of choice on behalf of the persons to whom duties are owed; in this way they structure the enforcement of duties, and thus also the interactions that those duties govern. The theory would say that the thing protected by rights is always choice, but of course each right does also represent some *thing*. The importance of the thing protected, though, be it speech, person, property, or whatever else, does not determine the existence of the right. If I have a duty not to come into your house uninvited and a duty not to whisper gossip about you to my neighbour, the will theory does not discriminate with respect to the stringency of the rights that correspond to those two duties—if you have equal control over the exercise of both of them, then both rights exist and neither is more important than the other. This theory, then, identifies rights by reference to the constraints they impose; a right's scope is a matter of the control that its holder has with respect to the constraint it associated with it.

B. The constitutional rights arena

The debate within rights theory by no means exhausts the conceptual and normative dispute about what rights are. We can also trace the dichotomy of value and constraint within one of the central conceptual debates within the theory of constitutional rights. One incarnation of the dispute concerns the question of whether constitutional rights essentially inhere in persons or whether they are legal mechanisms for delineating and limiting the scope of governmental action. One way of framing this question is to ask whether constitutional rights are 'personal' or whether they are 'rule-dependent'. Matthew Adler sets out these two possibilities and argues that, in effect, we must understand constitutional rights in one way or the other, because the two are irreconcilable.[4] We need not take up Adler's own question; elucidating the two positions he articulates will suffice to introduce the distinct conceptual views of rights I want to trace.

(1) Personal rights and rule-dependence

On one hand, Adler describes constitutional rights in terms of what he calls the 'personal rights thesis'. This thesis says that having a constitutional right is not exhausted by the fact of its holder's being in an advantageous Hohfeldian jural position vis-à-vis the state. The fact that the state has done something that is constitutionally impermissible, and which causes me to seek and deserve redress and remedy, on this view, does not express the full meaning of my having a constitutional right. For me as a litigant against the state to have a real constitutional right, something more must be true about me in relation to what the government has done. On this view, constitutional rights inhere in persons, and can

[4] Matthew D. Adler, 'Personal Rights and Rule-Dependence: Can the Two Coexist?', *Legal Theory* 6, no. 4 (2000): 337–89.

be vindicated even if their violation is not perpetrated by a particular rule. Adler elaborates as follows:

Certain actions by governmental officials are unconstitutional—and will be invalidated by reviewing courts at the instance of appropriate litigants—quite independent of the language, scope, or history of the legal rules that authorize, or are taken to authorize, these actions. That is to say: The unconstitutional actions can be characterized in terms that do not entail the existence of some legal rule with a particular scope, language, or history.[5]

A governmental action is unconstitutional on this view not in virtue of the existence of a rule made in a particular way but only when it actually infringes a protected interest of a particular person. This way of thinking about constitutional rights can be summarized by the idea that certain of our human interests are recognized by the constitution as being so important that their infringement is beyond the legal scope of the government's power. That power is justifiably limited, on this view, because of the immense value of certain human interests. Constitutional rights, on this account, protect that which we deem most valuable against infringement by the state. To illustrate this position on constitutional rights, Adler gives the example of torture as a violation of the due process clause:

If governmental official G tortures person P, P can get a damages remedy against G regardless of whether the rule that G was following licensed 'torture,' as opposed to 'appropriate measures, as necessary for national security'—indeed, regardless of whether G's action was authorized, or taken to be authorized, by any legal rule.[6]

It does not matter here what rule the state is acting on in infringing the interest at stake, because the interest—in not being tortured—is so important, so valuable, that the *conduct* is a violation regardless of the reason or rule that motivates that conduct.

In contrast with the personal-rights thesis, Adler suggests that the competing view of constitutional rights is characterized by the 'rule-dependence' thesis. This view says that

[i]n delimiting the conditions under which constitutional relief is available, constitutional doctrine sometimes entails the existence of a discrete legal rule, to which the litigant has some nexus, with a particular type of scope, language, history, or some other such property of discrete legal rules. For example, free-speech doctrine looks to whether the litigant has been sanctioned, denied a benefit, or otherwise set back by a rule that discriminates against certain viewpoints or speech contents. If so, the litigant's challenge is quite likely to succeed; if not, it is quite likely to fail.[7]

In other words, on a rule-dependence view, constitutional rights are the remedy of citizens who simply have a 'nexus' with unconstitutional rules. In a sense this seems like a thinner view of what constitutional rights are, but it primarily reflects a very different understanding of what they are there for. On a personal-rights

[5] Adler, 'Personal Rights and Rule-Dependence: Can the Two Coexist?', 340.
[6] Adler, 'Personal Rights and Rule-Dependence: Can the Two Coexist?', 341.
[7] Adler, 'Personal Rights and Rule-Dependence: Can the Two Coexist?', 341.

view, they are intended to protect people against the infringement of their important interests by the power of the state. They represent that which we have declared to be most valuable. On the rule-dependent view, individual litigants are essentially patrolling the boundary of the government's rightful legal powers, rather than being themselves of primary importance. One way of describing the two views, then, is to point out that each seems to be focused on a different subject. A personal-rights view takes constitutional rights to have individual persons, or, at least, citizens, as their main subject. A rule-dependent view takes the primary subject of constitutional rights to be the state, insofar as they control the proper conduct of government and its exercise of its tremendous power. So whereas the personal-rights account has things of paramount value—human welfare and human dignity—as its conceptual focus, the rule-dependence thesis views constitutional rights primarily in terms of constraining action—in this case, state action.

But in fact we can understand most constitutional rights in either of these two main ways. Adler gives the following illustration to further elucidate the different kinds of views, pointing to the first flag-burning case, *Texas v. Johnson*:[8]

> The Court there overturned Mr. Johnson's sanction, imposed pursuant to a Texas statute prohibiting the 'desecrat[ion] [of a]...state or national flag,' while at the same time leaving the State of Texas free to sanction Johnson pursuant to a rule against arson, assault, the destruction of government property, pollution, or some other such rule that was not targeted at speech. Johnson's successful claim in *Johnson* was premised upon the speech-targeted cast of the flag-desecration rule, not upon the innocence of his particular speech-act. Contrast *Johnson* with the case of the rule-independent litigant who has been tortured by police, demonstrates that to the satisfaction of a constitutional reviewing court, and secures a damages judgment under the Due Process Clause.[9]

Adler's illustration seems designed to show that the exercise of different constitutional rights can line up better with one or the other of the two conceptual views he describes. He contrasts the speech case with the due process case in the following terms:

> In the torture case, it is easy to see how the litigant's rights can be 'personal.'...Not only is she interested in the litigation—she has been harmed by the police action and will be benefited by the remedy—but the harm is to an aspect of her well-being that falls within the 'zone of interests' protected by the Due Process Clause, namely, the interest in not being tortured....By contrast, because Mr. Johnson could be an arsonist, polluter, assaulter, and so on...it seemingly remains open to question whether an individualized remedy for him is justified and whether his interest in speaking does indeed trump the general welfare. And is arsonous, polluting, or assaultive speech the kind of speech that falls within the 'zone of interests' of the Free Speech Clause? To be sure, Mr. Johnson does have a bare interest in having the flag desecration statute invalidated—he benefits from that remedy—but the same would be true of, say, a manufacturer of fire-starting fluids

[8] 491 US 397 (1989).
[9] Adler, 'Personal Rights and Rule-Dependence: Can the Two Coexist?', 344.

who prospers as a result of Johnson because she can now sell her product to flag burners. If it is not the case that the 'personal' rights of the fluid manufacturer are violated by Texas's flag-desecration statute, then why are Mr. Johnson's?[10]

This illustration makes it seem as though there really are two kinds of constitutional right, corresponding to the two theories of what they are. But in fact we can see both of the rights Adler alludes to in either of the two ways he describes. He implies, for instance, that it might not be easy to see how the flag-burning speech right could be seen as 'personal'. Mr. Johnson's real interest, he indicates, is in the litigation itself; Adler makes it seem as though because we do not know what the moral character of Johnson's act is—whether arsonous or assaultive or purely expressive—we cannot say that the constitutional act protects that interest directly in a moral sense. Rather, Adler suggests, the right in question seems morally directed at the rule against flag-burning. The right seems to be more oriented toward constraint than toward value. On the other hand, the suggestion is, torture is always morally wrong even if the police are engaged in an activity genuinely directed at law and order, so the right protects something that is of paramount value under any circumstances.

Both litigants—the torture victim and the flag-burner—have prudential interests in the outcome of the cases, and if they are successful in their challenges, both will be understood to be in advantageous jural positions. The reason the flag-burning case seems more susceptible to a rule-dependent view is that the pernicious activity at issue is the content of the rule in question. The constitutional rule (the First Amendment) is a constraint on the flag-burning rule (nearly all states have or have had some rule against burning the flag), and the system functions as a whole to structure and limit government action. A flag-burning rule and its content can be challenged by anyone it affects, regardless of whether its impact on them constitutes what might be thought of as the real target of the protection of free speech. The constitutional constraint—the right protected by the First Amendment—seems, in other words, to be independent of the value of the activity, since the speech in question could be valuable—political, say—or value-less—arsonous, for example, or tending to incite violence. The case seems, then, to be a kind of structural instrument in patrolling the state's rule-making conduct. But isn't this all-encompassing protection of speech precisely the point of the first amendment? The interest in free speech, a personal-rights theorist might think, is so important to each and every person, regardless of the moral character of any particular speech act, that it is constitutionally protected. The flag-burning case is just an instance of that protection.

On the other hand, we might say that while it is true that torture is always morally repugnant, and the interest in not being tortured is thus a crucial personal right, the due process clause is not only about important interests or values; rather, it precisely exemplifies the rule-dependent view of constitutional rights. The due process clause limits the *way* in which the state can conduct its business; torturing people is, on this view, outside the scope of its legal powers, and a constitutional

[10] Adler, 'Personal Rights and Rule-Dependence: Can the Two Coexist?', 345.

challenge to state action that involves torture is a kind of policing of the boundary of its legal power. Just as we could say that the flag-burning case exemplifies the constitution's protection of an important interest—in speech—as well as a kind of rule limiting the state's rule-making power, we could also say that in addition to protecting the personal interest in not being tortured, the constitutional challenge to police action manifests a rule limiting the state's conduct.

(2) Immunities and constraint

The important thing to notice, for our purposes, about the discussion of whether constitutional rights are personal or rule-dependent is that two conceptual views of rights emerge from that discussion. On the one hand, rights are viewed as being fundamentally about the valuable interests they protect on behalf of individuals; on the other hand, they are viewed as being rule-based constraints for limiting the agent they protect *against*—in the case of constitutional rights, the state. In the first case they are moral shields for important human interests; in the second they are cogs in the wheel of legal government. Another, slightly more abstract, way to understand these two views is described by Richard Pildes in terms of immunities and structure, where the 'immunities' view of constitutional rights maps onto the personal rights one, and the 'structure' conception maps onto that of rule-dependence.[11]

Pildes, like Adler, defines the two conceptual views as a precursor to arguing for a rule-dependent or constraint-based one. Pildes describes one concept of constitutional rights that he calls the 'immunities' view, which understands rights in primarily anti-aggregative, anti-maximizing, essentially anti-utilitarian terms. On this account, rights compete with collective goals. They 'emanate from some conception of the self; rights demarcate spheres of belief and conduct insulated from majoritarian preferences to enable fundamental attributes of that self to develop'.[12] Pildes says he believes this view to be the dominant one in public political culture. He is more explicit than Adler about what makes a given interest sufficiently valuable to warrant constitutional protection: interests become immune to majoritarian pressures when they are necessary for the development of fundamental aspects of the self. Freedom in the area of belief, he suggests, together with freedoms of conduct, constitute the basic spheres of development of autonomous individuality, and are thus of paramount value.

Like the personal rights account, the immunities view conceives of constitutional rights as shields against the state. Various rights protect a variety of interests, but, taken together, these rights construct a general shield or sphere of protection around each individual, which is taken to protect them against the government's intrusions.

[11] Richard H. Pildes, 'Why Rights Are Not Trumps: Social Meanings, Expressive Harms, and Constitutionalism', *The Journal of Legal Studies* 27, no. S2 (1998): 725–63; 'Two Conceptions of Rights in Cases Involving Political Rights', *Houston Law Review* 34 (1997): 323; 'Dworkin's Two Conceptions of Rights', *The Journal of Legal Studies* 29, no. 1 (2000): 309–15.

[12] Pildes, 'Dworkin's Two Conceptions of Rights', 311.

The second concept of constitutional rights Pildes describes is one he calls the 'structural' account.

> On this view rights are not justified as all-purpose shields that enable individuals to do as they like, regardless of majoritarian judgments; instead, rights deny the state the power to infringe individual interests on the basis of certain reasons but permit infringement on other grounds. Rights do not entitle persons as much as they channel the kinds of reasons upon which the state can constitutionally act in diverse institutional and other contexts. Conceived in this way, rights are still ultimately justified on the grounds of the individual interests they promote, but these interests are distinct, or promoted in distinct ways, from the way interests are conceived and promoted in the immunities conception. There is no general state duty of noninterference with such rights, but a duty not to interfere for certain reasons. There is no undifferentiated right to free speech, but rather a right not to have the state ban certain kinds of speech in certain settings and for certain reasons.[13]

Pildes's explication of the structural conception is more theoretically elaborate than the rule-dependent one. The structural view does not simply present constitutional rights as rules within a legal scheme that interacts with other rules to constrain the rule-making power of the state. Rather, it takes rights to be reason-oriented: conceptually speaking, it suggests, constitutional rights do not constrain government action directly, but rather limit the *reasons* on the basis of which it can act are limited.

Both the rule-dependent and the structural conceptions of constitutional rights view them as essentially constraining governance in certain ways, not substantively but formally, whereby rules limit rule-making. Yet because it focuses exclusively on limiting reasons in decision-making, the structural view seems to be even more polarized with respect to the value-based view than in the case of rule-dependence and personal rights.

Pildes's argument is based on his analysis of Dworkin's discussions of rights. Dworkin's own position within the conceptual dispute I have been outlining has itself been the subject of some debate. Pildes associates Dworkin primarily with the immunities conception of rights, an assertion that Jeremy Waldron contests. Dworkin's association with the immunities view is widely assumed because of his famous use of the term 'trumps' to describe rights, but Waldron argues that Dworkin in fact espouses the other, structural, conception.

Waldron, like Dworkin himself, describes two possible conceptions of rights—Waldron calls these the 'type *a*' and 'type *b*' accounts—which map onto the conceptual divide between the rule-oriented and the personal. Waldron describes the 'type *a*' view, one he argues is properly ascribed to Dworkin, as asserting that rights are 'constraints on the kinds of reasons that government may legitimately act upon'.[14] This account reflects the concept of rights we have so far

[13] Pildes, 'Dworkin's Two Conceptions of Rights', 311–12.

[14] Jeremy Waldron, 'Pildes on Dworkin's Theory of Rights', *Journal of Legal Studies* 29 (2000): 301.

identified in terms of structure, rules, or constraint. Dworkin himself describes this view as one he accepts:

> I wish to propose the following general theory of rights. The concept of an individual political right, in the strong anti-utilitarian sense I distinguished earlier, is a response to the philosophical defects of a utilitarianism that counts external preferences and the practical impossibility of a utilitarianism that does not. It allows us to enjoy the institutions of political democracy, which enforce overall or unrefined utilitarianism, and yet protect the fundamental right of citizens to equal concern and respect by prohibiting decisions that seem, antecedently, likely to have been reached by virtue of the external components of preferences democracy reveals.[15]

This theory is not about discounting people's actual votes, but about imagining each decision as involving a utilitarian calculus in which certain people express preferences that refer simply to discounting the preferences of others rather than to any particular substantive goal. These Dworkin famously called 'external preferences' and it is these that the reason-constraining theory is meant to eliminate as a basis for decision.

The view that Waldron describes as being 'type *b*' is the one that corresponds to those theories that fall on the 'personal rights' and 'immunities' side of the conceptual divide in rights theory. This view is one often associated with Dworkin because of his discussion of rights in terms of 'trumps'. Dworkin himself describes this view as suggesting that

> whatever rights people have are at least in large part timeless rights necessary to protect enduring and important interests fixed by human nature and fundamental to human development, like interests in the choice of sexual partners and acts and choice of religious conviction.[16]

There are, in other words, some aspects of human life that are 'fundamental' to development, and thus are so valuable that they warrant the kind of protection that rights status offers. This is, of course, the view that Pildes describes in terms of the 'immunities' concept of rights, and it corresponds to the 'personal rights' account that both Pildes and Adler see reflected in at least some Supreme Court jurisprudence.

Conclusion

In both rights theory and in the constitutional rights field, then, we find ideas about rights split into one of two types of conceptual characterization—that of constraint or that of value. In Chapter 4 I will turn from the primarily conceptual perspective on rights to a more normative one, illustrating the way in which

[15] Ronald Dworkin, *Taking Rights Seriously* (Cambridge: Cambridge University Press, 1977), 277.

[16] Ronald Dworkin, *Taking Rights Seriously*; 'Rights as Trumps', in Jeremy Waldron (ed), *Theories of Rights* (Oxford: Oxford University Press, 1984).

the dichotomy of value and constraint continues to underlie the debate. In doing so, I will also show how the dichotomy is undermined in that context, further destabilizing the mutual exclusivity of the two ways of conceptualizing rights. Neither an exclusively constraint-based nor an exclusively value-based theory of rights will generate the conceptual account that can underlie the model of public law rights.

4

Constraint and Value

In Chapter 3 I presented the dichotomous characterization of rights in terms of either constraint or value as a conceptual disagreement—a disagreement about the kind of thing a right is. But constraint and value can also be understood as substantive normative principles that circumscribe which entitlements we should think of as rights. So in this chapter I will turn to theories of rights that are primarily normative in nature. These theories either address directly the question of which rights we ought to have, or they refer to rights in normative arguments about how political society ought to be structured or how we ought to behave. My argument in this chapter is that even when we focus on rights' normative content rather than on their conceptual contours, neither of the elements of constraint and value is dispensable to a model of rights.

By way of introduction, recall that I take public law rights to be an instantiation of rights in two senses. They are, first, manifestations of the *concept* of rights; they are a species of the genus of rights, as it were. Second, public law rights are a particular *kind* of instantiation of the idea of rights because they are also a moral, political, and legal commitment to, or manifestation of, certain specific rights that people have. In other words, they, unlike the abstract idea of rights of which they are a manifestation, *do* present us with at least one kind of answer to the substantive normative question of which rights we ought to have. The model of public law rights that I will set out in the following chapters must therefore accurately capture the way in which public law rights are a species of the concept of rights more generally, and it must also accommodate the substantive norms that characterize public law rights.

If the model of public law rights is at once compatible with concepts of rights in the abstract sense and also includes certain substantive moral norms, however, the question arises: what is the relationship between rights' conceptual structure and their normative content?

I. Concepts and Norms in Rights Theory

When people disagree about rights, they normally do so in one of two contexts. First, theorists often disagree about what the concept of a right is—what is its nature and its form. Second, and much more often, ordinary people disagree about which rights we ought to have. These include lawyers, policymakers, and the individuals whose lives will be affected by decisions about rights. Sometimes this latter type of disagreement is of a very general kind—that is, someone might say 'My child ought to have a right to health insurance, even if I cannot afford to pay.' But very often this type of disagreement—particularly among lawyers, legal scholars, and policymakers—involves making interpretive, extrapolative, or extensional claims about rights in our existing legal system. These disagreements involve questions like: do we have a right to food, based on the best interpretation of the moral commitments represented by our human rights practice? The role of positive or socio-economic rights is perennially and pervasively subject to this type of disagreement, partly because of the difficulty of assigning duties in respect of these rights, where certain rights appear to be implied in, or as preconditions for the fulfilment of, other rights. Thus, the World Health Organization has derived a universal right to clean water from the human right to health.[1] Yet as demands for these interdependent rights accumulate, we have not yet reached any agreement about who, exactly, ought to be responsible for fulfilling them.

Conceptual theorists of rights quite often purport to refrain from committing themselves on these substantive questions of which rights we ought to have; but the everyday disagreements about which rights we ought to have often rely on some background notion of the kind of thing a right is, and, in particular, the kind of thing that grounds a given right. If someone wants to say that we ought to recognize a universal right to food, for example, he can say that the importance of the interest in food to each and every person warrants the elevation of that interest to the status of a right. Or if one thinks of rights as side-constraints or trumps that protect individuals against the potentially devastating impact of others' pursuit of their aims, then one might argue for a right to food on the basis that no benefit, individual or social, justifies systematically allowing some individuals to go hungry.

Conceptual questions about rights thus creep into substantive disagreements about them. And, of course, normative views creep in the other direction too, as it were, into the domain of conceptual analysis of rights. Conceptual theories of rights often privilege certain substantive moral ideas insofar as they suggest that rights are grounded on or justified by one thing or another: interest theorists of rights tend to be accused of privileging welfare over equal moral status, whereas will theorists of rights are conversely accused of unjustifiably limiting the grounds of rights to autonomy-based concerns.

The different concepts of rights are embedded in comprehensive moral and political outlooks that are in profound conflict with one another. To invoke the notion of a right taken from one of these moral theories in an argument for the recognition of a right in a given concrete circumstance will never succeed in convincing someone who is committed to the opposite conceptual view. Making an argument about the right to clean water based on an interest theory of rights, for

[1] World Health Organization, *The Right To Water*, Health and Human Rights Publications, Series 3, 2003, online at <http://www.who.int/water_sanitation_health/en/righttowater.pdf>.

example, will never persuade someone who thinks, as a Nozickean would, that a right like the right to health is not a real moral right at all because it is not capable of being universalized without creating conflicts between different claimants of the same right.

In light of these disagreements, the most useful account of rights for the purposes of my project would be one that made sense against the background of the mainstream moral views without taking sides in the deep moral disagreements between them. It is this kind of model of rights that I seek to articulate. I take the two major families of rights theories—the value-based and the constraint-based—each to contribute an insight about the *type* of normative consideration that justifies a right. The aim of my model is not to refute any particular theory of rights, but rather to bring to light the types of normative judgment that go into the recognition or creation of any given right, so that it can help to clarify the terms of many substantive disagreements about what rights we ought to have, particularly about those that pertain to the bearer(s) of a duty in respect of a given right.

II. Constraint, Value, and Normative Accounts of Rights

Normative accounts of rights, or accounts of rights that form part of substantive accounts of what morality requires, track the ethical gulf between consequentialists and non-consequentialists. On the value-based view, we have the idea that rights represent important, widely held values. Rights are seen as protecting, on behalf of individuals, those elements of human life that are essential to the development or well-being of the self. These mainly include the things that make each of us who we are: to identify them, we can begin at the centre of each of us, as it were, with conviction, thought and conscience, and proceed outward to the expression of that self into the world, to our protection of various forms of expression and conduct; finally, we show concern for the manifestations of the self in interaction with others through our protection of association and contract. On any value-based view, these are the aspects of human life that are deemed so important that they warrant special attention and protection. The emphasis is on the value that warrants limiting the government's actions: those aspects of the self that are crucial to our development or our well-being are taken to have paramount value. On this view, we could, without conceptual inconsistency, also include the aspects of human life that are materially necessary to human life and development such as basic subsistence, health care, and education.

This description of the value-based view might sound less like a conceptual view of rights and more like the substantive ethical view associated with (rule) utilitarianism. The basic thrust of both refers to human welfare and the goods necessary to the development of human life, which provide the normative basis for the creation and enforcement of rules. In the case of both value-based rights theory and a broadly utilitarian ethical view, too, obligations are not viewed as morally intrinsic but as generated by the importance of certain aspects of human welfare.

While the utilitarian ethical position and the conceptual views of rights I have characterized as value-based share a commitment to aspects of human well-being, the very idea of rights and of the kinds of strong or absolute pre-commitments they represent seems at odds with the consequentialist structure of the utilitarian view. Utilitarianism is not itself a rights based view, and thus to the extent that it is held up against an account of rights as morally fundamental, the difference between the two as far as their structure is concerned is striking. The constraint-based accounts of rights draw their content from rights' constraining *form*.

If the predominantly dichotomous characterization of rights in existing theories reflects the conflict between two types of moral theories—consequentialist and non-consequentialist—that has taken on a kind of adversarial character, one could perhaps be forgiven for assuming that a model of rights must involve *only* value or *only* constraint. I argue that this assumption about rights is mistaken; in the following, I will try to show that if one accepts rights to any degree, or uses the language of rights at all, then, whether one is a consequentialist or a non-consequentialist, one must somehow make room for the elements of both constraint and value in an adequate account of them.

Consequentialists and non-consequentialists have a bedrock disagreement about morality, and about the nature and existence of rights. Consequentialists argue that the non-consequentialist account of rights leads to intuitively strange conclusions, for example, about the desirability of letting many people die in order that one might survive. And non-consequentialists, by contrast, argue that consequentialism leads to similarly counter-intuitive results with respect to the permissibility of using or sacrificing people in the service of larger goals. That general argument is hundreds of years old and it is not the one I am taking part in here. Indeed, it would be misguided to claim that persons taking such divergent views would, in accepting both the elements of constraint and value in a model of rights, thereby adopt the *same* model. If that were the claim, it would imply that the consequentialist and non-consequentialist positions on rights are in fact the same, and that is clearly not the case.

Even admitting the existence of the two elements of constraint and value, consequentialists and non-consequentialists will give different accounts of which is more fundamental, or which grounds the other, what is the relative weight of the two, and so on. The two points of view would, in other words, interpret the two elements in different ways. My aim here is not to endorse one interpretation against the other. Rather, it is simply to establish that despite the fact that these two prominent theories of rights swathe themselves in the language of one element or the other, any sensible account of rights has to include both elements, however their interrelation is interpreted.

The elements of constraint and value are necessary building blocks in a model of rights. Even the most ardent utilitarian, if she accepts rights in some way, is committed to at least a functional notion of inviolability; and the most ardent formalist in regard to rights, I will maintain, implicitly incorporates some notion of value. I am not, in other words, trying to deny the core commitments of either moral position. I am making the much more limited claim that even accepting its core commitments, both positions have to acknowledge that rights involve some element of both constraint and value. The two sides will, of course, continue to disagree about the right way of thinking about the relative priority of the two, but, for the purpose of my own argument, I remain agnostic regarding that further debate.

A. Constraint

My argument for the element of constraint involves three main claims. First, I will point out that rights have a constraint-based form. Second, I will argue that this form entails a certain functional notion of inviolability. Finally, I will add that while consequentialists may dispute the more deeply moral notion of inviolability, some degree of its moral significance is suggested by the widely accepted set of general or human rights understood to apply equally to all persons.

(1) Form and constraint

In the dispute between consequentialists and non-consequentialists, one of the biggest controversies concerns whether or not consequentialists can defend rights. Many consequentialists argue that they can adopt a two-level view in which rights of some sort play a significant role. On that view, rights are ultimately justified instrumentally. On the other side, non-consequentialists argue that such a view is incoherent, either logically or morally or both. They argue that in order to adopt a rights framework one must also adopt a moral justification for those rights grounded in inviolability. There are many different versions of each of these two types of argument; my purpose here, though, is not to engage that debate. My concern, rather, is to show that people who accept the idea of rights, consequentialists and non-consequentialists alike, are accepting, in part, a particular formal idea, namely that of constraint.

The claim, then, is that rights take the form of constraints. This is an assertion about rights at a fairly simple or superficially common-sense level. Constraint, here, is to be understood roughly in terms of obligation or duty. This is the sense in which my having a right, for example, simply means that other people are constrained in the ways they can behave in certain respects. If I have a right that you not touch me without my consent, then you are prohibited or constrained from doing so. My property right means, among other things, that you are prohibited from entering my house without my permission.

The idea of constraint may seem best suited to these kinds of negative prohibitions, but in fact it functions in some sense to describe all rights. We can understand positive rights in terms of constraints: if I have a right to a certain level of health care, the effect or *manifestation* of that right is that unspecified others must do certain things to ensure that I obtain some degree of access to health care.

Their choices, their conduct, then, is, in certain respects, constrained by the existence of my right.

This is a very common-sense understanding of what rights are, and indeed the idea that rights are associated or correlated with duties is well known. Some theorists assert that rights just *are* behavioural constraints, or justified constraints, or some variation on that idea.[2] Hohfeld's taxonomy of jural relations is certainly the most well-developed systematization of this simple idea of the form of rights.[3] His system, in fact, is perhaps the best blueprint for articulating a specifically structural or formal view. He set out a set of eight normative positions that he called 'fundamental jural relations', dividing the positions into two categories—correlative and opposite. The correlative positions are: right (claim-right)/duty, privilege/no-right, power/liability, and immunity/disability. The opposite positions are: right/no-right, privilege/duty, power/disability, and immunity/liability.[4] The importance of these positions lies in their inextricable logical relation to one another: the correlative positions entail each other—so, by definition, then, your having a privilege to use my car *means* that I have no right (a no-right) to interfere with your using my car. Similarly, the position opposite to my having a privilege to use your car (such that you would have no claim to interfere with my doing so) would be my having a duty *not* to use it; you would have a claim against me if I did so. This is therefore a highly formal way of understanding rights. When we think of them in entailment relations with other norms, such as duties, we understand them in this structural way, in which the one exists by virtue of the other. What is a 'liberty',[5] for example, as distinct from a mere 'action', without reference to the absence of a corresponding constraint? Hohfeldian powers[6]—the ability to alter claims—are similarly distinct from mere actions: they can *be* powers only where there is something for them to act on. In short, then, the formal dimension of rights means that they are also forms of constraint: if a liberty entails a no-right, then it is a constraining form; if a right entails a duty, it is similarly constraining in a purely logical or formal sense.

[2] Judith Jarvis Thomson seems to fall into this category, for example, in her *The Realm of Rights* (Cambridge, Massachusetts: Harvard University Press, 1990); see also George Rainbolt, *The Concept of Rights* (Dordrecht, The Netherlands: Springer, 2006).

[3] Wesley Newcomb Hohfeld, *Fundamental Legal Conceptions as Applied in Judicial Reasoning* (Westport, Connecticut: Greenwood Press, 1978).

[4] Hohfeld, Fundamental Legal Conceptions as Applied in Judicial Reasoning, 35–7.

[5] Hohfeld uses the term 'privilege' in place of the term 'liberty', as he views the former as a more precise term, particularly in the legal context, than the latter. See his *Fundamental Legal Conceptions as Applied in Judicial Reasoning*, at 43–50. In practice, though, the two terms are essentially interchangeable.

[6] Hohfeld uses the term 'power' to refer to 'one's affirmative "control" over a given legal relation as against another', *Fundamental Legal Conceptions*, at 60; it is the opposite of legal disability ('no-power') and the correlative of legal liability, *Fundamental Legal Conceptions*, at 50. A liability in this context is not synonymous with a legal duty, but rather describes the condition of the person on whom the legal duty can be imposed by another; it is a liability, Hohfeld says, 'to have a duty created' *Fundamental Legal Conceptions*, at 59.

While we can understand Hohfeld's taxonomy as an elaborate systematization of the common-sense idea of rights and correlative obligations, some theorists of rights do not accept the Hohfeldian picture of the way rights and constraints interrelate. There is significant disagreement, in fact, among rights theorists, about the tightness of the correlation between rights and duties. Even on the weaker thesis about that correlation, however, rights still involve an element of constraint. One example of such a disagreement between rights theorists whose positions are, relatively speaking, quite close, is that between Joseph Raz and Matthew Kramer. Raz rejects the 'correlativity axiom', which says that rights are definitionally or analytically correlated to duties (as well as asserting that the other Hohfeldian relations are logically correlative). Together with several other interest theorists,[7] he objects to the idea that any given right is correlated with a single duty, since, among other things, rights seem to give rise to what Waldron calls 'waves of duties'—duties of forbearance, protection, remedy, enforcement, and so on.[8] On the Razian conception, rights are the *grounds* of duties, and logically prior to them. Highlighting the way in which rights and duties can come apart is one of the central features of his theory: he objects to the idea of strict correlativity on the basis that that thesis 'assume[s] that a right can be exhaustively stated by stating those duties which it has already established'.[9] In response to these arguments, Kramer does not dispute the dynamism and diversity of duties suggested by this kind of strictly interest-based view, but he stresses that each one is identifiably the logical correlate of a particular right.[10] The right to personal security, for example, can be said to generate a general abstract duty not to harm others, but it does not, as both he and Raz agree, mean that everyone is always under a duty to protect others from all injuries and accidents. Rather, the abstract right generates concrete duties not to assault, imprison, rape, kill, etc. Each of these concrete duties can be tied to a specific right that creates the relevant entitlements.

For the purpose of showing that constraints are somehow necessarily involved in what rights are, it doesn't matter who is right in this debate. The point is just that although they disagree about the tightness of the correlation, both accept the existence of the constraint in some way. Even on the more Razian view, as Waldron says, rights are 'the way interests generate duties'[11]— they are the grounds of constraints. So even if the question is left open about which duties will arise, and for whom, as a result of recognizing a given right, the fact that respecting or implementing rights necessarily involves constraints of some kind is generally accepted by everyone.

[7] Such as Neil McCormick in 'Rights in Legislation', in P. M. S. Hacker and J. Raz (eds), *Law, Morality and Society: Essays in Honour of H. L. A. Hart* (Oxford: Oxford University Press, 1977).

[8] Jeremy Waldron, 'Rights in Conflict' in *Liberal Rights: Collected Papers 1981–1991* (Cambridge: Cambridge University Press, 1993), 25, 212.

[9] Joseph Raz, 'On the Nature of Rights', *Mind*, 93 (Apr. 1984): 194–214

[10] Matthew H. Kramer, 'Rights Without Trimmings' in *A Debate Over Rights: Philosophical Enquiries* (Oxford: Clarendon Press, 1999).

[11] Waldron, 'Rights in Conflict', 212.

(2) *Constraint and inviolability*

The claim that rights take the form of constraints reflects the notion of duty or obligation; it also means that they embody the inviolability implied by the idea of constraint. If the form of rights is that of constraint, the implication of that form is that they manifest some kind of inviolability. The idea of inviolability I want to introduce here as associated with formal constraint is a simple, common-sense one: the idea is merely that if you have rights, you are inviolable in respect of those rights. They simply articulate certain things that people cannot do to you.

So my right to free speech, as we have seen, means that there are certain kinds of constraints on others not to interfere with my speech. Those constraints render me normatively inviolable in respect of the right they reflect. This inviolability obtains obviously enough in the case of negative rights, but, like constraint itself, it also obtains as an implication of the constraints associated with all rights. If I have a contractual right that you mow my lawn, then if you do not mow it you fail to be appropriately constrained by my right and you infringe my inviolability accordingly—in other words, you violate me in that particular respect.

The inviolability associated with constraint is sometimes thought of in different terms, but to the same effect: the demandingness or the peremptoriness of rights are characteristics entailed by their constraining form. This peremptoriness of the reasons associated with rights is often described by reference to the way that having a duty in virtue of a right makes that duty directed to the right-holder. It imbues the right-holder, in particular, with a high level of entitlement in relation to the duty. The example that is often used to illustrate this point refers to the difference between an obligation or duty to give to charity and an obligation or duty that one may have in virtue of a right. Although the duty-bearer may experience both obligations as equally important, there is a kind of priority associated with the right.

It is this constraining element that makes obligations associated with rights directed *toward* the right-holder. That is, the obligation established by or because of a right is owed to the person who holds it, who is its subject. It is this quartet of characteristics associated with the element of constraint—demandingness, peremptoriness, categoricality, and directedness—that create a functional inviolability in respect of the interest protected by the right.[12]

Even rights that do not seem associated with inviolability in the deeply moral sense of the term, such as the right of an administrative agency to take certain actions on behalf of the state, still reflect functional inviolability in the sense that they prohibit others from interfering with those actions for any reason, arguably, except for the weight of conflicting rights. In these cases, the element of constraint and priority associated with the enforcement of legal rights having a strong moral

[12] These features are widely taken to be particularly associated with the kind of things rights are; John Tasioulas has recently described rights' form, for instance, in terms of generating duties that are categorical and directed. See John Tasioulas, 'Taking Rights out of Human Rights', *Ethics* 120, no. 4 (2010), 657.

basis seem to carry over, or ride on the coat-tails, so to speak, of the rights framework itself so that the articulation of a legal right creates some degree of presumptive priority. Of course, in the case of all legal rights publically or democratically created, the constraint-based character of a rights framework in general also carries a moral priority associated with the process by which the right was created. If I have a right to health care, then, that right just is a strong consideration in favour of actions being taken in respect of that interest rather than others. It is precisely this presumptive priority associated with the directed obligations embodied by rights that gives them their anti-maximizing character: they are meant to indicate a certain *prima facie* inviolability of interests against infringement from the actions certain others might otherwise take in pursuit of their goals and desires.

(3) *The scope of inviolability*

The two claims I have made so far, that rights are associated with constraint and that constraint is associated with a certain kind of inviolability, might seem to lead to the conclusion that consequentialist and non-consequentialist views of rights are in fact the same. That conclusion is the one we would assert if we were making the strong argument made by non-consequentialists that two-level consequentialism, or consequentialism that incorporates a rights framework, is making a mistake, is logically or morally *incoherent*.

But this conclusion is not, in fact, the implication of my argument. My own conclusion concerns the basic elements of rights that each side ought to be able to accept in one way or another while still maintaining the fundamental uniqueness of its view. This is because my conclusion is a much more limited one: it says that even if everyone accepts the two claims I have made so far, consequentialists and non-consequentialists will continue to have a further and serious disagreement about rights, a disagreement on which my argument has no further bearing.

That disagreement concerns the nature and content of the idea of inviolability that goes along with rights. Inviolability can be understood in two possible ways. The first meaning of inviolability carries the connotation commonly associated with the term, namely, the strong moral motion that there are things people cannot do to one another. This is the view of inviolability taken by non-consequentialists.

On this view inviolability is a first-order moral idea and goes all the way down, as it were; it means that certain prohibitions on what you can do to someone obtain no matter how good the consequences of doing those things would be. The idea of equal rights, for those subscribing to this full-blooded notion of inviolability, is an ideal way of expressing the equal worth of persons. Asserting that persons have equal worth is a very abstract claim—it says little about just how much worth that is. And the idea of inviolability gives content to that abstraction. It answers the question of how much everyone is worth by insisting that everyone is protected against having things done to him or her in the service of even some very worthwhile goal. This means that the worth of each person is so great that it outweighs the importance of whatever beneficial consequence would arise as a result of violating him or her in some basic way. On this view, then, equal worth is understood in terms of inviolability. And equal rights express this rich notion of inviolability and equal worth. On this view, then, the element of constraint associated with rights operationalizes or makes manifest the idea of inviolability.

Consequentialists who accept rights accept the constraints that go along with them, but they view the nature and role of inviolability in relation to those constraints very differently. Consequentialists, like non-consequentialists, assert the equal worth of persons, but they understand that worth in terms of the importance of people's interests. They think that the best way of expressing the moral worth of persons involves something like counting everyone equally in a utilitarian calculus. Consequentialists adopt rights, then, not because the idea of equal rights just *is* the best way of expressing equal status, as non-consequentialists think it is, but because a rights framework is a particularly effective instrument for promoting and protecting people's interests, and certain especially urgent interests in particular. On their view, then, inviolability does not go all the way down; it is not, in other words, a morally foundational idea. This means that it is possible, on a consequentialist account, to say that there is a point at which inviolability is an interest to be calculated like any other, but that it happens to be a particularly important interest.

This disagreement between consequentialists and non-consequentialists is a deep and persistent one. But—and this is the important point for the purposes of my argument—the disagreement is unaffected by the acknowledgement that when you use the language of rights you import an element of constraint together with a certain kind of *functional* inviolability that goes along with that element. Non-consequentialists may argue, against two-level consequentialists, that it is incoherent to employ an instrument like rights based on a consequentialist foundation. But whether that is the case or not, the point I am making here is a much more limited one: whatever we think about its moral foundations, the rights instrument has a particular kind of character.

The full-blooded view of inviolability, then, is the one most often associated with rights, and it is the one non-consequentialists take to justify or ground them. Consequentialists, by contrast, view rights as ultimately justified in instrumental terms. But just because something is an instrument, that does not mean you can do anything at all with it. Different instruments have different functions in light of their intrinsic properties. A hammer, to give a facile example, is not an instrument with which it is possible to tune a piano. A screwdriver is not an instrument with which one can see things magnified—one needs something like a magnifying glass for that. Rights, similarly, having the formal property of constraint, therefore have the functional implication of some kind of inviolability. The kind of inviolability implied by the intrinsic property of the rights instrument, then, is only the thin or functional kind I described earlier, meaning that insofar as one has a right one is inviolable in respect of that right. The acceptance of a rights framework, therefore, entails at least the functional notion of inviolability—even a consequentialist, then, who accepts such a framework, is committed to at least this thin sense of inviolability.

But a further point of likely agreement between non-consequentialists and consequentialists is suggestive of a slightly more robust conception of inviolability associated with rights. As I said earlier, consequentialists often adopt rights frameworks because such frameworks are particularly useful to protect important interests. These interests are protected as rights precisely because they are viewed as extremely important, and it would be difficult to make sense of this importance if they were not protected on behalf of everyone. The right to be free from torture, for example, protects an interest whose importance would be difficult to make sense of if it did not protect all persons equally. Such interests, in other words, are important precisely because they are so vital to each of us simply in virtue of our personhood; they are therefore also generally understood to apply equally. When consequentialists adopt rights frameworks, in other words, they often do so precisely because of the special importance of those interests to every person. For example, the original two-level consequentialist, Mill, incorporated a framework of universal rights by creating a distinction between two types of utility: the one he describes in terms of reasons of 'ordinary expediency' that can be subject to calculations of the general good, and 'vastly more important utilities' that 'protect... every individual from being harmed by others either directly or by being hindered in his freedom of pursuing his own good'.[13]

However one justifies these frameworks of crucially important rights, then, they are generally viewed as applying *equally* to everyone. Among the rights accepted by two-level consequentialists, perhaps the most commonly adopted ones are also the most general or universal: basic human rights, basic autonomy rights, rights to physical integrity—these are ones that few who accept rights at all are inclined to reject. To the extent that one accepts the most basic framework of equal rights—however thinly one defines them—one also takes on board some specific ways in which people are *morally* inviolable. The enumerations of prohibited violations, taken together, describe a sphere of substantive moral inviolability around each individual. So, if consequentialists accept rights at all, and if they also accept some minimal notion of some rights that must be *equal* rights, such as general rights not to be tortured, or, slightly more robustly, autonomy rights, then they accept some degree of inviolability in two respects. First, they accept the functional inviolability that comes with the formal nature of the instrument of rights; and, second, they effectively adopt a thicker or more morally robust notion of the substantive moral gravitas of protecting certain interests on behalf of persons equally, as expressed by the adoption of frameworks of basic equal rights.

B. Value

Using the language of rights, I have been arguing, means that one accepts a certain formal idea of constraint and the functional inviolability in respect of

[13] John Stuart Mill, *Utilitarianism*, ed Colin Heydt (Peterborough, Ont: Broadview Press, 2011), 256.

protected interests it entails.. But any account of rights must also acknowledge an element of value. Consequentialist accounts of rights rely almost entirely on the idea of value—they argue that it is the value of persons, and more specifically the value of persons' well-being, that rights protect. Non-consequentialist accounts of morality accept an element of value as well, either explicitly or implicitly. My intention here is not to take up the quarrel between consequentialists and non-consequentialists about the relative priority, the appropriate weighting or correct interpretation, of these two elements. My intention, rather, is merely to establish that rights involve some element of constraint and some element of value. All that remains to make that argument, then, is to point out that even the most structural or constraint-based views of rights adopt or accept, however implicitly, some element of value underlying their formalism. As in the case of my argument for the element of constraint, I do not mean to suggest here that formalistic or rule-based views of rights are thereby *incoherent*. All I mean to establish is that an account of rights cannot be formal *all the way down*, as it were. By bringing out the element of value in several formalistic theories of rights, I will also point out the way in which the element of value gives rights their variable stringency.

In each of the formalistic theories of rights I will survey, I will point to two dimensions of value. The first is simply the value associated with the object of rights protection according to such theories, namely, individual inviolability. Moral inviolability underlies these theories in that it animates or motivates their construction of a rule system that is designed to foster inviolability. The second dimension of value at work within these formalistic theories is the prioritization of certain interests over others. These theories maintain, either explicitly or implicitly, that there is a set of interests that are eligible candidates for protection as rights. This set of interests is in effect selected for protection because they are *valuable* in some way. Even if a formalist theorist would argue that such interests are derived from the rule structure itself, that simply means that the interests thus derived are considered important *to* the animating value of persons and their inviolability.

The first element of value implicit in formalistic theories of rights, then, is the answer to the question of *why* we build a rule system around people's moral inviolability—why, in other words, we recognize people as morally and legally inviolable. There must be a reason for this construction, otherwise it would simply be empty rule-following. The reason is that the inviolability conferred by rights protects the value of persons; but the question remains of *how* to protect persons—or, to put the question differently, *in which respects* persons are morally inviolable. The particular interests protected by rights, on the formalistic views we will consider, are the ones judged most important to the protection of persons as inviolable. So the implicit value in these theories is the value of persons. That is a very abstract and apparently absolute idea; it is made more concrete through the elevation of some interests in a kind of hierarchy that rights actually protect. We will see, then, that each of the theories set out below is animated by the value of moral inviolability of individual persons; each one also emphasizes some more particular good, such as choice, autonomy, or personal property, whose protection is an instrument for that of the more abstract value of inviolability.

(1) Will or choice theories

According to the will theory, rights consist of duties together with the power to enforce or waive them. The right-bearer is the agent holding that power in respect of a given duty. The theory expresses the idea that rights protect the *choices* of individuals rather than their interests.

Hillel Steiner, one advocate of the modern will theory, asserts that rights protect only choices, and that it is thus an entirely formal normative system; that is, there is no 'justice test' to determine whether or not a right exists.[14] A right, he says, endows an individual with a 'discretionary domain'. Such domains, within which Hart suggested that right-holders are 'small-scale sovereign[s]',[15] are 'spheres of practical choice within which the choices made by designated individuals (or groups)'[16] must not be interfered with. The delineation of the sphere is made without reference to the content of the choices that will be made within it, but rather is demarcated by a number of powers. The ones Steiner specifies are:

(1) to waive compliance with the duty (ie. extinguish it);
(2) to leave the duty in existence (ie. demand compliance with it)
(3) to waive proceeding for the enforcement of the duty (ie. for the restraint of, or compensation by, the duty-bearer in the face of threatened or actual breach);
(4) to demand proceeding for the enforcement of the duty
(5) to waive enforcement
(6) to demand enforcement.[17]

An individual right-bearer, then, has an area of *'action-space'*. That area corresponds with some moral duty of others, so, as Carl Wellman puts it, 'John's claim not to be struck by others consists of the duty of others not to strike John together with his power to claim performance of this duty.'[18] The right, then, is more closely associated with the individual's control over its exercise than with the interest it protects.

The way the will theory identifies rights, therefore, is to look to who has control over the enforcement of duties. This poses several problems, since at an intuitive level many of the rights we believe ourselves to have are inalienable—that is, we have *no* choice about whether their corresponding duties will be enforced.[19] This seems to have the effect of removing from the conceptual category of 'right' what

[14] Hillel Steiner, 'Working Rights' in *A Debate Over Rights: Philosophical Enquiries*; Hillel Steiner, *An Essay on Rights* (Oxford: Blackwell Publishing, 1994); Carl Wellman, *Real Rights* (New York: Oxford University Press, 1995).

[15] In H. L. A. Hart, *Essays on Bentham* (Oxford: Oxford University Press), 183–4.

[16] Steiner, 'Working Rights', 262.

[17] Steiner, 'Working Rights', 240.

[18] Wellman, *Real Rights*, 80.

[19] MacCormick makes the point that it seems strange that claims can only qualify as rights if the claim-holders can both enforce and waive them, 195–9.

seem to be our most important ones—not to be murdered, tortured, or enslaved, for example. Moreover, because it views right-holders as bearers of will, the theory also restricts its ambit to those who have agency; so infants, children, the mentally disabled, and animals cannot, by definition, have rights.[20] These are problems that can be traced to the very formalism that defines the will theory; that is to say, it seems to be a system comprised entirely of rules with no real orientation to the question of *why* such rules should obtain. We are not interested, here, in the strengths and weaknesses of the theory for its own sake. Rather, we are interested in questioning whether there is some element of value inherent in the theory despite its professed formalism.

Steiner's response to this kind of criticism has several parts. First, he responds that in contexts like criminal law there *are* right-holders that correspond to the duties at issue, but these are not private citizens. Rather, they are the state officials whom he calls the 'power-possessors'.[21] This response defends the very formalism that the criticism seems aimed at, namely, that the theory does not make moral evaluation any kind of criterion in its recognition of rights: 'an action's being *rights impermissible* is not conclusive of its moral impermissibility'.[22] This distinguishes the will theory from both the interest-based theories we have already seen *and* the more deontological theories such as the Nozickean and the Kantian. For all these others, rights are *necessarily* related to moral permissibility—some, like the interest theory, leave open the question of which interests will be deemed most important from a moral standpoint, but none defines rights in such a purely formal way as the will theory.

One way in which the will theory incorporates an assumption about value, though, is in its normative emphasis on choice or autonomy: it makes the exercise of the individual will the primary or even exclusive object of rights protection. This elevation or prioritization of individual discretion entails a first-order commitment to the importance of autonomy, of individual freedom, associated with choice. While it is possible to construct or give effect to a formalistic rule system around choice, there is no reason why one would do so unless choice itself has value. Choice, in other words, is the background value assumption animating the operation of the will theory. Choice, that is to say, is normative within the theory. The will theory identifies a right in the control over the exercise of a duty. But to identify control over the exercise of a duty as a *right*, as distinct from a power (in the non-technical, non-Hohfeldian sense), implies that there is something *besides* control at work in the concept, and there is: something like the importance of self-determination or autonomy gives the idea of rights holders a normative dimension other than simply the idea of them as power-holders.

In practice, the value of choice animating the will theory plays out in the context of evaluative judgments made prior to the right-holder's exercise of discretion. Formalism suggests that interests generate duties *only* through individual choices made about which interests will be protected through enforcement. On this view, then, individual choice is what determines which duties will be required

20 See MacCormick, 'Rights in Legislation', 195–9.

21 Steiner, *Working Rights*, 261.

22 Steiner, *Working Rights*, 259.

and enforced. Interests can be rights only where the duties associated with them are both enforceable and under the control of their holder, and duties are therefore governed by individual choice about preferences, rather than by the moral importance of interests. On the interest theory, by contrast, the question of who decides which interests will take on right-status is an open one; it is thus perfectly acceptable for conflicts of rights to arise and be argued and *resolved* by a social group, a judge, or the state, as long as the conflict is decided according to the relative moral importance of the interests at stake.

But rights are discriminating: they protect some things and not others. And we do not individually decide which rights we will have. So it simply cannot be the case that rights protect preferences or individual discretion *simpliciter*. If I happen to have a preference for yellow tomatoes, that does not mean that I have any right in particular to yellow tomatoes that other people do not have. My preference for yellow tomatoes does not give me any special entitlement to them. When there is a question about whether or not some interest—like, say, access to sunlight in a building—ought to be protected as a right in some way, that question is not decided in the first instance by reference to the preference of the person claiming the right. In other words, whether the consumption of yellow tomatoes or access to sunlight from one's bedroom is innately good for human beings or not, for such things to become recognized as rights someone must independently *judge* that they are sufficiently important to warrant rights protection. Once a duty with respect to some interest has been imposed, the right-holder can exercise a choice about the exercise of that duty; but that exercise of choice only arises because of the *prior* judgment that the interest in question warranted rights protection.

This means that the will theory's claim—that a right is exhaustively described if we say that it protects a domain of discretion around each individual—is simply too limited to explain its other features: rights *do* protect individual discretion, but only in respect of certain interests, and the content of those interests is not determined by the right-holder. Even in the case of the rights the will theory explains best—private rights to person and property—an individual may have discretion over whether or not to enforce a right. He may decide to create or enforce a proprietary interest in a technological formula or trade secret, for example. But he cannot choose what *kind* of information he can elevate to the status of a right. Even if we think of more 'natural' rights, some kinds of interests—such as physical integrity—are protected, while others—such as an interest in having a certain minimal amount of personal space at all times—are not.

Choice, therefore, operates within a limited sphere of pre-existing duties in respect of protected interests. Here, I am using the term 'interest' in the thinnest possible normative sense: whether or not my right to my inherited mansion is a burden to me or not, and whether that right is a benefit to the state or to the general good or not, the right is nonetheless not described exhaustively by saying that it is a choice. It is a choice about some *thing* that will be protected in a way that not all my choices would be. I can perhaps choose to enforce or waive that protection, but I cannot alter the fact that, by virtue of the right having been conferred, such protection applies to the house rather than to anything else. And, to risk putting too much emphasis on what seems obvious, there can *be* no choice, no inheritance, no *right* at all, without the substantive interest to which the right entitles me.

The thing that any right protects, in other words, becomes protected as a right as a result of some evaluative judgment. The will theory can describe the way in which individuals exercise their value-judgments about which rights-protected goods are important to them, but it is silent about the fact that rights also reflect prior judgments that some things are specially valued and worthy of protection. This does not mean that such things are necessarily good for human beings but merely that human beings have judged them to be valuable. Rights therefore necessarily involve both a substantive interest and a judgment, moral or otherwise, that that interest is valuable in some way. The will theory therefore operates within a domain of value in the two ways I specified above. First, it reflects the value of individual choice to promote and maintain individual inviolability. Second, it reflects the value of certain interests above others.

(2) Side-constraints

A different theory that also purports to describe rights as being animated exclusively by what I have called the element of constraint or inviolability is that of Robert Nozick. The Nozickean view of rights as side-constraints differs from the will theory in several important ways, but the two share a formalism about rights. Nozick's theory, though, also makes implicit assumptions about rights and value.

Whereas the will theory, at least in its modern incarnation, distinguishes between 'rights permissibility' and moral permissibility, Nozick's theory views morality as relevant to the existence conditions for a right. The will theory values choice, and views rights as constraints controlled by the right-holder. Nozick, by contrast, says that rights 'determine the constraints upon your actions'.[23] In place of the will theory's 'domains of action-space', Nozick describes rights as spheres of moral inviolability, defined by a 'line (or hyper-plane)' that 'circumscribes an area in moral space around an individual'.[24] This view describes rights violations as 'encroachments' upon this 'circumscribed area' or as 'transgressions' of 'the boundary'.[25] This description of a domain of normative space echoes the will theory's similar view of rights' protection of individuals; but Nozick does not view rights as distinct from the moral content of duties in the same way as the will theory does.

Nozick does not set out to develop a substantive theory of rights. The statement—'Individuals have rights, and there are things no person or group may do to them (without violating those rights)'[26]—is the first in the book and his first premise. He begins with a Lockean state of nature, which includes the panoply of moral

[23] Robert Nozick, *Anarchy, State, and Utopia* (New York: Basic Books, Inc., 1974), 29.
[24] Nozick, *Anarchy, State, and Utopia*, 57.
[25] Nozick, *Anarchy, State, and Utopia*, 57.
[26] Nozick, *Anarchy, State, and Utopia*, 34.

rights that Locke thought it did.[27] Those rights present a picture of what Nozick calls side-constraints on action; these 'reflect the underlying Kantian principle that individuals are ends and not merely means'.[28] They 'express the inviolability of others, in the ways they specify' and 'reflect the fact of our separate existences'.[29] The moral importance of inviolability lies in the value of our 'separate existences'. This value involves the 'traditional proposals for the important individuating characteristic connected with moral constraints', which consist of one's

(1) [being] sentient and self-conscious;
(2) [being] rational (capable of using abstract concepts, not tied to responses to immediate stimuli);
(3) possessing free will;
(4) being a moral agent capable of guiding its behavior by moral principles and capable of engaging in mutual limitation of conduct;
(5) having a soul, together with 'an additional feature, the ability to regulate and guide [one's] life in accordance with some overall conception [one] chooses to accept.'[30]

These characteristics represent the features of persons' distinctness that is valued and protected by the theory. But moving from the abstract to the particular, we make sense of the value of persons, we protect their inviolability, *through* the protection of their interests. The value animating the Nozickean picture—that of individual moral inviolability—is a highly abstract one. That does not mean, however, that it is not a substantive value all the same. Nozick presents rights as spheres of moral inviolability. But it is impossible to recognize concrete rights without reference to the importance of the content of those spheres. Nozick *does* recognize their substantive content: he puts all the conceptual emphasis on inviolability itself, and thus on the thing being violated. It is impossible, moreover, to violate someone's moral status without also violating some describable concrete interest: this introduces the material dimension of rights' substance. The violation of a concrete, material interest is the vehicle through which the moral boundary is crossed. How could I violate a right of yours, in short, *without* violating some aspect of your well-being?

In invoking the Lockean account of rights, Nozick recognizes the necessity of substantive content to an account of rights. Incorporating the Lockean content of rights means that the Nozickean account already recognizes that some things are more important, more valuable, than others. In this case, the important things

[27] For this reason, Nozick's concept of rights might prove troubling to anyone who took a more Hobbesian view of the state of nature than Locke, or even who viewed the state as necessary to *some* part of a minimal moral concept of rights. See Bernard Williams, 'The Minimal State' in Jeffrey Paul (ed), *Reading Nozick: Essays on Anarchy, State and Utopia* (Totowa, New Jersey: Rowman & Littlefield, 1981), 31.

As Peter Singer points out, there is an entirely distinct view of justice and of rights from Locke's, which includes Hume, Bentham, and later utilitarians. Singer's point is that Nozick's concept of rights requires that we accept him on his own terms, that is, that we accept that rights, including the right to property, are a morally basic idea. See 'The Right to be Rich or Poor' in *Reading Nozick*, 45.

[28] Nozick, *Anarchy, State, and Utopia*, 30–2.

[29] Nozick, *Anarchy, State, and Utopia*, 48.

[30] Nozick, *Anarchy, State, and Utopia*, 48.

are the ones Locke recognizes as being protected by pre-political rights. Freedom from physical harm, from being killed, from having the things one is using in a certain way taken by force—these are the things Locke determines to be natural rights. Adopting the Lockean content for rights also brings with it the hierarchy of values implicit in Locke's own view.

To recapitulate, although Nozick's theory is a highly constraint-based one, it nonetheless contains an implicit hierarchy of value manifested in the interests it recognizes as rights. Adopting the rights content from Locke's state of nature brings with it precisely such a hierarchy in which personal freedom to use one's own self and things is only one important feature. Insofar as the goods described by Locke and adopted by Nozick are in fact particular, material ones, their selection suggests that the goods selected could have been otherwise. Locke—or God, for that matter—could have granted rights in other concrete interests, such as the necessities of life—food, shelter, or tools—or in a certain kind of treatment: we could all, to be frivolous about the matter, have been granted the right to be greeted with a handshake or a kiss.

The hierarchy of value expressed by rights is not identifiable only in Locke's own assertions about their divine origin; it is also manifested in the ways we evaluate rights when they come into conflict. Nozick frames these rights in negative terms so that this aspect of their value is minimized. To say that each of us has a right not to be killed, for example, suggests that the duties in respect of that right are all compossible.[31] To say, instead, that each of us has a right to life seems to create problems for compossibility of the kind we encounter when a group of survivors of a shipwreck must either all face death or kill one of their members to survive. But even if we limit the ambit of the interests rights protect to purely negative ones, so that they are framed, for example, in terms of freedom from being killed rather than a right to life, the fact of relative value—that some things are worse than others—is unavoidable. Suppose, for example, that I am driving a bus down a steep hill and cannot stop. I come to a narrow pass. On one side I see that the road abuts someone's house, and on the other side is a crowd of people. No matter what I do I will be violating someone's rights. Depending on the circumstances, I may be excused if the bus's brakes are failing, or I may not be, if, for example, I am driving drunk. In either case I am forced to choose between destroying someone's dwelling and killing a number of people. In this situation, two negative rights are in conflict, and my duties to both right-holders are not compossible. If I happen to think that property, or shelter, for example, are extremely important, and I elect to crash into the group of people, I will be more severely punished than if I crash into the house.

This is a fanciful example, but it merely expresses the thought that absolute compossibility of negative duties is a bit of a fiction. We are all constantly interacting with one another's 'spheres' of one kind or another and must choose which to violate. The set of interests we generally take uncontroversially to be inside

31 Compossibility refers to the possibility of fulfilling different duties at once; it is a term I borrow from Waldron; see, for example, 'Rights in Conflict'.

the boundary Nozick describes are the ones we deem most important, the ones it would be worst to violate. As I suggested when discussing the will theory, not every interest—even the various freedoms from intrusion—is protected. We do not have rights to personal space and privacy beyond a certain rather limited point, for example. And even once we enter the spheres themselves, where rights conflict, where we must violate one interest or another, some things are clearly more important than others. The idea of equal status suggests that harming people is prohibited and that all persons have an equal right to be free from harm, but in practice some harms are worse than others, and violations of the rights that protect those more valuable interests will attract more severe sanctions than others.

Implicit in the Nozickean side-constraint picture of rights, then, lies an assumption about value that manifests itself in two ways. First, the boundary that delineates the moral space belonging to each individual is not random: it surrounds and focuses on persons, and thus is animated by the value of persons' moral inviolability. Second, rights reflect a hierarchy of value in the way the material interests they protect are assigned: on this view, value is assigned to the interests inside the boundary; and the interests that are closer to the centre of the person, as it were, such as life and physical integrity, are protected more stringently than those we might describe as farther from the person and closer to the boundary itself; the latter might include minimal physical injury and harms to property or to privacy.

(3) Kant and rights: reason and formal equality

Nozick's account of rights as side-constraints is a highly formalistic one, but, as I pointed out, it nevertheless incorporates assumptions about interests and their paramount value in part through his adoption of the specific substantive content offered by Locke. In moving to consider a Kantian view of rights, we leave the specifically Lockean content aside and thus appear to move to a theory of rights that is still more formal and reason-based than Nozick's. Yet even here, in the Kantian tradition of thinking about rights, we find assumptions about value, about what is good for persons, which express themselves through rights.

When we consider rights in the Kantian tradition, it is important first to recognize that there are two ways of thinking about them that one can find in Kant's own ideas, one that is more specific and one more general. This division corresponds roughly to his categorization of duties into juridical and moral. While moral duties can only be enforced by self-constraint,[32] juridical duties justify, and can

[32] Juridical duties protect rights in a fairly specific sense that might be said to be similar to Nozick's conception of them. These duties concern acts, rather than intentions, and protect people's formal equality or 'external freedom'. They enable each person to pursue his or her conception of the good without interference from others. These duties are described under the rubric of private right, and reflect rights Kant described to things, to the will of others, and to persons as akin to things. These rights do protect interests in *things*, and rights *to* things are specifically described. But the animating idea here is not to protect things because they have value. Rather, it creates rights to things only because such rights enable individuals to pursue their own ends. These are mainly

be enforced by, coercive force.[33] While the juridical conception of rights describes equal freedom, the moral account describes equality of moral status. What the two ways of thinking about rights have in common, then, is twofold: first, both evince a commitment to equality among persons; second, both view that equality as modal rather than as the object of a moral teleology. Equality, in other words, is a mode of action rather than a goal.

This non-teleological character is what makes the Kantian and neo-Kantian deontological accounts of rights so focused on the discrete acts of individuals. Rights are, on this view, moral constraints on the wills of rational actors. It matters morally what each person does in each of his or her interactions. Rights do not protect values or valued goods. For Kant, the only unqualified good is the good will, which acts out of duty according to the moral law. This way of thinking about rights therefore appears to be wholly constraint-based, in that rights reflect the moral principle of equal status and structure interactions accordingly.

This non-teleological approach to morality, though, seems to have two main *loci*, namely the injunction on the agent's will to constrain his actions according to the moral law, and the injunction to treat the object or victim of a given interaction as an end rather than as a means. This double focus has led contemporary deontology to evolve into agent-centred and victim-centred accounts. And when we ask what rights are, or when asked to describe *rights* in particular, the question seems to refer primarily to the second injunction protecting the objects of interactions rather than the first. It is the object or victim, after all, whose inviolability is protected by rights. And here, in the consideration of inviolability, we see the recurrence of hierarchical value re-emerge as an assumption underlying the operation of even this heavily constraint-based theory.

As in the case of the will theory and the side-constraints accounts of rights, there is a background assumption here about the value of inviolability and

property and contract rights, then, and as such are not dissimilar to the side-constraints on action described by Nozick.

Kant describes juridical rights specifically *as* rights, but his inspiration of the Western rights tradition—which includes constitutional and human rights discourse as well as moral rights theorizing—also involved his wider conception of moral duties. These duties are the ones imposed through reason by self-constraint. Reason instructs us to give ourselves moral law, which Kant calls the categorical imperative and formulates in several ways. The most well known and well accepted of these formulations is the exhortation to treat the humanity in each person as an end rather than a means. On this more general view, the normative obligation to treat persons as ends in themselves means that persons have moral status simply by virtue of their personhood. Immanuel Kant, *The Metaphysics of Morals*, ed Mary Gregor (Cambridge: Cambridge University Press, 1996), 145: 'when the concept of duty concerns the internal determination of his will...the constraint that the concept of duty contains can be only self-constraint (through the representation of the law alone); for only so can that *necessitation* (even if it is external) be united with the freedom of his choice. Hence in this case the concept of duty will be an ethical one'.

[33] Kant, *The Metaphysics of Morals*, 147–8: 'To every duty there corresponds *a* right in the sense of an *authorization* to do something...; but it is not the case that to every duty there correspond *rights* of another to coerce someone....What essentially distinguishes a duty of virtue from a duty of right is that external constraint to the latter kind of duty is morally possible, whereas the former is based only on free self-constraint.' See also Mary Gregor, 'Kant's Theory of Property', *Review of Metaphysics* 41, no. 4 (1988): 758.

autonomy that gives rise to their normative emphasis. But even beyond this generalized value, where rights violations must be sanctioned and where rights conflict we see the operation of a hierarchy of valuable interests. It is one thing, after all, to say that rights protect people's entitlement not to be treated as a means, but it is almost impossible to spell out what that entitlement is exactly without referring to the interests or goods we as humans value.

If we look at a wide array of possible types of interactions, we can find some in which rights do not seem to be violated and yet in which one person is clearly treating another in some sense as a means to an end. If, for example, someone finds another person's face attractive, or interesting in some other way, and focuses their attention on that face in pursuit of their own pleasure, it is hard to imagine the person who is the object successfully claiming that even a moral right had been violated. Suppose, similarly, that John finds Susan's conversation on the telephone extremely interesting for reasons of his own and listens to it carefully, perhaps even writing parts of it down. If he reads what he has written later, thinking about it for his own reason, then while he has in *some* sense used her for his own end he has hardly violated anyone's moral right. Some types of interaction, then, in which one person is really only treating another as a means to his or her own end are morally innocuous and simply do not qualify as rights violations.

Similarly, we can compare interactions in which some rights do seem to be violated, and we can identify fairly clearly which violation is worse. Suppose, for example, that a hungry homeless person wanders into a supermarket and steals a loaf of bread. In doing so he violates the owner's rights through trespass and theft. Now suppose that he quietly wanders into someone's kitchen through the back door and steals the bread. Here we have the same technical violations, namely, trespass and theft, but in the latter case the violation seems more severe because the owner's security interest at stake is not only, or even primarily, proprietary in the technical sense; in this case her sense of safety and privacy in her own home has been violated, and the incursion therefore seems more sinister and offensive.

I offer these examples of different kinds of interactions only to make the simple point that we assign rights variability in their stringency. Most contemporary theorists of rights in the broadly Kantian tradition refer to harm as one of the crucial things rights protect against, so that rights' degree of stringency is associated with the degree of harm.[34] The basic idea here is that we have rights not to be unjustifiably harmed by another in the pursuit of his or her ends. Harm expresses a kind of negative value; it conveys the sense of a loss of some good or interest. Harm is, in short, always in relation to some interest.

Non-consequentialists do not simply argue that people have rights against harm, though; they argue more specifically against the idea that what matters morally is what happens in the world, rather than what people do. They therefore argue for agent-relative obligations. Such obligations involve what I can and cannot do to someone regardless of the consequences of my actions in respect of that

[34] See, for example, the role harm plays in the justifiability of constraints in Judith Jarvis Thomson's account of rights in *The Realm of Rights.*

person. We have already seen some of the classic examples of this kind of deontological, agent-relative thinking: it is impermissible for me to harm one person, for example, in order to save several others from the same harm. It is impermissible, to use Nagel's famous example, for me to deliberately twist a child's arm, causing her pain, to produce the consequence of her grandmother helping me to save my friends' lives.[35] This view of morality, and of rights, shares its basic non-teleological thrust with the Kantian account.

The point I want to make here is that the distinction between the teleological or consequentialist point of view and the non-consequentialist theories of Kantian derivation clearly lies in the emphasis of the latter on action and agency rather than mere occurrence, but both accounts share an underlying assumption about the kinds of actions or events that count as bad in the first place. That is, despite their insistent focus on agent-relativity, non-consequentialist, constraint-based accounts of rights rest on an implicit underlying assumption about 'badness' itself, and conversely about value. Once we see that rights necessarily protect valuable interests, we must acknowledge that they express a hierarchy of goods.

The characteristic focus of neo-Kantian or non-consequentialist accounts of rights is on the distinction between harm and non-aid, and on explaining the significance of that distinction. They rebut the idea that harm and non-aid are equivalent (Kamm calls this the *Equivalence Thesis*)[36] on the grounds that despite the fact that the same effects will be produced on a person—harm, say, or death—what matters morally, and the locus of the *right,* is not the good or bad effect but the attitude of the person causing the effect toward his or her victim.

But notice that even accepting that distinction between harm and non-aid, the bad effect, or disvalue to the victim's interests inherent in harming, is constant in both cases. That is, putting the normative emphasis on what an actor does rather than on what happens as a result of her actions cannot fully *isolate* what he or she does from the goods or interests her action affects. A person cannot aim at a bad effect without there being some bad effect to aim at. A negative consequence, in other words, may not be a sufficient or exclusive criterion by which to evaluate actions and assert the existence of a right; but some badness, or negative value, is nonetheless implicitly necessary, even on the constraint-based view, to evaluate action and find a rights violation. This necessity of disvalue or loss of interests to what constitutes rights violations implies that value cannot be dispensable to an account of what rights are. The theories of rights grounded in Kant's work purport to articulate rights as reason-based constraints on action. We are exhorted, so the theory goes, to treat the humanity in other persons with respect; that exhortation comes from our rational nature, and the humanity in others is associated with theirs. But, as is the case with the other constraint-based theories of rights we have canvassed thus far, the neo-Kantian theories rely on an understanding of

[35] Thomas Nagel, *The View From Nowhere* (New York: Oxford University Press, 1986), 175–82.

[36] Frances Kamm, *Intricate Ethics: Rights, Responsibilities and Permissible Harm* (Oxford: Oxford University Press, 2007).

what constitutes harm to the human person, and therefore, conversely, our rights protect what is of value to us as persons.

The normative focus of such theories is on the will of the agent, so that, as Nagel says, we violate the basic deontological constraint when we aim, intentionally, at evil. When we twist the child's arm, he says, we deliberately detract from her good. It is the deliberateness of that act, he emphasizes, that makes it run directly against the 'normative current'; but, underneath that deliberateness, or intention, lies the evil itself: the harm as disvalue, or loss of good. To return to the point I made at the outset of this section, it would be difficult to imagine a way of using a person as a mere means that had a wholly beneficial effect on them that we would nonetheless still describe as a violation of their rights. This is not to say that rights are actually just large units of utility. On the view I am advancing, the element of constraint is not normatively dispensable but rather is necessarily accompanied and underpinned by a hierarchy of value.

These background evaluative assumptions, though, of purportedly formalistic theories of rights are only one of the ways in which they illustrate rights' expression of paramount values. The other thread of substantive and hierarchical value we find in all these theories lies in the unavoidability of the material interests rights protect. Because rights always in fact protect interests—even if, according to the theorists they only do so incidentally—the selection of *which* such interests they protect, along with the ways in which conflicts between rights are resolved and with the variable stringency of rights, a framework of rights in practice always expresses a hierarchy of value.

Conclusion

The two questions most often asked about rights are: 1) what are they? And 2) what do they protect? The relationship between these two questions is at the heart of the central dispute within rights theory. Value-based views of rights such as the interest theory give priority to the second question, suggesting that what rights are is a function of the kinds of things, namely human interests, that they protect. That is, such accounts assert that a right just is something that protects an important interest or value. In the first part of this chapter I argued that although there may be disagreement about the extent to which it is logically or morally possible to derive rights entirely from the idea of valuable interests, once such rights have been recognized, then we must also recognize that they entail an indispensable element of constraint and inviolability. But just as the element of constraint is indispensable to what rights are, so, I have argued, the element of value is similarly indispensable. Value-based views of rights derive the element of constraint from the importance of human interests. Constraint-based or formalistic views of rights, conversely, describe rights in terms of the moral principle of equal status; that status, though, is animated by individual moral inviolability. Their emphasis on rights' formal anti-maximizing character, then, might make it seem that they don't have a notion of value. But—simply—they do—in two ways. First, they are animated by the value of individual inviolability, and, second, they rank rights in terms of relative importance, reflecting a judgment about the relative importance of the interests those rights protect. However we conceptualize the relation between the two elements, then, we must recognize both as necessary to any account of rights.

Taken together, the preliminary picture or model of rights developed so far is one in which rights involve the anti-maximizing, anti-aggregative properties inherent in the principle of inviolability, and are assigned to protect certain substantive interests according to a hierarchy of value. The existence and operation of a rights framework as a normative mechanism, in other words, expresses the principle of inviolability; the interests protected by the rights within that framework, together with their varying stringency, express a hierarchy of value.

This argument is obviously not meant to show that consequentialists and non-consequentialists are actually in agreement when it comes to rights, because their real debate concerns the relative priority, importance, and interpretation of the two elements. But that there *are* these two elements in an adequate model of rights, I have tried to show, is indisputable. A model of rights that claims the *joint* necessity of both the elements of constraint and value, then, reflecting both these two conflicting principles, must somehow make sense of the apparent dissonance involved in such a combination. The challenge of moderating that dissonance within the practice of rights is one I will address in the chapters that follow.

5

A Model of Rights

From Rights Theory to Public Law

In this section I will begin to construct a model of rights in general, and of public law rights in particular. A successful model of rights, I will argue, would be one that can analytically represent public law rights independently of their institutional context in a way that makes them translatable to the private sphere. It would also be one, though, that preserves the salient content from their moral context so that it can inform the answer to the question of which private actors these new, extrapolated rights ought to bind.

My claim that constraint and value are jointly necessary has so far been at the level of theory, and I have engaged with theories of rights to argue for the joint necessity of the two elements. In making the theoretical argument, I have avoided taking sides in the conceptual claims of both main types of rights theory about the conceptual coherence about the other side's view. But rights have important consequences in the real world, and the concept of rights we accept or assume affects their consequences, because that concept drives the way we identify them—the way we determine what is a right and what is not one. As long as we are working with several different concepts at the same time, therefore, it will be difficult to predict what their consequences will be.

The prevalence of the two main types of theories of rights has made it somewhat difficult to keep a clear grasp on what kind of thing a *public law right* could be, as a species of the genus 'rights', as it were, and so I will suggest a practical way of thinking about what it means to have such a right. I will, in what follows, construct a model of the genus rights—of rights in general—by extrapolating from constitutional and human rights. Why allow the conceptual model of rights in general to be partly determined by *these* ones? The development of rights thinking, and what has been called rights consciousness, is perhaps best reflected in the trend toward constitutionalization and protection of human rights. Insofar as our practice of rights reflects considered reflection on the kind of thing a right is, therefore, it seems to me to be reasonable to think that *this* practice of rights—the set of constitutional and human rights—must be granted some deference with regard to our best understanding of the concept of rights. I will therefore explore the question of whether these two kinds of positive law rights can be captured by either the constraint-based or the value-based theories of rights. In constructing a model of rights, this methodological approach is different from the exclusively theoretical approaches of both kinds of concept of rights, each of which begins with a different first-order moral perspective.

Finally, I will argue that although jointly necessary, the elements of constraint and value are not sufficient to a model of rights. I will first show that close consideration of public law rights supports the conclusion of Chapters 3 and 4, insofar as public law rights do not seem accurately captured by either a constraint- or a value-based concept of rights in general. On the basis of that conclusion I will construct a dualistic model of rights. I will next describe the distinctiveness of the public law context of rights in terms of their relational structure or setting and show how a model composed of only constraint and value is insufficient to account for that contextual element.

I. Constructing a Model of Public Law Rights

I have suggested that constraint-based theories generally fail to account for the role of value in what rights are. Conversely, value-based theories fail to adequately account for the element of constraint—the anti-aggregative character of rights—and the question of whom they obligate. These are both broad theoretical arguments, and I have engaged with them in previous chapters. It is my purpose here, therefore, to turn from rights theory to positive law rights—public law rights in particular—and to argue that even if we do not accept these theoretical conclusions of the last two chapters we nonetheless have reason to reject the claim of both types of rights theory to *exclusive* accuracy. Public law rights, I will suggest, imply that it cannot be the case that one kind of theory is true and the other false.

A. Constitutional rights

Constitutional rights can be said to obviously embody the constraint-based, even the deontological, concept of rights because, first and foremost, they impose duties on the state. They delineate a sphere in which state action will be legal, the boundaries of this sphere of legality being patrolled by constitutional challenges. This emphasis on constraining the state makes constitutional rights seem as though they are necessarily negative ones, protecting individuals against intrusion or interference from government. However, I want to be clear that although they embody the element of constraint, they are not thereby necessarily negative in the form of interaction they proscribe. In my introduction of the element of constraint, I emphasized that I mean constraint as a check on choice rather than action; the latter meaning is better captured by the term *re*straint, and would associate this element of rights with the negative form of interaction. *Re*straining someone means preventing him from doing something. And while constitutional rights partly function to limit the state's exercise of power, it is important to recognize that constitutions should not be seen only as restraints on government. Sometimes, rather, they *require* actions of the state. This is true at even the simplest level, in which procedural rights explicitly set out certain things the state *must* do, in its treatment of criminals, for example, that it might not otherwise do. But it is also a view of constitutionalism more generally that has been suggested by Waldron, for example,[1] and one that is actively practised by many constitutional jurisdictions: in Chapter 1 I described the way the German constitutional court takes the Basic Law to impose positive duties on the state; this view is accepted in other constitutional jurisdictions as well. The latter view of constitutional rights might be more accurately described as a *con*straint on the state, in that it directs the *choices* the state can make, the *way* it can do certain things, or requires it to take certain actions, rather than simply a *re*straint on its power.

Although constitutional rights thus clearly embody the constraint-based conception of what rights are, they also express elements of the other, value-based view. One of the ways in which constitutional rights are oriented to important goods, values, or aspects of human well-being is that they do not constrain the state in a general sense, but enumerate particular interests that are to be protected against the state: constitutional rights, in short, protect some things but not others. The state can infringe many areas of human life through regulation and criminal legislation without attracting constitutional scrutiny. Moreover, some interests, like property and liberty, can be infringed legally as long as the infringement conforms to due process. Other interests, however, like speech or, in some cases, gender equality, are in principle simply not susceptible to legal state infringement. Constitution writers select certain actions they prohibit the state from taking; their choices must be understood as expressing, therefore, a judgment about which aspects of human life they think important and valuable in particular ways. Furthermore, not all states protect the same interests; to the extent that there are differences, those differences must at least partly be driven by the ways in which citizens of different cultures value interests differently.

Constitutional rights can be roughly distinguished into two main forms, the substantive and the procedural; these categories might seem to track the two different conceptual views, procedural rights being more associated with the constraint-based position and substantive rights with the value-based one. Yet the constraint- and value-based accounts of rights seem to be identifiable in both the procedural and the substantive.

Procedural rights certainly seem to embody clearly the constraint-based concept of rights. These are not rights that determine what the state does or does not do, but simply declare that *when* it does certain things—such as interfere with people's liberty, as in the criminal or regulatory context—it must act according to the strictures of legality. This is expressed in a very straightforward way in constitutional provisions such as the due process clause of the fourteenth amendment of the US Constitution, or section 7 of the Canadian Charter of Rights and Freedoms. The former says that the state shall not 'deprive any person of life, liberty or property without due process

[1] See Jeremy Waldron, 'Rights in Conflict' in *Liberal Rights: Collected Papers, 1981–1991* (Cambridge: Cambridge University Press, 1993).

of law',[2] while the second states that 'Everyone has the right to life, liberty and security of the person and the right not to be deprived thereof except in accordance with the principles of fundamental justice.'[3] The Canadian charter also enumerates certain rights that it calls 'legal' ones, which explicitly regulate the state within the area of criminal prosecution.

Even in procedural rights of this kind, which seem most expressive of the constraint-based view, we find elements of value that cannot be entirely eliminated. Procedural rights, although they describe a sphere of inviolability, also invoke certain areas of human life as especially important so that they are out of bounds without due process. This explicit enumeration tracks political choices made on the basis of what people care about, since a constitution is not a theoretical treatise but a political document. And again, the United States and Canada, for example, differ even about the most essential sphere into which the state cannot intrude without due process of law: the American constitution explicitly enumerates property, while the Canadian one protects 'security of the person'.[4]

Substantive rights, which are laid out more explicitly in more recently adopted constitutions, such as rights to freedom of speech, religion, association, and mobility, express quite clearly the value-based view of what rights are. These are areas of human life or well-being that were deemed by the constitution's authors to be so important as to warrant the legal limitation of what the state can do even in pursuit of the general good. Not all interests are enumerated, and different cultures select different goods to protect and emphasize. The 2006 Afghan constitution, for example, protects women's rights through Article 22, which states that all citizens, 'man and woman, have equal rights and duties before the law', as well as through Article 54, which protects the family. It says that

> Family is the fundamental pillar of the society, and shall be protected by the state. The state shall adopt necessary measures to attain the physical and spiritual health of the family, especially of the child and mother, [and] upbringing of children.[5]

But the article goes on to put this protection in the context of a commitment to 'the elimination of related traditions contrary to the principles of the sacred religion of Islam'.[6] Japan's constitution is much more explicit about the singular importance of gender equality, even within the context of marriage and the family. Article 24 specifies that

> (1) Marriage shall be based only on the mutual consent of both sexes and it shall be maintained through mutual cooperation with the equal rights of husband and wife as a basis.

[2] *United States of America: Constitution* [United States of America], 17 September 1787, available at: <http://www.refworld.org/docid/3ae6b54d1c.html> (accessed 16 December 2014).

[3] *Canadian Charter of Rights and Freedoms*, section 7. Schedule B, Constitution Act 1982.

[4] Section 7, *Canadian Charter of Rights and Freedoms.*

[5] Article 54, Chapter 2, 'Fundamental Rights and Duties of Citizens', 2006 Constitution of Afghanistan.

[6] Article 54, Chapter 2, 'Fundamental Rights and Duties of Citizens', 2006 Constitution of Afghanistan.

(2) With regards to choice of spouse, property rights, inheritance, choice of domicile, divorce, and other matters pertaining to marriage and the family, laws shall be enacted from the standpoint of individual dignity and the essential equality of the sexes.[7]

Different states thus pick out different aspects of life as particularly important. The Estonian constitution sets out a discrete right for each person 'to preserve his or her ethnic identity';[8] the Indian constitution creates a discrete right for 'All minorities, whether based on religion or language' to 'establish and administer educational institutions of their choice';[9] the constitution of Italy, meanwhile, sets out rights for children born out of wedlock, stipulating that

(1) Parents have the duty and right to support, instruct, and educate their children, including those born out of wedlock.
(2) The law provides for the fulfillment of those duties should the parents prove incapable.
(3) Full legal and social protection for children born out of wedlock is guaranteed by law, consistent with the rights of other family members.[10]

Constitutional rights thus enumerate interests that are deemed to be of paramount value. This specific declaration of the goods to be protected as rights links constitutional rights to the value-based concept of rights. And perhaps the clearest expression of the value-based view is the inclusion in a great many state constitutions of rights to goods such as welfare, education, and health. Not all constitutions include such rights, and those of common law countries do so perhaps least, but many constitutions do include them, especially those adopted after the crystallization of human rights in international law. But this is not the only way of understanding these substantive rights. We can also conceptualize them in terms of constraint and the inviolability of the individual. These enumerations of important interests, after all, describe an area of individual well-being in respect of which the government's choices are constrained. A sphere of inviolability, it seems, can make sense either way: it can be viewed according to the important value of the interests within it, or it can be understood as a boundary that is to be considered morally inviolate, a boundary that expresses the equal dignity of all persons.

B. Human rights

Human rights are ones we have in virtue of nothing but our personhood. They are not linked to citizenship, nor are they specifically aimed at any particular respondent. While we can say something about constitutional rights simply by invoking the necessity of constraining the state from interfering with individual

[7] Article 24 [Matrimonial Equality], Chapter III, 'Rights and Duties of the People', Constitution of Japan, Effective from 1947.

[8] Article 49, Chapter II, 'Fundamental Rights, Liberties, Duties', Constitution of Estonia, 1992.

[9] Section 1, Article 30, Part III, 'Fundamental Rights', Constitution of India, 1950.

[10] Article 30, [Parental Duties and Rights], Title II, 'Ethical and Social Relations', Part I, 'Rights and Duties of Citizens', Constitution of Italy, Effective 1948.

freedom, to articulate what human rights are we really need to refer to their specific content. We do not view the right, for example, to wear a yellow shirt on a Tuesday as a human right unless we know much more about the context of the shirt-wearing. But much less contextual information would be required to argue that every person's right to a basic level of subsistence, for example, or his or her right not to be tortured, is a human right. The things—like freedom from torture, and subsistence—that seem relatively easy to identify as human rights, are, at least at first glance, distinguishable from an interest in wearing a yellow shirt on Tuesday by their clear and immediate importance to human life and well-being. Human rights, then, seem to embody a value-based concept according to which they protect important human interests or goods.

Human rights instruments enumerate a wide array of interests that individuals ought to have protected and fulfilled, such as rights to health care, to education, to their privacy and family life. These are interests that, when they have been protected, have been protected by states; but there is nothing in the basic ethos of these rights instruments that requires that we take a state-centred view of what such rights *are*. Rather, the emphasis in the human rights context is on the integral importance of these interests to human life, dignity, and well-being. If we look at the positive promulgation of human rights in international accords and agreements, this interest-based view seems to be borne out. The United Nations Universal Declaration of Human Rights,[11] to take but one example, sets out a series of interests that it elevates to rights status by virtue of the agreement of the signatory states. These include the interests protected by many domestic constitutions, but add a significant array of additional interests that are asserted to be human rights.

One of the features of human rights that reinforces this value-based view is that they do not distinguish in principle between what we might think of as negative and positive ones. Nothing in the many human rights instruments indicates that there is a difference, in terms of the conceptual question of what rights *are*, between those that enumerate freedoms from various kinds of harm and universal entitlements to valuable interests. In this respect, then, we can, without distorting their meaning, redescribe the interests enumerated by human rights instruments in terms of different kinds of protected goods: international human rights do not, then, differentiate between the good of non-invasion and the goods of, and necessary to, human sustenance and thriving. Article 12 of the Universal Declaration on Human Rights, for example, protects against intrusion:

> No one shall be subjected to arbitrary interference with his privacy, family, home or correspondence, nor to attacks upon his honour and reputation. Everyone has the right to the protection of the law against such interference or attacks.[12]

[11] UN General Assembly, *Universal Declaration of Human Rights*, 10 December 1948, 217 A (III).

[12] *Universal Declaration of Human Rights*, General Assembly resolution 217 A (III), 10 December 1948.

Section 1 of Article 25, by contrast, is an entitlement:

> Everyone has the right to a standard of living adequate for the health and well-being of himself and of his family, including food, clothing, housing and medical care and necessary social services, and the right to security in the event of unemployment, sickness, disability, widowhood, old age or other lack of livelihood in circumstances beyond his control.[13]

These two rights manifest the idea that not being brutalized is a good just as sustenance, health care and education are also goods. In many cases, declarations of human rights will fold various 'negative' and 'positive' interests into one provision that detail the different aspects of a given right. The UDHR's article on work, for example, addresses four different dimensions of that aspect of human life:

> Article 23.
> (1) Everyone has the right to work, to free choice of employment, to just and favourable conditions of work and to protection against unemployment.
> (2) Everyone, without any discrimination, has the right to equal pay for equal work.
> (3) Everyone who works has the right to just and favourable remuneration ensuring for himself and his family an existence worthy of human dignity, and supplemented, if necessary, by other means of social protection.
> (4) Everyone has the right to form and to join trade unions for the protection of his interests.[14]

We might say that sections (2) and (4) are specifications of more general rights to equal treatment and freedom from interference. Sections (1) and (3), however, protect the goods of work and remuneration in a more positive form.

In addition to their enumeration of what have conventionally been divided into negative and positive rights, human rights documents manifest the value-based conception of rights insofar as they emphasize certain aspects of various goods. In Article 26, for example, the UDHR sets out a general right to education:

> Everyone has the right to education. Education shall be free, at least in the elementary and fundamental stages. Elementary education shall be compulsory. Technical and professional education shall be made generally available and higher education shall be equally accessible to all on the basis of merit.[15]

In its second section, though, the article specifies that

> [e]ducation shall be directed to the full development of the human personality and to the strengthening of respect for human rights and fundamental freedoms. It shall promote understanding, tolerance and friendship among all nations, racial or religious groups, and shall further the activities of the United Nations for the maintenance of peace.[16]

So not only is education per se a universally important human good, as set out in section (1), it is recognized as having even greater value where it promotes the virtues of equality and respect. The protection of education is strengthened,

[13] UDHR, Art 25. [14] UDHR, Art 23. [15] UDHR, Art 26, section 1.
[16] UDHR, Art 26, section 2.

therefore, by section (2) where the good of education also promotes these values. The Declaration articulates one further way in which the value or good of education can be valuable in a particular *way*: section (3) asserts that

> Parents have a prior right to choose the kind of education that shall be given to their children.[17]

Where human rights instruments lay out this kind of specific provision it sometimes seems as though it is because, as in the case of the qualitative assessment of education, for example, the value of the good is increased when it is promoted in a particular way. This seems to be the case in the second section of Article 26 of the UDHR, which insists that the value of education is heightened where it is directed toward the more general values of dignity and equal worth manifested in the declaration; it has a slightly different overtone in section (3), in which the good of education is linked explicitly to the goods of family independence from state control and of parental direction of children's development. In fact, these two sections of the article might seem to be in tension: the parental right to choose the best type of education for their children is described as *prior*, perhaps because of this tension, but nonetheless the different aspects of the good of education here—the promotion of learned respect for the equal worth of others on the one hand and the possibly conflicting particular values that might be enshrined by parents on the other—are left to be interpretively worked out in particular cases.

Sometimes it seems as though the particular, specific aspects of valuable goods are articulated because the general right at issue has a history of failing to be protected in a particular way. The general right to subsistence in section (1) of Article 25, for example, is elaborated in section (2), which specifies that 'Motherhood and childhood are entitled to special care and assistance', and declares that 'All children, whether born in or out of wedlock, shall enjoy the same social protection.'[18] Whichever the reason for these kinds of elaborations on general rights, both indicate that the framers of the Declaration are seeking to promote the various goods they set out to the greatest possible benefit.

In their enumeration and specification of valuable aspects of human life, then, human rights undoubtedly conform to a value-based concept of rights. But in at least one respect, they also embody the other, more deontological view. When we considered constitutional rights, we observed that their special protection of citizens against state action made them two steps removed from the universal perspective of deontological rights; human rights, in contrast, *do*, at least in some abstract sense, adhere to the universal deontological ideal of protecting everyone equally against everyone. In the human rights context, rights protections are deliberately universal in their application. Article 2 of the UDHR establishes the universality of the Declaration's protections:

> Everyone is entitled to all the rights and freedoms set forth in this Declaration, without distinction of any kind, such as race, colour, sex, language, religion, political or other

[17] UDHR, Art 26, section 3. [18] UDHR, Art 25.

opinion, national or social origin, property, birth or other status. Furthermore, no distinction shall be made on the basis of the political, jurisdictional or international status of the country or territory to which a person belongs, whether it be independent, trust, non-self-governing or under any other limitation of sovereignty.[19]

The Declaration is therefore clear that all persons are the subjects of these rights. On the respondent side, the Declaration is equally universal. These rights are simply enumerated on behalf of everyone; no particular antagonist is specified for any given right, although in the case of the legal rights a state is generally implied to be the putative respondent. In its preamble, the universality of the rights respondent envisioned by the framers is clear: 'every individual and every organ of society'[20] is intended to take heed of the Declaration's injunctions.

In addition to this abstract universality of application, we might be able to interpret enumerated human rights conceptually as manifesting a broadly constraint-based conception in another way. We could, for example, take the articulation of crucially important interests, *together* with the theoretical universality of application, as instantiating a sphere of protection around individuals. Human rights, as manifested in their enumeration in international instruments, are heavily oriented to the subjects of rights—to the individual persons they protect. Perhaps *because* they do not emphasize whom is obligated to fulfil the entitlements set out, their focus is therefore exclusively on the entitlements themselves. Because they do not describe duties, but only rights, they can be seen as delineating a sphere around each individual.

This, we might say, is a sphere that has moral importance and that can constrain the actions of others. In other words, human rights documents do not specifically compel any particular agent to provide health care any more than they specify that any particular agent is prohibited from committing genocide or torture. What they do do, though, is to tie each of the interests they set out to the right-subject. All the moral weight is placed on the importance of *each* individual: *her* safety, *her* well-being, and *her* thriving are of paramount importance. And although the interests themselves are shown to have value by their elevation to the status of rights, part of the point of the document—of the rights framework itself—is to prevent actions from being taken—even for the purpose of promoting certain interests—that infringe the rights specified. Although they embody the value-based view, then, they do also embody the constraint-based one, in that they draw a sphere of moral importance around every individual, enjoining all agents to consider the normative significance of that sphere in all their actions.

To sum up this section of argument: it might appear at first glance as though constitutional rights and human rights represent the constraint-based and value-based conceptualizations of rights, respectively. But in fact both types of positive law rights embody the normativity of constraining action out of respect to individuals and *also* embody the normativity of value. They cannot, therefore,

[19] UDHR, Art 2.

[20] Preamble, UDHR.

be effectively explained and justified by one conceptual view to the exclusion of the other.

So public law rights bear out the argument that both constraint and value are jointly necessary elements in a model of rights. And indeed, to accurately capture those rights, we ought *not* to adopt one of the first-order moral principles in which theories of rights are so often embedded. Human rights, in particular, were *deliberately* crafted without reference to the justificatory principles that warrant their recognition: they represented, for their drafters and framers, a kind of second-order agreement on particular artefacts of rights practice, and this is their great strength in terms of their ability to attract consensus. They can be accepted as justified for different substantive moral reasons. Jacques Maritain, one of the participants in discussions leading to the United Nations Declaration, described the agreement on the enumerated rights in this way: 'Yes, we agree about the rights, but on condition that no one asks us why.'[21] Maritain describes the acceptance of the enumeration of international human rights by those who have different philosophical or justificatory standpoints as an agreement 'not on the basis of common speculative ideas, but on *common practical ideas*, not on the affirmation of one and the same conception of the world, of man, and of knowledge, but on the affirmation of a single body of beliefs for *guidance on action*.'[22]

But if we are to abstract from the *institutional* context of public law rights, we must also abstract from them as legal artefacts at least to the extent that they are divested of their exclusive attachment to the state as duty-bearer. This abstraction will render the model translatable to the private sphere. The model of rights in general, as I briefly outlined in the previous chapter, must restrict the specification of rights' conceptual content to (1) the constraining *form* that directs or narrows the range of choices for the actors they implicate, together with (2) the *type(s)* of normative facts or judgments that constitute the content they protect. In Chapter 4 I argued that two types of judgments about *value* are entailed by rights: first, the value of the individual person that is implied by the very form of the rights as a normative framework, and, second, the hierarchy of values that the content of the rights in that framework articulate. So rights can be taken to express normative facts or judgments about the relative importance of certain values to, and for, the individual persons they protect. Notice, though, that the conceptual content of this model of rights in general does *not* specify which facets of the person warrant protection; in other words, it does not take a view on *which* interests ground rights and therefore constitute the content of actualized rights. Rather, on this model, the conceptual content specifies only the form of rights—constraint— together with the conceptual inclusion of facts or judgments about values that warrant elevation to rights status. Any actualized right, then,

[21] As cited by Mary Ann Glendon, *A World Made New: Eleonor Roosevelt and the Universal Declaration of Human Rights* (New York: Random House, 2001).

[22] As cited in Glendon, *A World Made New*, emphasis added. For the importance of the agreement as a consensus about the guidance of action, see Joshua Cohen, 'Minimalism About Human Rights: The Most We Can Hope For?', *The Journal of Political Philosophy* 12 (2004): 190–213.

any right that we find in legal, political, or moral practice, will reflect a normative fact or judgment about value. When we recognize or assign a right, conversely, we must *make* the judgments of the types specified by the concept of rights. Public law rights, then, as instantiations or extensions of this general conceptual model, represent a certain set of normative judgments about a set of valuable interests.

II. Does a Dualistic Model Account for Public Law Rights?

Thinking of the model of public law rights in terms of thin conceptual content specifying that rights take the form of constraint and involve judgments about values is to envision a dualistic model of rights that does not refer to the state; it represents an extrapolation of the normative content of public law rights from their institutional origin in public law and thus seems responsive to the problem of institutional provenance. So on that basis we might want to formalize the model as follows. If we take the elements of constraint and value to be necessary and sufficient to create a model of rights, we would construct a dualistic model of *public law* rights that we can formalize something like this:

Every Public Law Right is a norm that
(1) Is oriented toward protecting the inviolability of individuals; and
(2) Assigns priority to certain important interests: (these interests are $I_1 \ldots I_n$ as defined by the overlapping content of the set).

Is this dualistic model, ('PLR'), an accurate account of public law rights? If it is, then the moral importance we assign to them can be transferred to the model and it can govern the application of public law rights to private law. The simple dualistic model does seem, at first glance, to describe public law rights.

But recall the objection from institutional provenance I introduced in Chapter 2: its concern is that public law rights are fundamentally or intrinsically *public* in some unspecified way, which would suggest that the context of the public sphere is somehow integral to what these rights are. This is partly a conceptual concern about accurately characterizing public law rights but it is also a worry about the translatability of public law rights to the private sphere, insofar as it is an insistence that the normativity of public law rights is specific to their public law context. There is nothing in this dualistic model that explains why the state is the exclusive bearer of duties in respect of the interests public law rights protect, and thus nothing that limits the model, in principle, to the public law context. That might, of course, seem to be an advantage, since the purpose of our project is to qualify *other* bearers of duties in respect of these interests, besides the state. But we cannot take advantage of this apparent benefit, since the model's *total* extrapolation from the public law context also means that it does not help to solve the problem of indeterminate applicability in the private sphere, the other of our two guiding methodological requirements.

If the dualistic model is *too* distant from the institutional context of public law rights, then, perhaps we can construct a model that includes the 'public' aspect of their nature: what can we add to the model to capture the public character of these rights? We might try 'Institutional Public Law Rights'*:

Every IPLR* is a norm that
1* – Is oriented toward protecting the inviolability of individuals;
2* – Assigns priority to certain morally important interests: (these interests are $I_1 \ldots I_n$ as defined by the overlapping content of the set); and
3* – Is held against a public body, most particularly against a state.

Does IPLR* capture public law rights? On its face, it seems much more successful than PLR in that it explicitly limits its ambit to the public sphere. This model takes the identity of the rights antagonist to be the aspect of public rights' context that is most relevant to what they are. The institutional model, however, would be a non-starter when it comes to applying these rights to private law, since by definition private interactions do not involve public bodies. But leaving that aside for the moment, we must first ask whether IPLR* is in fact an accurate model of public law rights after all.

This model would capture all of the rights entrenched in state constitutions; and these rights represent a large number of the source set of rights from which we are extrapolating. But the institutional model fails to capture the other central group of rights in this source set—human ones. Although human rights are institutionally *vindicated* by states, human rights treaties and declarations, as I argued above, are expressly designed to grant rights to individuals against any potential violator. In Articles 3 and 4 of the UDHR, for instance, it is proclaimed that 'Everyone has the right to life, liberty and security of person' and that 'No one shall be held in slavery or servitude', respectively, and the applicative scope of those rights are not limited. They are merely declared to inhere in everyone by virtue of personhood alone

The second paragraph of the Preamble asserts that the Declaration is in part motivated by the 'disregard and contempt for human rights' that have resulted in 'barbarous acts which have outraged the conscience of mankind'. This connection between outrageous barbarity and contempt for human rights suggests that these are rights against the worst kind of treatment, against disrespect for human dignity, and that such outrageous treatment and disrespect are themselves the evils that the entrenchment of human rights was intended to prevent. The identity of the perpetrator of such barbarism, therefore, does not seem, in itself, to be part of what human rights are. This dimension of public law rights does not seem to be captured by the institutional model, IPLR*, which extrapolates from the public law context only the formal identity of a public body.

In the development of the constitutional law of many states, as I elucidated in Chapter 1, the enumerated rights have begun to have some degree of horizontal application. While the UDHR makes this prescription most explicit, other jurisdictions have followed suit. Article 39 of the South African constitution, for example, requires that 'when developing the common law or customary law, every court, tribunal or forum must promote the spirit, purport and objects of the Bill of Rights'.[23] This approach, requiring that adjudication be somehow consistent

[23] South African Constitution, Bill of Rights, Art 39.

with the constitutional rights, was adopted by Canada through judicial interpretation,[24] and in the United Kingdom through the legislative passage of the *Human Rights Act 1998*, which required that British common law henceforward be developed in accordance with the *European Convention on Human Rights*. Both the German and Israeli constitutional courts have interpreted their basic laws to apply indirectly in horizontal interactions. The German right under section (1) of Article 2, for example, stating that 'Every person shall have the right to free development of his personality insofar as he does not violate the rights of others or offend against the constitutional order or the moral law', is one that inheres in every individual and applies, in some way at least, against all others.

This movement toward horizontal application both in the human and constitutional rights contexts suggests that while, on their face, or in terms of the historical understanding of the nature of constitutions, enumerated rights apply only against the state, in fact the more general understanding that prevails in the global rights discourse is that rights by their nature essentially express, and inhere in, the dignity of the human person, rather than merely expressing a limitation on the exercise of state power. However, we know that PLR, the dualistic model that referred *only* to orientation toward individuals and to important interests fails to capture something important about public law rights. And IPLR*, which included the *formally* public quality of the relationships in which those rights arise, is also insufficient to describe the set of rights we want to extrapolate to the private sphere.

In extrapolating *from* the institutional context of public law, we want to know what it is about the public law context, either normatively or conceptually, that justifies them in that context. So what, we might ask, is it about the context of public law rights that is necessary to an adequate model? As an answer to this question, the institutional model is a meaningless answer. It is to say, in effect, that to extrapolate the normative and conceptual content of public law rights one must reproduce public law rights exactly. That is simply to refute the normative mandate of developing private law rights that have the effect of protecting public law rights in the private sphere.

Extrapolating from the context of a practice, though, may seem to present a worry. Since the social practice of rights protection in the public sphere is morally important for differing reasons according to different moral theories, its justification is context-dependent. That is, the different reasons for accepting the practice could relate to its public law context in different ways; removed from that context we cannot be confident that the practice represents the kind of moral convergence that makes it important. In order to transpose the practice justifiably to a different sphere, therefore, we must render it *institutionally* context-independent without stripping it of the meaning and justification provided by its *moral* contextual situation.

[24] See *RWDSU v. Dolphin Delivery* [1986] 2 S.C.R. 573.

Therefore, we can only make the practice of rights protection in the public sphere independent of its context by incorporating the morally relevant contextual information *within* our model of public law rights. If a social practice is context-dependent, then in order to implement that practice in a different context we must understand what the practice *is* in a way that incorporates its original context. We could not, for example, intelligibly describe the practice of children going annually to strangers' houses and being given candy without incorporating the context of the holiday in which the practice occurs within our description. The model of a practice, in other words, must include the contextual information that is relevant to it. If the public law context is included *within* our model of public rights, then, the model will describe the practice as it truly is, albeit in different terms, and thus allow it to retain its moral importance while being detachable from the institutional context of public law.

Criteria (1) and (2) of the model of rights—constraint and value, respectively, cannot, therefore, be jointly sufficient conditions to capture the unique context of public law rights, because they do not incorporate the moral context of those rights that characterizes them specifically. The dualistic model (PLR) is, in other words, successful as a model of rights that is independent of their context, but the public law context of public law rights must, in an adequate model, somehow be taken account of.

III. The Problem of Translatability: The Structure of Public Law Rights

What does it mean to include the public law *context* within a model of public law rights? I will argue that the crucial contextual information that is morally relevant to the practice of public law rights protection is the nature of the relational or interpersonal structure within which, explicitly or implicitly, such rights arise. A brief taxonomy of public law rights with an eye to this problem of institutional context will begin to suggest that a structural, relational model of rights is best capable both of accurately accounting for what public law rights are in conceptual and normative rather than institutional terms, and of meeting the challenge of translatability, to operate successfully in the institutional context of private law.

As I illustrated in Chapter 1, the most common existing method for extrapolating rights to the private sphere generally proceeds on the basis that certain interests are prioritized by constitutional and human rights but not protected by private law. The current approach is thus a highly interest-based method of extrapolating from the public context to the private one. It does not, in other words, take any account of the structural dimension of the relation between individual and state that forms the context of public law rights. This interest-based extrapolative method for applying public law rights to the private sphere is flawed: the objection from the differing structures of public and private rights has something important to tell us about what would be necessary to a better method of extrapolation, as well as about rights more generally.

The structural worry begins with the observation that public law rights are polycentric while private ones are bilateral. In other words, one can think of the interests protected and balanced in private law adjudication as reflecting the moral and legal concerns of only two parties and of the character of *their* interaction. Public law rights, on the other hand, are polycentric in the sense that a right protects each individual's interest partly because of the importance of that interest *to* others, to the polity and its political well-being, and partly because of the way interests are interdependent. And, moreover, the state's position in contestations of rights is not that of a single agent, in the sense that the state represents and must yoke together all the interests, concerns, and well-being of all those it represents. Another way of thinking about this structure problem is that while the state acts not for its *own* sake but for the sake of pursuing some general goal, and its interests can be understood to be those of the common good, private law rights contests protect the autonomy interests of both parties: neither party's action or right is taken to stand for a more teleological justification of action. Thus, public law rights themselves have a structure that neither an exclusively interest-based account nor a dualistic one that includes a very thin element of functional inviolability captures, and it is that fundamental, relational structure that an effective extrapolative framework for applying them to private actors must explore, in order to *translate* public law rights into a more general conceptual model of rights that can, at the abstract level, *also* capture the nature of private law rights.

Consider the hypothetical instances of suggested extrapolation of public rights to private actors outlined in Chapter 1.[25] In each example, we can identify relational elements in the rights in question not entirely captured by the interests they protect that affect the way they must be applied. Freedom of religion, for example, can be expressed in terms of the protection of certain individual interests: it is composed, we might say, of interests in individual conviction, conscience, and thought. A Catholic, in other words, believes in the God of the Judeo-Christian bible, and in the divinity of Jesus Christ. But to be a Catholic, or any other kind of religious person, for the most part also involves an interest in association with a particular community. There is therefore an interest in association *with* that community as well as in having the interests of the community as a collective asserted and protected. That interest in the community is therefore a kind of associative or institutional component to the right,[26] and it is also linked in most cases with the freedom to express religious conviction in the form of certain practices, whose meaning is at least partly derived from their shared practice by the community. All these interests are of course deeply connected, in the idea of freedom

[25] See Chapter 1.

[26] Freedom of association, widely protected as a human right and in many constitutions, has the social dimension as an essential part of its structure: it is not an interest one can enjoy in a completely solitary way.

of religion, but in any given case of violation of the right, one or more of these interests might be particularly prominent or threatened.

Now contrast freedom of religion with the right to liberty or to security of the person. All these are generally conceived of as negative rights, violated by some active interference by another, and that is generally the extent of the consideration of their structure. But the rights to liberty or physical integrity, conceived of as negative entitlements, protect a narrower range of interests than freedom of religion and, most importantly, can be enjoyed by a solitary person on his or her own. And while some of the interests protected by freedom of religion can be similarly enjoyed in a solitary way—such as conviction, thought, and conscience—as a composite of all the interests I described—including the associative ones—freedom of religion cannot be enjoyed entirely solitarily. This gives freedom of religion a characteristically social dimension that is not easily translated into the distinctively individualistic structure of private rights.

The rights to racial and sexual equality, similarly, are enumerated as a kind of single interest in many human rights instruments and constitutions and yet also contain this variety of interests that include a social dimension: certain distinctions on the basis of sex are assumed to be universally permissible—men and women, for instance, are permitted to prefer partners of the opposite sex without accusation of discrimination. These equality rights are often conceived of as protecting the interest in equal treatment, presented as a kind of Kantian expression of equal worth. But, in actual practice, violations of the *right* to equal treatment only occur where they involve distinctions made on the basis of an individual characteristic, such as race or gender, that is in fact shared by a group of similarly situated members. Individuals, of course, are not protected in this way *as members* of the group, or at least not explicitly so; these traits are often protected because they are seen as unchosen features of the person. But there are of course other unchosen features—hair colour not clearly related to race, physical appearance, intelligence, certain talents and skills, etc.—that are permitted as grounds of distinction. The difference between those protected traits and those not protected is the association of the first set with *historical* mistreatment—even if only conceived of as detrimental differentiation—of members of the group of individuals sharing the characteristic in question. There is, in other words, a highly contingent, social aspect to what appears to be an individual interest protected by a right. That social dimension is fairly easily taken account of when the alleged discrimination or violation is committed by the state, since the state can be seen as having the public good as one of its aims, including that of all its members. Repeating humiliating historical mistreatment is one way in which, therefore, the state cannot be permitted to act. But why ought a private individual be held to account for such historical contingencies, or, for that matter, for promoting the public good? Again, simple focus on the interest protected by a given public law right does not in all cases allow for this contingent relational dimension to be taken into account, thus preventing its implementation in a different sphere.

Now consider the right to privacy, which was purportedly extrapolated to the private sphere in the case of the employee fired on the basis of a search of his office computer. Private rights to privacy primarily involve the interest in not being seen in certain contexts or in not having one's activities and thoughts widely broadcast to others without consent. The idea of 'reasonable expectation' governs much of the thinking in privacy doctrine in both the public and private contexts. But as a public right, privacy is protected in certain ways that are highly specific to the public context. In the US constitution, for example, the right to privacy is partly located in the fourth amendment's prohibition on quartering soldiers in individuals' homes. This has led, in American jurisprudence, to the idea of the home as being the primary focus of privacy protection, at least until the quite recent advent of new technologies that threaten privacy. The interest in privacy is also protected by public law rights against being forced to speak—*Miranda* rights, for example—and even in the fifth amendment protection against forced self-incrimination. In other constitutional contexts, the interest in privacy can also be identified in the right to security of the person, which, in the Canadian *Charter of Rights and Freedoms,* for example, is protected against invasion except in accordance with principles of fundamental justice. The interest in privacy put simply as 'the right to be left alone' is one of those rights that can, in theory, be enjoyed solitarily—in that respect it is relatively easy to extrapolate and translate its protection to the private sphere. But, as a set of interests manifested in these more institutional protections, it makes less sense to think of it as simply being an interest of a solitary individual with no social contacts. Many of the aspects of the public law rights to privacy involve police procedure—searches, seizures, interrogations, arrest, etc.—so that the interest is not simply in being left alone—since the police are entitled to *not* leave us alone—but in being treated in a particular way when the state *is* intruding on our private space. The fourth amendment privacy interest arising from the right not to have soldiers quartered in homes is similarly predicated on the fact that the state could, as a matter of its power, perhaps undertake to do so. So actions that, in the purely private context—such as searches, seizures, or forced inhabitation of our homes—would simply represent property offences such as trespass or theft, in the public context take on a more complex relational basis: the state is permitted to, or is going to, take these actions, but the privacy interest will curtail the *way* it does so. In a situation like that of the employer's search of the employee's computer, the privacy interest seems less like the property offence, or the offence involving broadcasting or even *looking* into the employee's business. Something in the context of the situation seems to make it more analogous to the privacy interest protected in rights against police actions: there are clearly *some* things an employer can do that would, in the absence of the contractual relationship, constitute a property offence, but that, because of that relationship, become sanctioned and thus also trigger the second dimension of the privacy interest that resembles the structure of the public law right.

Some public law rights, then, seem directly transferrable to the private sphere: these are the rights one can enjoy solitarily, such as physical integrity, simple privacy, thought, or certain basic freedoms of action. In the case of these rights, the private law right would protect exactly the same interest in the same way: private actors would be prevented from violating the interest in the same way, and for much the same reason as the state is. The possible *justifications* for their doing so might be different, but the relational structure of the right would look roughly the same.

Other public law rights, though, such as the freedoms of religion, association, and what we might call 'institutional' or 'procedural' privacy, protect an interest that makes little sense to think of as being enjoyable by a completely solitary person. Some of these rights are what we might call 'clubbable' in that they require the participation of others for their enjoyment, while the more institutional or procedural ones are predicated on the existence of some power that can, for some reason, violate certain interests without concern for the protection of person or property. These rights cannot be directly transferred to the private context; they require that an analogous relational context be present that somehow makes the potential private rights violator sufficiently similar to the state that the structure of the public law right seems to be present.

The set of public law rights—those to person and property—that can be easily and directly transferred to the private context must be taken account of by a theory of how private actors can be justifiably held to account for things like human rights violations. But beyond that justification—useful in contexts like international private law where little effective corporate responsibility for human rights violations exists—these rights are not the ones that are most problematic to extrapolate, largely because these *are* the interests that are already protected by the laws of property and tort. We begin to encounter real difficulties in extrapolating from the public to the private context when the rights at issue are those that cannot simply be enjoyed solitarily, and are rather 'clubbable' or involve some necessary analogy with the state in order for their structure to be present in the private context.

But if freedoms of religion and association, for example, manifest this kind of 'clubbability' in their enjoyment that creates a structural problem for direct extrapolation to the private sphere, there is another set of public law rights that seems to suffer from an even more extreme version of this relational complexity. Consider, for example, the hypothetical extrapolation I suggested of the right to vote, or to a fair trial. A purely interest-based or semantic extrapolation of these rights would seem utterly misconceived: the interests protected by the right to vote, for example, include, we might say, some kind of participation in social discourse or a sense of authorship of rules one must abide by. But surely *all* social discourse should not attract the kind of protection of everyone to participate in it equally that such a simple view would imply. Similarly, we must all live by many rules, in the private sphere, whose very point, in a sense, is that we agree to obey them *without* participating in their authorship. So the extrapolation to the employment context seems particularly problematic in this regard because the structure of the employment relationship is quite different from that of individual and state in certain fundamental ways: the employer is explicitly permitted to direct the purpose of the enterprise and the means of its implementation without consulting its employees. The state, on the other hand, is, at least in a liberal democracy, viewed as legitimate only when it forms and pursues its ends on the basis of the goals and preferences of its constituent citizens. But there does seem to be *some* analogy between the context of the state and that of the employer, in that both wield considerable power over interests that are crucially important to its participants—either citizen or employee—the exercise of which is partly manifested in the creation and enforcement of rules. Now whether or not that contextual similarity is sufficient to trigger these kind of participatory rights—such as the right to vote—in the private context, must surely be the subject of a much more nuanced analysis of the interests and vulnerabilities at stake for both parties. The important point, though, is that such a right could not be extrapolated to the private context *only* on the basis of a claim about its protection of an interest like participation in discourse, for example. A much more deeply structural analysis of the public law right would be required to delineate those private circumstances in which a similar structure and set of interests seem to arise.[27]

In the case of certain rights, such as the right to fair trial and the right to something like minimal subsistence—such as the extrapolation I hypothesized to a right to drinking water—the more institutional or social aspects of the right, such as that which seems to be involved in the right to vote, is combined with the dimension of the right that seems oriented to the public good. So if the right to vote is clearly meaningless for a purely solitary person—a monad, hypothetically—to enjoy, the rights to fair trial and to drinking water are even more structurally complex.

The right to fair trial, for example, has a number of dimensions and protects a number of interests. It has an individual aspect, whereby it protects the *dignity* of its subject. This is rather vague, of course, and although it might be enjoyable in a solitary way, it is more likely to be relevant where the individual is subject to the evaluative appraisal of others. So the individual interest involved in that right is in something like the non-arbitrary exercise of power—again, not something that makes sense to think of as being enjoyed by oneself. In addition to the dignitary harm that seems to be associated with the arbitrary exercise of power in itself, there is clearly an interest, here, in not being imprisoned or otherwise penalized unfairly; there is also the harm of the social stigma of criminality that will arise as one possible outcome of the trial. The interests protected by this right, then, that seem to be individual ones, only actually arise in the kind of relational context where a powerful agent threatens them.

Rights arise in the context of contingent relational structures. The structural or relational characteristics of a right thus refers to those aspects of the right that cannot be understood exclusively in reference to the interests of individual subjects, or to those interests together with the element of constraint as protected in a framework of rights. In the case of the right to fair trial, the relational dimension seems to involve the structure of vulnerability of the accused in relation to

[27] For a view of human rights duties as divisible into institutional and direct rights, see Thomas Winfried Menko Pogge, *World Poverty and Human Rights: Cosmopolitan Responsibilities and Reforms* (Oxford: Polity, 2002); Samantha Besson, 'Human Rights, Institutional Duties and Cosmopolitan Responsibilities', *Oxford Journal of Legal Studies* 23, no. 3 (2003): 507–23.

the finality of judicial decisions. In the absence of this positional or relational structure we would be less concerned about triggering the detrimental outcomes of physical coercion and criminal stigma. The right to fair trial also protects an interest that is not so much an individual one but a social, moral one, namely, the epistemic function of getting right answers—of finding out whether or not some accused person is actually guilty of some alleged offence. There is, in other words, the social good at stake of imprisoning only guilty people.

What does this structural analysis of rights tell us about how it must be extrapolated to a model reconstructed for the private sphere? The individual interests will be triggered where people are threatened with the exercise of power causing some detriment, where that detriment can be so severe that its potential arbitrariness would be harmful to the individual's dignity. Of course, most private actors cannot cause physical coercion like imprisonment—if they could, they would be subject to legal sanction under the laws of tort such as false imprisonment. But powerful social agents *can* cause other detrimental effects: losing one's job seems to be one possibility, though if there are many other jobs available this seems like an outcome that could be seen on a spectrum of harm to dignity. One of the individual harms that private agents can cause is that of blameworthy appraisal. The structural dimension of the public right tells us, though, that blameworthy appraisal analogous to the criminal sanction would trigger the right in its structural context only where the effects of that appraisal had certain characteristics: criminal stigma is a sign of basic anti-social personality or behaviour; it denotes an individual generally worthy of suspicion, or who is not trustworthy. This stigma is specific to the structural context of the relation between individual and state—in a private context like the employment one, or, say, in a store where one is thrown out for suspicion of shoplifting, the appraisal of blameworthiness can be more specific to the context and thus not trigger the same kind of social stigma. So this structural dimension of the public law right suggests that it can be triggered in the private context where a sufficiently general blameworthy appraisal takes place in the context of social discourse.

This brief taxonomy of the various dimensions of several quintessential public law rights illustrates the second aspect of the challenge in extrapolating such rights to the private context. An interest-based or simple semantic analysis doesn't tell us enough about the right even in its public context to be able to extrapolate it in a limited, principled way. An exclusively interest-based understanding of a public law right results in an extrapolated right whose contours are extremely imprecise; this imprecision in the definition of the right is exacerbated and multiplied when it is introduced into the institutional setting of the private law context, complicating the existing issues of judicial discretion in identifying appropriate duty-bearers. One might simplify this set of difficulties in the following way, acknowledging that the two institutional contexts assign duties in respect of rights very differently. In the public context, the state is the duty-bearer by definition, so the work of defining the scope and contours of a right is taken up by determining which interests the right protects, and what possible justifications for their infringement are legitimate and outside the scope of the right. In the private context, this question of which interests the right protects is still present, but there is an additional question, namely, who should bear the duties associated with these interests, and to what extent *their* interests should count as legitimate justifications for violating the right.

Let us take stock of the argument in the chapter thus far. In light of the conclusion that public law rights embody elements of both constraint and value, an adequate model will have to specify *both* those interests characteristically protected by public law rights and *also* specify that rights must function in a way that respects individual inviolability, thus prohibiting trade-offs or a moral calculus designed to promote those interests we identify as important ones at the expense of violating those of individuals. Taken together, those two elements together might seem to be jointly sufficient to capture our intuitions about rights and our social practice of rights protection. The dualistic model, though, does not capture the complex relational structures embedded in public law rights simply by the inclusion of the elements of constraint and value; such a model, therefore, despite meeting the challenge of translatability, is an inadequate extrapolative conceptualization of what public law rights are.

Its failure to fully describe the moral context of public rights means that it also suffers from another problem, namely the inability, necessary for a useful model of rights, to delineate their scope. The dualistic model (PLR) can say *what* rights protect, because public law rights articulate a set of particular interests. It does not, however, address the question of *whom* rights obligate; the dualistic model makes it difficult to say which of the situations in which someone's protected interest is infringed ought to count as rights violations. This brings us to the issue I will turn to in Chapter 6, namely, the problem of indeterminacy for a model of rights: delineating which situations warrant the recognition and possible enforcement of a right and which ones do not.

6

Indeterminacy

I. The Dualistic Model of Public Law Rights and the Challenge of Application in the Private Sphere

When we take public law rights out of the public law context—that is, when their exclusive duty-bearer is no longer the state—they become underdeterminate or indeterminate.[1] In one way this is simply an implication of translating rights from one institutional context to another: in their public law context, rights have institutional ties to the state, to interpretive doctrine, to constitutional theory. In the private sphere, they are cut free of these anchors and set adrift. The indeterminacy of new private rights of personal independence—that is, private rights protecting the interests enumerated by public law rights—is with respect to the duties they generate: for whom do they have normative implications, and what do those implications look like? It is this indeterminacy or underdeterminacy that leads to the unwieldy judicial discretion I described in Chapter 1 where constitutional and human rights are left to judges to apply among private actors. This problem of indeterminate applicability is really the flip side or the converse of the translatability problem of institutional context.

I have also alluded to the problem of the uncertain applicability of public law rights in the private sphere in intuitive moral terms: only in *some* private law circumstances do public law rights seem, intuitively, to justifiably apply. It is this problem of indeterminacy in respect of public law rights, and of a dualistic model of rights in general, that this chapter will be about.

The argument of Chapters 4 and 5 suggested that the elements of constraint and value are indispensable to a model of rights in general (I will henceforth

[1] I use the term 'indeterminate', henceforth, rather than 'underdeterminate'. This may seem controversial but I don't intend it to be. Since even on a dualistic model we know that a right protects a given interest, its normative implications are clearly not entirely indeterminate; in that sense, 'underdeterminate' would be a more accurate term. But because the dualistic model says *nothing* about the appropriate shape for the constraint associated with a given right, nor about *who* is to be constrained by the right, the underdeterminacy of rights is, *from the standpoint of potential duty-bearers*, in fact also a kind of *in*determinacy. The problem is, however, the same one whether we use the term 'indeterminate' or 'underdeterminate'.

capitalize the term in this context, 'Rights', to distinguish it from the more particular model of the set of *public law* rights) which looks like this:

Every Right is a norm that
(1) Is oriented toward protecting the inviolability of individuals; and
(2) Assigns priority to important interests $I_1 \ldots I_n$

The model of *public law* rights, as a specific instantiation of this general model, we have so far filled in with the interests we know public law rights protect, so that the model of *these* rights embodies the substantive normative judgments about interests left unspecified by the more general model of Rights. We called the dualistic model of public law rights 'PLR,' consisting of the jointly necessary elements of constraint and value but where the element of value is fleshed out. We formalized that model as follows:

Every Public Law Right is a norm that
(1) Is oriented toward protecting the inviolability of individuals; and
(2) Assigns priority to certain important interests: where $I_{1\ldots}I_n$ is defined by the core overlapping content of the set of constitutional and human rights.

With this model we appear to have addressed the objection from translatability in that we have abstracted the model of rights from any institutional context. But as we saw in Chapter 5, this model entails nothing *in particular* about the 'public' context of public law rights. It merely specifies the necessity of the anti-aggregative element of constraint and the inclusion of a type of normative fact or judgment, namely, that of value in the form of individual interests. So it seems that with the dualistic model we have abstracted too far, as it were, since it has no way of specifying which *private* interactions seem to belong to the moral context of public law rights. This means that PLR totally fails to address the problem of indeterminate applicability. Such a model of public law rights creates an impossibly unlimited scope for the duties rights generate in the private sphere, and thus it also creates a need for a principled limitation of that scope.

In order to develop a better model of public law rights that can overcome this challenge, we must return to the general model 'Rights', so that our model of public law rights does not violate the idea or concept of a Right. I will argue that a model of Rights that includes the element of its relational context is both a better model of Rights, and, when applied to the model of public law rights, fulfils this need for determinate applicability. The relational element in the general conceptual model, 'Rights', plays the role of normatively limiting the scope of rights and allowing us to reason from right to duty, thus answering the question of how to recognize or assign duties implied by rights. When we answer the question of *how* relational context impacts obligations with regard to rights in general in this way, and, in particular, *what kind* of relational contexts give rise to the kind of special protections associated with public law rights, we find that we also have an answer to the important question of how the scope of duties associated with personal independence rights can be limited in a principled way.

A. Rights and the moral minimum

A dualistic model violates the idea of rights—particularly rights that have some substantial moral dimension, such as public law rights and the core of private law ones—as a moral minimum. However they are understood to be morally justified, rights are generally taken to represent some idea of a moral minimum in respect of the way we must treat others.[2] This is a generalization, and most theories of rights will specify the careful way in which rights are picked out of all types of moral obligations in a slightly different way; the idea of a moral minimum is one I borrow from the political discourse surrounding human rights but its fundamental logic applies to other theories of rights as well. Non-consequentialists, broadly speaking, associate this minimum with agent-relative restrictions. Their idea of rights and of the distinct form of moral obligation they impose is associated with the prohibition on intentionally harming others. Rights impose a directed subset of moral obligations because although we may be morally required to help people in various ways, our obligation not to harm people is understood to be a special and distinct constraint on our action. On this view, then, rights track the distinction between harm and failure to aid; they are associated with the former rather than the latter, and tracking this distinction is a way of limiting the presumptively stringent obligations associated with rights to a certain kind of minimal moral requirement. A Kantian view of rights would take a more formal view of the moral requirements associated with rights, replacing the quantitative terminology of the moral 'minimum' with the idea of the categorical imperatives associated with perfect duties. Even from the standpoint of a purportedly formal, 'justice-independent' concept of rights like that of the will theory, the directedness of rights is emphasized in the powers over duty and enforceability that the theory specifies as necessary criteria for identifying a right. The enforcement of those powers associated with the small-scale sovereign are not necessarily morally justified, but in a system in which they are socially enforced, that enforcement requires some justification to those on whom the powers of the small-scale sovereign fall. From a consequentialist standpoint, too, if rights are to be recognized as imposing obligations that might conflict with what will produce the most overall good, then it clearly makes sense to recognize rights only in respect of those goods or interests that have the utmost importance. On both types of view, then, rights seem to represent a moral minimum of some kind.

There are thus several types of strictures employed by various theories of rights to limit the obligations rights can give rise to. Nonetheless, the idea of minimally moral conduct can, as a general extrapolation of those kinds of strictures, in principle apply both to negative prohibitions and to positive requirements: it can both forbid one from attacking someone else and also require that under certain

[2] Shue expresses this idea of minimally required treatment in terms of the justification of rights as 'demands': Shue, *Basic Rights: Subsistence, Affluence, and U.S. Foreign Policy* (Princeton, New Jersey: Princeton University Press, 1980), 14. See also Joel Feinberg, *Social Philosophy* (Englewood Cliffs: Prentice-Hall, Inc., 1973), 55–97.

conditions one must come to the aid of another. The key idea I want to draw from existing theories about rights is that rights are set apart from other moral requirements in that they impose distinct and presumptively stringent or peremptory obligations with respect to some set of actions that are most significant from some moral point of view. The idea of rights as expressing a normative[3] minimum thus cuts across the non-consequentialist/consequentialist divide, and it is therefore capable of grounding the three 'generations' of positive law rights, and, in particular, both the civil and political—often associated with negative prohibitions—and the socio-economic—often associated with positive requirements.[4]

In constructing new rights within the *private* sphere, it is particularly important that we take seriously this view of rights as expressing a moral minimum. This is because one of the most widely recognized problems with the application of public rights to the private sphere is that doing so will intrude on the freedom and other existing rights of the individuals who will bear the duties associated with them.[5] Some have, in fact, asserted that the scope of any such rights recognized in the private sphere ought to be delineated by the competing rights and interests with which the duties they impose would interfere.[6] Imposing new private law rights, then, creates a problem of justification that seems to present a special imperative to take the view of rights as expressing the moral minimum I outlined above.

B. Breaking down the binary of negative and positive

Under the heading of value, our model of rights will include the set of interests that are most commonly enumerated as both constitutional and human rights. The specific content of constitutional and human rights—the interests they enumerate—varies significantly. But we do nonetheless find a great deal of convergence in that set of rights. There is widest convergence on the most basic interests: in personal security, life, and liberty, as well as specific other personal freedoms such as conscience, thought, expression, religion, and association. There is also wide convergence on, broadly speaking, gender and racial equality and family status. Human rights, and many newer constitutions, grant some form of protection

[3] The type of normative force of the right will depend on its domain—legal rights will have presumptive peremptory force as against other kinds of reasons while moral rights will be correspondingly peremptory as against other kinds of moral obligations. Yet the peremptoriness of rights can be abstracted to the structure of rights more generally, as reflected in the element of constraint. This says nothing, however, about how legal and moral rights interact as competing in the more general normative domain as reasons for action, nor will I take a position on that.

[4] Shue elaborates the idea of 'basic rights', which represent the way we are required to treat one another at the most basic moral level, in terms of the interdependence of positive and negative rights. Shue, *Basic Rights: Subsistence, Affluence, and U.S. Foreign Policy*.

[5] See, for example, Jonas Christoffersen, 'Denmark: Drittwirkung and Conflicting Rights—Viewed from National and International Perspectives', in Dawn Oliver and Jorg Fedtke (eds), *Human Rights and the Private Sphere: A Comparative Study* (New York: Routledge-Cavendis h, 2007).

[6] Christoffersen, 'Denmark: Drittwirkung and Conflicting Rights—Viewed from National and International Perspectives'.

with regard to interests in basic subsistence or welfare, as well as basic education and health.[7] These, then, we will provisionally identify as personal-independence interests, and they will be carried, through our reconstructed model of rights, into the private sphere. This list is not meant to be exhaustive or fixed, and any such list will leave room for debate both about particular enumerations and about interpretation.

The first important thing to notice about this list of interests is that it does not differentiate, in principle, between negative and positive rights. When we focus only on the *valuable goods* protected by these rights, rather than also thinking about the form or structure in which they would be vindicated, what we have is a set of interests rather than a delineation of the negative or positive form of the obligations they impose. The inclusion of the element of value in the model of rights we are constructing, therefore, means that the model can recognize both negative and positive ones:[8] in a dualistic model, in other words, any right can be formulated in both negative and positive terms. If the valuable interest in question, for example, is physical security or physical integrity, we can think of it, and frame obligations in respect of it, in terms both of freedom from harm—a negative construction—and of health, or the absence of suffering—which would both construct the interest in a way that could easily generate positive obligations. The good of privacy, similarly, can generate obligations taking both negative and positive forms: the negative obligation would restrict the freedom of others—prohibiting looking, photographing, filming, or publishing, for instance—while the positive

[7] Human rights to these goods are well known, especially in the Covenant on Economic and Social Rights; many individual state constitutions also explicitly recognize rights to such goods in one way or another: see, for just a limited example of these, Constitution of South Africa, Chapter 2, Bill of Rights, section 26(1) Everyone shall have the right to have access to adequate housing, section 27(1) Everyone has the right to have access to (a) Health care services, including reproductive health care; (2) sufficient food and water and; (c) social security; Constitution of Japan, Adopted 3 November 1946, Art 25 (1) All people shall have the right to maintain the minimum standards of wholesome and cultured living; Constitution of the Republic of Latvia, Adopted on 15 February 1922, Art 111 [Health]; Art 112 [Education]: Everyone has the right to education; Constitution of Lithuania, Arts 52 [Old age and disability pensions, social assistance in the event of unemployment, sickness, widowhood, loss of breadwinner] and 53 [health, medical aid and services in the event of sickness].

[8] The terms 'negative' and 'positive', in the context of rights discourse, are used in a number of ways. In the political context, civil and political rights are generally viewed as negative, while social and economic rights are viewed as positive ones. The way in which I will use these terms, however, refers only the shape or form of interactions they describe. An obligation taking a negative form, for my purpose here, is one that we classically think of as an intrusion, in which A takes away something from B that was already in B's possession in a general sense. The 'something' that is taken away must be, in this context, something that already exists. So if A locks B in his garden shed, he takes away some of the freedom that B would have otherwise had, and this would count as an interaction having a negative form. If we suggest, however, that A takes away some of B's freedom by not giving her the use of his guest house, or by not giving her some amount of money, B is not being deprived of something she already had, and so, whatever else we might say about them, such obligations—if required—would count as positive in form. A positive form of interaction, then, is one in which A gives or expends something in respect of B's right. Another way of thinking about the two forms of interaction is that the negative form of obligation is one in which the violator takes an active role while the violated takes a passive one. A positive form of obligation, by contrast, can be breached even when the violator is passive with respect to some action.

obligation might require those others to build a fence, or establish a framework of, say, internet security. The constitutional interest in free speech or expression is in some places thought to require only that the actions of some not interfere with the speech of others. That construction of the interest imposes the negative form of obligation, but its positive form is less often thought to be required, so that, for example, the state is not required to build a platform from which a person can speak if he or she chooses to do so. Or the state might be prohibited, on the basis of the interest in free expression, from imposing content-based restrictions on speech on the internet; but the state is not required to develop and construct new electronic fora for similar expression.

Just as the inclusion of the element of value means that our model of Rights crosses the negative/positive divide, so, because of its conceptual thinness, the element of constraint we have developed can also function in respect of both negative and positive forms of obligation. As I have so far described it, this element simply means that rights impose constraints, and create, where they are recognized, a certain kind of functional inviolability. To impose a right, on this view, is simply to recognize or impose an obligation that gives rise to some inviolability. Constraints, though, can confer inviolability in this purely functional sense in respect of both negative and positive forms of interaction: constraint is conventionally associated with negative rights, but when a right imposes a positive obligation, it also imposes a constraint on the duty-bearer, restricting the choices she can make and the actions she can take.

When the set of rights interests, indiscriminate in itself between negative and positive forms of interaction, is *combined* with the thin and functional nature of the element of constraint within a single model of rights, the new set of reconstructed rights begins to take on an unwieldy, virtually unlimited scope. If my interest in health care is important, for example, why ought it not justify imposing duties on everyone in respect of it? The real problem here is that while each of the two moral principles animating the two elements I identified has a kind of internal, independent means of addressing this potential for indeterminacy and possible overbreadth, once we accept that rights necessarily involve both elements, those mechanisms for limitation are significantly weakened. In including the elements of both constraint and value, our dualistic model is deprived of the analytical resources associated with one-dimensional concepts of rights that would limit the circumstances in which rights arise to reflect the moral minimum. The dualistic model of rights—one that treats as jointly necessary two elements that conventionally animate very different theories—thus fails to address the challenge of creating new private rights for the private sphere, where they can in principle apply on behalf of anyone against anyone. This problem of indeterminate application is simply the consequence of a model that allows both concepts of rights to operate at the same time, as it were.

Duties associated with the element of constraint are conventionally limited by the negative form of rights implied by the idea of inviolability connected to constraint. The standard deontological account is that rights apply against everyone, and on behalf of everyone, because that account derives the interests rights protect from reason-based constraints. But because the constraint-based view of rights limits them in this formal way, their possible content is limited to conventionally negative rights. The deontological viewpoint, in other words, does not recognize rights to health care, for example, or education, or subsistence. It recognizes a framework of rights that is universal and that creates presumptively demanding or stringent obligations, but it limits the application of those rights to a fairly narrow range of interests.[9]

Conversely, the standard consequentialist account would narrow the range of interests that will be protected by rights on the basis of the importance of the interest. Only the most important, the most valuable, will be set aside from the calculus of general utility and assigned the special protection of rights. By including *both* the elements of constraint and of value, though, these limiting resources inhering in the two types of moral theory cancel each other out in practical terms. The deontological limitation of rights to negative ones (negative forms of interaction) can no longer function when the element of constraint is combined in the model with that of value. This is because the valuable goods identified by public law rights includes interests, such as health care, education, and welfare or subsistence, that appear to require a positive form of constraint, and that fall outside the limiting principle of the deontological account of rights. The inclusion of the element of value, left only to the limiting principle of consequentialism, means that rights will be identified only where the most value is: any claim about a right, on that view, will involve an assessment of whether protecting the right would protect or promote the maximal amount of one of the values in the set of rights interests.[10]

But the conceptual necessity of the element of constraint precludes this value-seeking type of limitation. If the true measure of what is required by the moral minimum, on an exclusively value-based view, is that which is most valuable, then a dualistic model that includes the anti-aggregating element of constraint deprives the consequentialist framework of its resources for limiting obligations to a reasonable scope. Another way of putting this problem, though I do not think my argument turns on this point, is to think of the problem of value- and constraint- based

[9] See Robert Nozick's discussion of compossibility, at pages 28–35, *Anarchy, State, and Utopia* (New York: Basic Books, 1974); also Hillel Steiner on the will theory's commitment to compossibility in 'Working Rights' in *A Debate Over Rights: Philosophical Enquiries* (Oxford: Clarendon Press, 1998).

[10] I have been using the terms 'consequentialist' and 'consequentialism' rather loosely. It must be acknowledged that consequentialism does not simply mean a maximizing or aggregating normativity. Consequentialists are confronted with a number of questions, including those of which consequences are important, and what to do when different important consequences pull in opposite directions. A utilitarian might take a maximizing approach, an egalitarian might take a distributive one, someone who doubts informational certainty might take a pre-commitment or rights based approach. See, for more on this idea of a menu of choices available to consequentialist reasoning, Amartya Kumar Sen and Bernard Williams, *Utilitarianism and Beyond* (Cambridge UK; New York: Cambridge University Press, 1982). Even taking this more nuanced view of consequentialist approaches, though, the problems of how to determine which consequences are important in the first place, and what to do if the good consequences, or the egalitarian distribution, pull in a different direction from someone's right, are questions that may cause problems without some independent account of constraints on how consequences can be pursued in the first place.

limitations on rights in terms of the distinction between agent-neutral and agent-relative reasons. Say that rights, on a consequentialist picture, if they are accepted at all, are those that represent the very highest value. Now because consequentialist morality is driven by value, it is comprised of a single type of reason—agent-neutral ones. It is this exclusive agent-neutrality, on a consequentialist picture, that allows for maximization: there is nothing special about what *I do*, so long as I respond to the reasons that pertain to us all to bring about the most value (however conceived). So, if violating one person's interest in liberty would maximize that or some other value to a sufficient degree, I am not only justified in doing so, I am required to do so. My actions—me, as an agent—have no special moral significance because the reasons generated by value are agent-neutral. Those who take rights to be morally fundamental, and in particular most deontologists, see the formalism of rights in terms of agent-relative constraints. This agent-relativity means that each right has a distinctive significance for *each* agent to whom it might pertain. When an agent comes across a putative right, he must say to himself—if this is a right, then it has implications for *my* actions: *I* must not violate the right of *that person*. It is that agent-relativity that prevents each person from violating a right for the sake of generating value, or for any other reason.

But of course on this way of seeing the elements of constraint and value, the dualistic model of Rights we have so far constructed will, because it embodies important values, generate agent-neutral reasons, and *also*, because of the individually oriented element of constraint, generate agent-relative ones. It looks, then, as though rights are a kind of multidimensional moral complex in which two very different types of reasons are forced together. Now the problem with this is that each type of reason gives agents discrete guidance about what to do—guidance that will sometimes conflict: whether to seek out and pursue actions that, viewed from an impartial standpoint, will produce the best outcome, or whether to consider the moral import of each action as it affects others on a kind of case by case basis. The dualistic model appears to ask agents to do both, or at least to be guided in both ways: it says that each of us has particular reason for not violating constraints in respect of a certain set of valuable interests. But if those valuable interests can be goods that seem to require both negative and positive forms of interaction, then it is just as important, on this view, that *I* fulfil the rights of each other person to health care, education, freedom of religion, and so on. How is this possible? And, more importantly, even if it is in principle true that I have *some* obligation to be guided by the constraints in respect of all these interests, *which* actions should *I* in particular take in respect of them?

C. The private sphere: the binary further undermined

This first problem, then, is that in extrapolating the set of rights interests from the public sphere—where they only impose duties on the state—to the private one—where, so far, no such relational limitation exists—rights would arise in respect of interests that are suggestive of both negative and positive forms of interaction, which would, in turn, undermine our ability to explain how rights are distinct from important interests. The second aspect of the indeterminacy problem is that imposing duties in respect of the set of rights interests extrapolated from the public sphere within interactions in the private one presents an exacerbation of the problem, because of particular features of the private law context itself. Without some further mechanism of limitation, a dualistic model would, in principle, create obligations that go well beyond what seem minimally morally required.

Protecting and respecting rights in the private sphere can require the obligated party to use or limit their use of their own resources—a positive form of interaction. Based on the examples I outlined above, this might seem to be simply an application of the problem of imposing constraints on choice and action in light of 'positive' interests such as health care. But the problem is not limited to those interests. Enforcing new duties on the basis of the set of rights interests in the private sphere also blurs the negative/positive distinction even in respect of interests that are generally understood to give rise to negative rights, such as freedoms of expression, conscience, and religion.

The idea that protecting even negative rights imposes costs is not a new one. The state, after all, must expend resources to protect the rights of its citizens in person and property through civil and criminal law. It accrues costs to protect citizens' procedural rights through the expenses of ensuring fair trials, humane treatment of prisoners, etc.[11] But in the context of private-sphere rights, even if we do not assert that some parties ought to actually *protect* some people's rights against others, the duties imposed on private actors in respect of rights directly can often come with a cost in terms of resources. If a mall owner, or a corporate owner of a whole town, is required to allow picketing, leafleting, or some other form of expression, on its property in respect of the rights of individuals to free speech, then that requirement, even as a matter of forbidding the property owner from intruding on or infringing the personal integrity of others, does not create only a negative form of interaction. The property owner's use of his or her *own* resource—the property—is directly constrained by the right. The application of the dualistic model of rights in the private-sphere context, then, would create what are effectively obligations taking a positive form in respect of what we ordinarily think of as negative, and minimally morally demanding, rights, such as freedoms of expression and conscience. In the case of free expression, for instance, I pointed out earlier that one positive obligation that might be required by the right—one that is in many cases rejected—would be the state's obligation to build or maintain some kind of platform for expression. Yet if we require a mall owner or some other private actor to allow his or her property to be used in service of some other person's expression, then a positive form of the obligation *would* effectively be imposed. In the private sphere, in other words, the apparently neat line I drew above between the negative and positive forms of obligation begins to

[11] See Cass Sunstein and Stephen Holmes, *The Cost of Rights: Why Liberty Depends on Taxes*, 1st ed (New York: W. W. Norton, 1999).

blur, because, in the private sphere, any action or expenditure one would require of private individuals in respect of even the 'negative' rights of others could entail an obligation to use or expend their resources in a particular way, thus taking the form of the positive obligation.[12]

This problem of indeterminate application and overbreadth, though, might seem to be overemphasized in the account I have given so far. After all, with respect to many public law rights, particularly the right to be protected against the very worst kind of mistreatment, such as torture, it does not seem so problematic to simply follow the norm where it leads, as it were, so that we enforce a duty not to torture against everyone. And indeed, this is the case in the United States—a state that does not practice horizontality—in respect of slavery, which is the only constitutional right to apply explicitly against everyone.[13] So in the case of certain acts, the overbreadth problem seems to be a misplaced objection. But in the case of most rights, like those of freedom of expression, freedom of religion, conviction, and association, the objection seems more measured. These rights are formulated, like the right against torture, in a basically negative form. Yet their violation in the private sphere can often involve positive obligations—as the French judge in the case of the Orthodox tenants found[14]—when it comes to imposing duties, and these obligations can seem unwieldy and unmanageable. The objection is even more pointed, of course, when it comes to rights framed in more general terms, such as those to personal security or physical integrity, whose form of interaction can be either negative or positive.

The problem, as I suggested earlier, is the undermining of the importance of rights as distinct from other obligations or from interests or values more generally. Having combined the elements of constraint and value in a single, composite model of rights, we are left without the robust resources of either of the two major moral theories to describe the way in which they are distinct. Non-consequentialists could rely on the idea of constraints differentiating rights from interests by being moral in a foundational and special sense, and thus of being clearly directed; consequentialists can similarly rely on the distinguishing ability of a hierarchy of values. Having extrapolated the set of rights interests from the public law context, it is unclear how we can avoid a problematic consequence. That is, that that those interests would impose the demanding constraints associated with public law rights on everyone. Consider, for example, a hypothetical case in which a six-year-old child sets fire to a church, destroying it. Imagine that it is the only church of a small religious group. Clearly their property rights

[12] For more on this idea, see Henry Shue, 'The Interdependence of Duties', in *The Right to Food*, International Studies in Human Rights (Netherlands: Martinus Nijhoff Publishers, 1984); 'Mediating Duties', *Ethics* 98, no. 4 (1988): 687–704; *Basic Rights: Subsistence, Affluence, and U.S. Foreign Policy*, especially Chapter Two, 'Correlative Duties'.

[13] *United States of America: Constitution* [United States of America], 17 September 1787, available at: <http://www.refworld.org/docid/3ae6b54d1c.html> (accessed 16 December 2014). Amendment 13 passed by Congress 31 January 1865. Ratified 6 December 1865.

[14] See Chapter 1, especially Myriam Hunter-Henin, 'France: Horizontal Application and the Triumph of the European Convention on Human Rights', in *Human Rights and the Private Sphere: A Comparative Study*, 124–5.

have been violated, possibly in addition to their security. But, freedom of religion being one of the special rights interests that form the content of the new private rights of personal independence we are creating, we must now also ask whether the right to freedom of religion of the group's members has been violated. If we consider freedom of religion to be at stake because it is a rights interest articulated in our source set, then it should be considered to have been violated *in addition to* the property rights violations. Yet although the group's *interest* in freedom of religion has been infringed, their *right* corresponding to that interest, I would intuitively suggest, has not. Similarly, if a neighbour puts political signs all over my house, my property rights have clearly been violated; my freedom of expression seems to be similarly *affected*, but my attendant *right* to expression, I would argue, has not been violated. Imposing new private obligations involving the special protections associated with personal independence rights on the basis of the set of rights interests we extrapolate from the public sphere, then, without further limitation on the scope of the duties they impose, creates the strong presumptive obligations associated with public law rights in circumstances in which they do not seem intuitively to be warranted.

II. A More Fundamental Indeterminacy in a Dualistic Model

So far I have described the problem of indeterminate applicability, of distinguishing *which* private actors ought to bear the new duties associated with new, reconstructed, rights, mainly in terms of the way the dualistic model of public law rights allows for both negative and positive forms of constraints in respect of the wide range of interests protected, and I have argued that this is a specially vexing problem in the context of private relations. Moreover, I pointed out that each of the moral theories animating the constraint-based and the value-based conceptions of rights have moral mechanisms for limiting the scope of rights. Constraint-based accounts limit the content of rights to negative forms of interaction and to a certain narrow range of personal and proprietary interests. Value-based accounts claim to limit their accounts to the *most* valuable interests, delimiting the scope of the duties rights will generate that way. These are both mechanisms of limitation, but they limit only the content of rights, in the sense of the things rights protect. What is lacking is a resource for a principled and measured assignment of duties even where there *is* a right whose content, whose element of interest, is uncontestedly worth protecting.

In fact this lacuna reflects a more fundamental indeterminacy that plagues a dualistic model of rights as a general matter—I have called this the model of Rights, to distinguish it from the more specific model of public law rights. This problem arose above in the context of the hypothetical case of the child setting fire to a church, affecting the interest in freedom of religion of some individuals but arguably not violating their right to that freedom. The more basic problem I refer to is the following: the dualistic model includes both the element of interest and the element of constraint, but it does not contain any mechanism by which one can say when the infringement of an interest constitutes a violation of the associated constraint. In other words, we need to be able to distinguish between an interest and a right; to do this, we need to be able to say when the special constraint associated with a right has been violated. And in order to be able to do that, we need to know *who is normatively implicated by the right's constraint, and what shape that constraint should take.* This is not only the practical problem of untethered public law rights becoming unwieldy and pushing too much of the moral deliberation into judicial discretion; it is not only a problem with the model of public law rights allowing for both negative and positive forms of constraint. It reflects a problem with models of rights even at the conceptual level.

A. Indeterminacy raises its ugly head in theories of human rights

Theorizing about the concept of rights, as I have been arguing, has become so polarized that most discussions simply accept one view or the other, or else try to avoid the dispute altogether. But in the context of human rights, the question of what rights *are* continues to be pressing for precisely the reasons I have been stressing throughout the book: human rights—and the 'fundamental' or human rights listed in constitutions—continue to be taken seriously in one way or another in political and theoretical circles. People argue for social change on the basis of human rights, and that often involves arguing for the recognition of new ones based on understanding existing ones, or, as in the case of our current project, trying to understand just how human rights generate duties, and onto whom. In this latter connection, there has recently been a strand of significant debate among rights theorists about how to understand the ways in which human rights impose duties that can counteract the international principle of state sovereignty; this is at once a question of the justification of human rights and one about onto whom they impose duties. So it is in this connection that some of the most recent discussions about theories of human rights has arisen. For our purposes the question of whether human rights duties can counteract state sovereignty, and to what extent the answer to that question can generate an explanation for the distinctiveness of those rights is mostly a non sequitur. But the discussion is illuminating for our project and the argument in this chapter nonetheless, for two reasons: first, the discussion has to some extent grappled with the problem that human rights suffer from indeterminacy; second, this discussion arising in the context of human rights is significant because human rights, as we have seen, embody the elements of constraint and value, and that dualism is becoming increasingly recognized in more recent contemporary thinking about them.

There are three generally accepted ways in which rights can fail to be sufficiently determinate. The first is the problem described recently by Raz as one of distinguishing between goals, values, and rights.[15] If rights are taken to be very

[15] J. Raz, 'Human Rights without Foundations', in Samantha Besson and John Tasioulas (eds), *The Philosophy of International Law* (Oxford: Oxford University Press, 2010), 321–37.

important interests, what additional conceptual content does the appellation 'right' import? One way of approaching this problem is to emphasize rights' constraining form. James Griffin,[16] for example, advocates a view of human rights something like those traditional ones I describe as formalist, in which the possible content of human rights is limited by the normative implications of their form: since they are a certain kind of constraint that protects people's choice-making agency in pursuit of their goals—being a 'self-decider'—the features of personhood that are intrinsic to, or necessary to, the capacity for normative agency, ought to be understood to be human rights.[17]

Raz points out what is in effect another problem of indeterminacy here—it is a problem of underdeterminacy, since, as he shows, it is nearly impossible to get enough content to get human rights going on this account, which ostensibly protects autonomy and liberty as the core features of personhood without reaching for aspects of the good, or interests of value, to flesh out the idea of protecting choice.[18] The objection Raz makes to Griffin in regard to human rights is essentially similar to the conclusion I argued for in Chapter 4, insofar as it observes that without recognizing the *content* of rights as an indispensible normative fact or judgment about what is sufficiently valuable to protect on behalf of individuals, one cannot, as it were, really get rights off the ground at all. Raz makes this argument by first showing how even persons whose autonomy and liberties 'were systematically denied, like slaves, [are] nevertheless persons'.[19] Deriving rights from an account of personhood that would survive the conditions of slavery means that the normative agency essential to personhood would have to mean only intentional agency. But that of course is the problem: since slaves have intentional agency, their rights to that aspect of their personhood could be protected even while they were subjected to conditions of slavery. But if a concept of human rights is to mean anything at all, it surely means that human rights are denied under conditions of slavery. And to avoid that problem Griffin makes the conception of the person as 'self-decider' thicker, which, as Raz shows, means that the aspects of life it incorporates becomes much less obviously minimal, and much less obviously principled.

Griffin quite explicitly extends the grounds of human rights beyond the capacity for intentional action. He includes conditions making its successful exercise likely, conditions such as the availability of education and information, of resources and opportunities. At every point he adds 'minimal'—minimal education and information etc. But if minimal means some information, some resources and opportunities, however little, it is a standard easy to meet, and almost impossible to violate. Just by being alive (and non-comatose) we have some knowledge, resources and opportunities. Slaves have them. Griffin, of course, does not mean his minimal standard to be that skimpy. He suggests a generous standard. But

[16] James Griffin, *On Human Rights* (Oxford: Oxford University Press, 2008).
[17] Griffin, *On Human Rights*, 14.
[18] Raz, 'Human Rights without Foundations', 326–30.
[19] Raz, 'Human Rights without Foundations', 327.

then we lack criteria to determine what it should be. My fear is that this lacuna cannot be filled. There is no principled ground for fixing on one standard rather than another.[20]

Raz and Griffin are writing specifically about human rights, but this particular task of marking out the 'normatively exceptional domain'[21] of rights as distinct from values by limiting the range of interests they conceptually generate introduces the third problem of indeterminacy for theories of rights more generally. As Raz argues, and as Griffin seems to acknowledge, the task of preserving rights' distinctive normative character—that is, solving the first problem of distinguishing rights from values more generally—'can only succeed if people do not have human rights to everything which will or may improve the quality of their life. For if people have such rights they are not exceptional.'[22] Griffin, too, regards the task of limiting rights to a normatively distinctive domain as essential: 'If we had rights to all that is needed for a good or happy life, then the language of rights would become redundant,' he says, since 'we already have a perfectly adequate way of speaking about individual well being and any obligations there might be to promote it.'[23]

But even in Griffin's attempts to derive the content of rights from some non-interest-based account of personhood, this third problem of the sheer multiplication of possible interests arises. It is this third problem to which Griffin's personhood account is directed; as he says, after the Enlightenment, 'the theological interpretation' of human rights was abandoned, and 'nothing was put in its place. The term was left with so few criteria for determining when it is used correctly, and when incorrectly, that we often have only a tenuous, and sometimes plainly inadequate, grasp on what is at issue.'[24] John Tasioulas interprets this as the task of enhancing the determinateness of the criteria governing the use of the term 'human right'. 'Success', he says, 'will consist in arriving at an account that is informative enough to yield determinate existence conditions' for identifying human rights and 'to guide us in fixing both their normative content and their weight in practical deliberation.'[25] Tasioulas characterizes this task as 'not primarily an exercise in lexicography or value-neutral conceptual analysis but rather in normative moral philosophy: greater determinateness is to be secured by locating the notion of human rights within the best overall understanding of ethics, showing that it earns its place there'.[26] This is of course a compelling point, and Tasioulas highlights the way that Griffin's conceptualization of moral

[20] Raz, 'Human Rights without Foundations', 329–30.

[21] This is how Raz characterizes what he calls 'The Traditional Approach' to human rights theory; even on the more political conception that interests him in the paper, though, it seems that he would share the view of rights thus described as marking out a 'normatively exceptional domain'—though in the case of his discussion of human rights in the chapter in question, the norms to which human rights are exceptional are at least substantially those of non-intervention and state sovereignty in international law.

[22] Raz, 'Human Rights without Foundations', 329.

[23] Griffin, *On Human Rights*, 8–9.

[24] Griffin, *On Human Rights*, 2.

[25] John Tasioulas, 'Taking Rights out of Human Rights', *Ethics* 120, no. 4 (2010): 647–78, 648.

[26] Tasioulas, 'Taking Rights out of Human Rights', 648.

rights emphasizes features of them familiar to us from will theory: 'Griffin', he says, 'briskly characterizes the modern sense of a right as an entitlement that a person possesses to control or claim something.'[27] Tasioulas acknowledges two 'threshold' problems of sufficient determinacy for an account of human rights, namely, too little substantive content to get rights going at all, and too few criteria for limiting the possible range of interests they protect so that human rights, *as* rights, become indistinguishable from valuable interests. He thus questions the capacity of Griffin's conceptualization of personhood to generate the content necessary to diminish indeterminacy in the intensional concept of human rights, given that 'personhood might consist in the bare capacity for intentional action together with some measure of its successful exercise'.[28] On this minimalist view of the person, Tasioulas refers to Raz's point that even a slave possesses this capacity, and thus arguably an unsatisfactorily small number of rights would be grounded by its protection. But, with respect to the second, upper threshold problem, if a richer conception of personhood is premised, there might be no limit to the features of human life that could require protection as human rights in consequence. Tasioulas's point is that personhood is a sufficiently variable concept that it can generate neither necessarily sufficient content nor a necessarily reliable upper threshold for the rights grounded by it. Tasioulas himself attempts to sketch a possible solution to this problem that looks, implicitly, something like our dualistic model of rights.

In developing what he appears to take to be a modest account of moral rights, he asks:

> Is there an informative explanation of the general notion of a moral right that does not mire us in philosophical controversies that are alien to the concerns of the human rights culture? What is at issue here is nothing so ambitious as a definition of moral rights nor anything so crass as an insistence that one take sides in the endless feud between the proponents of 'interest' and 'will' theories of rights.[29]

Having established this laudable goal, though, Tasioulas begins to question Griffin's agency-based account of human rights on the basis of his suggestion of what he calls a more pluralistic view of human rights—what he acknowledges to be a fundamentally interest-based one. Thus, far from trying to take sides in the debate between interest and will theories of rights, Tasioulas's discussion illustrates the difficulty of escaping the conceptual elements of constraint and value in discussing rights, and the fruitlessness of setting up views of the two types as having mutually exclusive purchase on understanding rights.

Griffin's view is essentially constraint-based, in that it takes human rights to be grounded in normative agency and generating protections for the aspects of human life necessary to the fulfillment of that human capability. While the exclusive primacy given to agency as a feature of personhood on Griffin's account make

[27] Tasioulas, 'Taking Rights out of Human Rights', 651, citing Griffin, *On Human Rights*.
[28] Tasioulas, 'Taking Rights out of Human Rights', 660.
[29] Tasioulas, 'Taking Rights out of Human Rights', 656.

it looks very much like a status- or constraint-based view, Tasioulas's arguments against it immediately advert to the necessity of interests to what rights are: he describes the aspects of personhood that could generate rights on Griffin's view as 'personhood *interests*'[30] (emphasis added) and goes on to argue that:

> Provided the threshold for generating a right is satisfied, and provided the right in question is suitably universal (possessed by all simply in virtue of their humanity), why should it not count as a human right even if nonpersonhood interests are also directly implicated in determining its existence and content? This opens the way to a more pluralistic account of the grounding of human rights than Griffin's personhood theory, one that can appeal to a number of different basic components of human well-being.[31]

I certainly do not make this point to claim that Griffin and Tasioulas are closeted will and interest theorists about rights, respectively, for, as Tasioulas points out, there is something about the 'feud'[32] between will and interest theories of rights that seems to be stuck, as is evidenced by the tendency among newer rights theorists to develop what they call hybrid theories possibly simply to avoid the 'crass'-ness[33] of being forced to take a side in the feud. I am not interested in 'outing' Griffin and Tasioulas here, quite the contrary: I am interested in illuminating the way in which a view of rights that does lean toward (presumably equal) status, and thus that includes mutual constraints, encounters natural and intuitive objections from the corner of values. And the resistance goes the other way, too: it is partly because of the importance of interests to views about rights that worries about their 'proliferation' and indeterminateness has come about. The intuitions of constraint and of value, in other words, seem to be drawn to one another and yet to hold one another at a certain distance like planets in orbit around one another: this reinforces the conclusion that these two poles are not mutually exclusive but are jointly necessary conditions for rights.

And indeed, Tasioulas's own view of rights bears this out: although in considering the range of possible grounds for and content of human rights he draws on the language of interests and values important to human life, in his sketch of what he takes a right to be, as a conceptual matter, he sets out three existence criteria that are entirely what I categorize as claim- or constraint-based. These are (1) that rights are '*Sources of duties*', meaning generating reasons for action in virtue of the object of the right that are *categorical* and *directed* in character; (2) that rights have an '*Individualistic grounding*' and (3) that individual moral rights are 'held by identifiable individuals; violations of the duties grounded by those rights entail the wronging of the right-holder'[34] (emphases added). Tasioulas's approach is dualistic in the way the model I have so far developed is, in the sense that he defines the conceptual content of moral rights in what he takes to be formal terms, then specifies that human rights will take the content of interests. The

30 Tasioulas, 'Taking Rights out of Human Rights', 662.
31 Tasioulas, 'Taking Rights out of Human Rights', 662.
32 Tasioulas, 'Taking Rights out of Human Rights', 656.
33 Tasioulas, 'Taking Rights out of Human Rights', 656.
34 Tasioulas, 'Taking Rights out of Human Rights', 657.

interests that will qualify as rights, grounding and, presumably, delimiting, them, will be established by moral reasoning.

Tasioulas's discussion, though, hints implicitly at the way such a dualistic model is conceptually insufficient because it underdetermines any given right. He describes the constraint element of rights, in his criteria listed above, but doesn't say how interests *become* duties for particular persons, nor what the shape of the duty is. This undermines at least two of the criteria he says will allow us to distinguish rights conceptually from interests.

First, consider his assertion that rights are 'sources of duties':

> Moral rights—or one paradigmatic manifestation of them usually referred to as 'claim rights'—are sources of moral duties or obligations (I use these terms interchangeably). The existence of a right to *x*, on the part of A, grounds duties on the part of others variously to protect, respect, and so on A's possession, access, and so on to *x*.[35]

Remember that the account is meant to be a way of distinguishing a right, when one encounters a purported one or a claim about one, from an interest or value. But A's right to *x*, on this account, already grounds duties in two unacceptably vague ways. First, it says nothing about who is implicated—Tasioulas says as much as this kind of account can say, when he says that duties will be imposed 'on the part of others'.[36] But how am I to know if I am one of these 'others' on whom A's right to *x* will impose an obligation? Nothing in this conception of rights tells me. For me, in other words, the very question we want answered is still open: am *I* to consider *x*, for A, a good thing, a valuable or valued interest, or am I to take it to be a right? And in fact Tasioulas seems to acknowledge this problem: he says that 'Griffin interprets rights as "claims," but A's claim on *x* may simply consist in a reason for A to pursue *x* or for others to help A acquire *x* or at least not obstruct him in his attempt to do so'.[37] That is, for others, A's claim may be a right or it may only be a reason of some other kind.

Second, even assuming I, as a purported or potential duty-bearer, take a conservative approach and assume that *I* should consider A's claim to *x* a right, on this model of rights the consideration of the purported right only tells me that the right grounds *various* duties: 'to protect, respect, and so on A's possession, access, and so on to *x*'.[38] Now on any kind of interest-based model of rights, these various *shapes* of constraint can apply to any duty-bearers. But Tasioulas's own formulation here emphasizes the indeterminacy of this fact in relation to a dualistic model, since, as a potential duty-bearer, I have no idea, by virtue of the conceptual content of a right, *what I am required to do* to fulfil my duty, assuming I am one of those who has one. Tasioulas is well aware of this objection, calling it the argument that rights ought to be 'claimable' in the sense that we can reason on the basis of the right's conceptual content to some conclusion about the identity

[35] Tasioulas, 'Taking Rights out of Human Rights', 656.
[36] Tasioulas, 'Taking Rights out of Human Rights', 662.
[37] Tasioulas, 'Taking Rights out of Human Rights', 656.
[38] Tasioulas, 'Taking Rights out of Human Rights', 656.

of duty-bearers and the shape of duties.[39] He rejects this idea, though, on the basis that it would, he says, cause welfare rights to be excluded—or 'demoted', as he puts it—from the domain of real moral rights, or, as he says, 'from the ranks of bona fide human rights'.[40] He doesn't say much about why this would be the implication of conceptualizing rights this way, but the likeliest explanation is that there is a view of rights, which I have called broadly formalist or deontological, which limits the shape of constraints it takes rights to embody to negative ones. Since welfare rights are normally taken to generate positive duties this would rule them out. This reasoning is based on the idea that the only way to build into the concept of rights information about the appropriate duty-bearer and the shape of the constraint is to do so in the manner of formal theories. But that, as I will argue in the following section, is not so.

The real indeterminacy problem in existing conceptualizations of rights—which we find creating a practical indeterminacy in creating new 'public law' or personal independence rights for the private sphere—is exactly the one I pointed out in Chapter 1: it is in the space or connection *between* right and duty. In terms of Tasioulas's model, simply recognizing that it is insufficiently determinate whether duties are created if we think of rights as claims but then solving that problem by stipulating that rights are special kinds of reasons—directed, exclusive, and individualistically oriented—simply does not solve the real problem of how we can tell *how* values become rights, how reasons *become* special reasons in the requisite way.

B. The right-duty problem reconsidered

The conventional or traditional way of understanding the link between right and duty is that of the correlativity axiom, which I introduced in Chapter 2 as the central plank in the disagreement between formal theorists of rights and interest theorists. For those who accept it, correlativity with duties is axiomatic to rights: it means that you can't have a right without a correlated duty—that the *logical* structure of a right is bound up with the duty it is correlated to. This idea is most clearly laid out by Hohfeld, whose taxonomy of rights as jural positions has been extremely influential. The idea here is that there is no such thing as a right, if there is no associated duty: the normative *connection* between right and duty (and between the other correlates on the Hohfeldian scheme, the privilege/no-right, the power/disability, the immunity/liability) is what constitutes the thing itself, as it were—both with respect to the right and the duty. You simply cannot have one, in a meaningful sense, without the other.

Now one thing to notice about the way I formulated the description of the correlativity axiom is that I described the right as being always correlated with

[39] Tasioulas, 'Taking Rights out of Human Rights', 656. Tasioulas here attributes the idea of claimability in this sense to Onora O'Neill, *Towards Justice and Virtue: A Constructive Account of Practical Reasoning* (Cambridge: Cambridge University Press, 1996), 128–53 and *Bounds of Justice* (Cambridge: Cambridge University Press, 2000), Chapter 6.

[40] Tasioulas, 'Taking Rights out of Human Rights', 657.

the duty rather than generating it or giving rise to it. This is because implied in the strict logical axiom of correlativity is the thought that right and duty come into being at the same time, as it were—you have both or you have neither. This is important because it is the central implication of the axiom to which the interest theory objected, when it was first articulated by Raz; that theory has proved extremely widely accepted by theorists, scholars, lawyers, and activists as a concept of rights.[41]

But even before we get to the rejection of the *axiom* of correlativity, we need to see that even for those who accept it, the connection between right and duty, or, more specifically, the directedness of the duty in relation to the right, is a contested question. This is because there is a version of the interest theory, that of Matthew Kramer—who accepts both the correlativity axiom and its implication for the logical necessity of a duty existing in relation to each and every right, or else no right being there at all—which accepts that rights protect interests and that the interests they protect warrant the duties to which they are correlated. That is, Kramer's version of the interest theory is that rights exist in both a logical and a justificatory relationship to duties.[42]

Kramer's version of the interest theory is nonetheless involved in what we have seen other contemporary scholars of rights refer to as the long-standing and perhaps somewhat stagnant feud that revolves directly around the question of how rights and duties relate to one another. This dispute is between the interest theory of rights as taken up by Kramer and the will theory, whose chief proponent in the debate is Hillel Steiner. Now Kramer and Steiner share a basic commitment to the Hohfeldian base or form of rights. Their conceptual accounts, therefore, move beyond the purely logical identification of rights as correlated with duties and make a further level of explanation. They each want to know, assuming one is presented with something that looks like a right and something that looks like its correlate duty, how one can identify the *holder* of the right in question. This seems to bring the inquiry up, as it were, from its logical base into the realm of the substantively human. What gives one person a right but not others?

By setting forth the necessary and sufficient conditions for the holding of a right, each theory in that debate is *specifying to whom any duty is owed*. The Will Theorists maintain that the direction of any duty is determined by the location of the authorization to waive or seek enforcement of the duty, whereas the Interest Theorists contend that the direction of any duty is determined by the location of the generally beneficial effects that are intrinsic to the fulfilment of the duty. These rival contentions generate the sundry points of controversy over which the Interest Theorists and Will Theorists have long quarrelled: points such as the status of certain persons (children, senile people, comatose

[41] It has been asserted as 'the received view' of rights by one scholar of rights: Grégoire Webber in 'On the Loss of Rights', in Grant Huscroft, Bradley W. Miller, and Grégroire Webber (eds), *Proportionality and the Rule of Law: Rights, Justification, Reasoning* (Cambridge: Cambridge University Press, 2014), 123.

[42] See, generally, Matthew H. Kramer, 'Rights Without Trimmings', in *A Debate Over Rights: Philosophical Enquiries* and, with Hillel Steiner, 'Theories of Rights: Is There a Third Way?', 27 *Oxford Journal of Legal Studies* (2007): 281–310.

people, and so forth) as potential right-holders; the status of individuals as right-holders under the criminal law; the distribution of rights under third-party-beneficiary contracts; the possibility of collective rights or animals' rights; and the conferral of rights by statutes such as minimum-wage laws. These and other related controversies lie at the centre of the division between Interest Theorists and Will Theorists. These are the matters which the two sets of theorists address when they joust with one another.[43] (emphasis mine)

As Kramer and Steiner make plain in the quoted passage, both sides in the debate take their question to begin *once a duty has been, or can be,* identified. Theories of rights have often referred to rights as 'directed duties' and this is, to some extent, what both Kramer's interest theory (I use his name repeatedly in connection with the theory to distinguish this type of interest theory from that of Raz) and the will theory have in common: each is a means of identifying right-holders by beginning with duties and then following them in a particular direction. The theory of rights is meant to tell us which direction to go, in pursuit of identifying the right, from the duty. The heart of the dispute is about the criteria to be used in determining the direction in which duties point toward their 'real', corresponding right-holders. In order to be able to identify claimants holding genuine rights, on either of these accounts, the duty must first be identifiable in order for the right to be identified. On Kramer's account of the interest theory, one must follow the direction of the *benefit* conferred by a duty in order to identify its attendant right. The will or choice theory identifies rights holders (and thus the rights themselves) with the location of *control* over the exercise or waiver of a duty (and its enforcement).

Theories like these, which accept the correlativity axiom, don't recognize the indeterminacy problem because it does not arise for them: as I said, you simply don't have a right whose normative implications might be unclear, because there is always a duty out there somewhere that embodies those implications, and you have it, moreover, in some sense *before* you can identify the right associated with it. But that is not as helpful as it seems, at least on the existing theories that accept the axiom. Both Kramer's and Steiner's accounts of rights, to take the most prominent of these, identify rights by beginning with duties. Their disagreement is what direction to go in from duty to right—toward benefit or toward control? So although at least for Kramer one could in principle still be presented with a right and not *know* who is required to do *what* in respect of it, that is not his chief concern, at least in his recent writing. His concern is to be able to identify not the rights but the *holders* of rights where a duty has been identified. This is just an entirely different question than the one we are interested in.

This is because there is a practical problem for these theories from our point of view, insofar as we begin with a normative mandate to protect a particular set of rights on behalf of individuals against a broader range of actors—against non-state as well as governmental agents. Our problem is to identify the moral structure of those rights in such a way that we can identify justified duty-bearers

[43] Kramer and Steiner, 'Theories of Rights: Is There a Third Way?', 298.

in respect of them. Since we begin with rights, then, in this endeavour, and look for justified duties, it is entirely unhelpful to be told that the way to identify rights is by identifying rights *holders*, let alone by looking for either benefit or control over an existing duty: we have the rights, at least pro tanto; what we are looking for is the justified duty-bearer of those rights. We want to follow the duties in the other direction, in other words, from the one pursued by these theories; we want to go from right-holder to duty-bearer, rather than the other way around.

So this is an impossible model for our purposes; but that problem is suggestive of the various compelling arguments against this kind of theoretically elegant but ultimately somehow narrow or limited view of what rights are. The weaknesses of this kind of approach to rights were identified and described by early interest theorists, particularly Raz and Waldron, and were part of the reason, it seems to me, why the interest theory became, as I suggested above, so influential. A theory of rights limited to their identification as certain kinds of implications or entailments of duties—be they associated with the benefit(s) flowing from a given duty or with control over its exercise—is a somewhat impoverished one. This could simply be because of a kind of circularity problem—what are we adding to our understanding simply by asserting that rights are simply correlates of duties?[44] To know which rights we have, on this kind of view, we only need to know which duties we have—the only further question is who holds the rights associated with these duties.

But our practical problem with the necessity to be able to identify duties in advance of finding their correlated rights indicates a more worrying moral problem as well, namely that we now normally take rights to enable people to protest particularly egregious treatment in a particularly powerful—and ostensibly effective—way. It is perfectly possible for someone to have the kind of grievance that leads them to assert the violation of a right—to have had members of her family 'disappeared', to have been subjected to physical cruelty, to have been coerced to work in degrading circumstances—without that person knowing exactly who is responsible for the primary violation, and, more importantly, without having a fully established table of duties of protection and promotion of their affected interests to refer to. As Waldron argues, a concept of rights seems morally impoverished if it does not allow us to say yes, a right of this person has been violated, or will be violated if something is not done to protect them from

[44] In 'A Right to do Wrong' in Jeremy Waldron, *Liberal Rights: Collected Papers 1981–1991* (Cambridge: Cambridge University Press,1993), Waldron illustrates the way rights have a content that goes beyond, as he puts it, 'merely the duties of the right-bearer perceived from a subjective point of view' (82). Moral rights, as Waldron illustrates, pick out some conceptual content that is not fully captured by simply focusing on a set of duties from the point of view of the agent to whom they are directed: 'by limiting rights to actions that are morally permissible', to give one way of describing the duty-generated account of rights, 'we would have to countenance some sort of lexical ordering whereby the morality of rightness and wrongness, duty and obligation, requirement and prohibition, even virtue and vice was allowed first in the field of action to pick out as its domain those actions that were of particular moral concern. The morality of rights would be allowed to enter the field only when that process had been completed, to clean up the leftovers, as it were. But *what* would be left over when the morality of rightness and wrongness had had its say? The answer seems to be: the banalities and trivia of human life' (83).

violence, to provide them with health care, and *then* for the question to become one of assigning or allocating duties on the basis of that moral position.[45]

But indeterminacy plagues existing concepts of rights, thwarting that moral imperative. We have established that constraint is the form rights take, and that constraining action or choice is part of their conceptual structure. This general dualistic position is the one that many, if not most, contemporary rights theorists and political theorists find themselves in. Rights are taken to protect interests and on that ground to both justify and require corresponding constraints; but the conceptual content of rights is in the position in which Tasioulas leaves it. That is, the conceptual content of a right does not itself sufficently *inform* the constraint it is taken to give rise to, either by way of justification or entailment or moral requirement or some combination. It tells us too little about the identity of those for whom rights will have normative implications, as well as about what the shape of those implications will be.

If we assume that we will begin with a right and try to reason our way to a duty, the inclusion of the element of value or interest in the conceptual structure of rights tells us what the corresponding substantive content of duties owed in respect of that right will have. A right to food will generate duties that have something to do with allowing the right-holder to have or to enjoy her interest in the good of food. But on this conceptualization of rights, the right to food tells us no more than that. It does not tell us who is implicated by any given rights, nor does it specify, for those who *are* so implicated, what shape the constraint on their choices and conduct will take, namely, positive, negative, institutionally oriented or individualistic, and so on.

Formalists or ostensible formalists about rights can of course argue that since their view limits real rights to the negative ones, this problem of indeterminacy does not arise, because rights are all compossible and universal. I have argued against the plausibility of this view in Chapter 4, but it is worth expanding on that argument in the present context.

The idea that formalists rely on is that it is possible for these duties in respect of negative rights to be universal and compossible. Even those who don't accept the dogma of the categories of negative and positive rights seem to accept it. But it is an idea past its prime. It is, in the real world, in fact not possible for my going about my own business not to affect the rights of (even) the seven billion. Consider, at a local level or small scale, my freedom from interference in my smoking habit. In my immediate area, my exhaled and second-hand smoke can cause harm to those around me; we cannot all enjoy the freedom from harmful interference at the same time. Now that seems a small example, but its logic applies to pollution and all forms of action that cause CO2 emissions, since those emissions have an effect, via climate change and its impact, on the freedom from harm and property

[45] This is partly the normative attractiveness of what Raz and Waldron described as the 'waves' of duties generated by interests (or rights) and rights 'dynamism'. See, generally, Raz, *The Morality of Freedom* (Oxford: Clarendon Press, 1986) and Waldron, *Liberal Rights: Collected Papers 1981–1991*, 212.

rights of those living in coastal and low-lying areas. My going about my ordinary economic business, too, affects those whose physical presence I need not enter. I can, in other words, and almost invariably do, cross the Nozickean boundary of moral space of at least hundreds of people in the Global South when I make choices about what clothes and food to purchase, how to obtain my goods, and so on. This has become a truism in the context of discussions of moral responsibility, globalization, and cosmopolitanism, but it is important to acknowledge in this context because it truly belies the dogma that negative rights can be universal and compossible. Not all of these impacts will be sufficiently serious or, perhaps, sufficiently structured so as to constitute rights violations, but my point here is only that we cannot rule out of hand the possibility that they would rise to the level of rights violations merely because I go about my business without physically interacting with anyone or their property directly. These impacts on distant others, moreover, happen because of mediating institutions, to be sure, but that only means that if I am to fulfil my negative duties to the seven billion, as it were, I need to do something to effect change in those existing institutional structures. And even then, air pollution and a shared climate undermine this classical fiction that is in any case based on an imaginary, and in every way distant, state of nature. So let us leave aside that perhaps attractive but impossible option of rights being neatly classifiable so that the general or universal ones—and thus arguably the most important ones—are compossible and unproblematic regarding who should be required to do what in the face of rights.

C. Can determinacy be externalized from the concept of rights?

The problem of indeterminate applicability of rights pushes the assignment of duties out of the normative sphere of a given right. Many people, since the widespread discrediting of the compossibility thesis, have pointed out that this leaves rights stranded and aloof from duties in a practical sense, since rights no longer obviously point, conceptually speaking, to the people and actions they implicate.[46] It has become difficult if not impossible to say on the basis of a right, considered in itself, what conduct, by whom, constitutes its violation. And without knowing when rights have been violated, it is much more difficult to put in place the discursive, political, moral, and legal sanctions that make rights an important and—in principle—powerful tool in our moral practice. But this problem has mainly been identified only as a practical one, rather than, as I want to claim, a problem for the current conceptualizations of rights even as a theoretical matter. There has been a barrage of complaints, since the birth of the more positive rights, the socio-economic rights, and the interest theories that have given them conceptual dignity, about rights becoming meaningless, toothless, or pointless.

And because the problem is taken to be a practical one—a failure to actually assign duties in respect of rights—rather than a problem with the conceptualization

[46] See Onora O'Neill, 'The Dark Side of Rights' in *International Affairs* 81, no. 2 (2005): 427–39.

of rights, the arguments to improve the situation have tended to be pragmatic rather than principled. Shue, Pogge, and others have made some variety of the argument that what matters is that rights' demands are met, meaning, because of their interest-based views, that rights will be fulfilled if right-holders are enjoying the good to which they are entitled by virtue of the right. Shue, for example, argues for the assignment of duties on the basis of a division of labour—a kind of rough and ready imposition of some elements of duty-fulfillment onto some persons and other such elements onto others. Even better, on these kinds of views, would be to give the assignment problem, both practically and normatively, to 'institutions' who can justifiably administer the allocation of constraints that will allow rights to be fulfilled.

O'Neill has similarly argued that rights are meaningless unless duties—she seems to be thinking of full-blooded moral as well as legal duties—are recognized/assigned directly on the basis of rights. And she wants to see a conception of rights that allows us to reason from rights to duties without the kind of interruption of being normatively lost—who *should* be affected by these rights?[47] Since we don't know, let's make sure *someone* is—and the subsequent pragmatic assignments of duties. The dualistic model of rights allows for constraints to be recognized on the ground or basis of a right but only after the right's own normative implications—namely those of the interest it articulates—have been exhausted. The considerations that go into the assignment of duties, on this view, are basically external to the right.

This externalization is a characteristic implication of an interest theory of rights or a dualistic one that takes rights' form to be one of constraint while allowing only the normative element of interest to be included in their conceptual content. It is evident in Raz's own recent description of the way the assignment of duties based on human rights—as distinct from the identification of their interest-content only—is a matter in some sense external to the rights themselves, to be decided partly on the basis of pragmatic, instrumental, and contingent facts.

> [Human rights] derive from three layers of argument: First, some individual interest often combined with showing how social conditions require its satisfaction in certain ways... The second layer shows that under some conditions states are to be held duty bound to respect or promote the interest (or the rights) of individuals identified in the first part of the argument. The final layer shows that they do not enjoy immunity from interference regarding these matters. If all parts of the argument succeed then we have established that a human right exists. Each layer presupposes the previous one, but to establish the conclusion of each layer requires considerations specific to it. So understood human rights enjoy rational justification. They lack a foundation in not being grounded in a fundamental moral concern but depending on the contingencies of the current system of international relations.[48]

[47] Onora O'Neill, 'The Dark Side of Human Rights', 427–39, 430–2, 'Agents of Justice', *Metaphilosophy* 32: (2001) 180–95, *Towards Justice and Virtue: A Constructive Account of Practical Reasoning*, and *Bounds of Justice*, Chapter 6.

[48] Raz, 'Human Rights Without Foundations', 345.

Now this is one plausibly practical way of assigning duties on the basis of rights conceived as protected interests. But I want to argue against this pressure toward externalizing the fundamental normative implications of rights from the conceptual structure of rights themselves. I will try to show that on a more determinate conception of rights, more normative information must be available, or immanent in the intensional aspect of the concept, that will inform more extensively the normative implications of rights for the recognition of constraints having a particular shape to particular duty-bearers.

III. Indeterminacy and the Insufficiency of the Dualistic Model

In Chapter 4 I argued for the necessity of the element of value by pointing out that rights cannot *only* be from or against intrusions and thus entirely formal. My argument there was partly that we know the element of value is necessary to the model of rights because all rights are inevitably and inescapably *to* something even if it presents itself as a right 'from' or 'against'. Now I want to suggest, conversely, that we can't identify, in some sense, even what a right is *to* by reference to an interest alone. We cannot identify the entitlement implied by a given right unless we know what would constitute its violation. We can't, in other words, know what a right is *to* unless we know what it is *from*. But here, unlike in Chapter 4, I am not focused on the goods that are the subject or content of the right, but on the action or choice limitation that *protects* the given good. The structure or shape of the protection of the good is as much a part of what the right is to as is an articulation of the interest it protects. If we don't know what could count as violating a right, in short, it remains conceptually underdetermined; it can't be meaningfully identified or accounted for.

To put this argument more formally we can state it as follows: (1) constraint and interest are jointly necessary to a concept of rights; (2) the necessity of constraint as an element of rights entails that we identify the constraint as part of the identification of the right; (3) the conduct that would constitute compliance with or violation of the right reveals the shape and content of the constraint by bringing into relief the kind of behaviour that is and is not permitted by the right. (4) Following from (2) and (3): to identify the content of the constraint in respect of a right we need to be able to tell whether it has been complied with or violated, or what such compliance or violation would look like. Therefore, (5), if we can't tell, when faced with some conduct by a given actor and a putative right, whether or not the putative right has been complied with or violated, we simply cannot say that the right exists. We cannot fully or sufficiently determinately know what a right is *to*, therefore, unless we can tell when it is complied with or violated and when it is not. It is *that* difference, rather than the importance of an interest followed by analysis of contingent facts about the capabilities of various actors, that distinguishes rights from interests or values more generally.

Premise (1), the joint necessity of constraint and value, I have already argued for in some detail in this chapter and the previous one and so I will take it to be true for the purpose of this argument. Premise (3) is essentially stipulative; it sets out what I mean by the content of a constraint. The conduct that would constitute a violation of a right is the content of the constraint because, as I argued in Chapter 4, constraint creates a functional inviolability. The meaning of functional inviolability is simply that there is a course of action that would constitute a violation and the constraint prohibits that course of action. The crucial premises are (2) and (4), and I will thus focus my argument on them. Premise (2) is what is necessary to distinguish rights from important interests; premise (4) is necessary to show, and the conclusion, (5), establishes, that the elements of constraint and value are not jointly sufficient to the nature of rights; the conceptual structure of a right must include some further content that can inform the particular conditions of its violation.

I will begin with the implications of the element of constraint for the model of rights. A right is very widely accepted to be a special kind of obligation—a directed one, or even an agent-relative one. This latter characterization means that for each person the right of another has a special normative implication *for them*, or, in the case of third parties to rights arising out of transactions like promises, it might have no implication for them.

The first thing this implies is that in order for a right to establish a directed obligation, each person must be able to or at least have some basis on which to *tell* whether the right of some other person has that kind of normative implication for them. The best existing method for apparently explaining how people can tell whether someone else's right creates a duty *for them* is the categorical one dividing rights on the basis of whether they are partly grounded in a relation (including a transaction)—these being the 'special rights'—or not—these being the 'general rights'.[49] Now it's true that special rights do seem to provide the information that allows us, and potential duty-bearers, to reason from right to duty from the right itself, as it were, without additional contingent information. These rights, then, don't seem to pose the problems of indeterminacy we are concerned about.

But that doesn't help us because the rights we are concerned with in respect of the normative mandate are either the kind that would be classified as general, namely, human rights, or they are ones that might be characterized as special, namely constitutional ones because they arise in the relation between individual and state; and the nature of our project is precisely to remove that ostensible 'specialness' so that these latter rights potentially apply to anyone against anyone, thus rendering them formally general.

And general rights are supposed to be ones that *everyone* has independently of any transaction or relationship. That latter requirement means that they are universal in the sense that everyone is a right-holder but also in the sense that everyone is a duty-bearer. But now we are clearly back to the problem of indeterminate

[49] The distinction is Hart's, most influentially and compellingly elucidated by Waldron, *The Right to Private Property* (Oxford: Clarendon Press, 1988), Chapter 4.

applicability: if I know that another person—and especially every other person—has a moral right to potable water, for instance, how do I know whether that right has any normative implications for me? I think it is reasonable to claim that if I can't tell, then the putative right in question can't be the right kind of reason or obligation—that it can't be sufficiently directed. Because if I am to be under a *special* kind of obligation that I owe directly *to* the person whose right is asserted; if that obligation is supposed to be a distinctive kind of reason having an elevated or peremptory status among my other reasons, then surely at a minimum I ought to have some way of *knowing* that I have such a reason. The right, in other words, has to be able to direct the obligation, not only in the abstract universe of theoretical rights, but in a way that potential duty-bearers can conclude on the basis of reasons arising from the right itself. Potential duty-bearers can only reason from right to potential duty if there is information in the idea of what a right is that tells them what kinds of judgments to make to determine whether a given right imposes a duty on them or not. One type of judgment is clearly the one about important interests, but that information has no specific bearing on whether or not a right directs *their* obligation toward the right-holder in the necessary kind of way.

This uncertain situation seems to be the one that has arisen from a widely interest-based or dualistic conceptualization of rights. On its basis, rights don't contain or consist of enough normative information to tell potential duty-bearers that they *are* duty-bearers and thus to direct their obligations toward the fulfilment of the right. In the absence of this normative content in their conceptual structure, we revert to the kind of post-right assignment of duties based on various contingent factors, capacities, institutional arrangements, and so on. Notice, though, that here even when duties *have* been thus assigned they have not truly been assigned on the basis of the rights themselves. The assignation of duties—the directing of obligations—is not informed by the normative content of the right.

Moreover, on this kind of picture of the assignment of duties, their allocation is contingent and must be *made* or *decided* by someone to assure that rights are fulfilled. This takes the agency for reasoning from rights to duties away from those who would be normatively implicated by that reasoning, namely, duty-bearers. It means that in the case of these supposedly general rights no one can tell whether or when a *right* has been violated as opposed to whether an *interest* has been curtailed and thus whether and when a constraint exists in respect of the interest except the person or agent doing the duty-assigning on one of the variously proposed contingent bases.

This seems like an absurd conclusion, since there would be only a few people (the duty-assigners) who could tell whether a constraint really exists and thus whether a right, as distinct from an important interest, exists. In fact the implications of this argument are contained in some of the early writing about the interest theory: Waldron, most notably, defined the business this way: 'Rights are the way interests generate duties.'[50] The nature of rights, that is, is coherently distinct from

[50] Waldron, 'Rights in Conflict', 214,

that of both interests and duties, and contains some analytic content that allows us to move from the former to the latter. On Waldron's phrasing there ought to be enough conceptual information in the 'rights' piece of that formulation to explain or at least to inform *how* we get from interests to duties. This is in contrast to the pragmatic picture on which duties are allocated external to, or after, as it were, the right. On this institutional-assignation picture, rights are not the way interests generate duties; rather, some decider makes an all-things-considered judgment about who should bear what constraint in respect of the importance of some interest.

We saw in Chapter 1 how public law rights have insufficient normative content for judges in the private sphere—how we need a model of rights that can assign duties in some fashion ahead of judicial adjudication—and this problem of indeterminacy plaguing the conceptually dualistic model of rights seems to bear this out. If they include the element of constraint—if they are conceptually distinct from important interests—rights' conceptual structure must include sufficient normative content or information that the judge, or potential duty-bearer herself, or an observing third party, can reliably reason from right to duty on a principled basis. On such a conceptualization, of course, each of these three—the potential duty-bearer, the judge, and the observer, might still disagree about the normative implications of the right even given its normative content. But on the model I am proposing here, at least their disagreement would hinge on a normative dispute about the implication of *information* that, because it is in principle part of the right itself, they can all share.

The same basic structure of argument applies to the premise that a potential duty-bearer must be able to reason reliably about just what, even assuming they reach the conclusion that some right has a normative implication for them, is required of them. Remember Tasioulas's formulation of A's right to *x*, which implied that some indeterminate others have some obligations to protect, promote, and respect A's enjoyment of *x*.[51] If the ground of A's right to *x* is the importance of A's interest in *x*, that does not in fact tell us anything about whose behaviour is or ought to be constrained by that importance, or what shape that constraint should take. You and I might easily reach different conclusions, given only the information that A's interest in *x* is important, about what we are required to do in respect of it, and there would be no way, in reference to the right itself, to adjudicate our dispute. All the stability and determinacy of the constraint necessarily associated with A's interest in *x* is in the authority of whoever decides that there is a right there. It is the decider who will determine what a violation of the right will look like, and thus create something distinct from A's interest in *x*.

And the problem of the failure of rights to adequately *direct* their corresponding constraints by providing sufficient normative information to their potential duty-bearers, a significant problem in itself, becomes magnified when we consider the implications of the directedness of obligations. As Tasioulas describes them, and as they are

[51] Tasioulas, 'Taking Rights Out of Human Rights', 656.

widely recognized, rights are not only directed but categorical[52]—perfect obligations to particular persons—and exclusionary or, as I have put the point, peremptory. It might be one thing for a reason purporting simply to guide one's action to fail to provide the necessary content for those to whom it might apply to be able to reliably identify themselves; it is almost incoherent for a reason that is supposed to override other considerations to be so indeterminate or even underdeterminate: the dualistic model thus leaves rights inadequate to the task of being the right kind of reason for their potential duty-bearers.

[52] Tasioulas, 'Taking Rights Out of Human Rights', 656.

7

Relationality in the Model of Rights

I. The Missing Piece

In Chapters 4 and 5 I argued that the elements of value and constraint are jointly entailed by rights. In Chapter 6 I showed why a dualistic model of Rights constructed on the basis of that joint necessity leaves out any further information about whom a right implicates and in what way. I argued that such an account of rights fails to explain how they become the requisite kind of categorical, exclusionary, and directed obligation they are taken to be, and thus that the dualistic model is insufficient: the elements of constraint and value are jointly necessary but not sufficient to what rights are. Something is missing from the model as so far developed.

The next question, then, is: what is that missing piece of right's conceptual content? Interest alone is insufficient to identify what exactly a violation of a right, as opposed to the infringement of an interest, would look like, since there are innumerable ways of infringing the various types of constraints that could be associated with a given interest, and no obvious way, certainly in the case of general rights, of knowing what constraints apply to which persons.[1] What type of normative fact or judgment[2] would supply the answers to the questions of 'why me' in the case of a potential duty-bearer and 'why her' in the case of the judge and observer, as well as to the question of what shape the constraint should take—what action or inaction, on the part of that person, will count as a violation of a given right?

I will suggest that the relevant norm concerns the relational context or structure in which any given right arises. The argument for the inclusion of a relational

[1] There is a very influential strand of thinking in the area of constitutional theory and human rights practice and theory, especially in Europe, which thinks of this as a question about proportionality—but that solution of course skips the step of establishing the duty-bearer and the shape of the duty. See, for example, Mattias Kumm, 'Who is Afraid of the Total Constitution? Constitutional Rights as Principles and the Constitutionalization of Private Law', *German Law Journal* 7, no. 4 (2006): 341.

[2] I refer to this missing content, and later to the element I claim supplies it, as a 'normative fact or judgment'. I mean by this to indicate that the requisite element will have to be a norm, either legal or moral. If it is a moral norm I do not wish to create confusion by referring to it as a normative fact (or judgment), only to indicate that I leave open the meta-ethical question of whether there are 'real' moral norms, and thus that some version of moral realism is true, so that the conceptual content of the right would have to be a moral *fact*, or that moral norms must emerge through the exercise of human moral assessment in which case even in the moral sphere the conceptual content of the right would have to be a moral *judgment*.

element within a model of rights will go as follows: (1) rights are formally relational; (2) because of this formal relationality, each recognized right in fact reflects a claim (and its recognition or acceptance) about the possible conditions of its violation; (3) the claim (and its recognition or acceptance) about the possible violation conditions of a given right refers, if only implicitly, to the interpersonal structure or relational context in which the right arises. In Part II of this chapter I will say more fully what I mean by the relational context or structure and what it means for a right to arise within such a structure. In Part III I will respond to some objections about including relational context within the conceptual content of Rights.

A. Formal relationality

(1) Directed constraints

Rights are formally relational. That is, they entail two poles or normative positions that are two sides of the same constraining form. This formal relationality, as distinct from the correlativity axiom, is the way the element of constraint implies both claim and duty. The object of the inviolability implied by the constraint—requiring or prohibiting certain actions—is the good protected by the right; in order for a right to retain its individualistic orientation, the good must be protected on behalf of a right-holder. This creates one pole of entitlement toward which the constraint is oriented. The constraint would be incoherent, though, if there were not some action—the action of some person(s)—to be constrained. This is what makes rights distinct from moral rules taken more generally: you may have a moral rule that constrains certain types of conduct—conduct motivated by an intention to cause harm, for example—where the other 'pole', the source of the constraint, is effectively morality itself. This bipolar fact about rights is evident in Hohfeld's taxonomy and its characterization of rights as types of relations; he refers to them as 'jural' ones, because he is working in the domain of legal rights, but insofar as the right/duty correlation is convincing in respect of moral rights, its implication is that these can be better characterized as 'moral relations'. And, as Griffin points out, we certainly have sufficient ways of understanding the moral importance of individual interests, individual well-being, and well-being more generally, as well as other types of moral goods that create imperfect obligations. In the case of obligations of these kinds, the 'thing' protected is identifiable—well-being, for instance—but the particular actions required in virtue of that thing are not part of the obligation itself.[3] In the case of rights, because they *are* directed obligations from particular persons toward particular persons, the action required or prohibited by the obligation constitutes the other pole of the constraint and thus the relationality implied by the form of rights.

[3] James Griffin, *On Human Rights* (Oxford: Oxford University Press, 2008), 8–9.

(2) *Claiming and formal relationality*

I have so far argued that rights are formally relational on the basis of their directedness; I now want to argue for their formal relationality on the basis of another of their features widely taken to be distinctively characteristic, namely, that rights are claims. It seems to me that understanding rights as claims is one of the broadest commonalities among theorists of them.[4] Hohfeld effectively substituted the word 'claim' for the way in which the word 'right' is most often used among non-specialists and specialists alike, to distinguish them more clearly from the other positions of strength in his table of jural relations—the privilege, the immunity, and the power.

Claiming is a compelling way of describing how rights operate, and what they are, because a claim has both a justificatory and a formal dimension, as rights do. That is, a Razian interest theorist could accept a view of rights as claims in the justificatory sense that a right is an assertion about the importance of an interest—an assertion, that is, that some aspect of the well-being of X is sufficiently important to *warrant* the imposition of a duty. And the claim need not be seen as exclusively voiced, as it were by X. The claim in this sense of the word can be voiced vicariously—by the moral community, by institutional authorities, by judges, and so on. It represents a moral judgment about the importance of an interest and the implication of a justified duty imposed in respect of it. On this view, the claim is exhausted, so to speak, at the point of the conclusion that the interest *is* sufficiently important to justify a duty, and the inquiry then moves on from the conceptual content of the right to allocating the burden of the duty thus justified.

On a formal view, of course, the claim is much more obviously synonymous with the right. The pervasiveness of the Hohfeldian view of rights as claims has led to many authors referring to rights as 'claim-rights' in order to distinguish the right from the other strong jural positions, as well as from interests alone. If the justificatory interpretation of rights as claims I sketched above conceives of the claim as a claim *to* the sufficient importance of a given good or interest, the formalist conceives of the claim as being *to* the control over the duty correlative to it. This is most clear in the case of the will theory, and it puts the voice of the claim, as it were, into the mouth of the right-holder herself much more deliberately and exclusively. Others could conceivably make a claim on the basis of a right, on this view, but they would do so as agents for the right-holder, because the claim is *to* a choice about whether to waive or enforce, broadly speaking, one or more aspects of a duty. Thus the claim is not about the specific content of the duty in a general or justificatory sense, but about its existence and execution in particular instances.

[4] One of the most influential accounts of rights as claims came from Joel Feinberg. See, generally, Feinberg, *Social Philosophy* (Englewood Cliffs: Prentice-Hall, Inc, 1973), 64, and 'Duties, Rights and Claims', *American Philosophical Quarterly* 3 (1966): 137–44.

(3) Right-claim as address

Stephen Darwall has developed the view of the moral claim as a particular kind of second person reason-giving.[5] His argument is not about rights in particular but about all moral claims, though he sees rights as a 'central' instance of the second personal character of reason-giving.[6] The fundamental tenets of the view involve the mutual accountability of persons and the reactive attitudes necessary to that accountability as fundamental to morality. If I tell you to stop standing on my foot, I am relying on your acceptance of a norm to which I refer in making that assertion. The key point Darwall makes is that moral reason-giving of this kind is not simply that 'people should not stand on one another's feet' and that that norm applies to the situation between us. Because if I tell you you should get off my foot, I am speaking to *your* acceptance of that norm—to your thinking that it applies to you as well as to me, and *also* to you as accountable to me. You are accountable to me because I have the authority to call you to account for the violation of moral norms, and your accountability recognizes that authority. There is a mutuality here as well, because my speaking to you as accountable to me, implying your recognition of my authority, also implies that you have the moral authority necessary to be accountable, to be responsible for your choices and actions.[7] So while the norms to which we refer in calling one another to account are shared norms of the moral community, the form of the address—the type of reasons expressed in the address—is in the second person; that is, it says that *you* should not have done that.

Even if the action implicates another person—so that the content of the address is 'you should not have stolen that lady's purse', there is a relationality in the form of the address because of the moral relation Darwall describes of *I* to *you*, which in the latter case refers not to the fact that you have done something to me, but to the fact that I have the moral authority to address you with second-person reasons where moral norms are concerned because I speak as a member of the moral community and I address you as a member of that community. Our shared membership in the moral community does not make the *address*, though, from me to you, any less second-personal and, in that sense, directed.

Now of course Darwall is interested in establishing moral reasons as second-personal more generally;[8] we need not accept that broader point to accept that rights, as claims, are forms of address in the way Darwall describes. But of course the problem with simply taking Darwall's analysis of the address as being second-personal and simply *applying* it to rights is that that would lead to the strange result that rights are, in respect of their second-personal and thus relational address regarding a norm, no different than all other moral rules in that sense. So one way of differentiating rights is to remember that they are characterized not only as claims, and as directed—both of which imply at

[5] Stephen Darwall, *The Second-Person Standpoint: Morality, Respect, and Accountability* (London: Harvard University Press, 2006).

[6] Darwall, *The Second-Person Standpoint: Morality, Respect, and Accountability*, 18.

[7] Darwall, *The Second-Person Standpoint: Morality, Respect, and Accountability*, 10–25.

[8] Darwall, *The Second-Person Standpoint: Morality, Respect, and Accountability*, 20.

least formal relationality—but also that they are, as reasons, expected to have a categorical and peremptory or exclusionary effect on the practical reasoning of their hearer; I will return to this aspect of their distinctiveness from other moral rules in a moment.

Another way, though, of differentiating them, is to understand their address as being two-fold: *both* second-personal *and* second-person-plural. If I tell you to get off my foot, not on the basis that if you don't I'll beat you up but on the basis that you *shouldn't* be on my foot, I can be giving you a reason in the second person that refers to your duty not to stand on people's feet. It can refer, in other words, to a general moral norm against foot-standing. And you can accept it on that basis: you can recognize that you have a duty not to intrude into the space of another's physical person without their consent simply as a matter of the moral rule against harming others, for example. Now I can also tell you that standing on my foot is such a significant problem that you should take my address to rise to the level of the peremptory, and get off my foot even if doing so would mean that you would get in the way, say, of the subway doors and prevent 100 people from getting where they need to go and cause tremendous delay, confusion, and a host of problems for many people. The idea behind rights as special kinds of reasons is that they are meant to convey that kind of peremptory quality, to contain and reflect the moral reasoning and judgments required to draw the conclusion that indeed getting off someone's foot (assuming, arguendo, that one has a right not to have one's foot trodden on) *is* more important than avoiding causing a pedestrian traffic problem; that, in other words, the assertion of a *right* means that such a moral judgment has been made, or is a fact, and that you ought therefore to take it to have that special kind of importance without my having to convince you. That second way in which a right is distinguished from a general moral rule involves the implication that there is another form of address involved in a right, namely, the address *to* the normative community from which it is drawn. This latter address is in the second person plural, where the *you* refers to all of the members of the normative community: when I assert a right, I do so on the basis that my authority to give you a second person practical reason *of that special kind* is backed up by the judgment of that normative community, *and* that that community *ought* to support my claim through some kind of sanction. This second form of address involved in rights claims is perhaps the reason that it might seem that part of what makes a right special is that it will be enforced—no remedy, so the saying goes, no right. The very existence of a right, on that latter view, involves its characteristic enforceability.

So where does this leave us with respect to rights' conceptual structure and formal relationality? Taking apart the right-as-claim, we find three features. (1) The norm of action or practical norm—a reason of law and/or morality. This norm is of the kind 'it is wrong to stand on the feet of others'. (2) The address in the second person to the actor who has or who could violate the right. This address says 'Do (not) do *x* action' because of (1). (3) The address to the relevant normative community to recognize and act on (1) and (2). Now (1) alone could describe all norms; the conceptual centrality of claiming to rights is manifested in (2), the second-person address *and* (3), the second-person-plural address, that is involved in the right as normative claim.

The two types of address involved in the right-as-claim further establish rights' formal relationality and also suggest that rights conceptually involve a normative fact or judgment of a relational kind: that is, pertaining to the relational structure of the context of any given right. This is for two reasons. First, the second-personal address element—(2), above—of the claim entails the conclusion of the argument I made earlier, namely, that for a right-as-claim to exist, there must be some hearer or intended hearer of the claim to whom the claim is specially directed. That person is the purported duty-bearer of the right because it is that person's actions or potential actions that will constitute the violation of the right in question and thus to *him or her* that the right will be particularly significant as a matter of practical reasoning in the right way, namely, as generating a directed and peremptory reason. This aspect of address, in other words, is the claim about the direction of the constraint. And this aspect of the claim already contributes to the formal relationality of rights, since it establishes a communicative and normative relation between claim-er and claim-ee: the person with the authority to make the claim and the person whose action or potential action constitutes the violation of the asserted right.

The address to the moral community—(3), above, the second-person-plural aspect of the claim—also contributes to the formal relationality of rights as-claims, because it must involve a shared normative judgment, or an assertion about such a judgment, between the claimer and that community about both (1), the norm itself, *and* (2) the *correct* direction of the address to a potential duty-bearer. That is, in order for the claim to go through, as it were—in order for it to be accepted or recognized as a right and enforced in some way—the normative community must recognize the judgment about the substantive value of the asserted right involved in the general norm (1), and must *also* recognize that the address to the person manifested in (2) is the right one—is justified as made *to that person*. So in a formal sense, the address to the moral community involved in a rights claim is part of what establishes one aspect of the constraint element of the right—the right will be in fact constraining if the claim goes through and is accepted by the moral community, *or* if it is normatively accepted in the practical reasoning of the person addressed in (2). But of course the acceptance of the moral community can also affect the practical reason of the person to whom it is addressed, and so (3) is thus doubly important to the constraining function of the right.

So far I have tried to show that the address or claim dimension of a right, and, in particular, (3), the address to the moral community for effectuation or support for the constraint, is what differentiates rights from moral rules more generally. Of course the *address* dimension of rights as-claims does not by itself establish their existence, normatively speaking, since in principle, if it did, a moral right could be established even if the claimer, the claim-ee, and the moral community all got it wrong, so to speak. The first aspect of a right-as-claim— (1), above, the norm itself—is thus also necessary: for a right to exist, the norm of action must also exist. But for the aspect of the claim made in the second-personal address,

(2), to be correct, and to be recognized, it must involve the correct content of the norm in (1) *and* the correct direction of the constraint entailed by the person addressed in (2). Since a purported claim, absent the norm in (1), cannot go through even if (2) and (3) by themselves are effective, in other words, the normative content of the claim must contain all the necessary information to establish it—to make it properly acceptable to its addressees. This means that the norm itself, absent any element of address, must involve both the value the right protects and the relational norm governing the context of the claim-er and the claim-ee. So in the claim aspect of rights, we find not only support for the fact of their formal relationality but also a hint, an abstract suggestion, that the relational context in which the claim is made is normatively requisite to whether the right is established or not.

B. From formal relationality to norms pertaining to relational context

In the above sections I described rights' formal relationality, and I used Hohfeld's model of axiomatic correlativity to buttress that argument. But of course there is something amiss there, since the dualistic model of Rights I have so far constructed, and am currently considering, does not take the correlative relationship between right and duty to be *axiomatic* in the sense that right and duty are simply two sides of the same coin. Yet the element of constraint is included in the model; does that not seem like the inclusion of a duty in the right itself? We have seen that interest theorists explain this by saying that the relation between right and duty is justificatory only; but that explanation, as I have argued, is not entirely adequate to explain rights' distinctively directed, constraining character. I want to now introduce a distinction that may help to clarify this subtle confusion.

Hohfeld was interested *only* in rights as formal objects. His scheme offers *no* account of what rights we ought to have or how that question ought to be decided or even considered. In a purely conceptual universe it is perhaps plausible to imagine purely formal rights; but in a world that includes experiences, things, and substances as well as concepts, such pure formality is, as I have emphasized, ultimately fictional. But now let us imagine, for the sake of clarification, the right as an object *in-between* the right-holder and the duty-bearer. Imagine the right itself as a kind of line (to imagine the simplest structure), which has one end pointing at the right-holder and the other at the duty-bearer. It does not matter, on this picture, whether the line represents only a justification, and, as the interest theory would see it, was drawn *from* the right-holder toward some duty-bearer, or whether it represents a *logical* relation between the two, so that we would have to imagine that it arose with both sides in place simultaneously. In either case, the line *creates* a relation between the two persons. And in that sense we can explain away its formal relationality on the basis that a line necessarily has two ends, and thus that the right, if properly conceptualized as a line in this way, simply could not be otherwise. The right is formally relational, on this story, only because it *is* or *creates* a relation; it need have no connection to any *substantive* norm pertaining to the descriptive or analytic relational structure in which the right arises, even to a very simply relational norm like equality.

But what I want to clarify, here, is that the formal relationality of a right is already suggestive that a right is also *responsive*, normatively, to facts or judgments concerning relational structures between purported right-holder and associated duty-bearer, just as it has to be responsive to value in the form of individual interests. And just as value is necessary to the conceptual structure of rights because rights are necessarily responsive to, and reflective of, value, relationality is necessary to their conceptual structure for a similar or analogous reason. Now for the purpose of our *present* project—namely, the normative mandate of recognizing a broader applicative moral and legal scope of public law rights—in creating this pictorial conceptualization of rights we need to take sides in the correlativity debate, because we cannot begin with duties and draw a line to right-holders; we only have rights—the public law rights—and we need to identify the correct private law duties associated with their holders. So we must adopt the picture of the line which begins with the right-holder and is intrinsically drawn toward the morally correct duty-bearer.

Now because rights are formally relational, the two ends of the line must point away from each other in a meaningful way; rights' relationality means that they connect normatively related but not identical things: that is the insight we should take from Hohfeld here. We should therefore imagine the line in magnetic terms, since a magnet is one *thing*, one *object*, but its two ends are attracted in exactly opposite directions and thus one of its properties includes a certain kind of dualism. The magnetic force in the representation will stand in for normativity, for the sake of illustrating the idea. In this illustration we need to restrict ourselves to moral rights because their normative force is easier to imagine, since legal rights—assuming legal positivism—will necessarily involve an explicit judgment by a third party—a line-drawing exercise by some human agent—that is difficult to illustrate. But the model will work for legal rights as well, as I will later show. I will call its magnetic poles the Northern and Southern ones, but this magnet is special because it responds to normative forces rather than to the Northern and Southern poles of the earth. But a right is like a magnet, insofar as it is a single bipolar norm whose poles are not drawn to the same thing. It must be a bipolar object, because of its formal relationality, and it must be a single object because it takes a constraining form that also contains its own justification.

So only one side of the magnet, let's say the Northern side, is attracted to value in the form of individual interests. This is on the basis that the element of interest is necessary to the model of rights. And because we don't take the line *only* to be a justification but also to be a constraint, we can't imagine it as a point arising at the right-holder's interest which we can then extend to the duty-bearer when we have (separately from anything to do with the right itself) chosen him. We have to imagine the magnetic line as a linear object which, because it extends from the point of the right-bearer, if we move it around arbitrarily, could bump into and constrain the wrong person. The right could not be a *normatively* directed obligation on such a picture because whoever *places* the other end of the magnet would be doing the directing, so to speak; the moral right has a correct person (or a range of correct persons) for whom the constraint *is already appropriate*. We know this because for a right to count in its given domain as a right, it cannot be a purely arbitrary constraint. While a legal right can point to the wrong person, *morally* speaking, and still count as a legal right, it would be incoherent to say a legal right constrains the wrong person *legally* speaking and is still a legal right. Similarly, a moral right is not assignable from the outside, so to speak, if it is going to count as a moral right; its status as a right is established by morality and we must discover where it points, as it were. Now of course this is precisely the point of contention between those interest theorists who think that a right is properly conceived of as a kind of point, sitting in the place of the right-holder's interest; but as I have said, even on this point of view, that is a misleading picture since the point will generate a connecting line to duty-bearers that is *justificatory*. So it is still correct to say that there could be appropriate and inappropriate duty-bearers at whom the justification can point. Just because an interest is important does not mean that the same constraints will be justified for everyone on its basis.

So let's imagine this line as a magnet whose force is normative: its Northern pole, the one that points to the right-holder, is attracted to value in the form of interests; what is the Southern pole attracted to? That is the question raised by the insufficiency, the unacceptable indeterminacy, of the dualistic model. Furthermore, we must add another layer of complication, since not all the magnetic lines (all rights) can be the same: we already know that the same interest will create different kinds of constraints—these have been rather generally grouped into three shapes or forms, namely, respect, protection, and promotion. Each of these three categories requires different kinds of action. To imagine this, we are going to have to oversimplify, but I don't think anything about the truth of the picture I'm painting here turns on this oversimplification. So let us imagine that each line has a minimal thickness—needle thin. That thinness corresponds with the requirement of forbearance—respect. Each of the other two types of action is an additional layer of thickness added to the line, so that the thickest lines are those that require all three types of action—and the particular range of actions that might be in-between on a more realistic picture of what actions are actually required. Now because of the directedness of rights, it is even more problematic for the Southern pole of the magnets to be arbitrarily pointed at someone, or to be pointed at someone to whom it is not attracted by magnetic—normative—force. In fact, because of its magnetic properties of attraction, we need to imagine that if it is forced to point at the wrong duty-bearer it will veer off, spin around as a misdirected magnet will do, and create more confusion—and disagreement—than clarity about whom the correct duty-bearer is. In other words, the magnets will align themselves properly. If the magnets are forced to point to people to whom they are not magnetically attracted, the wrong people will be forced to comply with actions that are not required of them.

The other possibility, of course, is that we do *not* conceive of rights in this way; that we do not take rights to be 'naturally' or intrinsically aligned between two persons. But in that case, we will have no idea how the lines should point and the attendant confusion will paralyse us into thinking of rights as, in a sense, fictional or aspirational—not, in other words, as rights. And in fact, this is the consequence that is developing from the strongly interest-based theories of rights that have taken hold in general political discourse. But to return to our argument, the directedness of rights means that we need to imagine the magnets as very strong reasons of the right kind, so that when they are pointed at someone that person is liable to take them to be categorical and exclusionary, and to allow them to guide their action. This means that the confusion created when they are pointed at persons to whom they are not attracted magnetically will be significant, and will interfere with people's proper practical reasoning.

The point of this abstract and protracted metaphor has been to illustrate that formal relationality can mean that rights *are* a relation, as our magnetic line is, between two persons, and thus that they create a normative relation. But the *magnetic* dimension of the line in the metaphor was meant to show that in the magnet two things are at work: the object that the magnet is—the thing that *becomes* a relation of a kind between persons—and the way in which the object is, because of its formal properties or conceptual structure, *responsive* to forces outside the confines of itself, and thus indicates through its formal relationality a relational context that is already significant to it. That is, the relation the magnetic line *creates* because it is an object arises in certain cases, where it arises there correctly, because it is responsive to *two* different types of force: in the case of magnetism those are the Northern and Southern magnetic poles. In the case of rights, the forces are normative: the Northern pole represents the normativity of value in the form of interests and it establishes the location of the right-holder. The Southern pole is attracted to the appropriate duty-bearer on the basis of the relational context between the persons. In other words, rights *are* a kind of relation, but they necessarily arise in response to *another* kind, which is in one sense external to them but which is necessary to their establishment, and thus necessary to their existence. Duty-bearers are properly identified in respect of interests, on this view, on the basis of whatever norms govern the relational structure or context between the two.

Now just as the picture of rights so far described tells us that rights necessarily involve value (because, as it were, that is the force to which one pole of our imaginary magnet will point) but not *which* particular interests are valuable, formal relationality and its implication that norms arising from relational structures or contexts are necessarily involved in their conceptual structure still cannot provide the specific norms to apply the model of rights, precisely because it is formal rather than substantive. But it can indicate that relationality is part of rights' conceptual structure, just as constraint is part of that structure because rights take the form of constraints. It can tell us, in other words, that rights involve *two* types of facts or judgments—that of value in the form of interests, and that of relational normativity.

C. Implicit normative facts or judgments about relational context

I have so far painted a picture, a metaphor for rights, that I hope clarifies the account I want to give, and I hope the picture itself has to some extent been persuasive that it is analogous to rights. But I will now argue for the role of relationality in a slightly different way. The general argument for the relational element in rights can be expressed formally, remember, as follows: (1) rights are formally relational; (2) because of this formal relationality, each right *in fact* reflects a claim (and its recognition or acceptance) about the possible conditions of its violation; (3) the claim (and its recognition or acceptance) about the possible violation conditions of a given right refers to a normative fact or judgment pertaining to the interpersonal structure or relational context in which the right arises.

In the previous sections I have argued for premise (1), and created a picture of rights' particular kind of formal relationality that I hope has been suggestive of premise (2). But that was only meant to be a suggestive illustration: here I will argue directly for the second premise. The argument for relational facts or judgments as the third element or dimension of the model of rights is formally analogous to the argument for the indispensability of value to the model.

The substantive facts or judgments about the normative implications of the relational structure or context of a right make up the third element in their conceptual structure. This becomes evident in much the same way that the element of value or interest becomes evident. In every right, an interest is *in fact* protected; that special protection as a right embodies a judgment that that interest is valuable in the domain of the right—legal rights protect legally important interests; moral rights protect morally important ones. Actual rights invariably—inescapably—consist of protected interests and thus normative facts or judgments about relative value. This means that we cannot dispense with an element of value in constructing a model of rights. Rights do not, however, necessarily arise in respect of any *particular* values. Their conceptual structure entails only a fact or judgment of that *kind*; in other words, whatever the *content* of those judgments about which interests are valuable, the *type* of judgment is necessarily part of what rights are. The fact that rights conceptually entail normative facts or judgments about valuable interests, therefore, does not specify which rights we ought to have. It is in this sense, as I have stressed, that this model is conceptually thin. What the model does tell us is that every actual right—as opposed to an imaginary, purely formal right with no content, if such a thing is possible, which in fact I anyway doubt—*reflects* judgments about the relative value of goods or interests.

When we look at rights in this way, to see what *kinds* of normative facts or judgments they *reflect*—which, as I have argued in Chapter 4 in relation to the element of value, we must do if we are to fully explain or understand any given right—we find relational norms in the concept of rights in exactly the same way. Rights become actualized as recognized or justified claims *about something*—thus asserting the value of some good or interest—*and* as claims addressed *to* some purported duty-bearer, as well as to the normative community in the domain of the right. They operate, in other words, by identifying, in advance or *ex post*, a violation of some interest that is claimed to be sufficiently important to warrant the recognition of a right. But as we have seen, one cannot identify a violation of a right without reference to some person in a position to violate the purported right, and to a type of action that would constitute the violation—to put this latter point more broadly we can call this the *shape* of the constraint. We can call this assertion about the person—or a person in a particular position relative to the claimant—and the action claimed to constitute the violation the *conditions of violation* of a right. These are the *Who* being required to do the *What* in respect of rights that are necessary to make them sufficiently determinate, just as there must be another kind of 'what'—a *thing* that each right protects. And just as the value of interests inevitably and silently underlies claims to their protection in particular cases, relational norms underlie claims about the possible conditions of violation that are prohibited by the right.

I want to suggest, in other words, that *every* right—even ones that have been categorized as general or universal (in the sense of being categorically non-relational)—contain implicit facts or judgments about the relational context in which they, or claims made on the basis of them, arise. Now this substantive relationality is obviously true in the case of 'special' rights that are said to arise on the basis of a relationship as opposed to those said to arise on the basis of a transaction. But this categorization is misleading. To call rights 'special' makes them seem like a deviation from the ordinary or like a categorically different kind of thing in the sense that they have a different conceptual structure. My argument will have the implication that there is no conceptual distinction between special and general rights; that, conceptually speaking, all rights are like the so-called 'special' ones in the sense that each reflects a judgment about the normative consequences of a particular relational structure as well as a judgment about the value of a good or interest.

Where I want to take issue with the existing categorization is not with respect to whether there is *any* difference between the so-called general and special rights, but about how to characterize that difference. The assertion that *all persons* are normatively implicated by a general right does not make that right free of facts or judgments about the relational norms relevant to it. Rather, it represents a judgment precisely that there *is* a norm pertinent to the relation of each person to each other person. Let us consider the moral right to be free from intentional harm. I choose this right to consider because it seems to be a case of one of the *least* intuitively relational rights. If any moral right exists that will apply against everyone and that does not, in principle, thus itself contain any necessary information about whom it constrains, surely this one does.

Now there is a considerable debate, still, about just what the normative relation between two persons is, in virtue of no particular contact between them, even among those who agree that every person *is* normatively implicated by a particular set of rights (the most obvious candidate set would be human rights considered purely as moral rights). But to assert that each and every person is duty-bound, constrained, on the basis of some other person's entitlement to enjoy some good, is in fact quite a bold relational claim. I am going to call it, henceforth, the *basic human relation*. But this is only to identify that it is a type of normative judgment that is fundamentally relational; it is not to give it any particular content. In fact it has a number of competing substantive conceptualizations.

We can imagine that one ancient and religious interpretation of that relationship is that both right-holder and potential duty-bearers are created by God. So when a potential duty-bearer considered the purported right of another person to be free from intentionally inflicted harm, her reasoning was not limited to what non-relationalists about right would have to claim, namely, that the interest of that other person is so important that is it a right, which itself somehow carries the meaning that *I ought not* infringe that freedom. If that were the only basis on which she took herself to be constrained then it would be very unclear how, if harming one person intentionally could prevent the harm of another five people, each of whom would, on such a view, *also* have rights protecting the same interest, the putative or potential duty-bearer wouldn't see herself as specially bound by the importance of each person's freedom from harm, even for her own action, to harm someone else. Rather, in order to reach the conclusion that a norm exists that is structured so that it has particular relevance to *her* actions in respect of each other person, or *any* other person (let alone a categorical and exclusionary one), such a potential duty-bearer always implicitly makes another step in her reasoning, the precise content of which will depend on her view of the basic *relational context* of persons considered simply as persons.

If the person is religious, for instance, he may think why ought *I* not harm *this* person? In other words, even aside from the normative importance of the value of the good of freedom from harm for everyone, why might *I* not harm *her*, if I can reduce overall harm by doing so? The norm pertaining to the relational context is particularly relevant to reasoning in respect of rights because of rights' formal relationality: in determining whether a given right exists in some relational context, one occupies the point of view of the potential duty-bearer to ask why the importance of the good protected by the right ought to create a constraint for *me*? And even from the impartial point of view, in order to make the judgment about the existence of a given right in a given relational context, one implicitly or explicitly relies in part on the norm governing that relational context, such as, in the case of the very general right to freedom from harm I have been considering, the norm of interpersonal equality in the context of the basic human relation.

There is therefore another norm, besides that of interest, implicitly at work in the recognition or explanation of rights, which, for the religious person, might be the following: if God created us both, we are both creations of God, and *equally* so. Or, for a non-religious person: if we are both members of the moral community, we are *equally* accountable to its norms and thus to one another as co-members. Or if the perceived normativity of the constraint for the duty-bearer is accepted on the basis of the requirement of a moral law to treat others as ends rather than as means, it applies to us for that reason because we are rational creatures; but the obligation does not depend on our relative capacity for reason. Accepting that *equal* membership in the moral community means that I have no more end-status than you do is part of the meaning of membership in the moral community on the basis of shared capacity for rational agency.

In other words, I want to suggest that these calculations of the non-interest-based reasons for a constraint to be oriented towards a *particular* duty-bearer—even in the absence of a relationship involving prior contact between the two people—rely on norms at work arising from the given relational context. First, there is in all these cases some good the two persons share in common. In the case of the first, religious reason for thinking there is the right kind of constraint, there is the shared creation by God; in the second case, shared membership in the moral community; in the third, shared capacity for rational agency. Second, there is, in all these so-called non-relational rights, such as in the right we have been considering to freedom from harm, a norm of equality between persons sharing one of these goods. From an impartial standpoint, equality can be relational only in the sense that it is comparative. But in the case of the point of view of the potential duty-bearer, the application of that norm involves taking the rights claimant and himself to be in a relational position normatively governed by equality. The fact that the good in question in each of these interpretations of the basic human relation is so fundamental to morality itself, so thin, and so universal, and the fact that the norm in question is equality and thus would apply, according to any of the moral theories I alluded to above, among *any* set of two people, does not make these two modes of relating, namely the sharing of the basic good in question and the norm of equality, any the less *relational*.

Equality, in these contexts, must involve an *interpersonal* relationality as well as a polycentric one. The agent-relative constraining form of rights forces the agent into considering the norm of equality as it pertains *interpersonally* between him and his potential victim, rather than only as it operates in a kind of distributive way, viewed from an impartial perspective.

This is because viewed only from an impartial point of view equality makes the potential duty-bearer a kind of enforcer, in which he is enforcing the equal position of the other person as a kind of third party against himself, also viewed from the impartial perspective. That is, he sees the other person and himself from an impartial standpoint, and, in order to decide how to regard this person-who-is-himself as constrained in respect of this other person, he asks himself 'what norm governs the relation among everyone?' He has to ask himself the question with respect to the norm for ALL humans because he can't, if equality requires that he take the impartial point of view, make any particular consideration for the fact that he, as a potential duty-bearer, is in a particular point of view facing a particular other person, in taking an action. He can only think about the other person as one of a class of persons, to which he himself also belongs. A class to which the norm of equality pertains.

But thinking this way means that he has to treat the right as an instrument. The norm of equality is not *integral* or *intrinsic* to the right, on such a view, and so he has to think that doing what the right tells him—not harming the other person—is just a way of *enforcing* the equal status of him and the other person, viewed impartially; of protecting that equal status as a good. But if a right is a constraint, and he takes the constraint to be instrumental, the right is no different from any other rule. It makes no sense to use the language of rights. If it's just a rule, then, abstracted to a sufficiently distant standpoint of impartiality, he could take the principle of equality to allow him to harm the one other person if it would better promote the ability of all other people to enjoy their equal status.

That is, the constraint of the kind that is particular to rights must be agent-relative. This is normally taken to be true by deontologists, but it's a problem for those who think rights involve valuable interests, since there is no reason why valuable interests would generate reasons having an agent-relative structure, being normally the sources of agent-neutral reasons. Rights, in other words, are structures in which agent-neutral reasons of value and constraints having an agent-relative structure are brought together. This makes no sense unless there is something that ties the interest to the agent to whom the constraint pertains. That something, I am contending, is the normative impact of relational form and the features of relationality that create that form.

Notice that the structure of this argument has been that when we look at well-recognized rights, such as the right to be free from harm—we will consider other rights shortly—there is a relational norm at work in the practical reasoning that leads to the conclusion that a particular duty-bearer has a given duty. The argument has not been, in other words, that the relational norm governs *instead* of the recognized norms that ground the type of so-called general right that seems so non-relational; rather, the relational norm is *implicit* in that reasoning and complementary to it. This is particularly hard to see, of course, where the relational norm in question operates to include all persons because the shared good in question is taken to be common to all persons, such as creation by God, rationality, or the capacity for rational agency, and so on, because only one piece of relational reasoning is necessary to implicate all persons. It operates, in this case, though, to distinguish possible right-holders and possible duty-bearers from those for whom such authority to claim and accountability to respond to claims is excluded. On the views of the basic human relation among persons I have alluded to, animals and objects, for instance, are excluded because they do not share the relevant goods in common with persons.

But more importantly, for our purpose in respect of our overall normative mandate, while it might be possible to think of many of the rights commonly categorized as negative and general without *emphasizing* the relational judgment involved in their recognition and application, the question of relational context becomes indispensable for recognizing rights that take the shape of positive constraints or requirements: it may be tempting to say, with respect to requiring positive actions to allow every human to enjoy his or her rights interests, that everyone should simply do what they can to contribute to the good of everyone who needs help in order to enjoy those goods. But this is problematic as a way of assigning rights. For one thing, it fails to contribute anything to the distinctiveness of rights: I rely here again on Griffin's point—we already have a perfectly good normative vocabulary for talking about the importance of people's well-being and the goods necessary to that well-being, and to the obligations that could arise on everyone to support the former by promoting the latter. Humanitarian obligations, obligations of beneficence, are in principle enough to account for that type of—everyone ought to do as much as he or she can to help others—argument. Of course we all should. But if rights are to mean anything, and if we take seriously the idea of rights taking the shape of constraints requiring actions on the part of others, then we need to be able to say more precisely who is required to do what in respect of such rights, and, more importantly, *why*.

So in principle I have obligations to Syrian refugees, but they may be imperfect obligations; does that mean that Syrian refugees have no rights to aid? Certainly not: their human rights would suggest that they are entitled to be provided with at least shelter, food, basic education, and health care. But if these are their rights, who bears the duties in respect of them? The arguments I have been making so far suggest that if we recognize those rights, then we must also engage in the reasoning process to identify the appropriate duty-bearer(s) associated with them. Do I have a duty in respect of those rights? Do you? What about my government or yours? What about the governments of Jordan, Iraq, Turkey, Lebanon, and Palestine? What about the people who live in those countries: do the citizens close to the border and the citizens far away from it bear constraints of the same shape in respect of the right-interests of the refugees? Does it make a difference to the shape of these constraints if *all* the refugees make their way or are forced into Jordan and Lebanon and comparatively few into Iraq? Does it make a difference if Iraq is itself in institutional disarray? What about the relative wealth of those neighbour countries? What about other countries? And, again, what about me? What are my duties in respect of those people's rights? Surely international institutions have moral obligations in respect of human rights, if only as agents for the obligations we all have. But this brings us back to the question of just what obligations in respect of those people's entitlements with respect to those particular goods we *do* all have. A full analysis of the normative situation of the Syrian refugees' rights would probably require at least a full chapter in itself, and that is not our central question in this book. But what the questions I have raised in connection with the particular human rights of those particular people have, I hope, gestured at, is that one of the considerations in understanding the appropriate shape of the constraints of every person who bears *some* duty in respect of those rights will involve a consideration of the normative significance of the relational context of the potential duty-bearer with the Syrian refugees, or with a person in the position of one of those people.

These questions cannot even begin to be addressed by the dualistic model of Rights, even as fleshed out in the dualistic model of public law rights. If we thus conclude that, as I have argued in this chapter, constraint and value are jointly necessary but insufficient for a model of rights—both in general and, by extension, for public law ones—and that the missing element in the model of Rights involves the relational context in which a right arises, our model of rights will be *three-dimensional*, and will take this element of relational, structural context into account, as follows:

Every Right^3 is a norm that

(1^3) Creates constraint(s) oriented toward protecting the inviolability of individuals;

(2^3) Assigns priority to certain morally important interests [as yet unspecified]; and
(3^3) Arises in the context of [some kind of] relational structure.

This model does not include the content of either of the normative judgments required in elements (2^3) or (3^3), namely, the particular interests the right protects and the particular relational context in which it will arise, respectively. Our model of *public law* rights, as a species of the more general concept, will thus follow the same conceptual structure. Because public law rights protect a relatively well-defined set of interests, though, we can add this substantive content to the model so that it will look, formally, like this: call it the three-dimensional model of public law rights—PLR^3.

Every PLR^3 is a norm that
(1^3) Creates constraint(s) oriented toward protecting individuals;
(2^3) Assigns priority to certain morally important interests: these interests are $I_1 \ldots I_n$ as defined by the overlapping content of the set; and
(3^3) Arises in the context of [some kind of] relational structure.

Obviously enough, though, this model does not yet tell us two important things: first, it does not tell us what exactly we mean by relational context; nor does it tell us, second, why relationality could be considered normative. Both those questions are important ones and will be taken up in the following parts of this chapter. Our new model merely indicates that relational context is somehow intrinsic to what public law rights are.

II. What is Relational Context?

A. Thin and thick relations and layers of relational norms

The implication arising from the previous discussions is that the best way of thinking about the element of relational normativity involved in rights is not binary, conceptually dividing rights into two kinds of thing—those with a normatively significant relational context and those without—but in terms of the relative thickness of a given relational context and layers of relationality. What I have been calling the basic human relation—the relational structure in which arise the rights each person has against each other person—is a very thin one whatever one takes its normative significance to be. But what I now want to show is that as relations become thicker, involving more complex connections between people, layers of relational norms begin to build up, so that the final picture of any given relational context in which a right is asserted or recognized will coherently generate a particularly shaped constraint. It will mean that in order to understand and explain the normative force of any given right, we will need to read it for two types of normative judgments: one about value, and one about the relational context of the right and its normative implications.

To get a sense of the ways relational structures can take various forms and become increasingly complex, let us consider one instance of the so-called general rights—the one we have been considering; the right to be free from intentional harm. Does some person in India, for instance, have such a right against me? If conventional understandings of rights have anything at all to say about the question, she does. But now what does that right actually entail? It takes the form of a constraint on my actions and choices in respect of the interest of that person in being free from intentional harm. So I cannot intentionally harm that person without violating her right. So far, on the basis of the basic relational norm we have said all we need to say to make that right determinate: we know that I have an obligation to her, and so do you, and so does every other person; we know what would constitute a violation of the right, and so the right is, so to speak, complete and determinate. We can recognize it as a right without difficulty.

But even the interest in freedom from being intentionally harmed by others generates constraints on *some* others that are thicker than simple forbearance. Police, for example, are required not to intentionally harm our hypothetical victim, but they are also required to step in if they see an action taking place that constitutes a violation of the forbearance-shaped constraint each person has, and protect her, if they can. A teacher, too, seeing one student bullying another student—intentionally harming her—seems to have an obligation to step in that either I do not have (though that seems an arguable point), or that is a stronger one than mine would be. A parent, an employer, even a witness, would seem to have some obligation in respect of the same interest (freedom from harm) that takes a different shape. This is all just relying on the point established by Raz's interest theory as articulated by Waldron's discussion of the 'waves of duties'.[9]

What is missing from that insight, though, is, first, a clear answer to the question of whether those duties are necessarily rather than only justificatorily implied by the constraining form that is the right or not—the interest theory would seem to answer no—and, second, *how* those interests generate each successive wave of duties, or, as I think we can more accurately put it, how one can tell which constraints properly attach to which duty-bearers in respect of the interest and what shapes those constraints properly take. The model of rights I have so far developed would suggest that the interest—freedom from intentional harm, for example—is misleadingly described as intrinsically *itself* having a particular form, since it can clearly generate positively shaped constraints as well as those of forbearance, but rather that the interest a given right protects necessarily also involves a constraint of some shape. It is relational context, rather than anything intrinsic to the interest, that shapes the constraint.

But now let us consider a right that is taken to have a negative form but that is not obviously 'universal' in the sense that while everyone has it not everyone obviously owes duties in respect of it, namely, freedom of conscience. Let us consider, again, our friend in India. Do I have an obligation in respect of her right to freedom of conscience? If not, then, on the basis of our model, we would have to say that she does not hold that right against me. So it is an important question—how

[9] Jeremy Waldron, *Liberal Rights: Collected Papers 1981–1991*, (Cambridge: Cambridge University Press,1993), 25, 212.

do we know? If we begin to think through who *ought* to have that obligation, it immediately begins to seem as though part of the answer will be relational, most simply because the right will impose constraints on actions that can violate the right. So far, the constraint operates in the same way as the interest in freedom from intentional harm; the complication arises because it is not enough to say that I am prohibited from limiting her right to enjoy the good of freedom of conscience, because the question of whether I *am* violating her right to that freedom, in contrast to infringing her enjoyment of the good, is the central one when it comes to establishing, recognizing, or understanding a right. There are ways that I could diminish her freedom of conscience, so to speak, to infringe her enjoyment of it: I could send her hate mail when she writes a letter to the newspaper expressing a view I disagree with: would that constitute a (moral) human rights violation? I could flood the newspaper with letters expressing another view, or I could write an editorial attempting to discredit her. I could threaten her and her family with worse forms of harm if she persists in her view. I could publically mock her or her family for taking such views; I could preach to all religious people that they ought to shun her, and so on. If, in doing any of these things, I was her government, I *would* be committing a violation of her freedom of conscience. But, just as myself, a legal scholar in Canada, personally unknown to her, even if I did any of those things it would not seem intuitively to count as a *human rights* violation.

Now adding physical proximity and personal connection—if, say, I were her friend or neighbour, I would still not, by doing the kinds of things I referred to above, intuitively be violating her right to *freedom of conscience*, though that seems to become less obvious as we add layers of relational complexity to our hypothetical context between her and a potential duty-bearer. Even if I were her neighbour, friend, or just as myself, it is certainly arguable that I have constraints of *some* shape in respect of the freedom of conscience of the woman in India: even if I cannot myself violate the right in any of the ways described above, I might be morally required to avoid contributing to the violation of that right by supporting her government in *its* actions. I might have a differently shaped constraint: I might be required to support institutions that would protect her against such actions. What if I were her employer? What if I were a religious leader in her Church or an elder in her community? What if I were in *both* the previous relational positions to her? What if I were her mother? What if I own the newspaper to which she wrote? What if I do not own it but have full editorial and managerial control over it? The way we answer these questions would seem to begin to delineate, the conditions of violation of the right in question: that is, in fully answering these questions in a fine-grained way we would come to a better understanding of what actions, by whom, would constitute a rights violation and thus where the right, as distinct from the interest, exists.

The general impression one can infer from this scenario and its possible varieties of relations, as well as the ones I suggested might be relevant in the case of Syrian refugees' human rights, is that the answers to the questions of *who* bears the duties generated by rights, and *what* the actions required by those duties are, are at least substantially informed by the relational structures among the right-holder and each possible duty-bearer. And in particular, I want to suggest, it seems that the thickness of the relational structure will affect the shape of the duty and the identity of its correct bearer.

B. Relational structures as molecular

Even if we accept my characterization of the normative relational basis for even the so-called general rights as deriving from the very elemental feature of the basic human relation, then it might be tempting to say that it continues to make sense to think of rights in categorically binary relational terms: those that arise in and are normatively responsive to *only* the basic human relation, and those—hitherto categorized as special rights—that arise in 'thick' relational contexts. There are two problems with this way out, however.

First, even in the case of general rights—rights involving constraints to the apparently negative interests—different relational structures will generate differently shaped obligations. The relation of shop owners to their customers in respect of the interest in personal security and life might be different than the relation of people passing on the street; it would certainly be arguable that they are. Similarly, for instance, tort law has in some cases begun to impose duties on so called 'hosts' who have parties at which their guests drink to excess to take steps to prevent their guests from then driving away. Clearly the *interest* would be the same, in the case of the host and passing strangers on the street, and yet the constraint is, at least arguably, quite different.

Second, and more important, the problem with the existing binary categorization of rights with respect to their relational element—either special or not—fails to capture the way in which relational structures actually give rise to norms that shape constraints. The problem with the way the special/general distinction works is that it requires that the normativity of relational structures in respect of rights be described in terms of relation*ships* in common categories. These are categories such as employer/employee, parent/child, husband/wife, teacher/student, and, most importantly for our present purpose, individual/state. Now I have been referring to these relationships when trying to suggest that even 'negative' rights, as well, of course, as 'positive' ones, will generate differently shaped constraints in the case of these different relationships. But, as our overall normative mandate in this book itself illustrates, knowing that a right or set of rights has arisen in the context of such a relationship and thus simply describing it as 'special' does not exhaust or usefully determine the role that that relationship plays in the normativity of the right, since it does not itself explain what it is about the relationship that shapes the constraint of the right in certain ways. It simply treats these rights as though there is something 'extra', normatively speaking, going on in the vicinity of the rights, and, moreover, that that 'extra'-ness is enough to warrant classifying these rights as different kinds of things from general rights. Now I want to stress that I do not deny, of course, that the fact that there is a clearly identifiable relationship that is pertinent to the shape of the constraint in these cases is relevant to understanding these rights. What I take issue with is the binary classification of rights into relational/non-relational where relationality is seen as in some way external to the conceptual structure of the right itself.

Instead, I want to suggest that each of these relationships is better understood as a relational *complex* or *structure* of more basic *elements* or factors that arise interpersonally, and that understanding the normative significance of each relational context as a kind of molecular complex of more elemental or atomistic analytical features will give us more specific guidance in understanding any given right. Some of these atomistic elements would be things like control, the sharing of very specific goods, affection, love, need, vulnerability, proximity, capacity, knowledge, and so on. Some of these elements are not in themselves obviously relational, at least in an interpersonal sense: a monad can have knowledge, for instance, though knowledge must be about or of something; rather, it is the structure of knowledge combined with, say, need, vulnerability, or affection, that makes knowledge part of relational complex in a given interpersonal context. It is when combined that these features give rise to more obviously *relational* structures, and those structures can give rise to what we more conventionally understand as relation*ships*. I want to stress, here, that this list of relational structures or their constituent elements is in no way exhaustive. Such a list of basic analytic elements that *can* contribute to relational structures would take a lot of thought to properly generate, and more space than I have here. But moreover, even if we had such a list, its constituents could be combined in a nearly infinite variety of ways so that a correspondingly vast number of relational structures or relation*ship*s would emerge. It is for this reason that it makes much more sense to approach given relationships, when considering their normative implications, by imagining them as molecular structures and deconstructing them into these analytical atomistic parts in order to understand the much more specific nature of the *particular* relational context in which a given right might arise. Relational contexts, understood in terms of their basic analytic structures, rather than in the 'named' categories of 'teacher', 'employer', government', and so on, make it clear that these basic relational features can be layered onto one another so that relational structures are better understood in terms of degrees of thickness, where the parent/child relation, for example, probably consists of many layers of analytical relational features, whereas the relational structure between neighbours consists of fewer such features and is thus best understood as thinner, rather than simply non-relational.

In order to clarify these two ways of understanding relationships as, on one hand discrete, fixed categorical phenomena such as 'teacher/student, employer/employee', and on the other hand as variable complexes of logically or analytically more basic relational features of experience is to think of the first, categorical approach as a 'top-down' way of looking at relational contexts and the second, analytically complex approach as being 'bottom-up'. The top-down view of relationality views relational context as pre-existing and largely fixed units in which individuals taking up relationships will thus take on certain roles associated with them, including the moral repercussions of those roles. But the bottom-up view insists on viewing any given relational context in terms of its component parts, as it were, so that each one, even ones that have the same name, such as three different employer/employee relationships, or three different teacher/student ones, can be understood to generate *different* normative implications based on the way each one reflects a distinct complex of factors. On this latter view, to understand, explain, or properly assign duties in respect of any given right, we must consider the normative implications of the *particular* relational context of the right and its possible duty-bearers. We would not consider general rights to be different kinds of things, but rather to arise in thin relational contexts in which the basic relational feature is that of the shared good—whatever we take that to be—among humans, and to generate particularly shaped duties on the basis of its moral significance.

These two ways of thinking about relational structures are reflected in the literature that has considered the possible moral implications of 'relationships' (I will use this word to describe the top-down view, for the sake of clarity) and those of relational 'structures' (I will use this phrase to describe what I have called the bottom-up view). The moral role of relations arises in two distinct but not unrelated discussions in moral philosophy. The first is the question that considers relationality to be associated with a partial point of view, and takes the *moral* point of view to be a characteristically *im*partial one, thus asking what justification there could be for taking relationships to be morally significant: the way this is generally thought about involves questions like why one might be justified in treating one's own children differently from others, or, more specifically, whether one might be justified in deviating from general moral rules where one's loved ones are concerned. This approach has characteristically been 'top-down,' considering whether a given relationship—such as those of parent and child, for instance—generates moral reasons, and if so, what those reasons are.[10]

The other thread of discussion has focused more closely on the question of 'distance' and its possible moral implications for obligation.[11] Again, it seems that the

[10] See, for some examples of this line of enquiry: Simon Keller, 'Four Theories of Filial Duty', *The Philosophical Quarterly* 56 (2006): 254; Niko Kolodny, 'Which Relationships Justify Partiality: The Case of Parents and Children', *Philosophy and Public Affairs* 38 (2010): 37; Veit Bader, 'Reasonable Impartiality and Priority for Compatriots. A Criticism of Liberal Nationalism's Main Flaws', *Ethical Theory and Moral Practice* 8 (2005): 83–103; Diane Jeske, 'Special relationships and the Problem of Political Obligations', *Social Theory and Practice* 27, no. 1 (January 2001): 19; David Miller, 'Reasonable Partiality towards Compatriots', *Ethical Theory and Moral Practice: An International Forum* 8, no. 1–2 (April 2005): 63–81; David O. Brink, 'Impartiality and Associative Duties', *Utilitas: A Journal of Utilitarian Studies* 13, no. 2 (July 2001); Thomas Donaldson, 'Morally Privileged Relationships', *Journal of Value Inquiry* 24, no. 1 (1990): 1–15; Gur Hirshberg, 'Situating Friendship: An Aristotelian Treatment of Personal Relations and Moral Choice', *Philosophical Writings* 10, no. 1999 (1999): 23–36.

[11] See, for some examples of this debate: Judith Andre, 'The Equal Moral Weight of Self-and Other-Regarding Acts', *Canadian Journal of Philosophy* 17 (March 1987): 155–65; Richard J. Arneson, 'Consequentialism vs. Special-Ties Partiality', *Monist: An International Quarterly Journal of General Philosophical Inquiry* 86, no. 3 (July 2003): 382–401; Marcia Baron, 'Impartiality and Friendship', *Ethics* 101, no. 4 (July 1991): 836–57; Gillian G. Brock, 'Does Obligation Diminish with Distance?', *Ethics* 8, no. 1 (March 2005): 3–20; Garrett Cullity, 'Asking Too Much', *The Monist* 86, no. 3 (2003): 402–18; Marilyn A. Friedman, 'The Practice of Partiality', *Ethics* 101, no. 4 (July 1991): 818–35; Violetta Igneski, 'Distance, Determinacy and the Duty to Aid: A Reply to Kamm', *Law and Philosophy* 20, no. 6 (November 2001): 605–16; F. M. Kamm, 'Does Distance Matter Morally to the Duty to Rescue?', *Law and Philosophy, The Moral and Legal Limits of Samaritan Duties* 19, no. 6 (November 2000): 655–81; Korsgaard, 'Creating the Kingdom of Ends: Reciprocity and Responsibility in Personal Relations', *Philosophical Perspectives* 6 (1992): 305–32; B. C. Postow, 'Care

assumption about the moral point of view clashes, to some extent, with the intuition that somehow distance matters. Now this line of argument and disagreement has largely assumed the binariness of obligations into negative and positive forms, and reasoned that since negative obligations are clearly not affected by physical distance or proximity—remember how easy it was to conclude on any basis that I have an obligation not to intentionally harm a far away stranger—the only real question concerning distance is whether it might matter to obligations of aid or rescue.

This latter line of thought has arguably been centred on, or at least driven forward by, Peter Unger's argument that even if we do have intuitions that we are justified in prioritizing our obligations to those 'close' to us, those intuitions are unjustified and ought to be reconsidered from the moral point of view.[12] But those intuitions seem heavily driven by common-sense morality, and that point of view seems to have been summed up by Bernard Williams's famous conclusion that if one is asking oneself whether or how one is justified in saving one's wife from a burning building in place of one or more others, one is simply having 'one thought too many'.[13]

Now we have to bear in mind several things about this debate. First, the widely recognized intuitions that 'distance' matters to moral obligation, somehow, together with widespread concern that those intuitions are morally problematic. At the same time, we have various points of view on why such intuitions are misguided, but, since intuitions are relied on fairly heavily even in analytic moral philosophy, there are also a number of attempts to explain those intuitions, and to offer reasons why we have them despite their being overruled, as it were, by moral argument. Finally, we have the point of view expressed by Williams and others, that those who say those intuitions are not reflective of moral norms are right, but that that does not make them *bad*, but rather outside the appropriate scope of morality. The situation, in short, is one of disagreement. The state of the literature on the proper role of relationality in moral reasoning reflects disparate intuitions. Now I do not claim to have a solution to this morass; rather, I offer to alter somewhat the terms of the debate. As I have argued, it is misguided to think of rights in strictly binary terms—as either negative or positive. Rather, one must recognize that rights are constraints that can require actions taking various shapes ranging from not engaging to assisting to promoting. Similarly, it is misguided to think of relationality in respect of rights in binary terms: relational structures are oversimplified when described as either non-existent in the case of general rights

Ethics and Impartial Reasons', *Hypatia* 23, no. 1 (2008): 1–8; Soran Reader, 'Distance, Relationship and Moral Obligation', *Monist: An International Quarterly Journal of General Philosophical Inquiry* 86, no. 3 (July 2003): 367–81; Samuel Scheffler, 'Relationships and Responsibilities', *Philosophy and Public Affairs* 26 (1997); Alan Thomas, 'Reasonable Partiality and the Agent's Point of View', *Ethical Theory and Moral Practice: An International Forum* 8, no. 1–2 (April 2005): 25–43; Susan Wolf, 'Morality and Partiality', *Philosophical Perspectives* 6 (1992): 243–59.

[12] Peter Unger, *Living High and Letting Die: Our Illusion of Innocence* (Oxford: Oxford University Press, 1996).

[13] Bernard Williams, 'Persons, Character and Morality' in *Moral Luck* (Cambridge: Cambridge University Press, 1981), 18.

or a kind of add-on to rights' justifiability and constraints in the case of special rights. We must instead think of the shape constraints impose when rights are recognized as determined partly by the interest protected but also by the *complex* of relational features of the interpersonal context in which a right arises.

To see the difference between the standard consideration of relationality in moral norms and the one I am suggesting here for rights, consider the focus of the discussion about relationality on 'distance'. Distance, in this line of thought, is sometimes thought of in complex terms involving a kind of concentric-circle model of obligations to those 'close to us' and sometimes in terms of strictly physical proximity. It seems to me that the real disagreement operating here is about the implications of the kinds of complex relational structures we actually think of when we consider relationality to be normative rather than about the normative implications of only *one* such relational feature, namely, in this case, physical distance. Relational structures *are* relevant to our obligations, as our intuitions would suggest, but only as a complex of relational features. Where more such features are present, or where they are themselves 'thick' or consisting of significant structures, the likely impact on obligation will be stronger. But we cannot say that any particular *type* of relational feature, like distance, or any particular relationship, like teacher/student, will necessarily generate any particularly shaped constraint, such as obligation to aid or to promote a good.

Consider, for illustration of this latter way of thinking, Frances Kamm's argument about why distance might—or might not—matter to moral obligations.[14] It is her method, and the assumptions it reflects, rather than her conclusion, that is important here, since we can find compelling arguments for various conclusions on both sides of the relationality debate in respect of obligation. The standard type of cases used to test and evaluate our intuitions about distance were set out by Peter Singer. These have become standard in the literature on the role of relational context in moral obligation, and they are intended to generate moral intuitions: assuming all I have to do is something extremely simple, in *both* cases, to save a drowning child, do I have a stronger obligation to assist that child close to me than one at a distance? The cases are also usually varied to track the ways in which different types of obligation may affect the intuition—there is generally a contrast between someone threatened by nature, such as the drowning case, or someone threatened by an accident who needs us to do something urgently—someone who needs to be driven to hospital in one's car, for instance—and someone who is hungry and needs us to feed him or otherwise give him something.

Kamm gives a variant of Singer's standard cases:

Pond: I am walking past a shallow pond and see a child drowning in it. If I wade in and pull the child out, my $500 suit will be ruined. Intuitively, I ought to wade in to save him.

[14] Frances Kamm, 'Does Distance Matter Morally to the Duty to Rescue?', *Law and Philosophy* 19 (2000): 655–81.

Overseas: I know there is a child starving to death overseas. To save him, I must send $500. Intuitively, I am not obligated to do so.

Kamm's argument is that part of what appears to be a moral question is really a methodological one; she suggests that the intuitive differences are a result of failing to properly equalize the cases, so that more than one intuition is being generated at once. She sets about equalizing the cases. Her new variants are:

Near Alone Case: I am walking past a pond in a foreign country that I am visiting, and I *alone* see many children drowning in it and I alone can save one of them. To save him, I must put the $500 I have in my pocket into a machine that then triggers (via electric current) rescue machinery that will certainly scoop him out.

Far Alone Case: I *alone* learn that in a distant part of a foreign country that I am visiting, many children are drowning and I alone can save one of them. To save him, all I must do is put the $500 I carry in my pocket into a machine that then triggers (via electric current) rescue machinery that will *certainly* scoop him out.[15]

In 'equalizing' *Pond* and *Overseas* to *Near Alone* and *Far Alone*, she identifies fine distinctions between the intuitions driving the cases and infers a number of relational features that are intuitively relevant to the moral outcome, and thus that must be *eliminated* in order to isolate the element she is interested in, namely, physical proximity or distance in the literal sense. The factors she considers are proximity, efficaciousness, salience (meaning that one can't take one's mind off the need of the other person for one's assistance—I think of this as perceived normative pressure), recognition (meaning that the victim or potential victim sees us and, as an additional factor, we know she does), as well as personal encounter. These factors that Kamm wants to equalize out of the cases for the purpose of considering our intuitions about the moral role of distance in obligation are precisely some of those that combine to form the relational complexes that structure relationships. She wants to reduce out or eliminate these factors by changing the facts of the cases to find out which one is controlling, and, more specifically, to isolate proximity to see whether it *alone* impacts our obligations.

What I want to argue, here, is that her method reveals precisely what it is intended to eliminate: our intuitions about relational normativity arise on the basis of these basic elements *in combination*; it is their combination that thickens relational structures and increases our sense that relationality is morally significant. If relational structure is morally relevant to rights in the way I suggest, it wouldn't be on the basis of *one* factor, for the most part, such as physical proximity, it would be on the basis of a layering of these various elements which, as they are combined in a given case, represent a holistic picture of the relational structure between two individuals; it is this complex relational structure that is likely to generate intuitions that the relation matters morally. These intuitions, in

[15] Kamm, 'Does Distance Matter Morally to the Duty to Rescue?', 657.

other words, are more likely to track the difference between different relational structures viewed in this complex way than to track single elements.

This is evident, it seems to me, from the way in which, as Kamm tried to equalize the cases for a single element, our intuitive response to the equalized case becomes *harder* to identify, and seems *less* likely to generate an intuitive consensus. So, for example, she wants to distinguish between physical proximity and efficaciousness; to do this she wants to eliminate the intuition that our obligations are stronger to those close to us *only* because we *can* help in a way we cannot when they are at a distance. We are asked to imagine 'Near alone' and 'Far alone' with the variation that I have very long arms so that I can help the distant child as easily as the near one.[16] This variant only produces the intuition, Kamm thinks, that I ought to help, if the part of me that is extended to the victim is the efficacious part. Thus, efficaciousness is isolated from nearness. If my very long *arms* were physically proximate to the drowning child in 'Far alone' but they were ineffective in assisting her, then we would have physical proximity (of my arms) but not of *me*—Kamm thus imagines several variations to the cases to eliminate the factors of recognition—if my victim sees me, looks into my eyes and implores me to help her, and personal encounter—if we have talked, if we know one another, if we have friends in common, and so on. The flip-switching variant, involving a remote-control button,[17] similarly, is meant to equalize for the extent to which an obligation, if imposed, would cause hardship for me.

To isolate the analytic feature of salience—what I am calling normative pressure—the possibility that I can't get the image of the needy person out of my mind—from that of recognition and personal encounter, she imagines a 'Door case' in which there is someone drowning just outside my door and I could help.[18] We don't see one another, but I know she is there—we are *proximate*—and that I am thus specially placed to help her. Does this proximity make a difference, intuitively, to my obligation to help? More pertinently for Kamm's immediate purpose, because the person is outside my door, I can't get her need out of my head. I carry it with me everywhere and think about it all the time. Now there may be another person, equally needy, equally unknown to me, whom I can help equally easily, somewhere far away—we seem to be back in switch-flipping territory here—what is the intuitive significance of the fact that I can't get the first person's need out of my head? Kamm thinks none, for the following reason: if, she claims, we had a mechanism by which we could choose to put the thought out of our heads, and there were *no other reason* why I ought to help her, that it would be permissible for me to use the mechanism and shut the thought of the needy person off.[19] In that case, my obligations to the near person and the far person

[16] She calls this the 'Reach' case: 'Suppose I stand in a part of France, but I have *very* long arms that reach all the way to the other end of France, allowing me to reach a child drowning in a pond at a distance... Intuitively, I think this case is treated as one where the child is near' (662).

[17] Kamm, 'Does Distance Matter Morally to the Duty to Rescue?', 663–4.

[18] Kamm, 'Does Distance Matter Morally to the Duty to Rescue?', 665.

[19] Kamm, 'Does Distance Matter Morally to the Duty to Rescue?', 665–6.

would once again seem to have more parity; by isolating only one element, the cases have been equalized.

I do not quarrel with Kamm's methodological point: it certainly seems true that we can manipulate our intuitive responses to such cases by arranging their facts so that only one relational feature is in play. If we want to know, specifically, *whether*, and *why* only *one* of these features has moral importance then we ought to follow Kamm's approach. But of course this way of thinking about our moral judgments in response to relations is mechanistic, and such an approach belies the usefulness of this kind of atomistic approach to relational structures and their normativity.

If a person is standing outside my door in need of my help, then the fact that I cannot get her out of my head is not likely to be *isolable* from the other factors. The normative pressure I feel—what Kamm calls salience—is likely due to my intuition that some complex of the relational factors at play, such as the person's need together with my ability to help her—my efficaciousness—together with some additional pressure I might feel from having *seen* her, empathized with the suffering arising from her need of me. I might feel the moral arbitrariness of my good fortune in being in a position to be efficacious in respect of her need, reflecting my awareness of the norm of equality governing our basic human relation as it pertains to our immediate situation. So whether or not it is appropriate to flip a switch to cease the feeling of normative pressure to assist the person will depend on what one thinks of the moral significance of these other factors. It might be the case, for instance, that the capacity to feel that normative pressure in response to looking into the eyes of a person in need and whom I can help is part of what makes me a moral person.

I need not take a position, here, about the accuracy of Kamm's conclusions in these cases; what is revealing, though, about her methodology, is how obvious it seems to be that *when combined*, these various factors increase the likelihood that our intuition that the person in question has a moral obligation to the other increases, or that our differing intuitions converge on that conclusion. She wants to isolate the various features to see which one is controlling, morally speaking—proximity, in particular, in this case—but her method would seem to reveal that the *type* of normative judgment about which people are actually substantively disagreeing, in all these questions about the role of relationality in respect of morality, is a relational *kind* of judgment. It is about what the basic human relation requires, both with respect to humanitarian obligations and rights, when it is layered, and thus the relational structure made thicker, with various other elements such as the ones Kamm suggests, namely, need, efficaciousness, recognition, personal encounter, salience or normative pressure, proximity, and perhaps others as well. So the moral significance of relational structures will tend to be molecular, as it were, rather than atomistic.

In the case of the atomistic factor of recognition, of course it will make an intuitive difference in some way to whether I take myself to have, or in fact have, an obligation to some needy person, if we look each other in the eyes; because, if I choose not to help her, then in addition to her other struggles, she will experience herself as being abandoned by me. If I *know* her, if I am her neighbour or friend, that sense of abandonment, for instance, will be worse. If I am a doctor, it will be accompanied by a sense that she is not even worth giving the kind of care that I give to people all the time. And of course I will know all of that; so of course once I see her and know she recognizes me and so on, I will know that my choosing not to help will be that much worse. Similarly, of course it makes a difference to my obligation to help if I *can* help, since we cannot require of someone an action they simply cannot perform. Similarly, the cost of the action to me will have an impact on how much I value helping the other person—how important I take her life to be in comparison to my time, my money, and so on, and the more factors present that enable her to *know* how costly or costless it would be for me to help, the more she will experience her predicament worsened by the knowledge that she is being treated as so much more worthless.

If, in other words, we just want to know whether physical proximity all by itself matters to moral obligation—and I am not saying it does or does not—of course we have to carefully control for these other factors, precisely because our intuitions that relations including *all these different elements together* are clearer, stronger, and subject to greater agreement.

But there are two purposes at work here, and Kamm's is not the same as mine: I am simply interested in showing what I mean by relational structures in contrast to either an atomistic or a pigeon-hole kind of view of relationships considered outside the context of their actual, specific structure in a given situation—that of 'teacher', that of 'employer' and so on. I used Kamm's methodology to show that to the extent that it makes intuitive sense to say that relationality matters morally, its significance will be based on the complex of more basic analytical features that come together in particular structures.

That is why I have deliberately avoided the question, naturally prevalent in the literature about *whether* relationships can generate reasons or obligations or warrant the agent's prerogative to prioritize those close to her, of how to define a relationship. I have suggested that neither of the two approaches to relationality in the literature relating to its normativity—what I referred to as the top-down or relation*ship* question, and the bottom-up, *atomistic* question—are directly pertinent to the relational element of rights. Although both approaches often begin by asking what a relationship is in the relevant sense, that is, such that it can generate moral obligation, both are in fact engaged in precisely the normative reasoning that I am contending is entailed in judgments contained in recognized rights. That is, these approaches are not defining relationship for the sake of establishing anything ontologically, but rather for the sake of reasoning normatively about which relationships, or which aspects of relational structures, generate moral reasons. My claim, remember, though, is not, with respect to the model of Rights in general, that any particular relational structures generate any particular relational norms, but rather that the recognition of a right necessarily involves *some* judgment about the normative significance and implications of whatever the relational structure actually is in which the right in question is being considered.

The third element in the model of rights is thus relational in the sense that it reflects a normative fact or judgment about the relational structure in which a given right arises, is considered, recognized, or explained. Those relational facts or judgments account for the shape of the constraint in the context of a *particular* relational structure between right-holder and duty-bearer. So the fact that we think there are moral rights to life and liberty as a 'universal' matter reflects two judgments, on the view I am advancing: one is about the relative value of the goods of life and of liberty; the second is that the basic human relation gives rise at least to constraints of forbearance in respect of those interests. If we think the state has additional constraints in respect of those interests, it is because the relational structure operating between individual and state gives rise to those constraints. So the conclusion is that we *find* relational normativity in every right, reflecting those judgments. That does not tell us *why* such relational structures are normative—that is the purpose of Kamm's larger question—nor does it tell us, without actually unpacking the relational context of any given right, *which* relational structure is at work and generating normative judgments about its significance to the shape of constraints.

III. Two Kinds of Objections

I must now address two kinds of objections to my argument that relationality is the third dimension in a model of rights. The first is an internal objection, meaning that it accepts that relational structures have normative significance in respect of assigning rights but claims that this significance is already captured by one or the other of the elements in the dualistic model. It thus would imply that the two elements in that model are jointly necessary and jointly sufficient; this I will call the objection from *reducibility*. The second is an external objection insofar as it rejects the inclusion of relational norms in a model of rights at all. So, like the first objection, it takes the elements of constraint and interest to be jointly sufficient as well as jointly necessary, but for a different reason: it considers relationality to be inappropriate within the conceptual structure of rights. I will call this the objection from *impartiality*.

A. Objection from reducibility

This objection goes as follows: relational structures do seem to be operating within rights, informing the shape and even the specific content of constraints, but their normativity is already part of the dualistic model of rights; it is, in other words, reducible to relationality somehow implicit in the element of interest, or to relationality implicit in the element of constraint. These objections will go through if the impact of relational context on the shape of constraints is fully explicable by reference to the view of interest or constraint as it may contain relational implications.

(1) *Is relational structure reducible to the element of interest?*

Let us begin with the argument that the significance of relational structures is already present in the claim that rights protect interests. One might think relationality is reducible to the element of interest in this way for several possible reasons. The first is that just as each right is a protection of some good or interest, it is a protection of that interest *against* something: the protection of the right to life means that the interest is not just in life but in not having the enjoyment of one's interest in life improperly abridged. We can think of this as the 'relational description' of interests, and one might argue that it accounts sufficiently for the formal relationality rights manifest. We can perhaps best describe this objection in relation to the idea of *value*. We might argue that if a right protects something of value, then what it protects against will be whatever diminishes the value of the thing protected. Would this way of thinking about interests adequately account for the ways in which relational context informs the shape of constraints?

One possibility would be to say that the significance of the relational structure is that it is what gives rise to the possibility of harm to the interest; by focusing on harm to interests, or to the diminishment of their enjoyability to the right-holder, one could say that rights only arise in certain relational contexts. If the interest is sufficiently important to warrant the imposition of duties, it will, presumably, impose duties wherever duties are relevant *to* the interest. Where, in other words, the interest *can* be harmed or protected or promoted from a particular direction—by a particular person.

The relational context would then only be important because it is within that context that the interest is threatened. So of course there is a relational context in which my right to freedom from harm arises, because it will arise wherever there is a threat of harm—that threat must come from somewhere, and a right can only arise where that threat comes in the form of, or from, another person.

This way of thinking would mean that relational context is a proxy for the principle that valuable interests generate obligations on everyone to help as much as they can, or to help in ways particularly important to the interest. Not, in other words, to diminish the value for individuals in the interests rights protect. One could say that the moral importance of interests generates obligations on those in a position to violate them. The normativity of relational context would then simply be an extension of the principle that everyone ought to have *some* duty imposed on them in respect of an interest that is sufficiently important, and that the shape and content of the duty will directly reflect the person's ability to affect the interest. The potential for harm to a given interest is *magnified* in different relational contexts, and so it is not relationality that is generating normativity, here, but the importance of harm to interests. This account seems most persuasive in the cases where the constraint involved requires non-engagement, or ones conventionally called negative. The Nozickean 'bubble' or 'hypersphere' model of rights might seem appropriate here; and in fact there is a general assumption that negative rights are the ones where distance or relationality have no bearing because the normative focus is on the victim since she carries her bubble of normative protection around with her.

But this won't work, first, because, even in the context of negative forms of interactions, threats to interests are *created*, and where there is such a threat there *is* a relational structure in a meaningful way that arises through the actions by which the threat is created. Being in a position to violate the most basic norms involves the creation of risk; as one philosopher of the law of interpersonal obligations has emphasized, 'risk imports relation'.[20] That is, to create a risk involves implicating some class of other persons who could be affected by your action. The moral implications of creating risk thus involve the ability to foresee *who* will be potentially affected; and the potential victims' well-being will depend, whether they know it or not, in part on how carefully you conduct your actions so as not to violate them in the way made possible by the risk.

Moreover, rights normally categorized as negative generate constraints of various shapes, and these different shapes cannot all be explained by reference to threatened harm. The right to freedom of conscience is in principle a negative one, but of course it will impose other constraints as well—it may also generate obligations on educators, parents, and employers, for example. Do those obligations arise because those people are in a position to affect the interest in an especially *powerful* way? Or because the relational norm at work in those contexts is, as a more general matter, one of support, care, and the promotion of interests of the students, children, and workers? Or, in the case of the employer, because so much of the employee's hours of wakeful productivity are in some way occupied by the employer; because his livelihood and thus his ability to enjoy so many other interests is thus bound up with his employment, or because his social standing among his community is bound up with his social standing within his occupational setting, a matter over which his employer has control? Reasoning about these matters will affect the particular duty-bearers implicated by a given right and the shape of the constraint imposed on them. But it is implausible to think that each subtle difference in the array of possible duty-bearers in the case of freedom of conscience described above can be explained by reference only to harm to that interest.

This brings us to the second problem with this objection of reducibility. Once we move beyond negative constraints of forbearance—which our dualistic model requires us to do, remember, because neither interests nor constraints are intrinsically 'negative'—without the element of relational context we can't even always say *what would constitute an infringement of an interest.* When you define an interest simply in terms of a good or aspect of well-being, that does not by itself outline the possible ways in which the interest could be affected that will count as morally

[20] Ernest J. Weinrib, *The Idea of Private Law* (Cambridge, Mass.: Harvard University Press, 1995) 160.

problematic. So if someone doesn't have enough water, their interest in water is engaged: they need water; if no one *took* water from them, or is taking water from them, that engaged interest is not an infringement of a prohibition. The right to water, though, is more than a prohibition, it is (as a legal and political matter) a socio-economic right and is normally considered to have a positive shape: if our thirsty person has a rich neighbour who has lots of bottled water and she doesn't share it, is *that* an infringement of the interest? What if the neighbour is also her father or brother or friend? We can say the interest is in water, but not that there is a right to water such that a positive constraint can be recognized, without thereby saying whether, if someone fails to give water to someone who needs it, that constitutes a violation of the right: *more needs to be said* to figure that out. Does that make the right to water 'special?' I would have thought that if general rights are supposed to be ones that everyone has, the exclusion of the right to water on this basis would be an unfortunate result.

The same problem arises in the case of all possible forms of mistreatment or failure to respect rights in which knowing what the interest in question is does not tell us when it counts as being infringed; such cases are certainly those in which the good in question itself involves some kind of interaction, such as health care, education, and procedural and political rights. The one thing we do know about the right to education, for example, is that it is widely taken to impose a duty on states to provide their citizens with some level of education. It is my contention here that the right to education thus cannot be fully explained as a moral matter without recognizing that that right, as an instance of our thin model, counts as a right and consists of *two* types of normative judgment: the first concerns the special value of a good or interest; the second concerns the normative implications of the relational context of the right. In the case of the public law right to education, the substantive normative judgment about value that is instantiated in the right is that education has a particular kind of importance; the substantive normative judgment about its relational context is the one that says that there is a duty to provide a certain level of education in a relational structure like that of the individual and the state.

Another possibility for reducing relational context to the element of interest would be to say that the harm is of a different *kind* in certain relational contexts, even to the same interest. So the harm to a given interest might be not only *worse* in the context of certain relational structures, thus being quantitatively different—if someone very strong hits me the harm will be worse than if someone very weak does so—but it might also be qualitatively different: a violation of the right to be free from intentional harm, for instance, might be a different kind of thing if the violation is coming from my father than from a stranger or from a teacher. Still, to account for these differences only by reference to the element of interest one would have to describe each right in terms not only of the interest in a reasonably general sense—freedom from intentional harm—but in terms that are specific to each type of relational structure in which the harm would be of a different kind: I would thus have a right to freedom from harm from my teacher, a different right to freedom from harm from my mother, and another to freedom from harm from my neighbour. If we were to take this approach, a right whose content is, or ought to be, relatively easy to understand would become a dizzyingly increased number of rights. Even if this way of describing the role of relational context in terms of interest were normatively plausible—that there is simply a different interest at stake in each of my rights not to be hit by various people—it would be a terribly cumbersome approach to try to identify the correct duty-bearer in connection with rights in the way we currently describe them in practice, namely, to the protection of interests generally described.

Moreover, though, it does not seem to me that the kind of account given above is actually one in which the element of relational normativity is in fact reduced in the sense that it is normatively eliminated into the consideration of the importance of an interest. Because if we were to *describe* each interest-in-a-given-relation differently, thus giving rise to as many rights for each right-holder in respect of each general interest as they have distinct relational contexts, we would still have to make a judgment about the normative implications of the relational context at issue in order to describe the interests properly. To describe the special kind of wrong that is abuse by a teacher as distinct from that of a parent and so on, we would have to reach the conclusion that *those* are the relevant relational contexts in which it is necessary to re-describe the interest in not being abused, for instance, on the basis of reasoning about the role of the relational context. The distinct relational normativity therefore is not in fact reduced into the element of interest, on this kind of account, it is rather *made separately* and then formally included in the element of interest, but to no real advantage, as I will argue below.

(2) Is relational context reducible to constraint?

So far I have outlined some ways in which relational structure might seem to be in fact a feature of the element of interest; what about the element of constraint? This way of thinking about the normative role of relational structures in rights would certainly seem to account for rights' formal relationality, in the following way. Part of my argument for the element of relational context as rights' third dimension involved the premises that rights necessarily protect interests *and* involve constraints and that the constraints are thus bipolar. The line-shaped magnet I described that is drawn on one pole to valuable interest could simply be said to be drawn on the other pole toward the *violator* of the constraint. But of course that avoids the question of how one determines who counts as a violator, since it does not explain what actions count as the right kinds of infringement of the interest such that they amount to a violation. If we take the element of constraint to be purely functional, as we would if we accepted moral rights from an interest-based perspective—taking the element of interest to be doing all the normative work in any given right, so to speak—it would be difficult to see how, from within constraint itself, we could explain the reasons why only certain people seem to properly attract obligations in association with rights to, say, health care, freedom of religion, freedom of expression, and so on.

But we might think that relational context is reducible to the element of constraint if, for example, we consider that although rights protect interests, the employment of a rights *framework* emphasizes the directedness and agent-sensitivity of rights, and that these features of rights carry with them the normative force of the separateness of persons, hence the orientation of constraints toward individuals, and of some degree of equal inviolability arising from the anti-maximizing feature of rights. On this kind of view, we could argue that one could, with sufficient moral reasoning, derive the norms governing the various relational structures from these basic normative features associated with the element of constraint. What I have called the basic human relation, in particular, whatever one takes it to be, governed by a relational norm of equality, would seem particularly at home within the element of constraint. Even if this were so, though, it would not account for the role of more complex relational structures in shaping more complex constraints in respect of the same interests in, say, freedom from intentional harm. In the case of moral rights it would be difficult on this view to account for the significance of the 'worse-ness' of the violations of the same right within different relational contexts, a problem I described when considering reducing relational structure to interests. So if it is worse for my mother to beat me up than it is for a stranger to do so, an account of rights that takes relational structure only to refer to equal inviolability among all persons would not explain why the right not to be beat up might impose special constraints on my mother not only not to beat me up but to protect me against others, to help me to learn to protect myself, to advocate for me at school or in other contexts, and so on. On this view, my mother might have those obligations but they would have nothing to do with my right not to be beat up.

(3) *Is relational normativity external to rights?*

This last possibility, if one finds it persuasive, might suggest another way of reducing relational structures out of rights, namely, simply to recognize the normative significance of relational structures but to externalize that significance from the conceptual structure of rights. One might say, for instance, that there are independent relational norms at issue that are *also* violated when the interest is infringed that makes things worse. If this were the case, we might say that the apparently necessary role for relational context in shaping constraints within rights is in fact reducible to the fact that rights arise in situations where there are also relational norms that are separate or external to the right. This seems implausible to me for the reasons I discussed when arguing for the dualistic model's indeterminacy. If we take the normative role of relational structures to be entirely external to rights, we will still be making normative judgments about the significance of relational contexts in respect of rights because we will rely on those judgments to some extent when assigning duties in respect of rights. Without the element of relational structure within a model of rights, though, we have no way of reasoning directly on the basis of the conceptual structure of the right to the duty it generates. And we would then be back to the situation where we wouldn't be able to understand and explain a right and the duty it generates partly by recognizing the normative judgment involved in assigning the particular content and shape of the constraint to particular people. We would not be able, in that case, to recognize that a disagreement about which duties arise in respect of a right is in fact a disagreement about what the *right itself requires*, and the directedness of the particularly shaped constraint associated with a given right would thus not be explicable by reference to the right. We *can* think of relational context as being relevant to the assignment of duties in respect of rights but external to them, but since the assignment of directed duties is precisely what distinguishes rights from interests then relational context is inevitably part of what determines what the right in question requires, *as a right*, and, like the elements of interest and constraint, it is indispensable to what rights are.

B. Objection from impartiality

This objection is perhaps the most compelling and the most important, it seems to me, because it seems to come from an intuition about the universal importance of rights and about the importance of their inhering in the right-holder, rather than being subject in any way to relations she may have. I take the most persuasive form of this objection to go something like the following: including a normative judgment about the relational context of a right within its most basic conceptual structure seems to discount the importance of the rights that we hold against everyone; this seems in some cases very counter-intuitive—*surely my right not to be tortured doesn't depend on my relationship with my torturer?*

It is most important to be clear that the three-dimensional model of rights does *not* mean that we *ought* to take relational contexts into account when assigning rights where currently we do not. Rather, my argument is this: if we look carefully at *any* recognized right, we will find there a judgment about the normative implications of the relational structure or context of the right. Now in many cases this relation may be a very thin one. It may be what I have called the basic human relation. And this relation, one might object, is so thin as to be trivial—its recognition does nothing to help us to understand those rights in which it is the only relational context at issue, and so it makes more sense simply to say that relational context only functions in the way I have been arguing in the so-called special rights.

Three further important responses to this objection. First, with respect to the point about the thinness of the basic human relation and its consequent so-called triviality where rights are concerned, this seems to me simply wrong. On the contrary, this interpretation of rights forces us to focus our attention on the normative implications of the basic human relation that we *do* take to be the site of the most important rights. If we begin to understand *that* relational context as normatively significant, and to think carefully about why we take it to be significant, we may in fact begin to see that it generates stronger moral requirements than we think, because we won't be focusing on the badness of the action, we will be focusing on the importance of complying with—in the context of this particular relational structure—whatever we take the normative implications of the relational structure to be.

Second, even in respect of the most universal rights, such as the right not to be tortured, a variety of possible violations will exist, the distribution of which cannot be explained only by reference to the universality of the right. So my duty to interfere, somehow, if I think torture is occurring, might well be normatively implied by the right against torture. This is an absolutely uncontested point in the case of the state, which we take to have obligations of protection and promotion in respect of all kinds of 'negative' and thus apparently universal and non-relational rights. As I have been emphasizing, the duties in respect of those rights, to say nothing of rights that require engagement and the provision of goods, will be different for differently situated individuals and agents: that 'situation' is not trivial—the way in which rights generate duties goes *through* the situated-ness of potential duty-bearers, or their relational structure to putative rights holders.

Finally, it is important to recognize that some of the rights we now take to be the *most* universal have developed in reflection of historical practices and contingencies, so that the way in which torture, for example, is defined, is *in fact* relationally sensitive: according to the legal instruments that prohibit torture it is by definition an act committed under certain relational circumstances: by an agent of a state, for example, with a particular kind of intent that pertains to the relation between individual and state.[21]

The objection from the impartiality of morality has a more technical or professional incarnation among theorists that means that the element of relational context as necessary to a model of rights looks like precisely what many moral theorists *don't* want to see (though, it has to be said, common sense morality certainly seems to allow us to take special care of those closest to us). To put the point slightly more technically, because rights are directed and peremptory, the obligations we have to those close to us will, on the view I'm suggesting, override the humanitarian obligations we have to everyone else. To this I would have to refer to the arguments I have made regarding the conceptual implications of including the element of constraint within the concept of rights: rights must generate

[21] Article 1 of the United Nations Convention Against Torture, specifies, for example, that:

> For the purposes of this Convention, the term 'torture' means any act by which severe pain or suffering, whether physical or mental, is intentionally inflicted on a person for such purposes as obtaining from him or a third person information or a confession, punishing him for an act he or a third person has committed or is suspected of having committed, or intimidating or coercing him or a third person, or for any reason based on discrimination of any kind, *when such pain or suffering is inflicted by or at the instigation of or with the consent or acquiescence of a public official or other person acting in an official capacity.* It does not include pain or suffering arising only from, inherent in or incidental to lawful sanctions. (emphasis mine).

Convention Against Torture and Other Cruel, Degrading or Inhuman Treatment or Punishment, Adopted and opened for signature, ratification and accession by General Assembly resolution 39/46 of 10 December 1984, entry into force 26 June 1987, in accordance with article 27 (1).

agent-sensitive reasons if they are to foreclose the permissibility of maximizing or aggregating individual interests to justify sacrificing the violation of a single one.

But also, humanitarian obligations can be very strong: if we take these to be based on human need, just for the sake of illustration, the moral demand on my resources and yours would be very strong indeed. Now that does not mean that each person I ought to help has a *right* to that help; but *that* fact does not mean that my obligation to help them is not a strong one—it just means that it is not a directed one. I might be required on the basis of my children's *rights* to provide for their sustenance, education, and health care, as well as the development of their agency and moral powers. The implications of those obligations being rights *would* mean that I would have to fulfil those rights before I give away *all* my resources meeting my humanitarian obligations. But so much is, I think it is safe to claim, in fact quite uncontroversial, at least from the standpoint of conventional morality: hence the fable from Dickens of Mrs Jellyby,[22] who devoted all her resources, time, and energy, to a project to assist the impoverished; a noble cause, but the *extent* of her devotion to it led her to utterly neglect her own children and to impose unfair burdens on them.

Understanding rights in the way I suggest would prevent me from channelling so many of my resources into my children that I have nothing left to help others: rights are directed, categorical, and exclusionary, but the *actions they require*, as I have been arguing, are underspecified on existing accounts except in the extremely general categorical terms of negative and positive forms of obligation. If we knew, more specifically, what it is about the parent–child relation that gave rise to *rights* in respect of those interests in health, education, and so on, we might also be able to say that fulfilling the right requires meeting some level of satisfaction of the good in question—the famously 'minimal levels' approach to limiting the indeterminacy of the obligations imposed by rights—and the idea of our children's 'rights' would not be so amorphous and thus would not be susceptible to vaguely justifying the total expenditure of their parents resources, in some cases, on their fulfilment.

Conclusion

In order to answer the question of which private actors ought to bear the duties associated with new rights and which ones ought not to, we need to understand the moral distinctiveness of public law rights. That distinctiveness—the answer to the question of *which rights* we have or ought to have, rather than the question of what rights are—is captured by the variable content of elements (2^3) and (3^3), namely the particular interests judged to be valuable *and* the particular relational structure that warrants the recognition of constraints of a particular shape in respect of those interests. The moral distinctiveness of the rights that arise

[22] Charles Dickens, *Bleak House* (London: Chelsea House Publishers, 1987).

between individual and state is important to our model both for its accuracy and its usefulness. Understanding that distinctness, explaining the special protections of public law rights against the state, will allow us to transpose that distinctness to the private sphere, so that private relationships can be similarly distinguished from one another. Practising rights on the model I am offering—recognizing new ones, understanding or explaining existing ones, or applying existing ones in a different context—will require that we say more, in respect of a given relational context, than that the constraint takes the shape it does 'because the right is operating in the relational structure of teacher and student'. To make the moral case or explanation convincing, one has to be able to say what it is about that relational context that delineates the constraint in the way it does. To break the relationship down, as it were, to unpack or deconstruct it, into its constituent social and moral parts. And that deconstruction is precisely what I will do to public law rights in Chapter 8.

8

Relations of Dependency and the Model of Rights

I. Argument for Interpersonal Dependency as the Third Pillar in the Model of Rights

Which private relations ought to be made subject to new, personal independence rights extrapolated from the public sphere? If *all* such relations ought to attract the special scrutiny associated with the relationship between individual and state, then the applicative scope of the new rights seems unlimited, raising the problem of overbreadth associated with judicial discretion and legal uncertainty. I have so far been arguing that we can sort out the private relations that ought to be subject to new private law rights by focusing on those that are structurally analogous to the one between individual and state. Of course the reason *why* the application of public law rights to private law has become an increasingly important issue is that the dynamic that characterizes the relation between individual and state has begun to appear in non-state relations. But now the question remains: what *is* the structural dynamic at work in the relationship between individual and state that is morally salient for the determination of these other cases?

Our social world is characterized by a vast, intricate web of interdependent relationships of varying degrees of thickness, ranging from my daily encounter with strangers in a subway car to my interactions with my bank and my employer to my relationship with my friends and family. Although these are all relationships in some thin sense, they are very different from one another in virtually every practical respect. Yet all these relational contexts share one structural commonality that is important to our analysis of relational structures: the parties in all relational contexts occupy a relational form in which they share a relative perspective of normative magnification:[1] this means that what each of them does with respect to the goods they have in common has a special importance for them both. And because all relations are grounded in some way in a good or interest that is common to both parties, the relational form always involves some small degree of interdependence of its parties. Thicker relationships, the ones we might think of

[1] The phrase 'normative magnification' is borrowed from Thomas Nagel's discussion of deontological reasons in Nagel, *The View From Nowhere*, (New York: Oxford University Press, 1986), 180–4.

as being real and full-blooded, are partly characterized by the kinds of affective interdependence associated with trust.

Relations therefore always create some measure of dependency, but in most cases that dependency is mutual; normal relations of friendship and commerce can be reasonably described as ones of *inter*dependency. But there is a subset of relations in which a sufficiently substantial degree of dependency arises that, I will argue, the obligations associated with the special normative scrutiny of relationality we apply to the relation of individual and state also arise. In this chapter I will explore the concept of dependency, and argue that this is the particular type of relational context that ought to apply to the model of rights we extrapolate from the public sphere to the private one.[2]

Dependency involves an increased vulnerability of one party to another.[3] It is a relational structure that links power and need, or power and vulnerability, so that the vulnerability of one person is specific *to* the influence of another. A person can be vulnerable on his or her own if he or she is weak, for example, physically or socially in some way. Such vulnerability can pertain to natural forces—droughts, floods, and so on. Dependency is the structural relation that converts vulnerability—a general condition that can pertain to anyone and everyone—into *violability*—a condition that pertains to another person. One does not say one is violated by an act of nature; one is violable with respect to some agent, or specifically, to some action undertaken by that agent. Moreover, dependency arises with respect to a particular good or goods: if I am dependent on you, in other words, it must be possible to say what it is in respect of that I am dependent on you. While relationality in general, therefore, is a form of experience that aligns vulnerability to or power over another with the importance of goods, dependency is a species of that more general form in which the morally salient features of relationality—value and vulnerability—are isolated and focused so that the benefit and burden of relationality fall disproportionately on the two parties.

There are three main parts to the argument that dependency is the type of relational context that should govern our reconstructed model of personal independence rights for the private sphere. The argument will exemplify the method I set out in Chapter 2, of treating theory and practice as operating in a reflective equilibrium, each informing and limiting the other. In Part II, I will examine in some depth the idea of dependency itself; I will argue that upon

[2] Before proceeding to the arguments for dependency, we must be clear that we are looking for a particular type of relational context to act as the third element in our model of rights. The dependency I will discuss, therefore, is perhaps better termed 'interpersonal dependency'. This clarification is meant to indicate that when referring to 'dependency' in this regard I am not referring simply to that which is contingent, such as the location of a party that depends on the weather on a particular Saturday. Such contingency is not unrelated to the relational context of interpersonal dependency, but a more particular meaning of that term, related specifically to the relational context between agents, is the one with which we are concerned here.

[3] In this sense it is a relational state that typifies and intensifies the relational form itself, and therefore carries with it an amplified degree of relational normativity. Relational form in general, as I define it, involves a vulnerability to, or power over, another, in respect of some interest or good.

close inspection it contains and expresses certain central features, and I will define it in those terms. These features, I will suggest, are characteristically understood as having normative significance in their own right, and I will thus evaluate the concept of dependency partly in terms of widely accepted ideas about morality. In the third Part I will argue that these features of dependency correspond to the relational features I identify as characterizing the one between individual and state. This part of the argument, therefore, will turn from morality more generally to the practice of rights protection. Part IV will bring together these two strands of argument, in that it will explore the ways in which dependency is important to rights more generally. It will suggest that the moral status of dependency identified in Part II is tied to the normative imperative we impose on the state's relation of dependency with its citizens, and thus that understanding the relational structure of the state and its citizens in these terms can help to explain certain characteristic features of existing public law rights. In Chapter 9 I will illustrate the way in which this third piece of conceptual equipment, the relational context of dependency, will allow the model of rights to impose new rights within the private sphere, but also to limit their scope of application in two main ways.

II. Defining Dependency

Dependency is a concept most often discussed in connection with social inequalities. It seems to arise as a subject of interest for social and political argument in the context of patterns of inequality in gender and class relations. Women, so this kind of discourse goes, are either biologically or socially constructed—or both—to be the bearers of, and caregivers to, the most truly dependent members of society, namely, infants and children, the elderly, and the infirm. Their role as caregivers thus creates a kind of derivative dependency in which women must be cared for by others; and that derivative dependency has created a patriarchal structure in which the family provides for the dependent members of society, while men, being at the head of the family, are independent members. Dependency on the state, on this way of thinking, is, for its more vulnerable members, conventionally secondary to dependency on the family or on other social institutions such as cultural and religious ones.

But that discourse of dependency is not the one that I will pursue. Rather, I will argue for a less purely social, more analytic understanding of dependency as a subset of all interpersonal relations. I will argue that the conventional polarization of that kind of social discourse of community and dependency away from the discourse of individual rights is misguided, in a sense, because dependency is, analytically speaking, the potential enemy of personal security, and thus also of autonomy and dignity. I will argue that, far from belonging solely to the discourse of social and group-based inequalities, interpersonal dependency lies at the heart of even the conventional political philosophy that views the relation between individual and state as the real locus of moral rights. Dependency underlies that relational context, and is therefore integral to a full understanding of the individual rights that arise within it. Moreover, in a more general sense, dependency consists of certain features that are widely understood to attract moral responsibility, and it is thus at home in the more conventional and widespread understanding of rights as being primarily directed at, or justified by, the protection of autonomous security, and of dignified treatment. If we think security is what rights protect, I will argue, then we must recognize that dependency is what rights scrutinize and supervise. In this section, I will focus on distinguishing four facets necessary to the concept of dependency as I will use it, and as it is apposite as the third dimension in our model of public law rights. Part of the reason for the appropriateness of dependency as the relational feature integral to rights is that the features that, I will argue, it consists of are all ones normally taken to have some measure of moral significance, and to attract moral responsibility.[4]

There are several inherent components in the idea of dependency as I will use it. First, it is relational in a simple sense: something can only be dependent if it is dependent *on* something else. Second, dependency connotes need or vulnerability:[5] the dependent thing needs the primary or independent thing for its existence in whole or in part. A drug-dependent person, for example, does not actually require the drug to *survive*, but, because of the addiction, forms a need for the drug to maintain his or her well-being in a particular respect. He or she experiences the relation to the drug in this way, moreover, in terms of need.

The third and fourth facets of the concept of dependency are closely related to one another, as well as to the second one. These are the idea of power and of a role for will or agency. I refer to the third facet in terms of power, but I mean to emphasize the factual ability of one person to affect what happens to—to affect the interests of—another.[6] This idea obviously implies the element of need described above: in a sense, something dependent on something else is in the first thing's power. But it also begins to suggest the implications of the concept for interpersonal relations. Power, here, refers to the fact that one person *can* actually affect the interests of another. If I am in a position to hit you and I have the physical ability to do so, then I have the power to hit you.[7]

But power on its own does not exhaust the idea of the dependency. Whether or not you will be hit by me does not exclusively depend on whether I can hit you or not; it also depends on how I conduct myself or exercise that power. In other

[4] In her claims about the rights of future generations Annette Baier argues for the moral relevance of dependence and interdependence: 'The rights of past and future persons', *Responsibilities to Future Generations: Environmental Ethics*, Ernest Partridge, ed (New York: Prometheus Books, 1981): 171–83.

[5] Robert E. Goodin, *Protecting the Vulnerable: a reanalysis of our social responsibilities* (Chicago: University of Chicago Press, 1985).

[6] For an argument for human rights duties that emphasizes this aspect of action, see, for example, Elizabeth Ashford, 'The Inadequacy of our Traditional Conception of the Duties Imposed by Human Rights', *Canadian Journal of Law and Jurisprudence* 19, no. 2. (2009): 217.

[7] For a discussion of some circularity in the idea of following the norm where it leads, identifying duties where right-violations have occurred, see Steven R. Ratner, 'Corporations and Human Rights: A Theory of Legal Responsibility', *The Yale Law Journal* 111, no. 3: 443–545.

words, it depends on how I choose to act in the exercise of my power. If I can hit you, then, to some extent, you are in a position of dependency in relation to me with respect to being hit: that aspect of your well-being is now dependent on how I determine my course of action.

This idea of determination or choice of action is the fourth facet of dependency. It is obviously related to the element of power—having choice without power does not produce dependency—and it also narrows the scope of the concept to beings capable of determining their conduct or of choice. The third and fourth facets of dependency—those of power and determination or choice—are also linked by the idea of control. Control can refer both to power—'to have power over, to rule'—and that of choice over a course of action. It seems plausible, then, to say that to be in a relation of dependency is to have some aspect of one's well-being subject to the control of another.[8] Having introduced the importance of control to the impact one can have on another, to someone's ability to influence vital interests of others, there is an intermediate factor between power and control, on the one hand, and impact and vulnerability, on the other. That intermediary is the relevant course of action of the more powerful party that links his or her control and his or her impact on the interests of others. In the context of an analysis of dependency, this intermediary factor is crucial to limiting the right and obligation of the parties in a principled way. I will refer to this 'course of action' piece of the dependency analysis as the *undertaking*.[9]

It is important to distinguish the way in which I mean the term from the one sometimes used to signify a responsibility voluntarily undertaken, as in, 'I undertake to get the project finished in time'. Here, I mean an undertaking to refer only to the course of action itself, without the element of intentionally taking on the duty in respect of the interest in question. So if I undertake to employ you, I can be taken to be acting voluntarily and my actions in the context of that undertaking will be given the scrutiny associated with voluntary action. The point is that this responsibility obtains for the impact I might have on your rights interests even if, in the course of hiring you, I do *not* specifically undertake any obligations in respect of your dignity, equality, family status, freedom of expression or association, etc. But even absent this element of voluntary intent to take on the responsibilities new rights will impose, the idea of the undertaking can help us to solve the problem of limiting the obligations associated with new rights where the distinction between negative and positive obligations has been compromised.

A rich and well-armed person and a poor and vulnerable person who are physically proximal to one another are both subject to ordinary duties to avoid harm. But we can also say that the two exist in a relationship of both vulnerability and

[8] For more specific discussions of the significance of dependency in tort liability, see Stephen R. Perry, 'Protected Interests and Undertakings in the Law of Negligence', *The University of Toronto Law Journal* 42, no. 3 (Summer 1992): 247–317; Hugh Collins, 'Ascription of Legal Responsibility to Groups in Complex Patterns of Economic Integration', *The Modern Law Review* 53, no. 6 (November 1990): 731–44.

[9] Perry uses the term in a related but slightly different way in the context of liability for purely economic loss in 'Protected Interests and Undertakings in the Law of Negligence'.

proximity, and thus relational models of responsibility will have a difficult time limiting the obligations of the more powerful party to restraint from harm. Yet it seems counter-intuitive that in the absence of some *other* relational factor, the rich gun-toter ought to also have obligations to protect the weak person from *other* possible harms, and even to *aid* him, simply by virtue of the power asymmetry between them. But now imagine that the reason why the rich gun-toter is proximal to the weak person is that he is a floor supervisor for a contractor producing low-cost goods for a giant corporation. The weak person can occupy a number of different possible positions in the scenario: he can be a worker on the factory floor, he can be a resident living near the factory, he can even potentially be a family member of the worker. Now the power asymmetry between the two parties does not stand alone as the moral criterion for attributing responsibilities, because it exists within the context of an undertaking: the 'course of action' susceptible to the greatest control of the most powerful party is the factory itself, the manufacturer of the goods in question for the profitability of the corporation. This is a very simple addition of contextual information, but it is an important one. Because now we can say that the undertaking is the locus of the dependency relation; it is the context that creates and sustains that relation, and rights and obligations based on affected interests and power, therefore, will be restricted to the ambit of the undertaking.

We no longer need to say simply that the weak and vulnerable worker is less powerful than his armed factory supervisor; we can make a more nuanced evaluation and say that the undertaking is the context in which the power and vulnerability are morally relevant. Under that analysis, the more powerful person's obligations will be limited in two main ways. First, they will arise only in respect of those vulnerable persons whose vulnerability arises in respect of the undertaking itself. This means that we cannot extend the obligations to say that the more powerful supervisor will owe all the obligations in question (protection, aid, etc.) to everyone he passes on the street at the end of the workday. Second, the more powerful party's obligations will arise only in virtue of those interests in respect of which the other person's vulnerability is caused or significantly exacerbated by the undertaking itself. The dependency analysis, therefore, operates within a sphere of the undertaking that is the nexus or fulcrum of the relational structure.

The control of action that is integral to this conception of dependency refers not to any and all possible actions taken by a more powerful party in any situation of proximity or ability to influence the interests of others. It refers specifically to an undertaking by that party, the conduct of which will be held to certain standards in the treatment of those affected *by* and vulnerable *to* the operation of the undertaking in particular. This focus on the undertaking as the basic sphere of rights and obligations also means that the responsibility for the impact of the undertaking will flow to the agents most powerful *in respect of that undertaking*. While the armed supervisor will be responsible for non-harm, that person is not the person who controls the undertaking itself; responsibilities to protect or even possibly to aid will run upwards, so to speak, to where the control is greatest for the undertaking. This means that although the worker's immediate *vulnerability* is greatest to the supervisor, his *dependency* is sharpest relative to the corporate governors who can actually control the conduct of the undertaking and its impact.

It is, in essence, the way we define the relationship in question, because it is the context in which the parties interact and are morally significant to one another. It is, in other words, the context of normative magnification to which I referred at the outset of this chapter. The factory supervisor, for example, might live next door to a slum in which many very poor people live. His position vis-à-vis the worker, however, is distinct from that in relation to his neighbours. His obligations to the workers flow through the dependency relation between the corporation he works for and those he employs; whatever obligations of humane treatment and non-harm he owes the workers, he owes them in the specific context of the undertaking in which they are involved. Even if his personal neighbours are equally *needy* or *vulnerable*, relative to him, we would define his obligations to them only in terms of any relation of dependency between them. Simply being powerful relative to needy people who are close by is not necessarily going to create obligations on him to aid or protect them. That does not mean that there are *no* obligations in respect of one's neighbours, but just that they will be defined by any dependency that exists between then in the context of the undertaking involved in living next door to someone— to being a neighbour.

Having power—simply *being* the factory supervisor in the poor country—is relational in the sense that one can only have power in respect of something else. But merely *having* power is also an abstract condition, even if it is, in theory, relational. The significance of the undertaking is that it is the concrete expression or manifestation of power in the world. The undertaking is not meant to have a kind of moral authority *independent* of the dependency relation, it is important because it is a concrete manifestation *of* that relation. An undertaking on which people depend in various ways is a *manifestation* of the abstract relationality of dependency: it involves power (expressed in action) that threatens the interests of another. It is not a manifestation of power simply in the sense that having a naturally strong body is concretely powerful; an undertaking is an expression of power through action taken voluntarily. It is thus the context in which power connects with the moral importance of voluntariness. And we can say the same kind of thing about vulnerability and dependency: vulnerability is, like power, relational in only an abstract sense. Dependency, though, is specific not only to the more powerful party; it is, as I explained above, also specific to a particular good with respect to which the depending party has some kind of prior enjoyment or legitimate expectation of enjoyment.

The important thing about the undertaking in the analysis of rights I am offering is that it allows us to think about the more powerful party's conduct as a *sustained course of action* rather than a single act. The importance of the sustained course of action in the context of the model I have developed is that it attracts expectations and reliance that are necessary to the conception of dependency, rather than simple need, as I have defined it. The undertaking, as a sustained course of action, is distinct from the actor's power simpliciter, because it distinguishes power from control. Power is more abstract than control—it can exist in the absence of particular action. Control is what the state has over the individual because the coercive capacity of the state manifested in its undertaking creates a kind of *potential* for detriment, or threat, to well-being, and therefore threatens security. An action that leads to a harm is *evidence*, in a sense, that the security of the good that has been harmed *was*, prior to the action, under threat, however briefly. An undertaking and dependency just *is* a threat to the security of the affected party by the more powerful party. The control the more powerful party has over the undertaking is also the control he or she has over the threat, and, if the control is great enough, and the affected interest important enough, over the personal independence of the depending party as well.

Undertakings on which someone is dependent are also a kind of specific context of action—a circumstance—in which the acting party is presumed to benefit from the action; the dependency is a way of expressing the fact that some other person is particularly vulnerable to be burdened by that action. The undertaking is therefore also a context in which a rights violation expresses a particular unfairness arising from the action of the more powerful and benefitting party. This kind of comparative way of thinking is often limited to the specific good for which the undertaking was instigated: so, for instance, both the corporation and the sweatshop worker derive some benefit from the operation of the factory—profit and employment, respectively. There is nothing to suggest that the two parties ought to benefit from the undertaking equally in respect of that good; the rights analysis means, rather, that we recognize that the undertaking represents the exercise of freedom and the pursuit of value for one party that can impose significant burdens of other kinds on the other party.

A final word about undertakings. The interests that will count as new private personal independence rights will be those whose enjoyment depends on how the respondent conducts his undertaking; thus the rights that will be recognized will depend on how we define the undertaking and then consequently determine its scope. How will we define the more powerful party's undertaking? This may seem a particularly pressing question, since claimants will, one may think, always seek to draw the scope of the undertaking more broadly, and respondents will try to draw the scope more narrowly. The nature and purpose of the undertaking will thus be controversial because it seems as though it is that definition that will partly govern the success of rights claims.

In fact, the definition of the undertaking is less likely to be susceptible to such widely diverging interpretations than might at first appear. First, remember that the question is not what the *moral* or *legal* undertaking appears to be, only what the agent actually seems to be setting out to do, and doing. The question where rights are concerned is not in fact what the subjective or objective *purpose* of the action is—whether we define it as 'conducting a business' or 'running a global enterprise'. The question is whose interests—and which interests—are instrumentally involved in the action. If an interest is instrumentally involved in some undertaking, however we define its nature or purpose, then we look to see whether the person whose interest is so involved depends for their enjoyment of that interest on the party controlling the undertaking.

The undertaking will be the course of action which brings together the various interests of a set of parties within the *use* or *benefit* of the action. It is a kind of but-for test: if the interest at stake would not *be* threatened but for the action of the more powerful party, then there is a presumption that the undertaking of that party, whatever its purpose, includes the interest within its scope. We can also pose the question the other way: if the 'face value' interpretation of the undertaking is contested by a respondent, saying, in other words, that the rights claimant's interest is not within the scope of his undertaking because the undertaking is actually narrower than it appears, we can ask whether the respondent's course of action, his undertaking, would look exactly the same if the claimant and his interest were not involved.

Undertakings are morally significant, then, only as manifestations of dependency, and in parallel with relationality itself: undertakings are the context that *joins* the obligations flowing from voluntarily taking action (in pursuit of values, goals, and in exercise of one's freedom and autonomy) with those that arise in respect of the vulnerable and needy. If dependency is an abstract relational form that links the morality of voluntarily exercising one's power with vulnerability to those actions, undertakings and the interests they threaten are the concrete manifestations of those relations in the world. As I define it, then, interpersonal dependency consists mainly of these two features: first, an agent's exercise of power over, or conduct affecting, another in the context of the agent's undertaking; second, the actual impact of that action on the other's well-being.

The final facet of dependency is that of trust. Relying on another for support seems to be part of the idea of dependency. And indeed the idea of some aspect of one's welfare as being vulnerable to the manner in which another conducts his or her actions implies that dependency seems to involve the entrusting of one's goods to the care or conduct of another.[10] But the trust implied in the idea of dependency here is not necessarily the one we most often think of in connection with interpersonal relationships, namely, that of *affective* trust or of delivering one's goods to the care of another in the confidence that that other person will take care of them *because* they care about them, or about us.

After all, we sometimes talk about dependency in a looser way that seems to refer entirely to this aspect of affective trust: I can say to an employee 'I'm depending on you to do a good job on this project', without invoking the full moral significance of interpersonal dependency in the specific sense of the term I have in mind. A poor person, begging on the street, can call to a passerby—'Please give me a dollar, I depend on your help to be able to eat today'. Clearly these uses of the term have some things in common with the kind of interpersonal dependency I mean to invoke; but the kind of dependency that can give rise to rights where one of the enumerated interests are involved will require more than

[10] This is close to the definition of dependency in the context of a possible tort involving economic loss, namely, entrusting one's goods to the care of another, given by Perry, 'Protected Interests and Undertakings in the Law of Negligence'.

a merely subjective assertion on the part of the person claiming dependency that they entrust some aspect of their well-being to the care of another.

Rather, the facet of trust here embodies the idea that in a context of dependency one is not, in a more objective sense, fully in control of the care of one's goods oneself. This *can* be because of full-blooded, affective trust attitudes, but it can also be for other reasons that do not necessarily involve the relinquishing of control over the care of our own goods and interests in what we ordinarily think of as purely *voluntary* terms. Our interests can be effectively entrusted to another as an outcome of some process or series of events in which we are only one minor agent.

Our social world is characterized by a vast, intricate web of interdependent relational forms, and this web requires that we relinquish some control over what happens to us: when we live in a modern society, we must make ourselves vulnerable to the conduct of others with respect to certain of our goods or interests. This is true even where we would not ordinarily or intuitively think that dependence is the main feature that characterizes a situation. Take, for example, the case of two motorists arriving at a stop sign from opposing directions. Each motorist relies on the other to respect his or her security, to minimize the risk inherent in the fact of two cars approaching each other at speed. The fact that the motorists rely on the rules of the road to enforce that security means that they do not have to think about trusting the other's concern for their security; they can rely on the prudential concerns of the other that will, they hope, motivate them in a way that will in effect protect their security. But a relation of dependence, or in this case, of interdependence, arises in such situations regardless of the presence of laws and the prudential motivations of the actors. This is effectively just to make the Hobbesian point that when we leave the state of nature and enter society we relinquish our natural rights—in this case this means having total control over one's interests. The idea is that the interdependency on which any kind of security rests, that exists wherever there is risk in the state of nature, is transferred to the state in political society so that the insecurity produced by interdependency is mitigated.

When the motorists are at the stop sign, it is true in a technical sense to say that their dependency for their security is on the state to make and enforce traffic laws that can motivate other drivers to minimize risks, but when the motorists are actually at the stop sign, or are rushing past one another on a busy highway, the idea that our dependence is entirely on the state is really just an abstraction: we do, in fact, by driving on the highway with others, relinquish some measure of control over what happens to us to others, so that we come to depend on their conduct in the context of risk, for our security. My interests can be entrusted to some other agent where that agent *takes* control of them so that I acquiesce, either through prudence or necessity.

Before we leave this important issue of how dependency arises, and the role that affective trust and voluntary entrusting of goods to the care of another plays in the analysis of interpersonal dependency, we must canvass more closely the question of how the dependency comes about. I am not suggesting that dependency can be reduced to the moral significance often attached to the voluntary assumption of obligations; far from it—what I am suggesting is that the analysis I offer *brings together* the moral significance of vulnerability—the ability of one person to affect the interests of another—with the moral significance we attribute to actions voluntarily undertaken and the risks to others that these actions pose.

This analysis also invokes a third way in which we attribute moral responsibility, namely, the unfair distribution or allocation of burden and benefit. The thoroughly relational nature of this analysis invokes the idea that a party can attract obligation by engaging in an action that creates vulnerability to the outcome of that action not *only* because of the element of voluntariness in the undertaking of the action, but also because the benefit of the relational form that arises as a result of the action falls disproportionately on the more powerful party, while the burden of that action falls disproportionately on the less powerful one. In other words, the concept of interpersonal dependency I am advancing here involves three of the most widely accepted ways of understanding how moral obligation is generated: the vulnerability of vital interests, the voluntary undertaking of action that creates a relational form, and the principle of fairness in the distribution of burden and benefit within a relational form where there is considerable power asymmetry and where the vulnerability arising from the undertaking is significant.

III. Unpacking the Relation of Individual and State

> *If it be asked, what security, what* fence *is there*...against the violence and oppression of this absolute ruler? *The very question can scarce be borne. They are ready to tell you, that it deserves death only to ask after safety.*
>
> Locke

We can characterize our relations in the modern world as ones of interdependence in a basic sense. But that de facto interdependency rests on a relationship that is better characterized as one of dependency, namely, the one between individual and state. That relational context is the one in which our legal culture has come to assign individual rights that have a strong moral dimension, such as constitutional, human, and domestic civil rights. In constructing a model of rights based on such public law ones, this aspect, their relational context, must be accounted for. My primary aim in this section is therefore to unpack that relation. I will argue that its main features are the ones that also characterize dependency in the way I have defined it, and that dependency is therefore the best candidate to embody the third, relational dimension in the structure of a right. The relevant question here is: what is the most important feature of that relationship? The obvious answer to this question seems to be: power. States have a monopoly on coercive force.

This answer to the question is supported by virtually all political philosophy concerning the nature of the state: individuals in the state of nature have a right to use force to defend their interests; when these individuals become members of civil society they no longer have that force-right. It is precisely the advantages of a single agency having that force-right, as compared to the chaos and injustice caused by each person acting as judge and enforcer of his own claims, that justify the state. But in the transition, so described, from the state of nature to the state of society, we move from a condition of de facto 'natural' inviolability, in the sense that we can protect and defend ourselves against violations of our interests, to a condition of de facto vulnerability, or *violability*, because, within the state, we no longer have that force-right. For Hobbes, this total violability of individuals within civil society with respect to their sovereign is justified because it is the state that best rectifies the de facto violability of individuals in relation to other individuals.[11] He makes an exception for a right of self-defence against the state in cases where the state threatens one's life[12]—a matter to which we will later return.

From the perspective of Locke and Rousseau, this individual violability within civil society created an additional moral problem and thus required a moral solution: the establishment of individual moral rights against the violative capacity of the state.[13] For Kant, too, the same individual moral rights obtain against other individuals as against the state; and because the state is required, in his view, to enforce those moral norms, it acquires a special kind of moral authority over everyone.[14] In this condition of society, then, with respect to the state, individuals become violable as a de facto matter but inviolable as a moral matter. So in this latter, post-Hobbesian tradition, it is not only against other individuals that the state of civil society protects us, but against the state itself. Notice, though, that with respect to the transition to civil society there are two kinds of threat—that from other individuals, calling for the inception of the state, and that from the state itself—but both these threats pertain to the same problem: that of human *violability*. In both cases, too, such vulnerability is a de facto problem: it manifests the fact that there will always be some other, more powerful individual who threatens one's interests, as well as the fact that the state, by its nature, is simply more powerful than any individual.[15] The result of the fact of human violability, both with respect to other individuals and to the state is that, from the standpoint of legal culture, we create *de jure* inviolability to individuals by granting legal rights against other individuals and by protecting moral rights against the state.

[11] Thomas Hobbes and Edwin Curley (ed), *Leviathan* (Indianapolis: Hackett Publishing Company, Inc., 1994), Chapter XIII, 74–8; Chapter XVII, 106–10. In Chapter XVIII he defines the condition of '*propriety*' as one wherein 'every man may know what goods he may enjoy, and what actions he may do, without being molested by any of his fellow-subjects' (114).

[12] *Leviathan*, Chapter XXI.

[13] John Locke, *Second Treatise of Government (1690)*, ed C. B. Macpherson (Indianapolis: Hackett Publishing Company, Inc, 1980); Jean-Jacques Rousseau, *The Social Contract; and, The Discourses* (New York: A. A. Knopf, 1993).

[14] Immanuel Kant, *The Metaphysics of Morals*, ed Mary Gregor (Cambridge: Cambridge University Press, 1996).

[15] Hobbes alludes to these two types of violability when he discusses commonwealth by choice and commonwealth by force: in both cases, he argues, the motivation to submit to the common power arises from fear: 'men who choose their sovereign do it for fear of one another, and not of him whom they institute'; but in a commonwealth by acquisition, 'they subject themselves to him they are afraid of' (Chapter XX, 127).

This aspect of simple power in the relational context of individual and state—the ability of the state to affect the important interests of individuals—manifests two of the central features of dependency I outlined earlier. One party's having power over another's interests also means that the second party is vulnerable to the first in respect of that interest. This correlative structure of power and vulnerability seems central to the relationship between individual and state, and also to the reasons for which we think of individuals as having moral rights against the state.

Even for Hobbes, whose argument is not premised on any pre-political moral rights, our natural inviolability—our force-right to defend all our interests—is only renounced in the political state because in the state of nature *violability* is such an enormous problem. In his state of nature the inviolability we had—our right to defend our interests—was de facto, not moral or normative. So even where we imagine there to be no pre-political moral rights, there is still reason to think that those rights obtain once we make the transition to political society; human violability was such a central problem for Hobbes that it was the catalyst for his development of the laws of nature. Of course it seems that Hobbes also did not consider us to have moral rights against the state, since he thought absolutist government the only kind that could preserve peace. But remember that Hobbes also thought that where our life is at stake in the context of civil society we are entitled to resist in self-defence, even against the state.[16] For Hobbes, we enter into the state to diminish the violability of our lives, and thus where *that* violability is threatened by the state we have just as much reason, as well as the right, to resist the state as we would to resist other individuals in the state of nature.[17]

One way of putting the Hobbesian view of the matter is to say that he viewed the legitimacy of the coercive power of the state with respect to each individual as bounded at the point at which it threatens that individual's life. This is because the justification of the state, for Hobbes, is founded on the protection of human life. And here we must address an objection to my argument that the relationship between individual and state is characterized purely by power imbalance. When I initially considered the nature of the relational structure between individual and state, the answer I suggested was power. I pointed to the famous formulation of the danger implicit in that power—the state presents a concern from a rights perspective because it has a monopoly on coercive force. But of course, in the Weberian formulation, the importance of the state in fact lies in its monopoly on the *legitimate* use of coercive force.[18] So now we might object that this suggests that it is not just power simpliciter that we are concerned with, but legitimate power, or authority. If we take this point seriously, we might say that the way in which the state constitutes a concern for individuals from a relational standpoint

[16] *Leviathan*, 1412. 'If the sovereign command a man (though justly condemned) to kill, wound, or maim himself, or not to resist those that assault him, or to abstain from the use of food, air, medicine, or any other thing without which he cannot live, yet hath that man the liberty to disobey.'

[17] *Leviathan*, 1412. 'the obligation and liberty of the subject is to be derived, either from those words [– *I authorize all his actions* –] or else from the end of the institution of sovereignty, namely, the peace of the subjects within themselves, and their defence against a common enemy.'

[18] Max Weber, *Sociological writings* (New York: Continuum, 1994).

seems to have to do not only with the state's special power to infringe interests but with the fact that the exercise of that power is in some way accepted as authorized.

Yet legitimacy can imply not only the justification of the state but its justness. And this latter element is not present in all, or even most, of the relational contexts between individual and state where public law rights apply. Perhaps, then, it is not the moral legitimacy of the state that is relevant to its relation with individuals where rights are concerned, but the fact that individuals, broadly speaking, follow the rules it makes for governing their conduct. If individuals do, in general, abide by the rules the state makes, then its power over them is much more extensive than mere coercion: it would suggest that it includes the second major element of the relation of dependency, namely, that of the ability of one party to willfully guide or determine the course of the other party's life in some way. In respect of the state, this element of control is perhaps epitomized in the state's legislative function. Its very purpose, in some ways, is to set out rules for governing behaviour. Individuals, then, are to some extent limited in their ability to decide for themselves what they do and what happens to them by the fact of the state and their abiding by its rules.

The major features of dependency therefore seem to underlie the relation between individual and state, the main locus of public law rights. But what about the element of trust within the definition of dependency? In reference to this element, as well as to the general tendency of individuals in a polity to follow the state's rules, and thus to be in a relation of dependency with it, the problem of legitimacy seems to recur: after all, in some states it can be said that individuals are subject to the state but that they do not follow its rules for any reason beyond sheer fear of its coercive power. This kind of circumstance, surely, is not one in which we can say that the well-being of the citizen is *entrusted* to the care of the state.

But remember that the dimension of trust in the definition of dependency referred less to an affective attitude and more to the fact of reliance. Similarly, citizens do not necessarily follow the state's rules and acquiesce in its control over them as a matter of choice, but that does not mean that they do not, in fact, do these things. Simply as a descriptive matter, we do not tend to assume that we as individuals have the right, broadly speaking, to coercively defend our own interests within the political state. This is true with respect to aggression against or coercion of other individuals even in the case of important goods such as housing and sustenance; but perhaps more importantly we generally assume that we cannot, as a matter of course, resist the imposition of the rules imposed by the state. But why not? Perhaps because we assume our political institutions to be more or less just. This would be a kind of normative renunciation of our right to defend our own interests: we cannot resist the coercive force of the state, on this view, because, for whatever morally justificatory reason, we ought not to. On a view of the state based in hypothetical consent, it might seem that where the state's institutions are basically just and legitimate then we normatively relinquish our right to protect all our interests against the state, thereby creating the problem that the state, however legitimate, is in a unique position to infringe those interests.

There is also the opposite extreme, however, of injustice in political institutions: what is the unique concern about the state *qua* state in the context of a dictatorship? There, the state's forceful *exercise* of power—its actual use of force, rather than its legitimate monopoly on that force—is a much more direct reason for concern about infringement of interests. Here there is not necessarily any *renunciation* of the right to protect one's own interests, but simply the descriptive fact that any such attempt at self-protection will be futile. But even in such a case the state *qua government* seems to represent a particular kind of concern from the perspective of individual rights, and this indeed is the typical situation in which much human-rights law is in effect engaged. But if the state *is* effectively just a kind of band of gunmen, and if we might therefore be inclined to say that its rules are not laws, why does it continue to have any special status at all from the standpoint of public law rights?

What I have called normative renunciation, then, is one possible way of thinking about the relationship of justification or legitimacy and violability, so the link between them is both necessary and causal: violability in the state of nature creates a normative prescription for either consent or contract that legitimates the coercive power of the state; that legitimacy then gives rise to a further, normatively rooted violability *to* the state within civil society. And in an illegitimate polity, we do not view ourselves as *renouncing* our right of self-protection but simply as being coerced into the non-exercise of that right—in this situation subjects are obliged, to use Hart's vocabulary,[19] rather than obligated, to follow the state's rules. But a more nuanced descriptive view of the relationship between legitimacy and violability is also available. What I have in mind here is a polity in which—as in most actual states—full legitimacy is not available on the basis of real consent or any other criterion, but a polity whose institutions and governance are not, generally speaking, obviously unjust or dictatorial.

On one hand, a well-functioning democracy that maintains the rule of law, respects minority and human rights, and provides some minimum standard of living for its worst-off citizens seems a good candidate for legitimacy. On the other, obvious oppression or popular revolution seems to be one clear way of identifying illegitimacy. But there is clearly room on the spectrum between these two examples for political entities that we might call states, whose rules we might acquiesce in calling laws, but which fall variously along all shades of the spectrum in between those two poles of legitimacy and illegitimacy. But in all of these cases we would worry about individual *rights*—we regard the problem of individual rights as clearly engaged with respect to the state. Why is that?

Leaving aside its de facto monopoly of the use of force, what is it about the state, in other words, where there is neither perfect justice nor perfect legitimacy, which makes it the central antagonist of individual rights? Most states, after all, fall somewhere in-between the two poles of justice and injustice I described, and in those states, I would venture to suggest, most citizens follow most rules most

[19] For Hart's seminal discussion of rule-following see H. L. A. Hart, *The Concept of Law* (Oxford, Clarendon Press, 1975).

of the time. Even an illegitimate state is a state by virtue of the fact that it makes rules for the polity and that citizens follow those rules; it also enforces the rules that it makes. So it decides *how* conduct is to be governed by rules, and then it enforces those rules. Important interests are threatened in different ways at both stages.

The state's coercive and legislative capabilities as twin indicators of power and rule-making are the two crucial structural features of its relation to its citizens. If real legitimacy is not always available as an explanation for the individual's renunciation of his or her right of self-protection vis-à-vis the state, but if coercion simpliciter is not itself sufficient to explain the state's historically special role where rights are concerned, then we need to reconsider the particular nature of the state's power, and the way in which the renunciation of the right of self-protection contributes to that power. This brings us back to the state's legislative capacity as a facet of its relation to its citizens. Acquiescence to abide by the state's rules means that we effectively relinquish the right to protect our interests. This puts the state in a position to use coercive force against us to infringe those interests—because of the general assumption that that use of force will be acquiesced in. So mere acquiescence in abiding by the state's rules (or in not exercising our force-right to protect our own interests) creates a power structure in which the state has a capacity and individuals have an incapacity in a very unqualified sense. The real problem with the state's monopoly on coercive force does not arise or derive from its *use* of that monopoly—its actual exercise of power—but from the capacity imbued in it by our acquiescence in that monopoly in such a way that it is *always* in a position to infringe our interests. It is not its coercive acts, then, but its coercive *capacity* that presents the problem for individual rights. It has a *de jure* capacity to infringe our interests as well as a de facto one. Acquiescence rather than legitimacy—a descriptive rather than a normative standard—is what gives rise to the descriptive violability of individuals by the state. The central features of dependency, then, are manifested in the relational context of individual and state, and this manifestation offers one reason to accept dependency as the type of relational context that constitutes the third element in our model of rights, and thus also as the relational condition in which the special protections associated with these rights should arise outside the context of the relation with the state.

There are, of course, at least two other important features of the state's relationship with its citizens, features that can contribute to both the interest protected by rights and to the structure of those rights. I raised some of these structural issues relating to rights to fair trial and to gender equality and religious freedom in Chapter 5, where I argued that the structural distinctness of such rights must be taken account of in reconstructing them for the private sphere. And the dependency analysis *can* take account of the structural issues to a significant degree, because where there is dependency with respect to those particular interests, such as in the case of employment, with respect to equality, or of media control with respect to the public discourse issues surrounding the structure of the right to fair trial, the structural context of the public law right at issue is likely to be reproducing itself between the more- and less- powerful parties to the dependency. But there is another facet to these issues that we must acknowledge, namely, the way in which the structure of the individual's relationship to the state informs the interests at stake between them.

The first such aspect of the individual/state relationship is that the state effectively controls the dignitary status of its citizens, or, even, of those in its territory. It does this, at the first level, by granting citizenship status to some but not all persons who would seek it, or who would seek to build their lives on the state's territory. It does it, too, in the way in which it can and does draw distinctions even within its citizenry. The state extends privileges such as driving licences, and grants rights such as the right to vote, to drink, to smoke, to gamble, and, more importantly, to marry, to retain custody of one's children, and to practise certain professions. The state creates and reinforces other distinctions, such as race, gender, and class hierarchies—or it does not do so—but the way in which it treats various groups within society affects the social standing, and the dignitary status, of those individuals. The state, through its executive branch, has the power to act coercively against its citizens, to arrest, question, and imprison them, to inspect their buildings and supervise their child-rearing. In all of these ways, the state affects or controls the dignitary status of those living within its territorial domain. This means that the dignitary status of citizens is always a subject of their dependency on the state, and it is always one of the interests at issue in the structural dependency between them.

This is a more difficult aspect of the relationship to extrapolate to the private sphere, but, once identified, it can be seen to be at issue in certain extreme relational settings. An employment dismissal, for example, might or might not carry the kind of comprehensive denigration of dignitary status exercised by the state: it might arise, for instance, where the relation at issue is sufficiently coercive through circumstances of dependency, such as in a company town, or where the dependency on employment is extreme, such as in an export processing zone. But that is an assessment of an interest that may or may not be at stake that must be determined with respect to each right on a case-by-case basis because it hinges on the particular nature of the dependency relation.

The second feature of the individual's relationship with the state that is not easily extrapolated to the private sphere is that the state, particularly in democratic settings, purports to, and is taken to, speak and act in the citizens' name. It has a representative character that seems to be unique, and that similarly affects the way in which its actions can affect individual interests. This feature of the relationship arises whenever the state acts coercively against an individual, because it seems worse, at the level of the interest involved, to be cruelly treated by an agent who purports to act in one's own name than by someone who acts only in their own interests. This representative feature is more difficult to extrapolate to the private sphere, although that does not mean that it can never arise, and we should, in reconstructing public law rights for the private sphere, be attentive to it.

Both the dignitary and the representative character of the individual's relationship with the state seem to arise in cases in which the interest at stake between private individuals arises in what appears to be a 'public' context. So, for instance, where a person is expelled from a mall for distributing political leaflets, judges will sometimes find that the mall is a quasi-public space of some kind, and that this somehow contributes to the wrongness of the owner's exercising their property rights in that particular way. Sometimes rights advocates in the private sphere emphasize this 'public' quality of goods, such as water, to argue that individuals ought to have a right to that good. Their arguments tend to run through the 'public function' analysis, so that the more powerful actor can be said to be acting in some way similarly to the state. I have outlined some criticisms of this approach in Chapter 1, but here we can see how it is conflating several things that ought to be kept distinct.

One aspect of what appears to be the 'public function' of some actors is their power over individuals—teachers, care-home operators, and massive media corporations are examples of some of these. But the dignitary and representative character of the state's relationship with individuals seems to arise more pointedly in the context of truly public *goods*. Water, for instance, is not a public good in that it can be enjoyed by, and is necessary to, each individual by him or herself. But the *system* of infrastructure that links cities' homes, businesses, and water resources, and cleans and treats the water, is a good that begins to seem less like an individual one and more like one that must be enjoyed by many people together.

Some goods, though, are even more distinctly public in nature: language rights, for example, are not an interest that can be enjoyed by a single person in a solitary way—language is inherently social, though not inherently the subject of dependency in the way education and health care are.[20] Similarly, and perhaps more to the point in this case, we might think of the function of very large or monopolistic media corporations as performing a good that is inherently public in function because it occupies the space of public discourse. It is the relation between publicness in *this* sense of inherently and *necessarily* interrelated spaces—either literal or figurative, in the case of discourse—that can raise both the dignitary and representative interests at play in the individual's relationship with the state in a way that is somewhat distinct from the issue of power and even dependency.

If a town has only one newspaper, for example, or only one public space such as a mall, then those whose opinions or persons are in some way ejected from, or denigrated in, that space, are treated in that way in some sense by the public itself, and their 'public' interests in dignity and in authorship over public discourse can be at stake. These interests are, as I have attempted to show, features of the individual's relationship with the state that are difficult to extrapolate to the private sphere in a way that the interests enumerated in rights instruments are not; but they are not irrelevant to the private sphere, as I have suggested, and they can in some cases be relied on to buttress and to deepen the dependency analysis.

[20] For discussion of the nature of public goods, see, for example, Denise Réaume, 'Individuals, Groups, and Rights to Public Goods', *University of Toronto Law Journal* 38 (1988): 1–27.

IV. The Justification of Rights Against the State: Control, Authority, and Violability

In this section I will bring together the argument from the first section, that dependency consists of features that attract moral obligation, and the argument from the second section, that these features of dependency are the ones that characterize the relationship between individual and state. Here I will argue that interpersonal dependency is integral to the normative ground of the state's moral obligation—both in respect of individual rights and in respect of the rule of law. This is because, I will suggest, dependency is closely associated with the more conventional and widespread understanding of rights against the state as being primarily directed at, or justified by, the protection of security and of dignified treatment in the face of claimed and exercised authority. If we recognize that the stable enjoyment of goods that allows for autonomous self-direction is what rights protect, I will argue, then we must recognize that dependency is what rights scrutinize and supervise.

The normative ground of the state's moral obligation is broadly associated with the importance of individual security. By security, here, I mean the protection against violability in two related ways: first, the ability to form and pursue one's plans under conditions of dignity because of the absence of the constant threat of invasion and brutality; and second, the ability to be self-directing because of the stability of expectations.[21] Conditions of violability, in other words, can destabilize expectations to the extent that self-direction and dignity are threatened or impossible to sustain.

In the Kantian rights tradition, the ability to direct one's actions in accordance with the rational will is a fundamental moral premise. For Kant, this dimension of autonomy was as basic as being guided by reasoning rather than by inclination and instinct. Being self-willed, in this perspective, does not have *interpersonal* dependency as its primary antagonist, but it can be said to be threatened by human dependency on, or control by, certain goods or interests. But even from this viewpoint, the need to be self-directing in relation to others arises because of the autonomous capacity of others: to threaten others' capacity to be self-directing, in such a context, is associated with treating them as a mere means, because it does not take into account, and respect, their full humanity.

For Rousseau, there was an even sharper emphasis on the state's normative imperative to respect and protect autonomy. On this formulation of the normative

[21] I do not mean 'expectations' here in the sense of what might be morally required as a general matter, what are sometimes called 'legitimate expectations', such as the legitimate expectation of privacy, for instance. Rather I mean it only in the sense of creating an atmosphere of stable predictability in the enjoyment of goods. This is why the fact of a good having been *created* by the more powerful party is significant: where a good comes into existence because of someone's actions, it is impossible to rely on that good ahead of time, as it were—to require it for the capacity for stable autonomous pursuits. I use the term, in short, in the sense in which Bentham defines it—see the quote from his *Principles of the Civil Code* in this section.

basis of the polity, to be dependent on one's instincts and inclinations is to be reduced to a kind of enslavement, even to exist only as an animal.[22] To have one's will subjugated to that of another person, though, is viewed as perhaps a worse predicament, associated, in the political context, with slavery and tyranny.[23] For both Kant and Rousseau, the imperative to move to a political condition of a certain kind is animated by the possibility that under this particular condition, human autonomy can be enhanced, because the individual can become the lawgiver as well as its subject. This strand of reasoning is perhaps especially pronounced in Rousseau's particular version of the social contract, which involves the political participation of everyone to create a political will that is truly general rather than private. The operation of the general will, then, can be said to fulfil the normative imperative to preserve the independence of individuals from one another's private control, including—especially—from that of the governing agent.[24]

It is one thing, we might think, for the moral importance of security to be defended by the major progenitors of the natural rights tradition, since deontological rights are associated with autonomous self-determination, and individual security and secure expectations are necessary to autonomy. Yet Bentham, too, who was, of course, perhaps the original naysayer of natural rights, demonstrates the importance of security in this connection. The significance of security, as Bentham describes it, lies in the importance of expectations to autonomy and dignity:

> To form a precise idea of the extent to which importance ought to be given to the principle of security, we must consider that man is not like the animals, limited to the present, whether as respects suffering or enjoyment; but that he is susceptible of pains and pleasures by anticipation; and that it is not enough to secure him from actual loss, but it is necessary also to guarantee him, as far as possible, against future loss. It is necessary to prolong the idea of his security through all the perspective which his imagination is capable of measuring.
>
> This presentiment, which has so marked an influence upon the fate of man, is called *expectation*. It is hence that we have the power of forming a general plan of conduct; it is

[22] Jean-Jacques Rousseau, 'Discourse on the Origin of Inequality' in *The Social Contract and the Discourses* (New York: A. A. Knopf, 1993); he asks whether, for example, in renouncing his liberty man 'degrades his nature, places himself on the level of animals enslaved by instinct' (74).

[23] Rousseau, 'Discourse on the Origin of Inequality'.

[24] In 'On the Social Contract', for example, Rousseau describes the passage from the state of nature to the political condition he describes as being one in which man 'gains the equivalent of everything he loses, along with a greater amount of force to preserve what he has', because in the latter condition he 'obeys only himself and remains as free as before' (Chapter VI). In the civil condition, he says, man acquires 'moral liberty, which alone makes man truly the master of himself. For to be driven by appetite alone is slavery, and obedience to the law one has prescribed for oneself is liberty.' The transition is thus associated with the freedom from enslavement to animal instinct: 'This passage from the state of nature to the civil state produces quite a remarkable change in man, for it substitutes for instinct in his behavior and gives his actions a moral quality they previously lacked. Only then, when the voice of duty replaces physical impulse and right replaces appetite, does man, who had hitherto taken only himself into account, find himself forced to act upon other principles and to consult his reason before listening to his inclinations' (Chapter VIII).

hence that the successive instants which compose the duration of life are not isolated and independent points, but become continuous parts of a whole.[25]

The obligation to ensure individual security is, he argues, imposed on the state because of its unique law-making function, since 'law alone', he says, can create such security:

A feeble and momentary expectation may result from time to time from circumstances purely physical; but a strong and permanent expectation can result only from law. That which, in the natural state, was an almost invisible thread, in the social state becomes a cable.[26]

The special imperative here comes from the state's special power to create and control that security.

That special power—its coercive and legislative capacity—manifests the main features of interpersonal dependency; the relational context of dependency between individual and state, therefore, seems to be inextricably connected to the rule of law. This normative imperative imposed on the state is recognized across the spectrum of the rule-of-law discourse from the fully substantive, Fullerian moral ideal to the more formal or procedural account of it.[27] Security, in both the literal sense of non-invasion and in that of expectations, then, is a precursor to self-direction; it is associated with the normative imperative imposed on the state both from the deontological standpoint, which prioritizes the stable ownership of property precisely because such stability is necessary to autonomy, and from a consequential standpoint that views security and autonomy as themselves central human goods. On either view, though, security is compromised by having one's goods or interests controlled by someone else; in other words, by a condition of dependency.

Having authority over someone—being able to tell them what to do, attracting their obedience—is more obviously threatening to autonomous security than controlling the goods they rely on. The question, then, is: when does controlling what happens to someone, jeopardizing their security, become threatening to their autonomy and security in the relevant way? When does it begin to resemble authoritative control over them? When you have sufficient control over someone's good or interest, you control the choices they can make in respect of that good, and, therefore, you have an important control over their ability to form and pursue plans. You influence their security to the extent that you have control over the good or interest in question. If the extent of your control is very small—if, say, you can only reduce their choices to a very tiny degree, or if the good is relatively

[25] Jeremy Bentham, 'Principles of the Civil Code' in *The Works of Jeremy Bentham*, ed John Bowring (Edinburgh: W. Tait Publishing, 1843).

[26] Bentham, 'Principles of the Civil Code'.

[27] Seminal views along this spectrum include Lon L. Fuller, *The Morality of Law*, rev. ed (New Haven: Yale University Press, 1969); Joseph Raz, 'The Rule of Law and its Virtue', in *The Authority of Law: Essays on Law and Morality* (New York: Oxford University Press); Albert Venn Dicey, *Introduction to the Study of the Law of the Constitution* (New York: Macmillan and Co. Ltd., 1897).

unimportant—then the degree to which you can affect their security and autonomy is similarly curtailed.

So when do you have control over someone's good in the relevant way? At a minimum, this kind of control exists in respect of goods people rely on. We can be secure, in the relevant sense of stability in our expectations and physical freedom from invasion, despite the fact that we do not have or control some interest; if we do not already have some requisite degree of control over some interest, then, our security is not compromised when someone else controls it. Existing physical security is the epitome of an interest with respect to which dependency is always threatening to security. This is because of the importance of expectations to the ability to form and pursue plans or choices. We form and pursue our goals in light of what we know the world to be like, in both the general sense of our understanding of how things work and the particular sense of what we reasonably believe or know to be true in our own lives. I cannot make a plan on the basis of being able to fly because I cannot do so. Similarly, I make plans for myself based on what goods I have available to me to use. In short, I form my plans on the basis of my expectations.

Interpersonal dependency is threatening to security in a special way, therefore, because it concerns reliance rather than simple need, and it therefore involves expectations that are associated with the former rather than the latter. The very meaning of expectations, in the sense in which Bentham used the term, refers to those things that we know we will have continued use of. This can be seen more clearly if we clarify the distinction between need and reliance. Both involve some agent and some good. The distinction lies in the role expectations play in the way the good and the agent are connected: in the case of need, the agent does not enjoy the good in question, and therefore does not make that good the basis of any plans or expectations; in the case of reliance, the agent enjoys the good in some way, and therefore the good can form part of the agent's plans and expectations. You cannot rely on something, in other words, that you do not have nor have any expectation of having. Interpersonal dependency is a relational condition: two agents exist in relationship to one another in respect of some good they have in common in some way; when one of them has sufficient control over the other's enjoyment of that good within the scope of an undertaking of the more powerful party, their relationality is characterized by dependency. Interpersonal dependency therefore involves not only reliance or dependence on some good, but on a particular agent who has control of it.[28]

[28] To this framing of the relational context of public law rights, and thus of new private rights, in terms of goods one already enjoys in some way, one might object that this will privilege an existing distribution of goods, and that that distribution is unfair from the outset. The model I have proposed for protecting people's rights more broadly, in other words, will still leave many people without access to the basic or primary goods necessary to a decent life, and to which, it might be argued, everyone has a human right. The new rights in the private sphere are extrapolated from the public law context. This means that their content must go *through* public law in an important way. For instance, there is currently no full right to have medical care provided for one as a public law right. This means that that care is not directly one of the rights interests and that there is no private law right to such care. If there were such a right widely recognized in constitutional jurisdictions and human rights instruments, then its content could be extrapolate and reconstructed for

But now two things seem to have emerged in respect of dependency that must be distinguished. On one hand, you can be dependent *on a good*; this means that your well-being is dependent on it in such a significant way that it might be said that the good itself is necessary to your security. Subsistence is such a good: if I do not subsist, I do not survive. In this way, our enjoyment of certain goods themselves can control the choices we can make in a very basic sense. The importance of this kind of good seems to be manifested in the enumeration, in various contexts, of positive rights. This kind of dependence on a good means that, wherever we find that good controlled by someone else, we are dependent on that person to the extent of their control. We are dependent on the state in this way because, under the conditions of the modern regulatory society, the state controls, through legislation and regulation, virtually *all* interests, including these vital ones on which we depend in the most fundamental sense

On the other hand, you can be dependent *on a person*, which means that your enjoyment of some good—not necessarily one of the essential ones just described—is controlled by them and that therefore in some way they can limit your choices. I have said that in this kind of case the moral importance of the dependency pertains to the expectations and security of the depending party. This type of dependency is associated with what I called a negative form of interaction—someone taking away or diminishing your enjoyment of something you already have—and thus this type of dependency gives rise to negative rights because these *always* refer to goods you already enjoy and which already therefore form the basis of your expectations. We are dependent on the state in this way in virtue of its authority over us: the state can affect our choices in respect of many goods.

Where these two types of dependency conflate, where you are dependent on an agent in respect of some good on which you are also dependent, the level of control the depended-on party has over the depending party greatly increases; the relation of dependency, in such cases, is enhanced. This is perhaps why these kinds of circumstances are the ones that attract the greatest moral and legal scrutiny. Because we are dependent on the state in both ways, our relationship with the state constitutes a relational context of significant dependency. The state is in charge both of expectations—because of its rule-making power—and of goods on which we depend—because of its coercive power. The state's control over expectations gives rise to the importance of our negative rights against it, while its control over goods gives rise to positive rights against it. The relevant relational

the private sphere within the context of dependency relations. This means that the model will, in effect, pass certain injustices that exist in the public law context through to the private one. And if we want to criticize the unfairness of the distribution of goods, or of the absence of certain rights, we have to criticize public law rights directly against whatever standard of evaluation we have in mind. Because of the extrapolative method, the criticism of private law rights under my model must be against public law rights, rather than against some independent theoretical principle of justice. If you have complaints about the denial of private claims to things for which no public law right or private law right exists, the remedy is not going to be a directly private one. Rather, you will have to back to the public context for a remedy that will then pass, through the extrapolative method, to the private sphere.

circumstance to which we should logically extend the stringent obligations we impose on the state, therefore, is the one where one party has sufficient control over another party's enjoyment of some good so that, in the relation between them, it can be said that the second party *depends to some sufficient extent on the first party for her enjoyment of that good.*

Where the good in question is one of the rights interests, we can assume that these two types of dependency conflate: the widespread enumeration of a core set of goods in constitutions and human rights instruments seems to indicate that these goods are crucially important to human life; that, even, to have a minimally dignified life in which it can be said that individuals are able to be autonomous, these goods must be protected. In other words, we can understand the importance of these goods or interests to be such that they are the ones we as humans most widely depend on. Where a relation of dependency exists in respect of one of these goods, therefore, then *in respect of that good* it can be said that the type of dependency that characterizes the relation between individual and state arises. The special protections of reconstructed public law rights, then—which I have been referring to as ones of 'personal independence'—will, in those narrow circumstances, apply.

Robert Goodin offers a model for social responsibility that is relational in something like the sense I have in mind, but where responsibility tracks vulnerability together with proximity.[29] The main thrust of Goodin's account is to argue that the morally salient feature of our special obligations is not voluntariness but vulnerability. He wants to pin the intuitive notion of moral responsibility to protect and aid within relationships involving special obligations (parent, policeman, fireman, etc.), on the vulnerability inherent in those relationships.[30] The important feature of these obligations, and the relations of vulnerability in which they occur, for Goodin, is that the vulnerable, in them, are owed not only negative duties of forbearance, but also positive duties of protection and aid.[31] He argues that since vulnerability, rather than voluntariness or any other particular feature of these relations, is what attracts responsibility, the moral paradigm of obligations of protection and aid can be extended outward to encompass other relations of vulnerability.

Goodin stresses that vulnerability is a relational circumstance, thus implying that the obligations it produces are not ones of charity but are directed ones, falling on those to whom the vulnerable people are vulnerable. He claims that vulnerability is like dependency, in that both imply a weakness or need *relative* to something else, and he claims that the two are simply cognates of one another.[32] But of course vulnerability, as I will later argue, is in fact only a very weakly relational notion, in the interpersonal sense necessary for directed duties. As Goodin acknowledges, one can be vulnerable to acts of nature as well as to acts of persons.[33] So he needs some further feature of relationality on which to hinge the directedness of the duties

[29] Goodin, *Protecting the Vulnerable*, Chapter 2, 16.
[30] Goodin, *Protecting the Vulnerable*, 28.
[31] Goodin, *Protecting the Vulnerable*, 16.
[32] Goodin, *Protecting the Vulnerable*, 110, n. 3, and 112.
[33] Goodin, *Protecting the Vulnerable*, 110–12.

advocates. The feature he selects is that of proximity. His account incorporates the moral significance of proximity in the attribution of responsibility. In expanding obligations to aid and protect from special responsibilities to more general social obligations he picks up on both vulnerability and proximity within those relationships. He therefore wants to expand the intuitive responsibility we ascribe within special obligations to include others where proximity creates vulnerability.

Goodin frames the responsibility for protecting the interests of the vulnerable in consequentialist terms: the more powerful party is responsible for creating the better consequences in respect of the interests of the vulnerable party (more specifically, in relation to those interests in respect of which the vulnerability exists). In order to mitigate the unwieldiness and unworkability of this very general obligation, he relies on the idea of proximity as a limiting mechanism,[34] using a kind of Humean concentric-circle model of responsibility. He takes the position, something like that of Hume and Sidgwick,[35] that the responsibilities we have to the vulnerable will not become overly demanding and unwieldy because we will in fact be in a better position to help those closer to us (and that, conversely, those closer to us will be more vulnerable to us). Goodin acknowledges that this is effectively a consequentialist model, even one with a utilitarian flavour (insofar as the promotion of interests can be equated with the promotion of welfare)[36] but he insists that in practical terms the injunctions and prescriptions his model would set out would be accepted by non-consequentialists as well.[37]

There are important differences between his account and the one I propose, most importantly in light of this matter of the importance of the agency or control of the more powerful party. A relational model of rights where power is the only relational feature that attracts obligations is one that creates absolutely unlimited responsibility for both positive and negative forms of interaction. If I have power over you, as your employer, for example, then it is not clear, on such an exclusively power-based model of obligation, why I would not have duties to aid and protect you, just as much as I am specially prohibited from harming you. Even if we do think that more powerful agents ought to have *some* obligations of aid and protection, in such situations, the power-based model does not explain why there still seems to be an intuitively irresistible hierarchy of obligations ranging from prohibition to protection to aid.

[34] Goodin, *Protecting the Vulnerable*, 120–2.

[35] David Hume, *A Treatise of Human Nature*, ed L. A. Selby-Bigge, 2nd ed. (Oxford: Clarendon, 1978), 241; Henry Sidgwick, *The Methods of Ethics*, 7th ed (Chicago University of Chicago Press, 1962).

[36] Goodin, *Protecting the Vulnerable*, 114–16.

[37] Goodin, *Protecting the Vulnerable*, 117. Goodin makes this argument by claiming that 'Over the broad range of action implications, there is no... tension between [consequentialist and non-consequentialist accounts of protecting the vulnerable.] Protecting the vulnerable, for the most part, need not entail lying, cheating, stealing, killing, or any other violation of nonconsequentialists' *thou shalt not's*. It would usually just be a matter of reallocating time, energy, money, and other resources to those who would otherwise suffer grave harms. None of that would violate any of the standard prohibitions that nonconsequentialists place on our actions.'

Also, power is a very general relational idea: one can be powerful by having authority over particular people—as in the case of employment—but one can also be powerful simply by virtue of one's resources, either military, political, or economic. So if one is the only employer in town, then one would have significant power in relation to everyone in the town, even to those who are not already employees. The power-based model does not account for any difference that might exist among different individuals in the town, especially in regard to obligations to aid and protect. We might think, for example, that obligations to protect employees from harm, even to provide them with health care on the job, exist in such situations, where those same obligations might not so easily obtain against all the individuals in the town. Power, then, like vulnerability, is a relational concept to be sure, but it is relational in a very abstract sense: it does not lend itself especially well to the kind of directedness of obligations that would be imposed upon private actors under the application of the reconstructed, extrapolative model of public law rights we have been working with.

Vulnerability is a similarly abstract relational phenomenon: it can, as Goodin accepts, apply to floods, storms, and earthquakes. A person can be vulnerable without any intervention of others whatsoever: a person with two broken legs is a vulnerable, less powerful person, relative to almost everyone, just as a very wealthy person, or a very well-armed person, is very powerful relative to almost everyone. So although there is relativity in the phenomenon of both vulnerability and power, neither one is sufficiently directed for a model of rights.

Goodin responds to this problem by introducing the fact of proximity as a way of limiting the obligations that could flow from such an abstract and general relational account. There are several possible problems with an account that hinges on proximity, whatever we may think of proximity as a relational phenomenon capable of generating obligations in a more general sense.[38] First, it is not clear that proximity in itself is morally significant: it seems possible to reduce it to one of a number of other relational phenomena. Perhaps, for example, the fact of proximity is morally important for the consequentialist reason Goodin relies on, namely, that of effectiveness and practical relevance of aid. This idea is that we are always in a better position to help those close to us than to help those far away. Perhaps, though, proximity matters because, in a circumstance where a person sees a drowning child in a pond they must look into that child's eyes and help them or leave them to their death. The importance of that 'looking in the eyes of others' idea could relate to something like an account of relational normativity according to which there is something important about these interpersonal moments of moral action that is crucial to morality itself, and to the sustenance of normative conduct. But that importance could relate to something more like Parfit's idea of interpersonal justification in evaluating the

[38] For accounts of relational normativity that refer to proximity see, for example, Soran Reader, 'Distance, Relationship and Moral Obligation', *Monist: An International Quarterly Journal of General Philosophical Inquiry* 86, no. 3 (July 2003): 367–81; Jeremy Waldron, 'Who is My Neighbour: Humanity and Proximity', *The Monist* 86, no. 3 (2003): 333–54; Deen K. Chatterjee, 'Moral Distance', *Monist: An International Quarterly Journal of General Philosophical Inquiry* 86, no. 3 (July 2003): 327–32.

moral status of actions.[39] Or it could refer to the fact of *knowledge* of the plight of those vulnerable to us. Most likely the intuitive importance we ascribe to proximity involves some combination of all these factors.

Goodin's account is one of *social* responsibility, not specifically one of rights. So far as it goes, therefore, it may be perfectly appropriate. But the problem with using an account like Goodin's in respect of *rights* is that vulnerability and power are excessively vague relational ideas, and proximity is similarly vague and seems to rely on too wide a plethora of moral bases for its normativity.

Whatever else we may say about them, rights are distinct obligations in their directedness, and this is reflected in their element of constraint. Although Goodin uses vulnerability and dependency as interchangeable, my account of the latter is distinct in precisely this dimension of a more particular and directed relationality. The differences between Goodin's account of responsibility and my own are primarily twofold, and they make the model of relationality I offer more appropriate for rights and duties than is an account like Goodin's.

First, the moral significance ascribed to vulnerability on Goodin's account is, as he says, directed at affected interests. This is the feature of relationality that attracts responsibility nearly exclusively on his account. On mine, though, it represents only one of the facets of dependency—that of need or vulnerability. The generality of that feature of responsibility is limited, on my account, by reference to the other major facet, namely, that of power and even undertakings. Goodin's exclusive emphasis on need rather than on control over action as the primary source of responsibility means that he has to reject one of the central, intuitively appealing sources of moral responsibility, namely, voluntariness.

If we take on an obligation, clearly, we are responsible for its performance. In respect of human and constitutional rights we are often talking about obligations *in*voluntarily imposed, and so this might not seem to be relevant in that context. But the scope of imposed obligations to protect, aid, and forbear is simply too broad and unwieldy when grounded only on a victim-oriented principle like vulnerability. The role of the actor in attracting responsibility to himself for the plight of others is reflected in my account through the facet of undertaking and control in the concept of dependency as I define it. On my account of it, dependency arises in respect of some good that the vulnerable party is already enjoying: a usage of the term dependency such as 'I depend on strangers to feed me' has little or no place in my use of the concept. On my account, relations of dependency give rise to rights and obligations because the interests of vulnerable parties are in some sense *already* controlled by the more powerful party in the course of their carrying out of some undertaking. This means that the account draws not only on the moral status of extreme need, as Goodin's does, but *also* on the moral status of the responsibility to others we take on when we undertake to act in the world.

The second way in which my account of dependency differs from Goodin's model based on vulnerability is related to the first. I define dependency as creating

[39] Derek Parfit, *Reasons and Persons* (Oxford: Clarendon Press, 1984).

some measure of insecurity and thus as threatening to *self-direction*[40] because of both the elements of control *and* vulnerability, rather than simply to neediness. And again, the difference between insecurity and need involves the dimension of expectations I described earlier: this means that the obligations that can be recognized in respect of rights will differ on the basis of whether or not the good being enjoyed by the vulnerable party was created by the more powerful party, and thus on whether or not the vulnerable party would be enjoying the good in the absence of the more powerful party's undertaking. If not, then only procedural rather than substantive rights will arise in respect of those interests.

The importance of control—rather than simply of neediness and proximity—and the undertaking by a more powerful party as the nexus of dependency is illustrated by the rights we hold against the state. Public law rights (particularly constitutional ones) are often conceptualized as 'trumps' in a rather vague sense against the state. What this means is that the state can take measures based on a utilitarian calculus or on a conception of the good that is restricted by the requirement to do so in a way that respects certain interests of its citizens. Now if we take power and vulnerability as the relational form that gives rise to rights, this picture of rights against the state looks fuzzy. The state is powerful, by virtue of its economic and coercive capacity, and individuals are vulnerable in a variety of ways. This should mean that states, as a rule, have obligations to forebear from injuring individuals, but also to aid and protect them. It should mean that in respect of *all* individuals, since all individuals are needy. Now even if we introduce the element of proximity to this picture, many public law rights are excluded from it—not all participatory rights, nor all welfare rights, are accorded to individuals within the state who are not citizens. Yet these individuals are equally vulnerable and equally proximal to the state as to its citizens. What is the difference, then, between these individuals and citizens when it comes to the state? One answer might be—nothing; states should extend rights protections to all proximal persons who are vulnerable to it. But then why would proximity be defined territorially, and vulnerability measured only within that territory? If we think this account is adequate for states and public law rights, then if a wealthy state, with a wealthy population, exists next to a developing state, with a poor population, why ought the wealthy state not owe greater obligations to the individuals who are neediest—their political neighbours—and who are also proximal, compared to their own citizens? On such a view, the United States ought to owe *greater* obligations

[40] I deliberately use the term 'self-direction' here rather than 'autonomy' because although they may in fact be technically synonymous, autonomy is a term very often associated with formal accounts of the grounds of negative rights. The description of autonomy as an *interest* or valuable *good* is arguably seen as problematic because there is a sense in which pure or formal autonomy cannot be directly enjoyed or not enjoyed, which is perhaps why much of the argument for rights to goods have been directed at the necessity of certain goods in creating *conditions* that make autonomy feasible or plausible, rather than formally possible. In using the term self-direction, then, I do not mean the pure capacity to direct one's will, but the interest in actually making choices that enable one to pursue one's plans.

in respect of constitutional and human rights to Mexicans, for example, and Haitians, than to most of its own citizens. While some might be drawn to such a conclusion, it does not make much sense of the overwhelming bulk of actual practice.

On the model I have developed, though, the practice of public law rights protection makes more sense. It makes sense, in particular, of one of the most commonly accepted accounts of rights, namely, that they are 'trumps' or presumptively prioritized reasons to prevent the state from taking certain actions in pursuit of the general good, or in a utilitarian calculus. Rights protect individuals, on this view, whose vital interests might otherwise be trampled by a majoritarian rush to achieve certain goals. On this view, or any view like it, the state is engaged in a particular kind of undertaking, that of governing within a given territory, within the scope of which dependency relations will be scrutinized by rights protection, and vulnerable interests thereby protected.

The specific content of the state's undertaking is a matter for political philosophy, and will in any case vary slightly to some extent from state to state. China, for example, might seem to be engaged in a different type of undertaking from that of Iran or France. But in the broad sense within which all these states might be thought to owe certain obligations in respect of rights to their citizens, the state's undertaking is basically the same across this spectrum of variation. It seeks to pursue goals, usually in the name of the people subject to its laws, which further some good or goods seen to be in the interest of those people. Within that undertaking, it establishes rule and dominance in the form of coercion, and it pursues particular goals through legislation. These create dependency relations with those subject to the rules and the coercive force, and public law rights protect their affected interests within the dependency thereby created. While perhaps disputable in a number of its details, this account explains citizens as involved in a special way in the state's undertaking, in addition to being dependent on it simply in virtue of its power. This helps to distinguish citizens from non-citizens, especially in the case of neighbouring states' populations who might be particularly vulnerable.

In addition to making better sense of public law rights in general than purely vulnerability- or power-based models do, the account of rights in terms of dependency and security can help us make sense of the different special protections and emphasis respectively placed on two particular sets of rights. First, compare the kind of rights against physical harm associated with due process, and also with anti-torture and anti-genocide norms, against socio-economic ones. I compare these two because they essentially protect the same basic interests, namely, life, physical liberty, and physical integrity. I will call these goods 'personal material' ones, to distinguish them from the personal but non-material ones such as rights to free expression, religion, and the like. But despite protecting the same type of goods, the first type of rights is generally given greater priority in one way or another than the second. 'Conventional' views of what constitutes rights are associated more with the first than with the second: both private law *and* public law protect the first; and, while public law does protect the second, the practice of constitutional and human rights emphasizes the first rather than the second in a number of ways.

Deontologists would likely argue that this is because the first type are negative rights while the second type are positive rights, and that the difference in priority can be traced to the moral importance of the distinction between harm and non-aid. But even from a more consequentialist standpoint we can explain the difference between these two in terms of the directness of the degree of threat to secure self-direction their violation entails. Where the good in question is as important as the one in physical liberty and integrity, then, its control by another party creates a dependency and a threat to autonomy in a way that the control of goods we may need but do not yet enjoy, such as the ones protected by positive rights, does not. In both cases, the goods in question are ones on which, it can be argued, we inherently depend; but the first type of rights involves the additional derogation of security implicit in the violation of expectations. This also makes sense of the fact that states are allowed to infringe these goods as long as they do so in accordance with due process norms, because following certain procedures stabilizes expectations in respect of them.

Now consider a second comparison, also involving what we might think of as traditional or classical rights and more contemporary socio-economic ones. This time the comparison tracks what are often referred to as first- and second-generation rights, namely, civil and political ones as distinct from positive, socio-economic ones. Socio-economic rights include the various rights to subsistence as well as to health care and education, while civil and political rights include not only the right not to have one's physical integrity compromised without due process but, more pertinently for our purpose at the moment, also the rights to free expression, conscience, thought, religion, and association. As in the previous comparison, the difference between the two sets of rights would be interpreted in the same way from a deontological point of view, namely, in terms of the form of interaction: in both comparisons, the first type of rights reflects intrusions. The distinction in both cases therefore tracks the one between harm and non-aid, making the first a greater moral priority from a deontological perspective. From a consequentialist standpoint there is less of a principled distinction between the two possible types of rights. In the case of the first comparison, as I suggested earlier, if we think there is some difference in the degree of protection between the two we might defend that position from a consequentialist perspective by arguing that although the goods are the same types of interests in a general sense, upon closer inspection the personal nature of the first type may have special significance. That personal character may relate to the role of autonomy as a good: in the first case it may be threatened more directly than in the second. Similarly, in the case of the second comparison, we might think, from a consequentialist standpoint, that the difference lies in the fact that here we have two different types of goods—as distinct from the more conventional view that these are two different types of rights—where the first is inherently related to security because of its specifically personal character.

We can, however, leave aside the differing roles the form of interaction plays in the two moral views and simply interpret the two comparisons in terms of security and dependency directly. In both comparisons, rights of the first type—in the first case, protecting what I call the 'personal material', and, in the second, the civil and political—are associated with security directly, because, in both cases, dependency in respect of the goods in question is directly threatening or problematic for self-direction and self-determination. One has one's choices limited in a directly physical sense when one's bodily integrity and freedom are curtailed and controlled by someone else. And with respect to the first set of rights in the second comparison, the non-material goods of freedom of expression, thought, conviction, and so on, are ones which, by virtue of their intimate importance to our ability to form and pursue plans, give rise to a direct threat to security *when* they are the subject of a dependency. In other words, to have either one's body or one's thoughts and convictions closely controlled by someone else, as in a condition of interpersonal dependency, is to have one's security curtailed in that context to the extent of the dependency.

If we turn to the second set of rights I set out in both comparisons, namely, the socio-economic ones, we find the protection of goods that are also important to security. There are two important differences to be noticed, though, that make these rights distinct from the standpoint of dependency. The first is that although these are *goods* on which we depend by virtue of their importance to us, where we do not already enjoy them the closeness of the dependency relation we have with those who might control them is diminished because of the absence of the element of reliance and *its* importance to security. From the standpoint of dependency, in other words, there is an important difference between goods one already enjoys and those one does not. There is a difference between *depending* on a good and its being *beneficial* to us. It is therefore hard to imagine goods we truly depend on, but for which we might not exist, which we do not to some extent already have. That is, we depend on food and water. There might arguably be intrinsic relations of dependency in respect of those involved in undertakings involving control over food and water—though the implications for the content of the rights would need to be spelled out in much more detail. It is in respect of the goods we depend on *absolutely* that the distinction between humanitarian obligations and duties in respect of rights becomes harder to draw. But we depend on those things in very absolute terms, and the only point about that level of dependency is that *lesser* degrees of control would be required for a dependency *relation* to obtain between persons. It is that relation and its implications for rights and duties, on my account, that delineates that difficult distinction. It is difficult, too, to argue that many other goods fall into the category of such basic sustenance. Even goods very basic to a decent life, let alone a good one, would require a greater degree of *control* over them to generate a relation of dependency. This would be true in cases such as electricity, internet connectivity, and so on.

Moreover, and perhaps more importantly in respect of these rights, some goods, such as that of health care—as distinct from physical integrity—and education, are ones that *consist*, in part, of relationality and dependency. The very possibility of health care and of education only arises where there is someone else to provide them. Dependency and interdependency are therefore constitutive of what these goods *are* in a way that they are not in the case of physical integrity. To put the point at its simplest, you can have physical integrity and freedom, in a basic sense, before you ever encounter other people. But you cannot have health care or education simply on your own. Where goods are created by others, relationality and interdependency—or even dependency—become necessary to their value. Enjoying the good of health care, in other words, *means* that you are to some extent dependent on the person providing that care, and, similarly, receiving an education involves being dependent on the person who is teaching or educating you. Dependency certainly *can* be problematic for security in respect of these goods when it is sufficiently extreme. But because *some* degree of dependency is part of what such goods are, being in a relation of dependency in respect of one of them is less directly threatening to security than it is in the case of goods like bodily freedom or freedom of conscience.

Of course, in respect of both of the sets of rights where dependency represents a direct threat to security and thus to self-direction and those in which it represents an indirect threat, there is much more to say than this about the complexity of the matter. In modern society, the distinction between goods one *can* simply obtain for oneself and those that consist, in part, of relationality and even some dependency becomes much more difficult to draw in absolute terms. But the distinction does offer some guidance, as there might be said to be an element of it present in, say, the intuitive difference between taking water out of a wellspring people are using, potentially depriving them of its potability or stability, and being in control of a water treatment plant or system of regulation in a modern urban centre. And, moreover, however difficult it might appear to be to draw the distinction in some cases, when we contrast the two types of rights I set out—one involving truly direct threats to autonomy in the context of dependency, and the other requiring some dependency and interdependency for their very existence—the interpretive roles of autonomy and dependency in making sense of the difference in special protections commonly attached to the two sets begins to make at least some sense.

9

The Model of Rights in Practice

I. Six Cases: The Need for Principled Limitation of Scope

Extrapolating rights from the public sphere to the private one, I have argued, requires adopting a model of them that takes seriously their deep relational structure. Such a model will allow us to limit the circumstances in which we apply the special protections associated with public law rights. Consider, for illustration, six cases in which it has been argued that public law rights ought to apply to private actors.[1] In which of these ought a new private law right be recognized and enforced?

(1) (*Power Monopoly*) Catherine Jackson, a resident in the town of York, Pennsylvania, received service from the Metropolitan Edison Company, a privately owned and operated corporation, licensed by the Pennsylvania Public Utility commission.[2] Under the company's general tariff filed with the Commission, it had the right to discontinue service to any customer on reasonable notice of non-payment of bills. Ms Jackson became unable to pay her electricity bill. Representatives of the corporation visited her home to inquire about the meter, and several days later her service was discontinued with no further notice. She filed suit against Metropolitan under the Civil Rights Act,[3] seeking damages for the termination and an injunction requiring Metropolitan to continue providing power to her home until she had been afforded notice, a hearing, and an opportunity to pay any amounts found due. Metropolitan was a heavily regulated monopoly in the provision of power to the area. The Supreme Court found that there had been no state action, and dismissed Ms Jackson's claim. Ought a private, personal independence right be recognized here? And if so, to what?

(2) (*Hospital*) In Billings, Montana, James Michael and Gloria Jeane Taylor[4] went into hospital at St Vincent's, a denominational hospital formerly operated by the Sisters of Charity of Leavenworth, which also happened to be the only hospital in Billings to have a maternity ward and obstetric service. The couple

[1] Although each of the situations below actually occurred, I will reconstruct the facts of each in somewhat simplified terms for the sake of analytical clarity.

[2] *Jackson v. Metropolitan Edison Company* 419 US 345, 42 L. Ed. 2d. 477.

[3] *Civil Rights Act* of 1871, 42 USC §1983.

[4] *Taylor v. St Vincent's Hospital* 523 F 2d. 75 (1975).

were expecting their second child to be delivered by caesarean section and had elected to have a tubal ligation performed at the same time. They requested the procedure from the hospital and were denied. The Taylors brought suit against the hospital on the grounds that it had violated her right to privacy under substantive due process in the fourteenth amendment. The district court initially issued an injunction ordering the hospital to permit the procedure, but in the intervening period the Church Amendment (§ 401b) had been passed, permitting denominational hospitals to refuse to perform sterilizations. The court found that there was an insufficient connection between the hospital's monopoly status and the state to find 'state actions' or that that the hospital had acted 'under colour of law' (as the District Court judge had found). The appeal was therefore denied. Ought Ms Taylor's constitutional right to privacy, or her human right to personal security or to equal treatment be reconstructed and a private right recognized in this case? If so, what duties would it impose?

(3) The next case (*Transit Radio*)[5] involves passengers riding a municipal bus operated by a private transport company, Capital Transit, licensed by the District of Columbia. The company initiated a 'music as you ride' programme, under which radio programmes were received and amplified through loud speakers. Capital Transit granted Washington Transit Radio (hereafter 'Radio'), also a private corporation, the exclusive right to install, maintain, repair, and use radio reception equipment in Capital Transit's streetcars, buses, terminal facilities, waiting rooms, and division headquarters. Radio agreed to contract with a broadcasting station for programmes to be received during a minimum of eight hours every day except Sundays. Radio contracted with Station WWDC-FM to provide this service. Several passengers protested and took the case to the Court of Appeal, which remanded the case for further proceedings in conformity with its opinion which included the statement that 'In our opinion Transit's Broadcasts deprive objecting passengers of liberty without due process of law.' The Supreme Court reversed the Court of Appeal's denial of a rehearing, and found that no state action had occurred and thus that no public law rights had been violated. Leaving aside the state action doctrine itself, ought some *private* personal independence right be recognized in such a case?

(4) The next case (*Nursing Home*) involves a care facility, a nursing home, that decided to move a patient to a lower level of care, a decision that would reduce his well-being.[6] He sought either to prevent the facility from doing this, or, at least, to be involved in the decision-making process, to be given reasons by the doctor, as well as sufficient notice of the decision.

(5) The next case (*AIDS Drugs*) involves the more general circumstance of impoverished victims of AIDS, in which some have argued that the human right to health care imposes an obligation on the pharmaceutical companies

[5] *Public Utilities Commission v. Pollak* 702 S. Ct. 813.

[6] *Blum v. Yaretsky* 102 S. Ct. 2777 (1982).

who control the intellectual property rights to the drugs that would save or treat those patients, and thus who also control the licensing of their production and sale.[7]

(6) The last case has a more obviously international dimension, and involves a large multinational company—in this case Pepsi-Cola—operating a bottling plant in rural India (call this case *Pepsi*). The nearby village complained to local tribunals and courts because Pepsi was taking water from the local ground in such a way as to threaten the stability of the water supply in the village for drinking water in the longer term. The question in the case was whether its licence to draw water out of the ground was illegal because of the effects it was having on the local water supply. Some argued that Pepsi was violating the local residents' human rights to water.[8]

In Chapter 5, I argued that a successful model of public law rights would both explain the majority of those rights on which there is greatest convergence and also meet the challenge I called that of indeterminate applicability, namely, the capacity to delineate, in a principled manner and in advance of application, which private law relations will be subject to rights scrutiny and the imposition of new duties. In the previous chapter I addressed the first prong of these two requirements, arguing that dependency is the relational context both best suited to the model of rights from a moral standpoint and also, relatedly, the one that best explains and describes the practice of public law rights protection. Here I take up the second prong of the challenge: to demonstrate the capacity of the three-dimensional model to determine and limit the scope of circumstances in which new private personal independence rights will be recognized and duties imposed. I will illustrate this benefit of the model by illustrating the way the analysis it gives rise to would apply to the cases described above, and by arguing that this analysis is capable of limiting in a principled way the obligations that would be imposed in those situations in a way that a simpler power- or-vulnerability-based model is not.

[7] See, for example, Barbara Alexander Cochrane, 'Lack of Access to HIV/AIDS Drugs in Developing Countries: Is there a Violation of the International Human Rights to Health?', *Human Rights Brief* 8: 12; Joanne Csete, 'Several for the Price of One: Right to AIDS Treatment as Link to Other Human Rights', *Connecticut Journal of International Law* 17: 263; Marjorie Cohn, 'The World Trade Organization: Elevating Property Interests Above Human Rights', *Georgia Journal of International & Comparative Law* 29: 427.

[8] For some discussion of this topic, see, for example, Saby Ghoshray, 'Searching for Human Rights to Water Amidst Corporate Privatization in India: Hindustan Coca-Cola Pvt. Ltd. v. Perumatty Grama Panchayat', *Georgetown International Environmental Law Review* 19: 643; John Scalon, Angela Cassar, and Naomi Nemes, 'Water as a Human Right', *International Union for the Conservation of Nature Environmental Policy & Law Paper* 51 (2004); Stephen C. McCaffrey, 'A Human Right to Water: Domestic and International Implications', *Georgetown International Environmental Law Review* 5 (1992): 1; Peter H. Gleick, 'The Human Right to Water', *Water Policy* 1 (1998): 487.

II. The Merits of the Three-Dimensional Model of Rights: Limits on the Applicative Scope of Obligations

On the model I have developed, a new private claim in respect of a personal independence right would be recognized where a relation of dependency exists within the scope of an undertaking[9] of the more powerful party in respect of one of the set of rights interests. The relevant features of dependency in this model are as follows: first, dependency occurs where one party substantially controls the goods of another such that he or she can create a threat to that good; second, dependency occurs with respect to goods one is in some sense already enjoying; the role that dependency itself plays within what makes certain goods valuable, such as health care and education, means that dependency within an undertaking and dependency in respect of one of these goods is less morally objectionable than it would be in the case of goods not inherently involving dependency, such as personal security. This latter limitation means that substantive obligations on more powerful parties in a dependency relation can obtain where the good at stake is one that was not created by that party; where it was created, or substantially created, by the undertaking itself, then only procedural obligations in respect of it will apply.

The major alternative model to the one I have offered is something along the lines of the vulnerability-based account of social responsibility set out by Robert Goodin.[10] In brief, it asserts that where significant vulnerability exists between persons who are also in proximity to one another, then the special obligations to both protect and aid that we find in special relationships like those of parents and children will obtain. Scholars seeking to attribute responsibility for human rights violations to corporate actors have developed a similar model of responsibility in a number of ways.[11] These models focus more on power and influence and less on vulnerability,[12] but they similarly combine one of these features with proximity and actual infringement of certain interests to find rights violations.

[9] Stephen R. Perry, 'Protected Interests and Undertakings in the Law of Negligence' *The University of Toronto Law Journal* 42, no. 3 (Summer 1992): 247–317.

[10] Robert E. Goodin, *Protecting the Vulnerable*, (Chicago: University of Chicago Press, 1985).

[11] See, for example, Elizabeth Ashford, 'The Inadequacy of our Traditional Conception of the Duties Imposed by Human Rights', *Canadian Journal of Law and Jurisprudence* 19, no. 2. (2009): 217; Baez et al., 'Multinational Enterprises and Human Rights', *Yearbook of International Law* 8: 183; Adolfe A. Berle, 'Constitutional Limitations on Corporate Activity—Protection of Personal Rights from Invasion Through Economic Power', *University of Pennsylvania Law Review* 100, no. 7 (1952): 933; Jonathan Clough, 'Punishing the Parent: Corporate Criminal Complicity in Human Rights Abuses', *Brooklyn Journal of International Law* 33: 899; Abigail Gosselin, 'Global Poverty and Responsibility: Identifying the Duty-Bearers of Human Rights', *Human Rights Review* October–December (2006): 35; Ivar Kolstad, 'Human Rights and Assigned Duties: Implications for Corporations', *Human Rights Review* 10 (2009): 569–82.

[12] Steven R. Ratner, 'Corporations and Human Rights: A Theory of Legal Responsibility', *The Yale Law Journal* 111, no. 3: 443–545.

Such models sometimes refer to 'spheres of influence' of corporate actors,[13] which is a not too dissimilar approach from Goodin's, although such accounts tend to be less well developed from a moral standpoint than his.

Focusing on power, or on spheres of influence, like the focus on vulnerability, attempts to limit the possible obligations of more powerful actors to less powerful ones by reference to proximity. But these models are designed to expand, rather than to limit, responsibility, and they do so; they expand it, however, too far, and cannot limit potential obligations in a way that makes their application feasible and justifiable. This type of power/vulnerability + proximity model, as I will illustrate, would find obligations in respect of the rights asserted in virtually every one of the examples I set out above and will analyse below. It is difficult to imagine, in fact, assertions of rights violations of this kind that would *not* be caught by this type of theory, which makes these accounts fail the second condition of adequacy for a model of rights and obligations I set out, namely, that of indeterminate applicability.

The three-dimensional model of rights reconstructed from the public sphere, or personal independence rights, limits the kinds of possible application of the obligations they impose on private actors in two main ways. These limits reflect the morally salient aspects of dependency relations identified in the preceding section. The first limit simply manifests the way dependency relations are threatening to security in a way that relations characterized by normal private interactions characterized by interdependence are not: the special obligations associated with personal independence rights will be restricted to relational circumstances of interpersonal dependency within the scope of an undertaking of the more powerful party. The second limit on the application of obligations associated with personal independence rights in the private sphere reflects the distinction between threats to existing goods within dependency relations and threats to goods created by the more powerful or controlling party. The moral importance of stable expectations with respect to why interpersonal dependency is normatively important to rights means that the obligations this relational context can enhance are limited to those pertaining to goods the depending party already enjoys in some way. The role that dependency plays *within* certain goods, as I argued earlier, means that being dependent on others for them is less morally objectionable than dependency in respect of goods that were not created.

These two latter moral features of dependency mean that obligations in respect of new rights can be limited in two main ways through this analysis. The first is simply that, as I indicated above, these special protections can only apply to goods one is already enjoying in some way. The second is that differing types of obligations, procedural and substantive ones, respectively, reflecting differing degrees of protection, will apply to goods one has created or partly created and those one has not created.

[13] David Weissbrodt and Maria Kruger, 'Norms on the Responsibilities of Transnational Corporations and other Business Enterprises with Regard to Human Rights', *American Journal of International Law* 97 (2003).

There are two major ways of creating a dependency relation. Both involve the creation of risk to the enjoyment of goods: the first is the risk to existing goods; the second is the creation of a good that is itself one on which we depend in some vital way, and the operation of an undertaking on which individuals rely or depend for their enjoyment of that good. In the first case, substantive obligations can be imposed, prohibiting the controlling party from diminishing the depending party's enjoyment of the good. In the second case, the inherent dependency within the good itself means that we would not prohibit the controlling party from making a decision that would threaten or diminish the depending party's enjoyment of it, but, in order to protect the expectations and autonomy of the depending party, procedural obligations in respect of such decisions and actions to remove the good from the depending party could be imposed. These would correspond to the kinds of procedural obligations we impose on the state in its executive and administrative functions, namely, transparency, notice, hearing, and the giving of reasons.

The three-dimensional model of rights would therefore limit the wide array of possible obligations involved in reconstructed rights for the private sphere in two main ways: (1) such obligations would be limited to dependency relations; (2) within that class, we would distinguish existing from created goods. When enjoyment of existing goods occurs, substantive obligations can arise. When enjoyment of created goods occurs, procedural obligations can arise.

These two limits on the applicative scope of obligations inhere in the third element in our model of rights, namely, that of the relational context of interpersonal dependency. These limits mean that the three-dimensional model meets the two facets of the major problem characterizing the two-dimensional model of rights, consisting only of the elements of constraint and value but excluding that of relational context: that the interests protected by these rights could be described in terms of either negative or positive forms of interaction, and thus the conventional distinction between negative and positive rights is effectively lost.

In the *three*-dimensional model of rights I have described, the relational element of dependency does not exactly preserve the distinction between negative and positive forms of interaction—and the limitation to negative obligations in the private sphere—because sometimes individuals will be required, on this model, to limit their use of their resources, or even expend resources, in respect of someone's right. But the limiting features of dependency allow us to think of that distinction between negative and positive in a new way. Because of the importance of expectations to autonomous security, the element of dependency would limit obligations in respect of the rights interests to circumstances in which the good in question was already being enjoyed to some extent. This would mean that although sometimes individuals would have to expend resources in respect of another's right, someone would never be required simply to aid another person to achieve or enjoy some good that they did not already have or have good reason to expect to have access to. The three-dimensional model would only impose such obligations, rather, in circumstances where one party had *created* a dependency by creating a risk to some good already enjoyed.

So a person would not be required, on this account, to save a drowning child in a pond as a matter of the child's right. But, if the person had *developed and created* a pond, and had failed to take reasonable steps to protect children from falling into it, then, having created the risk through the undertaking, the person might be required to assist the child once the harm materialized. The analysis would also mean, for example, that a hospital would not be required, as a matter of its obligation to respect individual private rights, to admit and treat sick people at its doorstep. It would mean, though, that obligations would be imposed on it in respect of the rights of those it was already treating. But, because the good in question—the health care of the patient—is one that the hospital created or substantially contributed to, its obligations in respect of the right would be procedural rather than substantive. In other words, the hospital would have the freedom to choose to diminish a patient's level of care, but only where its actions in doing so respected the person's autonomy and dignity by following the procedural requirements of notice, hearing, transparency, and non-arbitrariness. These obligations would count, in a strict sense, as positive in form, because the hospital would be required to expend resources and accept costs to fulfil its procedural requirements to treat its patients with dignity in diminishing their enjoyment of a good. But on the basis of the limitations drawn by the three-dimensional model of rights, that positive obligation would not be endless; it would have delineable contours.

The role dependency plays in the nature of different types of goods, too, creates a further type of limitation on the scope of obligations the model would impose. Remember that I set out two broad types of goods in relation to dependency. The first includes those goods that are themselves so crucial to autonomy that dependency in respect of them is inherently problematic—these include the very personal goods such as free expression, thought, and conviction, as well as the personal material goods such as bodily integrity and physical liberty. The second type refers to goods which include some degree of relationality or dependency by their nature: health care and education are the clearest examples of these, but in a modern society one might say that in circumstances of rental housing, there is a degree of dependency inherent in that good as well. This distinction means, remember, that if a good that is the subject of a dependency has been created by the controlling party, then his or her obligations in respect of that good will be limited not only to the particular party that is depending, but also will be limited to procedural rather than substantive obligations. This latter limitation, in particular, is not designed to take account of the autonomy of the controlling party, but in fact it does that to some degree. In imposing only limited obligations on parties in respect of goods they have themselves created or significantly contributed to the creation of, we effectively grant them increased freedom in respect of goods they create. This, together with the effective limitation of obligations to relations of dependency that the controlling party has created either through the creation of risk or through the creation of one of the goods enumerated by the rights interests, on which, to varying degrees, people intrinsically depend, means that obligations are in fact linked to voluntary behaviour, so that the model has the effect of respecting the autonomy of potential rights respondents.

III. Illustrating the Applicative Implications of the Three-Dimensional Model

I will illustrate these various limiting implications of the three-dimensional model for obligations by returning to the cases that I outlined at the outset of this chapter, circumstances in which it has been alleged that private rights, or something like them, ought to be recognized in respect of some kind of public right. All of the cases are ones in which some have suggested that public law rights ought to be interpreted more broadly in order to recognize duties: in the cursory analysis that follows, though, I will argue that the application of the three-dimensional model of rights would impose obligations in only five of the cases, and, in several of them, only partial obligations.

The three-dimensional model of rights, it must first be pointed out, makes sense of all those circumstances in which a private actor violates the physical freedom and bodily integrity of another, so that situations in Nigeria, for example, that are the subject of some intensive theorizing about how to understand corporate responsibility for human rights violations,[14] would be dealt with relatively straightforwardly in terms of the analysis I have introduced. Where goods such as bodily integrity and physical liberty that are themselves crucial to autonomy are put at risk, and thus made subject to dependency, as they are in actions such as physical assault, executions, or torture, the controlling party is understood to have violated personal independence rights, and to have violated, in particular, substantive obligations not to diminish the enjoyment of those goods.

The cases that are more difficult to make sense of, as I suggested earlier, are ones in which the violation would not already count as such in existing private law if the parties were in a common jurisdiction where there were clear existing private law rules and enforcement—such as those in which the obligations that would be imposed if rights were recognized seem to be more conventionally positive in form. The six cases argued to be ones in which public law rights ought to apply that I outlined at the beginning of the chapter are all of this latter type. With the analytical tool of the three-dimensional relational structure in hand, we are now in a position to distinguish those cases in which a right ought to be recognized on a principled basis.

From the standpoint of a theory of responsibility that refers to power/vulnerability + proximity, the cases might look very similar to one another: all involve something like a 'positive' form of obligation; all involve a very large, in some cases multinational corporation, on one hand, and what appears to be a rather helpless

[14] See Adam McBeth, 'Crushed by an Anvil: A Case Study on Responsibility for Human Rights in the Extractive Sector', *Yale Human Rights & Development Law Journal* 11 (2008): 127.

individual on the other; all involve very important goods that clearly form part of the set of rights interests; and all could take place outside of any one jurisdiction. But that conclusion would have problematic implications for the scope of those new obligations. Why, for example, if each of the corporations owes obligations to the particular individual in these cases in respect of their rights, would they not also owe obligations to other individuals whose rights are at stake but with whom they are not in a specific relationship? Why would Pepsi-Cola not be obliged to clean the water in addition to not removing it all? Why would Pepsi not have to take some actions in respect of all the citizens near its Indian operations in respect of their human right to water? There may be answers to some of these questions in the various different existing mechanisms for applying public law rights to private actors, but if they cannot recognize the differences between the cases in addition to their similarities, then it seems unlikely that such mechanisms would be capable of answering all these further questions in a principled way.

The questions we will ask in each case to determine if a right ought to be recognized refer to the three elements of our model of rights. The first question is *whether the good in question is one of the rights interests*. The second is *whether there is a relation of significant dependency in respect of that good*. If both these questions are answered in the affirmative, a right of some kind is presumptively recognized. The third question concerns the type of constraint a possible right would impose; it asks *whether the good in question was substantially created by the controlling party* or whether the depending party was enjoying it prior to the dependency relation.

In the previous chapter I set out the two central features of interpersonal dependency—power, or the ability to actually affect the interests of another, and control, or governance over that power, and, consequently, over the ability of the other person to enjoy the good in question. In addition to illustrating the way in which the three-dimensional model of rights can operate to limit the obligations imposed by the new set of rights, the analysis of the cases will flesh out some important nuances of the second question—whether a significant relation of dependency exists in the context of the undertaking. In light of the major features of that relation, there are several important considerations for establishing dependency.

The first of these considerations is how much choice the depending party has in respect to the good in question. This is a function of at least two things: (1) to what extent can the depending party enjoy and make choices about the good in question in the *absence* of the undertaking, and (2) are there alternatives available to the depending party? If there is a direct threat to a good because of the undertaking, the answer to (2) is always no. If there are alternative avenues by means of which the less powerful party can enjoy the good in question, can the individual access the available alternatives?

The second major consideration in establishing a dependency relation involves the amount of control the independent or more powerful party has in respect of the good in question. Factors that affect this control will include (1) whether the independent party contributes to the unavailability of alternatives—such as in monopoly situations. If so, then she exerts maximal control over the dependency itself. Situations of risk to existing goods such as drinking water are the prime example of this level of stringency, as well as monopolies or holdings amounting to a vast market share making the resource effectively scarce.

If she does not contribute to the existence of the unavailability of alternatives, the next question is (2) whether her undertaking *benefits* from the unavailability of alternatives. A monopolistic business, for example or a small group of businesses each sharing a very large share of the market, has much greater discretion over price and other production processes than a small operation competing in a large market. If so, then there is an intermediary level of dependency, because the undertaking is itself partly a product of the dependency relation, and will therefore tend to promote and sustain that relation. The next factor contributing to control is: (3) can she make unilateral decisions in respect of the other party's enjoyment of the good?

In answering these questions, the general principle is that the less choice is available to the less powerful party with respect to the good in question, and the more the independent party is able to control that good and through it the other party's conduct, the greater the extent of the dependency.[15] This attribution of responsibility for rights to more powerful parties in a dependency relation obviously turns partly on the moral significance of agency and choice, as well as on that of vulnerability and need. The restriction of the analysis to an *undertaking* in which the parties are linked through the good in question serves to limit responsibility on the basis of action taken voluntarily by the more powerful party. But if voluntariness is morally important, we must also pay attention to that of the depending party. So one question to bear in mind in examining the cases below is how we should evaluate the voluntariness of the depending party *to* the dependency, and how that voluntariness, if any, contributes to our analysis? For the sake of clarity and simplicity, we can set out the analysis required by the three-dimensional model as follows:

When analysing a situation where A makes a right claim against B in respect of some good G where A asserts that B is infringing or has infringed her enjoyment of G, on the basis of the three-dimensional model, the following analysis will take place.

1 – is the good one of the Rights Interests? If yes, we assume that G has been deemed sufficiently important to everyone that it can be said that A depends in some sense on G itself.

2 – is there a relation of dependency between A and B in respect of G? If yes, then some right will be recognized to protect G, and a constraint of some kind will be imposed on B's actions.

- i) How much choice does A have over her enjoyment of G?
    - a. Does A have available alternatives to enjoy G?
    - b. Can she access them?

Negative answers to these questions will tend toward the recognition of a dependency relation.

[15] For some discussion of the way in which control over goods can amount to something like authority, see Hugh Collins, 'Ascription of Legal Responsibility to Groups in Complex Patterns of Economic Integration', *The Modern Law Review* 53, no. 6 (November 1990): 731–44.

ii) How much control does B have in respect of A's enjoyment of G?
  a. Does B create or contribute to the unavailability of alternatives?
  b. Does B's undertaking *benefit* from the unavailability of alternatives?
  c. Can B make unilateral decisions in respect of A's enjoyment of G?

Affirmative answers to these questions will tend toward the recognition of a dependency relation

3 – did B *create* G or, more specifically, A's enjoyment of G? If yes, then the constraint on B in respect of the right will be a procedural one; if no, then the constraint may be a substantive one.

With this analysis in hand, we can now turn to a more nuanced exploration of the six cases of private relations in which a violation of a public law right is alleged.

(1) Power Monopoly

Ms Jackson lost her electric power without notice or hearing. Is electric power one of the rights interests? Under the circumstances of modern social life, power is the only way to heat or cool one's home, often to cook one's food as well, to say nothing of its necessity to virtually all forms of communication. It is therefore relatively straightforward to conclude that electric power is a good recognized as having paramount value under the rights to life, personal integrity, subsistence, or welfare. Not all these rights are recognized in many constitutions, but the first two enjoy very wide convergence. We can therefore answer (1) by concluding that the good in question is one of the rights interests.

The more significant question here is whether a relation of dependency exists between Ms Jackson and Metropolitan Edison Corp. The court's rejection of Ms Jackson's claim was based on the state action doctrine, and its details are therefore not relevant here because the court was looking for a *formal* nexus between the state and the company such that the state could be said to actually have acted through the company. Both Ms Jackson's claim, however, and the dissenting opinion of Justice Douglas, emphasize not the formal features of the situation but the moral salience of certain of its relational features in respect of rights. Ms Jackson claimed, for example, that the corporation's monopoly status was highly relevant to the moral equities of the situation, and Justice Douglas's intuitions as expressed in his dissent seem to agree. The fact of the corporation's monopoly meant that Ms Jackson had little choice over her enjoyment of power, because there were no available alternatives to her. It might be said that a person in her situation could somehow purchase power from a different source, such generator power, or some other energy source, but her financial situation precluded those possibilities, thus answering question (2.i) in the negative.

How much control did Metropolitan Edison have over Ms Jackson's ability to access electric power? Here the corporation's monopoly status seems to determine the answer quite clearly. That status was state-created, and thus it does not seem that the company can be said to have created or contributed to the lack of alternatives; since the monopoly was state-conferred, the corporation was also subject to state restrictions above standard corporate regulations. It does not seem, then, either, that Metropolitan Edison necessarily *benefitted* from its monopoly status, since, presumably, it might have been subject to price controls imposed by the state. But it clearly *could* make unilateral decisions in respect of Ms Jackson's power supply, since it did so even in disregard of the requirements of its own public tariff. It seems, then, that there is a dependency relation here, and that the good involved is one susceptible to rights protection. Justice Douglas's intuitions pointed in the same direction: 'I agree', he said, 'that doctors, lawyers, and grocers are not transformed into state actors simply because they provide arguably essential goods and services.'[16] In other words, the essential quality of the interest at stake is necessary but *not sufficient* to recognize a right in respect of it. Justice Douglas goes on, though, to say that

> In the present case, however, respondent is not just one person among many; it is the only public utility furnishing electric power to the city. When power is denied, a householder, the home, under modern conditions, is likely to become unlivable.[17]

In other words, it is *both* the important value of the good in question *together* with the relational context at issue in which this Justice's intuitions lead him to recognize a rights violation, and his analysis is fundamentally in accord, therefore, with the composite model of rights I offer. He criticizes the court for rejecting the essential quality of the good and the importance of its monopoly status individually, arguing that 'its underlying analysis is fundamentally sequential rather than cumulative'.[18] In his moral estimation of the situation, 'it is the aggregate that is controlling'.[19]

Justice Brennan, in a separate dissenting opinion, agrees with the significance of both the importance of the good in question and of the relational context in which it was withdrawn. He argues that the possible benefit of allowing a diversity of corporations to create diverse sets of rules for themselves is 'simply not relevant when the private company is the only electric company in town',[20] and concludes that 'at a minimum, due process would require advance notice of a proposed termination with a clear indication that a responsible company officer can readily be contacted to consider any claim of error'.[21] It is, then, the unilateral and unrestricted quality of the company's ability to make decisions in respect of the individual's receipt of power that troubles both dissenting judges, and that supports the conclusion that a relation of dependency did in fact exist in the case.

So although a right would here be recognized, under the analysis I offer the third question would clearly be answered affirmatively: the corporation *did* create or substantially contribute to the good in question, and thus the form of the constraint imposed on it in respect of the right ought, as the claimant asserted and the dissenting judges agreed, to be procedural rather than substantive. So it

[16] *Jackson v. Metropolitan Edison,* para 361.
[17] *Jackson v. Metropolitan Edison*, para 361.
[18] *Jackson v. Metropolitan Edison*, para 363.
[19] *Jackson v. Metropolitan Edison*, para 360.
[20] *Jackson v. Metropolitan Edison*, para 373.
[21] *Jackson v. Metropolitan Edison*, para 374.

is not the case that the power company owes electricity to individuals, even given its monopoly status and the importance of the good. But if they *deny* service to individuals, they must do so in accordance with principles of due process. As Justice Brennan points out, this requirement could have wider implications in other cases: 'the majority's analysis', he suggests, 'would seemingly apply as well to a company that refused service to Negroes, welfare recipients, or any other group that the company preferred, for its own reasons, not to serve'.[22] This, he asserts is an untenable and perhaps even absurd result; his insight suggests that procedural norms imposed in respect of rights may seem minimal—and in most cases of this nature they will be—but they will also extend to cover cases in which the failure to act fairly in one's delivery of a good can attract penalties.

The importance of the limiting function of the three-dimensional model in a case like this might be obscured by its facts: Ms Jackson *was* already enjoying the good as a function of Metropolitan's undertaking when it revoked her enjoyment of it. In the absence of the dependency analysis of the kind I have developed, though, a court faced with such a circumstance might consider itself to be confronted by the question of whether or not the power company had a positive duty to Ms Jackson in some way: after all, although she was seeking only a procedural remedy, we might argue, that remedy would recognize what seems like a positive form of obligations—for Metropolitan to incur costs taking specific actions to provide Ms Jackson with power, even if only for a limited period of time. This might seem to a court as though it would recognize a more general positive right on a power company or on a monopolistic corporation of any kind, or on any corporation providing a necessary good. The limiting function of the three-dimensional model of rights distinguishes the position of Ms Jackson from others in the town or outside of it who might *not* be enjoying the good already: in other words, the right recognized by the three-dimensional model would *not* impose a more general positive obligation on the corporation to provide power to everyone within its purview, a conclusion that the court in such cases seems extremely wary of even indirectly approaching.

(2) Hospital

The case of Mrs Taylor and St Vincent's hospital is similar to the power case in that it seems likely to turn on the monopoly status of the corporation. The good in question, after all—access to contraceptives—is claimed, and accepted, to be that of privacy, but would also be protected by a human right to determine the size of one's family, and also by the more basic right to personal integrity. The question of the hospital's monopoly on obstetric and maternity services answers both parts of question (2), relating to the availability of alternatives and to control. The hospital might not contribute to the unavailability of alternatives, but it does likely benefit from that unavailability in two ways: first, its business interest is furthered

[22] *Jackson v. Metropolitan Edison*, para 374.

because it will be called on for service from any individual in the area who is in need of such care; second, because it does not have to compete with other hospitals for that service, it can pursue its own values—such as non-contraception—more freely than it might be able to otherwise, since it will not lose the business of its pregnant clients who wish sterilizations to other hospitals. It is therefore in a position to make unilateral decisions about Mrs Taylor's family planning.

So it seems that here, too, a personal independence right would be recognized. And, like the power case, the good in question is not one that Mrs Taylor could obtain on her own—it is a good that inherently involves relationality because it involves the care of a doctor. In that way, it seems that the hospital creates the good and need only observe certain procedures in rejecting patients' requests for tubal ligation, which it did in the case of Mrs Taylor. In this case, though, there is a difference from the previous one, which could suggest that in fact a substantive obligation to allow the service could obtain. In the power case, the decision to withdraw power was made by the same agent—the company—as the one who actually withdrew it. In the *Hospital* case, though, the corporation does not perform surgeries, doctors do. If the hospital owners wish to adhere to their religious tenets in the undertaking of providing health care, they may do so. But the same freedom of conscience protected by religious freedom ought to apply on behalf of doctors as well, particularly given that the hospital enjoys a monopoly status not only in respect of its patients but also in respect of the medical staff it employs. If no doctors were willing to perform a tubal ligation, then, the hospital would be within its rights to refuse as long as it did so in accordance with due process. If, however, a doctor at the hospital *did* want to agree to perform the procedure, then the hospital would be exercising a different form of restraint from that of failing to provide a service. Refusing to provide a service can be seen as simply the non-performance of a positive obligation; refusing to *allow* someone to take an action that he or she *wants* to take, and could otherwise take, especially if that refusal is contrary to the doctor's conscientious convictions, takes on the character of denying goods—liberty and freedom of religion and conscience—that it did *not* create.

(3) Radio Control

In the case of the passengers riding in the transit system, it seems clear enough that the good is one of the rights interests, since it affects liberty, privacy, and perhaps even freedom of expression, since that right is often analysed as involving the interests of the audience to be able to choose what they want to hear. The interest at stake here, involving as it does access to an audience that might have to listen to the broadcast every day for several hours a day, in a place that is for all intents and purposes a public space, also seems to involve the freedom, openness, and impartiality of public discourse that are necessary to participatory rights. The question (2) of whether a relation of dependency exists between transport passengers and the corporation is less clear-cut. On one hand, it seems true that the individuals at stake do not have available alternatives in the way of public transit, and thus that they have no choice over their enjoyment of privacy and freedom in that context. And, like the hospital and the power company, the monopolistic status of the transit company means that it does not create a relation of dependency but likely benefits from it, subject to state regulations. And the company can make decisions about what gets played in the transit system once it is established that having radio there at all will not constitute a public inconvenience.

But there does appear to be more choice on the part of individuals here than in the other cases so far canvassed. For one thing, it might be said that individuals could choose to use private transportation, such as car or bicycle, or carpooling, and thus that the dependency is not as severe as in the case of the power company or the hospital. Also, the passengers can be said to have nothing forcibly imposed on them, since they can always get off the bus if they do not like what they are hearing. Or passengers could perhaps be said to be able to simply choose not to listen, or not to pay attention. They will not, after all, suffer the kind of detriment from getting off the bus that they might in the case of the power company, for example. It seems, then, that there are some more available alternatives here than in the other cases, and therefore perhaps in principle the broadcasting of radio is inoffensive to the goods at stake because there is not a sufficient dependency relation between the parties.

But the choices available to the passengers are not as great as they might seem, particularly in relation to the interest at stake that relates to the formulation of opinions and views in the context of public discourse. After all, the problem with the broadcast of one-sided or otherwise biased information is that the passengers might not *know* that it is offensive to them until after they have already been forced to hear it. Furthermore, and more problematically, the good of a free and fair public discourse is not one that can be enjoyed exclusively by any one person: even if one woman chooses to get off a bus, or to put on her headphones, because she finds some misogynistic commentary offensive, she cannot bar other passengers from hearing the same material, and perhaps from being persuaded or influenced by it in a way that will affect her. The real dependency is in respect of the good, therefore, in the sense that while the individual may have an alternative to the transport company's service, she may not have the option of creating an expression of her own point of view in the context of that public discourse. The court found, in that case, that there was no rights violation because there was no state action; in his dissent, however, Justice Douglas seemed inclined to find state action because of his intuition about the power relation involved in the transport company's undertaking. He argued that although one must expect to forfeit some degree of privacy and choice over what to hear when in public, he also conceded that

> In one sense it can be said that those who ride the streetcars do so voluntarily. Yet in a practical sense they are forced to ride, since this mode of transportation is today essential for many thousands. Compulsion which comes from circumstances can be as real as compulsion which comes from a command. The streetcar audience is a captive audience. It is there as a matter of necessity, not of choice.[23]

[23] *Public Utilities Commission v. Pollak*, para 468.

So perhaps the availability of alternatives to individual passengers is illusory, and therefore a relation of dependency does exist in such a case. It is important to note here that although the good in question—freedom from invasive and partial discourse in a public place—takes place within the transit company's property and therefore would not in a strict sense exist without it, that is not a sufficient link to show that the transit company created the interest; plainly the goods of privacy, liberty, free public discourse—however one wants to frame the interest here—are not created by the transit corporation of the district of Columbia. If a right is to be recognized on the basis of the value of the good and the dependency relation involved in the case, it can be a substantive right, compelling the company to do something beyond simply notifying its passengers of its course of action and hearing their perspectives on the matter.

(4) Nursing Home

In the *Nursing Home* case, the good in question is that of health care, or, if the decision would clearly harm the patient, it might perhaps be framed as a violation of the right to personal security. If the decision to diminish care would actually threaten the patient's life, then the interest in life would be at stake. The interest in question is thus capable of being framed as one or more of the rights interests. If the patient is in a nursing home, then there is clearly some measure of dependency here, to the extent to which the patient cannot enjoy the good of the health care she is receiving at the existing level on her own. But this is partly because this interest is one in which dependency is inherent in the good itself. Caring for the sick is not something one can do for oneself.

But what about the choices available to the patient in this case? Surely there are other care homes available—this is not a case of monopoly. The patient entered the care home voluntarily, and the dependency therefore seems to be mitigated by some measure of choice on the part of the patient. If the patient has family or others to act on her behalf, then even if she is not capable of making those choices herself, she does have those alternatives available to her in principle and she could access them. What if those alternatives exist but she does not have family or anyone else to act on her behalf? What if she is, by the time of the transfer, not in a condition to research and contact other care homes? It is also possible that the home is the only one anywhere near to her family or relatives.

But here we might take into consideration the principle of 'last chance' from the doctrine of causation. Goodin refers to this principle in his analysis of cases of people who have become vulnerable either in whole or in part through acts of their own choice, or who are somehow otherwise complicit in the situation in which they find themselves.[24] After all, if a person cannot access alternatives to some good—electricity or health care—because they cannot afford it, surely

[24] See Goodin's discussion of comparative and contributory negligence in *Protecting the Vulnerable*, 128.

the cause of their not having that good cannot be exclusively some act or decision of the corporation. Clearly in many if not most of the circumstances I have described, and particularly in the ones that are more extreme and more likely to seem like rights violations, like beatings or terrible and humiliating treatment in factories and private care facilities, the *cause* of the person's condition is not uncomplicatedly the corporation's act. It is also the one that makes them choose to participate in the corporation's undertaking, and this brings into play social factors of inequality, poverty, and other forms of social dysfunction. The question is whether an individual can access alternatives to the good that is the subject of a dependency relation, and whether the independent party (B) has control over the vulnerable party's (A) enjoyment of that good.

The last chance principle of causation says that although there may be a long chain of causal factors that bring two people together in a particular way, or that makes someone vulnerable in a particular way, *including* acts taken by their own choice, once they are in that vulnerable position, then it is the act of the more powerful agent—the corporation contracting with the factory, or employing the nurse—who stands between the patient or employee and the bad treatment he or she receives. On this view of things, once the patient is in the care home, she may well be in a position of vulnerability and inability to choose that she would not have been in prior to entering the home. And while it may be true in a very abstract sense that the patient *could* in theory go elsewhere for care, and thus that the corporation's control is not so very great, the actual inability of the vulnerable party to act on those theoretical choices does benefit the home because they may make decisions that negatively impact the patient's care without losing her business.

But having concluded that a dependency relation does exist in the *Nursing Home* case, where the patient is sufficiently vulnerable for one reason or another, and thus that a personal independence right ought to be recognized there, to the extent that the patient was enjoying a particular level of care provided by the facility, it can be said to have created that good. So there is a right here, according to the model, but, because it is a created good, the home's obligation is not substantive but procedural. It *can*, therefore, move the patient to a different level of care, but the process of its decision-making will be supervised. It must provide the patient with notice and hearing, and must offer reasons that relate to a reasonable understanding of the nature of the good itself, so that, in the sense that it is thus predictable, it is not an arbitrary decision.

(5) AIDS Drugs

In the *AIDS Drugs* case, the good in question is clearly closely related to subsistence and survival, at least for the patients in question, and is thus even more obviously one of the rights interests. And there is a significant power imbalance between the patients and the corporations, one that even looks like dependency, since the fate of the patients in respect of the good in question depends on the decisions made by the corporations. But, in this case, the specific good in question—the AIDS drugs—is not one that predated the dependency relation. This means not only that the drug companies created the good entirely, but also that in fact there is no dependency relation here in the relevant sense. To see why this somewhat counter-intuitive conclusion is true, we only have to recall that dependency does not obtain simply in cases where someone is needy and another person is able to provide for that need (even at relatively little cost). If that were the case, then any very wealthy party, any state, ought to be held to have duties in respect of the AIDS patients' need. And while it certainly seems true that there are moral obligations on some of those parties to respond to the needs of those who are suffering and ill, there is no dependency between the needy and the powerful here. Dependency, remember, requires that the needy party is already enjoying the good or interest in question, so that that enjoyment is threatened by, or is under the control of, the undertaking of the more powerful party. *All* of the questions in the analysis based on the three-dimensional model of rights *begin* with the premise that the purported rights claimant is enjoying whatever good the right would be recognized to protect.

So, therefore, although there is a private right to life and to health care, in this case, unlike in the nursing home one, there is no such right, on the part of the AIDS patients, that would impose an obligation on the drug companies in respect of it.

This latter conclusion would seem undesirable to those human rights activists who try to argue for policy changes on the basis of the human rights of the patients and the responsibility of the corporations in respect of those rights. But, I want to suggest, rather than being a weakness of the three-dimensional account of rights I have introduced, such a limitation is in fact its greatest strength: as I have pointed out repeatedly, one of the major—and justifiable—objections to applying or reconstructing public law rights to the private sphere is that of what I have generally called indeterminate applicability, or, more specifically, overbreadth. The simple application of public law rights to private actors, without a further, more principled mechanism of limitation, would produce a raft of obligations on all private actors that seems highly counterintuitive. The model I have introduced, by contrast, limits both the existence and the form of obligations imposed on private actors in respect of rights interests, so that those obligations would not only be restricted in number and in scope, but, because the limitation is a principled one, would be predictable in advance.

(6) Pepsi

Consider one final example. In the *Pepsi* case, the relevant question is whether the three-dimensional model would recognize a personal independence right in the case, and, if so, what kind of obligation it would impose on Pepsi in respect of it. The good in question, the water, can only be one of the rights interests if its enjoyment is closely connected to subsistence. So not all citizens of India, for example, could claim this nexus of enjoyment and subsistence. But for those who depend on the resource in question for their drinking water, the answer to the first question appears to be yes. Pepsi-Cola created a risk to the residents' enjoyment of that good when they began to use their property in such a way that it became clear that they *could*, as matter of their power, sufficiently deplete the resource to threaten its future availability for the residents.

Now the question concerning dependency will turn on the choices available to the residents. If the effect of Pepsi's undertaking was only on one well, and there were others nearby, then there would clearly be available alternatives. If water was available for purchase locally, then *some* of the residents—those who could reasonably afford to buy it—would not be in a relation of dependency with the corporation in respect of the water. In this case, the corporation can control and limit the residents' enjoyment of potable drinking water not by making rules, or restricting service, as in the case of the hospital and the power corporation, but by the scale of their operation, their much greater resources, which give them property rights over the land, and their licence for the use of the water, which they can pursue and defend through extensive legal costs. So a right of some kind is presumed. Whether the corporation will have a substantive obligation imposed on it—not to remove the water at such a rate that the removal will threaten the viability of the resource—or a procedural one, will depend on whether the good and its enjoyment were created by the controlling party, the corporation, or not. In this case, although the corporation owns the land and rights to use the water, the residents enjoyed the good independently of Pepsi's undertaking; that enjoyment pre-dated the dependency that was threatened by it. The restriction could be a substantive one.

The various possible relationships in which the three-dimensional model will recognize personal independence rights and impose obligations are significantly limited, compared to the spectre of all private individuals owing duties in respect of all these rights interests. This means that the moral importance of the rights and freedoms of private individuals is taken account of in the three-dimensional model. For one thing, most private relationships are simply not classified as dependency relations, because these involve power balance but are not exclusively defined by it and include the factor of whether a good was pre-existing or created. So, for example, the various intuitive concerns we might have about owing our friends and neighbours obligations in respect of freedom of expression and racial equality will not materialize because these are simply not relations in which it can be reasonably be said that our friends depend on us to any significant degree for their enjoyment of those goods. If, on the other hand, the relations are not between individual neighbours but involve a large corporation which buys a significant portion of a region's property—especially including space that was once public and thus made free expression a good those residents already enjoyed—then, in taking on those properties it also creates a relation of dependency with the residents of the town in respect of their enjoyment of the good of free expression. We might, therefore, recognize that those residents have the right to free expression within that relationship, against the property-owning corporation, that they do not have against one another.

The analysis of the cases I have outlined here would allow us to assign obligations in this kind of case in which there is often a strong intuition about the moral equities of the situation. But it would also allow us to explain the intuitive distinction between, say, the employer of a factory worker in an export-processing zone, one in a 'company town' in northern Canada, and a small independently owned business with few employees. Similarly, we can explain the distinction between a media company like Clear Channel or Comcast,[25] which owns a significant majority of radio stations and media content, respectively, and one like a small, independently owned local newspaper, in respect of control over content and expression. In contrasting the various types of actors in these cases, the interest in question remains the same—employment and expression, respectively—and the vulnerability of the individual might also be the same. The salient difference is not simply that of the naked power of the larger corporation—that could give rise to a raft of duties to *many* other vulnerable parties in need of protection or aid—but that of a dependency relation within the context of the more powerful party's undertaking or course of action.

[25] See my discussion of these corporations in the Conclusion.

Conclusion: Implications for Private Law

The right way to conceptualize the relation between rights and duties is contentious in virtually every branch of thinking about, and of practising, rights protection. The extension of constitutional rights to private individuals in many jurisdictions causes manifold difficulties of implementation. The question of who ought to bear the duties associated with human rights is equally problematic. The complexity of the matter of rights and duties is at the heart of the challenge of implementing the normative mandate I set out in this work, namely, the protection of public law rights within the private sphere. The model of Rights I have developed is one that can offer a new piece of conceptual equipment, as it were, with which to tackle the problem of identifying rights and assigning duties.

In the context of the project of constructing new 'personal independence' rights for the private sphere, it is an innovation because it allows us to extrapolate a model of public law rights that is capable of accounting for the importance of the relationship between the right-holders and duty-bearers of those rights—the individual and the state—and of analysing that relationship as integral to those rights. This analysis of the deep structure of rights in general, and of public law rights in particular, is new, and offers not only a helpful analysis for the application of public law rights to private actors, but also a fresh take on the matter of rights and duties more generally. The analysis implies that interests will become rights and generate duties both where the interest itself is deemed sufficiently valuable and where there is a relation of dependency in respect of the interest-holder and some other agent: where that dependency relation is sufficiently substantial, such that the threat to or control over the interest in question is serious, the special protection associated with public law rights will arise in the form of a new, private law right. The duty associated with that right would follow the controlling party in the dependency relation.

As I indicated in the previous chapter, this analysis can make sense of private responsibility for human rights, while limiting that responsibility in a way that makes intuitive sense and does not open a floodgate of right and duty claims that would render the language of rights utterly meaningless. But, as I have insisted throughout this work, the rights that will be constructed to reflect the protection of human rights in the private sphere will be private rights: even if they are brought to a court of human rights, they will be specifically *private* human rights, with an analysis that is in at least some ways distinct from that of public human rights. I have not, so far, begun to elaborate the nature of these new rights in the context of private law. To fully elucidate the doctrinal implications of this study for tort, contract, and property would require another book. But it would also be inadequate to end this work without some further indication of the direction in which such a study would go, and a gesture at the concrete implications of new, extrapolatively reconstructed private law rights.

The analytical template I created through the extrapolative model of rights, remember, can be simplified as follows. A private right-claim can be made in respect of one of the core Rights Interests[1] where there is a substantial dependency relation in respect of the interest in question. So, if an employee is prevented from, say, using the bathroom on a long shift so that she is urinating into a plastic bag under her sewing machine, she can make a claim in respect of the right to physical integrity, privacy, and reasonable working conditions. The claim can only be made, however, against the actor upon whom she is dependent in respect of that interest, in this case the analysis would consider those imposing the strictures on her: candidate duty-bearers would include her immediate supervisor, the general manager of the plant, the owner of the contract working for the garment company, and the company itself. The party, among those candidates, with the greatest degree of actual control and latitude to pursue their own interests with respect to the worker would be the one upon whom the duty would be imposed. A simpler case involving, say, a tenant evicted summarily for late payment of rent, would identify a right by reference to the interest in housing (by itself or as an aspect of minimal subsistence) and to an identification of dependency in respect of that interest. The degree or severity of the dependency would affect the stringency that the duties imposed would attract.

The most important distinction in this reconstructed model of rights is between goods or interests that are the objects of dependency that were created or substantially created by the more powerful party (like the case of housing or the care in a nursing home), and those where the dependency involves only the more powerful party's risk or threat to the enjoyment of a good that is itself the object of a dependency (like water and food used for subsistence), where the good itself was not created by that party—even if the more powerful party has a proprietary interest in the good. In the case of created goods that are the object of a dependency, a rights claim can only be made for procedural limitations on the way in which the more powerful party can withdraw access to the good from the depending party. In the case of goods having inherent dependency not created by the more powerful party, a right-claim can be made to block the actions of the more powerful party more substantively.

[1] See Chapter 5.

I. Core Rights and Private Law

These new private law personal independence rights can affect all three of the main branches of private law. Since the model of rights is a relational one, one might be inclined to assume that contract, itself a relational form, would be the area of private law most appropriate for the imposition of new rights and duties. In the nursing home case, the duties imposed on the home in respect of the patient's right to health care—even if they are, as I indicated, procedural in nature—would be of two kinds. First, we could say that the owners of the home were being limited in the way they could exercise their proprietary rights, although, in this case, that analysis seems inapposite, since the physical care of another person is hardly the object of a proprietary interest. Second, and more fittingly, we could say that the home's freedom to create binding contractual relations is limited. The relation between the home and the patient, is, after all, a contractual arrangement for care. Presumably, then, the home can contractually impose limits on its obligations to care for the patient. If the patient suffers because of those limits, her recourse is limited under the contract. Since one branch of the new private rights I set out under the dependency analysis is a procedural one, involving requirements of transparency, notice, hearing, and reasons, it might seem that any imposition of new *procedural* duties would be imposed precisely because a contractual relationship already exists in virtue of which the more powerful party has created the good in question. This would be true of the nursing home case, the tenant case, and other cases, like private prisons or private water providers, where the corporate actor is providing a good because of a contractual relation. Addressing these considerations would require a much more intensive study of contractual rights, but here I will simply suggest that this somewhat intuitive inclination towards contract as the doctrine best suited to accept the new private personal independence rights is misguided.

Contract is a relational form, to be sure, but it is also almost entirely concerned with voluntary obligations. The kinds of rights we are concerned with, in implementing the normative mandate, are not ones that are created by acts of will. Insofar as contract is the law of voluntary obligations, then, new private law personal independence rights would not seem a natural fit. Now the enforcement of contracts is, in a sense, only the background of contract law—a substantial part of contract doctrine is concerned with when courts *won't* enforce the contract, or where it won't enforce it as written, but will read in certain terms interpretively to impose what are essentially involuntary obligations on the parties. Some doctrines, such as promissory estoppel, deal with obligations that are acquired in a less explicitly voluntary way. Others, such as those of unconscionability and public policy, are expressly concerned to refuse to enforce contracts where the obligations they purport to create are morally or socially problematic. So one can imagine that new private law rights could, for example, inform the interpretation of contractual terms, or inform the content of the vaguer notion of what constitutes conduct that is unconscionable or contrary to public interest. But in cases where a contract *was* the reason for a relationship and for the creation of a good, such as the care home or even a hospital case, the court (or a legislature) could only create procedural obligations by reading into contracts implied or standard terms in respect of private rights of personal independence. While this is a possibility, especially given some of the normative resources of contract—the doctrine of unconscionability and the emphasis on reliance interests in the case of promissory estoppel in particular—it fundamentally mischaracterizes the nature of the new private rights in question.

For one thing, situations in which a relation is created because of a contract—the operation of a water or mining company, for example—are not necessarily ones in which the relationship of dependency with respect to the interest in question will be a contractual one. In the *Pepsi* case, for instance, the corporation was certainly operating under a licence from the state, but the local population affected by the threat to the water resource was not a party to that relation. Contract law is largely defined by its restriction to the privity relation, and those most affected by powerful parties are very often those not in a position to contract with them directly. Even in cases of employment, such as those I described in the free trade zones, contractual relations are present all the way from the employee up to Gap or to Walmart, but Gap and Walmart structure their operations so as to deliberately avoid having direct contractual relations that would create ownership of and responsibility for the factories in which their garments are produced. The same way in which they avoid regulatory burdens, in other words, would create conceptual and practical problems for the imposition of new personal independence rights duties on these parties—who certainly qualify for them under the dependency analysis—through the doctrinal mechanisms of contract law.

Even aside from the privity problem, then, these are rights that people have regardless of whether anyone has voluntarily undertaken their corresponding obligations. The point of the reconstructed model is that they arise where one of the interests on which people inherently depend where those interests are substantially controlled by one party over another. If new personal independence rights are introduced, the major *effect* they will have would seem to be on property rights. If, for example, a Pepsi bottling plant in India is forced to limit its annual water use, for example, then its proprietary right to the land or the use of the water through licence is restricted.

In fact, because of the way in which private actions will in virtually every case be curtailed by the imposition of new duties, and particularly because of the way that private actors may be forced to expend resources or use their property in a way that they would not have chosen to do, *all* impositions of duties in respect of these new rights will impact property rights. In one way, then, the interaction and balance between human rights—especially new private ones—and property rights is perhaps the most important one, and thus also one that requires a much more intensive analysis than I can sketch here. In another way, though, even taking that importance into account, property doctrine itself is unlikely to be the direct recipient of new rights and duties because property rights are enforced partly through tort actions. This brings us, then, to tort as the area of private law that is best suited for the application of new duties in respect of private human rights.

Tort is the domain of law that creates involuntary obligations on private individuals, and is thus, simply for that reason, structurally well suited for the application of new personal independence rights.[2] It is also the branch of law through which property rights are often vindicated, and is for this reason also well suited for this kind of legal reform. New private rights can function as both sword and shield in tort, creating new causes of action for rights violation and new defences against existing tort actions where property rights are being vindicated. Moreover, there is an internal relationship between the relational model of rights extrapolated from public law ones and the primary structure of tort itself, which has developed to manage the increasing interdependencies of the modern social world, and especially to supervise the risks to crucial personal interests associated with those dependency relations.

It is clear enough how the doctrines of property and contract provide for the kind of stability of expectations Bentham was concerned about. The negative rights protected by tort law are basically similar to the ones enumerated against the state. Tort law supervises and scrutinizes the creation of risks. To create a risk is to create a dependency of some kind. A risk is a possibility that something, usually something negative or harmful, will happen—in the context of private law, risks involve the possibility of injury. Once a risk has been created, the good or interest that is at risk is effectively entrusted to the conduct and care of the agent who is carrying out the risky activity. If I create a construction project, there will be risks to those who live nearby, perhaps, of falling into a hole or of being injured by falling objects. Whether or not those injuries occur is, therefore, partly governed by how I conduct my work—whether I place barriers and scaffolding around dangerous areas, whether I hire competent tradespeople, whether I place signs warning passers-by of any possible remaining risks. In this sense, then, the interpersonal relation of dependency *is* the one scrutinized by tort law.

Private action attracts liability according to the two elements I originally set out as the basic components of dependency, namely those of power and choice: the first element, remember, refers to the *act* of 'carrying on' a course of action, while the second refers to a 'mode' or 'standard' that governs personal behaviour. The element of power, in this context, refers to the action itself, and its causal relation to possible injury. The second element refers to the capacity of the acting agent to control the action, to guide his or her conduct, in other words, in a way that governs its likely impact on others. So again we find reference to the twin ideas of action itself—or, in the case of dependency, to the actual impact the action has on another party—and of the governance of that action and its impact.

The notion of risk in private relations I have been describing, moreover, can be thought of in terms of the overlap of the importance of goods and control

[2] I have argued elsewhere that in its justification for the interests it selects to protect, tort must directly take account of the public provenance and normative status of public law rights: Jean Thomas, 'Which Interests Should Tort Protect?', *Buffalo Law Review* 61 (2013): 1.

over goods that I suggested lies at the heart of the most stringent rights. And indeed the special obligations associated with personal independence rights, imposed on both private individuals and on the part of the state, obtain where the good or interest in question is a particularly important one: in the case of private law, injuries to the person are the ones most widely protected. And in the case of public law rights, the ones protecting us against torture, death, and other violent exercises of power against our physical person are some of the most widely accepted.

II. Personal Independence Rights and Tort Rights—Interpretive Implications

Where new personal independence rights are introduced into private law, therefore, they will be most at home, and most effective, as introduced to, and developed in, the doctrine of tort. Introducing new rights into tort doctrine, though, immediately raises the question of the best interpretation of tort law. In tort, as in the areas of constitutional and human rights theory, the question of what tort rights *are*, and the concomitant questions of what tort is *for*, what the best interpretation of it is, are highly contentious. The theoretical or conceptual questions about rights, remember, bear directly on the way in which a theory—be it of constitutional, human, or tort rights—identifies and imposes duties. Where the rights in question are legal ones (even if they are also, in some sense, morally grounded), the coercive implications of identifying duties make what might otherwise seem an academic and abstract question—what is the right way to conceptualize rights and duties in, say, tort—into a very important practical one, both morally and legally.

So choosing an interpretation of tort law and tort rights on which to ground the introduction of new personal independence rights is a matter of some real importance. In what follows, I will argue that the extrapolative model of rights I have introduced bears directly on the interpretive question of what tort rights are, and suggest that this interpretive implication will, in turn, facilitate the structural assimilation of new private human rights into tort doctrine.

In introducing rights reconstructed according to our extrapolative model of public law rights into tort law, it might seem simplest, and thus most effective, to select the dominant interpretation of tort as it exists, and graft the model we have developed onto that interpretive model of tort rights. Now currently the most dominant theory of tort, at least in the United States, is a consequentialist or economic one. Simply accepting this theory of tort, therefore, proves problematic right away for applying its interpretive implications to our model of new private rights. The economic analysis, after all, does not prioritize the idea of tort law as a rights framework at all—rights can be determined, on this kind of view, by reference to best consequences, however identified. If our model were aligned with that view, then it might require that, in a given case where a dependency was present, the value represented by the interest at stake ought, presumptively, to be the one promoted in that particular case. But the kind of rights we extrapolated from public law—constitutional and human rights—are, whatever else we say about them, clearly not framed so that the duties they impose are to be determined by a utilitarian calculus of some kind. That is, after all, why they form a *rights* framework first and foremost. And this aspect of those rights is embodied in the element of constraint in our model that generates some presumptive priority *over* consequential considerations. So, on that score, the economic analysis of tort will prove problematic for the introduction of rights, unless we simply say that, as in constitutional law, the state—in the form of the court—can make utilitarian calculations that are limited or restricted by the new rights we are constructing. This approach would, in effect, make these new tort rights function under a different interpretation altogether from the tort framework. Since we are concerned to make the new private rights cognizable to existing doctrine, that is, structurally consonant with it, this way of setting out the interpretive theory of tort to work with seems problematic.

Of course, as it turns out, we do have another possible contender for the best interpretation of tort law, namely, some variant on the rights based or wrongs-based view, the most common of which are the ones grounded in corrective justice. The fact that we are interested in introducing a new rights framework that necessarily contains an element of constraint might seem to militate in favour of this kind of interpretation of tort law. There are two objections to this approach, however.

First, as I will illustrate in more detail below, the current rights based interpretation of tort—the corrective justice one—is, because it *is* corrective, limited in the kinds of interests it conventionally recognizes and protects. Because it is corrective, it can only protect rights that are thoroughly negative in structure; as we have seen, the inclusion of the element of value and the panoply of publically selected rights interests in our model of new private rights creates a problem for a theory of rights that can only impose duties for infringements of traditionally negative rights.

The other problem with this approach is more practical: while, within the most narrow confines of the debate about tort theory, the division between wrongs-based or corrective approaches and loss-based or economic ones is a live one, in legal practice the argument between the two approaches is much more murky, and also tends to be divided along the lines of jurisdiction rather than theory. So, for example, in the United States and a few other places, the economic approach has gained a significant judicial foothold, while in Canada and the United Kingdom a more loosely corrective approach is still more dominant.

By now it may have begun to become clear how the model of rights I have introduced will have more relevance in this debate within tort law about how to assign duties than simply the pragmatic point about effectiveness of implementation. On one hand, tort theory presents us with a view that views tort rights as being oriented to promoting some values—efficiency, deterrence, most common among them. On the other hand, we have tort theorists arguing against that view on the grounds that tort law protects rights, and thus ought not to be determined by reference to a consequential calculus. In other words, in trying to determine what the right relationship between rights and duties in tort law ought to be, tort theorists are divided primarily between a value-based view (albeit a consequential one) and a constraint-based one.[3] The apparent irreconcilability of the positions in this debate might make it seem as though a composite model of rights such as the one we have begun to develop in previous chapters is simply not going to work within tort doctrine. But in fact the reason for the debate between these two branches of tort theory is that neither one—perhaps unsurprisingly, given the results of our more wide-ranging exploration of rights debates in a variety of fields—can adequately explain long-standing tort doctrines that suggest that tort recognizes both rights and compensates for injuries.

On one hand, tort theorists have responded to the fact that tort law has become substantially taken up with automobile and industrial accident cases and cases of consumer injury. Viewed through this lens, tort seems to have become, or perhaps has always been, about how to deal with losses. In all these types of cases, after all, plaintiffs seek redress from the court because they are suffering a loss, and the question in such cases is whether the court ought to leave the loss where it lies or shift it to someone else. But, as corrective justice and other wrongs-based theorists of tort point out, all these theories that view tort as about allocating losses do not adequately explain some of the central doctrinal features of tort. For one thing, although make-whole monetary awards are the standard remedy in many tort cases, injunctive relief and punitive damages are also available remedies, both of which point to constraining the defendant's behaviour as one important tort function in those cases.

Also, many torts do not require proof of damage or loss to establish liability. Trespass, for example, is an offence for which a defendant can be held liable although her action caused no impact on the plaintiff's property whatsoever. Intentional torts, moreover, which are even more explicitly concerned with the defendant's fault, similarly require no proof of loss or damage to establish liability. The tort of battery can be established even for kicks or touches that are unwanted, regardless of whether they caused any material impact on the plaintiff. Finally, in order to establish liability—not all losses are shifted, even where they are foreseeable—the defendant's conduct must have been a wrong *to* the plaintiff; this gives the plaintiff standing to seek redress.[4] This requirement is often called the duty of care.

On the other hand, wrongs-based theories of tort also seem to fail to explain something essential about tort doctrine that points away from wrong and toward loss as its main function. If we see tort as being about wrongs, many argue, we would expect it to be about punishment. Now it is true that punitive damages are available as a tort remedy, but they certainly do not exhaust the scope of those remedies. Just as the allocative views fail to account for the diversity of tort redresses available, so do the wrongs-based views fail to account for the emphasis in tort doctrine on making the plaintiff whole rather than punishing the defendant. The wrong, in fact, if the defendant's conduct is viewed that way, is measured—especially in negligence and accident cases—by the magnitude of

[3] Goldberg and Zipursky outline the two major views of tort along these lines: see John C. P. Goldberg and Benjamin C. Zipursky, 'Torts as Wrongs', *Texas Law Review* 88, no. 5 (2010): 917–86.

[4] See Goldberg and Zipursky, 'Torts as Wrongs', 27.

the plaintiff's injury, rather than by the seriousness of the tortious conduct. Loss-based theorists of tort argue that where the state is in the business of preventing and punishing wrongdoing, it does so directly—as in the case of criminal law. If tort's concern were with wrongs, this argument suggests, it is not clear why the defendant's payment goes to the plaintiff rather than to the state, as it does in the case of crime.

It is easy to see, even for a non-specialist in tort, how one might respond to these kinds of arguments on both sides. And of course the availability, within tort doctrine, of examples to counter both sides of this debate about the best interpretation of legal rights in tort only serves to weaken the case of either side in the debate to exclusive accuracy. In moral theory, after all, when deontologists and consequentialists present one another with counterfactuals that undermine the principles at issue, those counterfactuals depend, for their persuasiveness, on agreement at the level of intuition—the way the counterfactual is framed, therefore, its context and details, can be very important and can make comparisons difficult.[5] But in the case of the dispute about the best theory of tort rights, the counterfactuals are neither reliant on intuitions nor dependent on the way they are constructed: they all form parts of a single body of doctrine—tort—which, at least to some extent, an adequate theory of that doctrine ought to be able to account for in some way.

And now we find another parallel between the disputes surrounding the best way to allocate duties in constitutional and human rights law and theory and the debate in tort theory about how duties ought to be imposed in that field. In both cases, the major camps are divided between constraint-based and value-based views, and in both cases the dispute is entrenched so deeply partly because there is a body of positive law that must reasonably be accounted for. In the case of tort this is the body of tort doctrine, in that of rights theory more generally it is the body of constitutional and human rights that I called our 'source set'. And just as the value- and constraint-based views fail to account fully for the range of rights in the source set in the context of public law, the wrong- and loss-based views fail to account fully for the range of doctrine in the case of tort. This parallel, then, points to the way in which the model of rights developed here militates in favour of an interpretive position about how to understand rights in tort law.

The composite model of rights so far developed would explain tort law's emphasis on remedial entitlement to compensation because of the normative dimension of value or interest: instead of simply asserting that the loss is merely 'included' in the wrong, or that compensation is tort law's way of 'undoing' the wrong, this view would explicitly assert that tort law has developed to protect a specific range of important human interests. It would interpret existing tort rights as representing the protection of those interests in the context of certain relational states (which resemble, though they need not be identical with, the dependency relation at work in personal independence rights) such as dependency in respect of a created risk.

[5] On the equivalence of hypotheticals, see F. M. Kamm, *Intricate Ethics: Rights, Responsibilities and Permissible Harm* (Oxford: Oxford University Press, 2007), 112.

This interpretation of tort law would be successful, first of all, simply as a way of accounting for existing tort doctrine: all tort rights represent a human interest protected against the conduct of others where those others create circumstances of risk and dependency, and where the injury occurs, thus creating a setback to the interest. The new, reconstructed rights would therefore simply represent an expansion of the range of interests tort law protects in respect of a particular relational context that is similar to the one already scrutinized by tort rights.

The intuition driving the normative mandate I have been working with is widespread. The contribution of this book has, I hope, been to introduce and defend an analytical framework for new private law rights reconstructed by extrapolating from public law ones. This contribution is relevant in the area of theory because of the introduction of the relational component to the model of rights. Many theorists of rights are specifically concerned about the relationship between right and duty because it seems that the moral problem of effective enforcement of public law rights depends upon that analysis. As Henry Shue says in 'Mediating Duties',

> The powerful international actors—like the major national governments, the large transnational firms, and crucial international organizations like the IMF—exercise the greatest nonnatural power on the planet. If these social forces cannot be subjected to moral constraint—that is, made to fulfill negative duties—our lives will be buffeted by unruly giants under no compulsion to pay most of humankind any heed. And if their gargantuan force cannot be at least in part harnessed for the solution of some of our species' worst problems—that is, made to implement some positive duties—the lost opportunity will be spectacular.[6]

The relational component of the model I propose addresses not only the challenges of institutional provenance and indeterminate applicability—of identifying which private actors can justifiably be held to account for their conduct infringing interests protected by constitutional and human rights. It also introduces one possible mechanism by which to make the step from the identification of important interests to the identification of duties imposed in respect of those interests. The dependency analysis I have introduced is in some ways simply a development of many of the intuitions of scholars and judges grappling with this difficult problem. As early as 1952, Adolf Berle identified a problem relating increasing corporate concentration to the vulnerability of individual rights against corporate actors:

> Apparently the community has wanted or needed the results of large organizations more than it feared [their] existence. It follows that the protection of the essential freedoms instinctive in Anglo-American law and in the American democracy involves the development of at least two bodies of law... The first is a requirement that the collectivized organisms essential to the economic life of the modern state shall be so handled that they can and do acceptably perform their functions of supply and growth. The second is that

[6] Adolf A. Berle, 'The Developing Law of Corporate Concentration', *The University of Chicago Law Review* 19, no. 4 (1952): 661; Adolf A. Berle, 'Constitutional Limitations on Corporate Activity—Protection of Personal Rights from Invasion Through Economic Power', *University of Pennsylvania Law Review* 100, no. 7 (1952): 933.

within them, and as an offset to their necessary organization and power, the basic rights of individuals shall be as scrupulously protected against them as they were against the erstwhile political state. Thus we are merely retracing in this field a legal history analogous to that of the taming of feudal institutions since Magna Carta, seven centuries ago.[7]

And in that same year, in one of the Supreme Court's state action cases in which the doctrine was developed to exclude private actors from any kind of rights scrutiny, *Public Utilities Commission of District of Columbia et al v. Pollak et al*,[8] Justice Douglas wrote a dissent protesting the failure to see the moral analogy between corporate conduct and its impact on individual rights and that of the state, even if the formal nexus is not proved. He made his case in terms that did not use the term dependency, but that seems to anticipate this kind of moral basis for the identification of duties. The case involved a challenge to a private transport company contracting for the city, running its bus service. The challenge was against the use of the transit passengers as an audience to broadcast messages of various kinds. Justice Douglas articulated his concern as follows:

The present case involves a form of coercion to make people listen. The listeners are of course in a public place; they are on streetcars travelling to and from home. In one sense it can be said that those who ride the streetcars do so voluntarily. Yet in a practical sense they are forced to ride, since this mode of transportation is today essential for many thousands. *Compulsion which comes from circumstances can be as real as compulsion which comes from a command.*

The streetcar audience is a captive audience. It is there as a matter of necessity, not of choice. One who is in a public vehicle may not of course complain of the noise of the crowd and the babble of tongues. One who enters any public place sacrifices some of his privacy. My protest is against the invasion of his privacy over and beyond the risks of travel.[9]

To close, I will simply offer one final example of the practical and moral significance of 'compulsion which comes from circumstances' through the operations of dependency. On the night of 18 January 2002, 911 operators serving Ward County, North Dakota began receiving panicked phone calls from the residents of Minot, the state's fourth largest city. 'I don't know what it is but there was a huge, huge crash', one caller explained. 'There's smoke everywhere outside.' A railway train carrying anhydrous ammonia for fertilizer had just derailed nearby. Its explosion released almost 250,000 gallons of the compound near one of the town's residential neighbourhoods. Electricity was down, and so residents who smelled fumes frantically tuned their battery-operated radios to KCJB AM 910, the designated local emergency broadcast station, for news. But, according to Eric Klinenberg,[10]

[7] Adolf A. Berle, 'Constitutional Limitations on Corporate Activity—Protection of Personal Rights from Invasion Through Economic Power', *University of Pennsylvania Law Review* 100, no. 7 (1952): 933; see also Adolf A. Berle, 'The Developing Law of Corporate Concentration', *The University of Chicago Law Review* 19, no. 4 (1952).

[8] 72 S. Ct. 813, emphasis added.

[9] 72 S. Ct. 813, 468.

[10] Eric Klinenberg, *Fighting for Air: the battle to control America's media*, 1st ed. (New York: Metropolitan Books, 2007).

KCJB, and every other radio station in town, were not reporting any news or information about the anhydrous spill... Instead, all six of Minot's name-brand stations—Z94, 97 Kicks, Mix 99.9, The Fox Classic Rock, 91 Country, and Cars Oldies Radio—continued playing a standard menu of canned music, served up by smooth-talking DJs trading in light banter and off-color jokes while the giant toxic cloud floated into town.

Clear Channel Communications, Klinenberg notes, owned all those licences; upon purchasing the signals in 2000, the company 'replaced locally produced news, music, and talk programs with pre-packaged content engineered in remote studios and transmitted to North Dakota through digital voice-tracking systems'.[11] The event in Minot has become infamous, and a lightning rod for free speech and media reform advocates. A man died because he was unaware of the toxicity in the air, though, and the case is thus also illustrative of the coercive and rights infringing potential in a circumstance such as that one.

Clear Channel has become a smaller media giant in the years since Minot, but others have risen to threaten various rights: Comcast, for example, the largest cable provider claims to reach approximately 110 million American viewers. It is trying to negotiate a deal to acquire NBC, including MSNBC, without being deemed a monopoly. If successful, it would control one in five television-viewing hours. FreePress.com says the following about the proposed merger:

Comcast already owns cable networks that would otherwise compete with NBC cable networks—after the merger, many popular channels on the cable menu would be controlled by one company and would no longer compete against one another for viewers. Instead, expect to see more re-purposed, re-packaged content on all Comcast-controlled channels, and less new original programming.[12]

The potential for infringements of individual rights to free expression and freedom of the press arise in this kind of circumstance, in addition to the threat to more fundamental interests in non-harm exemplified by the results of Clear Channel's control in the Minot incident. The Center for American Progress performed an empirical study of talk radio in the United States, and found that 'conservative talk radio undeniably dominates the format':

- Our analysis in the spring of 2007 of the 257 news/talk stations owned by the top five commercial station owners reveals that 91 percent of the total weekday talk radio programming is conservative, and 9 percent is progressive.
- Each weekday, 2,570 hours and 15 minutes of conservative talk are broadcast on these stations compared to 254 hours of progressive talk—10 times as much conservative talk as progressive talk.
- A separate analysis of all of the news/talk stations in the top 10 radio markets reveals that 76 percent of the programming in these markets is conservative

[11] Klinenberg, *Fighting for Air*.

[12] 'The Structural Imbalance of Political Talk Radio', A Joint Report by The Center for American Progress and Free Press, 21 June 2007, <http://cdn.americanprogress.org/wp-content/uploads/issues/2007/06/pdf/talk_radio.pdf>.

and 24 percent is progressive, although programming is more balanced in markets such as New York and Chicago.

This dynamic is repeated over and over again no matter how the data is analysed, whether one looks at the number of stations, number of hours, power of stations, or the number of programmes.[13]

The ideological orientation of the Center is made evident by its use of the term 'progressive' rather than, say, liberal, but nonetheless, its evidence does show that there is a significant imbalance in the political climate in American talk-radio. Comcast, for its part, has launched its own content platform, which it calls 'Right Network'. This is obviously a right-wing operation, ideologically speaking: in addition to its ubiquitous use of the term 'right' in its publications, it describes its television content as follows:

> the lineup focuses on entertainment with pro-[A]merica, pro-business, pro-military sensibilities—compelling content that inspires action, invites a response, and influences the national conversation.[14]

Many people are concerned about the concentration of media power, and many liberals are concerned about the ideological domination of the airwaves. On an interest-based, power-based, or vulnerability-based view, one might conclude that Comcast, for example, ought to owe duties in respect of individual rights to free expression, and these duties might follow Comcast wherever it goes, so to speak—even in those markets where it is not dominant, or where other stations have an impact on the broadcast market. Its power and dominance could even be argued to warrant the imposition of some positive obligations in respect of these rights. On my account, though, personal independence rights to freedoms such as expression and conviction could be recognized against a corporation such as Comcast in those limited circumstances where the corporation is clearly in a relation of significant dependency with individuals. There will always be difficult cases, even following the analysis I have developed; but a case such as the one that occurred in Minot, North Dakota, would not be so difficult, and would recognize rights not only to non-harm but to freedom of expression, political participation, and conviction on behalf of those residents, so that their public law rights to those goods could be rendered truly effective and meaningful.

[13] 'The Structural Imbalance of Political Talk Radio',1.

[14] 'Company Overview', RIGHTNETWORK: All That's Right With the World, 8.

Bibliography

Adler, Matthew D. 'Rights against Rules: The Moral Structure of American Constitutional Law'. *Michigan Law Review* 97, no. 1 (1998): 39.

Adler, Matthew D. 'Personal Rights and Rule-Dependence: Can the Two Coexist?' *Legal Theory* 6 (2000): 337–89.

Alexander, Barbara Cochrane. 'Lack of Access to HIV/AIDS Drugs in Developing Countries: Is there a Violation of the International Human Rights to Health?' *Human Rights Brief* 8 (2001): 12.

Alston, Philip, ed. *Non-State Actors and Human Rights*. Oxford: Oxford University Press, 2005.

Alston, Philip, and Katarina Tomasevski. *The Right to Food*. International Studies in Human Rights. Netherlands: Martinus Nijhoff Publishers, 1984.

Andre, Judith. 'The Equal Moral Weight of Self- and Other-Regarding Acts'. *Canadian Journal of Philosophy* 17 (March 1987): 155–65.

Arneson, Richard J. 'Consequentialism vs. Special-Ties Partiality'. *Monist: An International Quarterly Journal of General Philosophical Inquiry* 86, no. 3 (July 2003): 382–401.

Ashford, Elizabeth. 'The Inadequacy of our Traditional Conception of the Duties Imposed by Human Rights'. *Canadian Journal of Law and Jurisprudence* 19, no. 2. (2009): 217.

Bader, Veit. 'Reasonable Impartiality and Priority for Compatriots. A Criticism of Liberal Nationalism's Main Flaws'. *Ethical Theory and Moral Practice* 8 (2005): 83–103.

Baez, Cristina, Michele Dearing, Margaret Delatour, and Christine Dixon. 'Multinational Enterprises and Human Rights'. *Yearbook of International Law* 8 (2000): 183.

Baier, Annette. 'The Rights of Past and Future Persons'. In Ernest Partridge, ed., *Responsibilities to future generations: Environmental Ethics*. New York: Prometheus Books, 1981, 171–83.

Bantekas, Ilias. 'Corporate Social Responsibility in International Law'. *Boston University International Law Journal* 22, no. 2 (2004): 309–47.

Baron, Marcia. 'Impartiality and Friendship'. *Ethics*. 101, no. 4 (July 1991): 836–57.

Beitz, Charles R. *The Idea of Human Rights*. Oxford: Oxford University Press, 2009.

Belobaba, Edward P. 'The Charter of Rights and Private Litigation: the Dilemma of Dolphin Delivery'. In N. R. Finkelstein and B. M. Rogers, eds, *Charter Issues in Civil Cases*. Toronto: Carswell, 1988.

Bentham, Jeremy. 'Principles of the Civil Code'. In John Bowring, ed., *The works of Jeremy Bentham*. Edinburgh: W. Tait Publishing, 1843.

Berle, Adolf A. 'Constitutional Limitations on Corporate Activity—Protection of Personal Rights from Invasion Through Economic Power'. *University of Pennsylvania Law Review* 100, no. 7 (1952): 933.

Berle, Adolf A. 'The Developing Law of Corporate Concentration'. *The University of Chicago Law Review* 19, no. 4 (1952).

Besson, Samantha. 'Human Rights, Institutional Duties and Cosmopolitan Responsibilities'. *Oxford Journal of Legal Studies* 23, no. 3 (2003): 507–23.

Blanco, Veronica Rodriguez. 'The Methodological Problem in Legal Theory: Normative and Descriptive Jurisprudence Revisited'. 19 *Ratio Juris* (2006): 26–54.

Brink, David O. 'Impartiality and Associative Duties'. *Utilitas: A Journal of Utilitarian Studies* 13, no. 2 (July 2001): 152–72.

Brock, Gillian G. 'Does Obligation Diminish with Distance?' *Ethics* 8, no. 1 (March 2005): 3–20.

Center for American Progress and Free Press, 'The Structural Imbalance of Political Talk Radio', 21 June 2007. <http://cdn.americanprogress.org/wp-content/uploads/issues/2007/06/pdf/talk_radio.pdf>.

Center for Human Rights and Global Justice, Human Rights First and Human Rights Watch. 'By the Numbers: Findings of the Detainee Abuse and Accountability Project', vol. 18, no. 2 (G), April 2006 <http://hrw.org/reports/2006/ct0406/>, 6, 19–20>.

Chatterjee, Deen K. 'Moral Distance: Introduction'. *Monist: An International Quarterly Journal of General Philosophical Inquiry* 86, no. 3 (July 2003): 327–32.

Chemerinsky, Erwin. 'Rethinking State Action'. *Northwestern University Law Review* 80, no. 3: 503–57.

Christoffersen, Jonas. 'Denmark: Drittwirkung and Conflicting Rights—Viewed from National and International Perspectives'. In Dawn Oliver and Jorg Fedtke, eds, *Human Rights and the Private Sphere: A Comparative Study*. New York: Routledge-Cavendish, 2007.

Clapham, Andrew. *Human Rights Obligations of Non-state Actors*. Oxford: Oxford University Press, 2006.

Clough, Jonathan. 'Punishing the Parent: Corporate Criminal Complicity in Human Rights Abuses'. *Brooklyn Journal of International Law* 33 (2008): 899.

Cohen, Joshua. 'Minimalism About Human Rights: The Most We Can Hope For?' *The Journal of Political Philosophy* 12 (2004): 190–213.

Cohn, Marjorie. 'The World Trade Organization: Elevating Property Interests Above Human Rights'. *Georgia Journal of International & Comparative Law* 29 (2001): 427.

Collingsworth, Terry. '"Corporate Social Responsibility," Unmasked'. *St Thomas Law Review* 16 (2004): 669.

Collins, Hugh. 'Ascription of Legal Responsibility to Groups in Complex Patterns of Economic Integration'. *The Modern Law Review* 53, no. 6 (November 1990): 731–44.

Collins, Hugh. 'Utility and Rights in Common Law Reasoning: Rebalancing Private Law Through Constitutionalization'. *LSE Law, Society and Economy Working Papers* (June 2007).

Csete, Joanne. 'Several for the Price of One: Right to AIDS Treatment as Link to Other Human Rights'. *Connecticut Journal of International Law* 17 (2002): 263.

Cullity, Garrett. 'Asking Too Much'. *The Monist* 86, no. 3 (2003): 402–18.

Darwall, Stephen. *The Second-Person Standpoint: Morality, Respect, and Accountability*. London: Harvard University Press, 2006.

Davidson, Donald. *Inquiries into Truth and Interpretation*. Oxford: Clarendon Press, 1984.

De Feyter, Koen. *Privatisation and Human Rights in the Age of Globalization*. Oxford: Intersentia, 2005.

Dickens, Charles. *Bleak House*. London: Chelsea House Publishers, 1987.

Dicey, Albert Venn. *Introduction to the Study of the Law of the Constitution*. New York: Macmillan and Co Ltd, 1897.

Donaldson, Thomas. 'Morally Privileged Relationships'. *Journal of Value Inquiry* 24, no. 1 (1990): 1–15.

Dworkin, Ronald. 'Rights as Trumps'. In *Theories of Rights*. Oxford: Oxford University Press, 1984.

Dworkin, Ronald. *Taking Rights Seriously*. Cambridge: Cambridge University Press, 1977.

Fedtke, Jorg. 'South Africa: From Indirect to Direct Effect in South Africa—A System in Transition'. In Dawn Oliver and Jorg Fedtke, eds, *Human Rights and the Private Sphere: A Comparative Study*. New York: Routledge-Cavendish, 2007.

Feinberg, Joel. 'Duties, Rights and Claims'. *American Philosophical Quarterly* 3, (1966): 137–44.

Feinberg, Joel. *Social Philosophy*. Englewood Cliffs: Prentice-Hall, Inc, 1973, 55–97.

Friedman, Marilyn A. 'The Practice of Partiality'. *Ethics* 101, no. 4 (July 1991): 818–35.

Friedmann, Daniel, and Daphne Barak-Erez, eds. *Human Rights in Private Law*. Portland, Oregon: Hart Publishing, 2001.

Fuller, Lon L. *The Morality of Law*. Rev. ed. New Haven: Yale University Press, 1969.

Gardbaum, Stephen. 'The "Horizontal Effect" of Constitutional Rights'. *Michigan Law Review* 102 (2003): 388.

Ghoshray, Saby. 'Searching for Human Rights to Water Amidst Corporate Privatization in India: Hindustan Coca-Cola Pvt Ltd v. Perumatty Grama Panchayat'. *Georgetown International Environmental Law Review* 19 (2007): 643.

Gibney, Mark, and R. David Emerick. 'The Extraterritorial Application of United States Law and the Protection of Human Rights: Holding Multinational Corporations to Domestic and International Standards'. *Temple International & Comparative Law Journal* 10 (1996): 123.

Gleick, Peter H. 'The Human Right to Water'. *Water Policy* 1 (1998): 487.

Glendon, Mary Ann. 'Knowing the Universal Declaration of Human Rights'. *The Notre Dame Law Review* 73 (1998): 1153.

Glendon, Mary Ann. *A World Made New: Eleonor Roosevelt and the Universal Declaration of Human Rights*. New York: Random House, 2001.

Glendon, Mary Ann, and E. Abrams. 'Reflections on the UDHR'. *First Things* (1998): 18.

'Global Compact Sustainability Report 2013' at <http://www.unglobalcompact.org/docs/about_the_gc/Global_Corporate_Sustainability_Report2013.pdf>.

'Global Compact' brochure and explanatory publications at <http://www.unglobalcompact.org/docs/news_events/8.1/GC_brochure_FINAL.pdf>, <http://www.unglobalcompact.org/docs/news_events/8.1/after_the_signature.pdf>,

'Global Compact' 2011 implementation survey at <http://www.unglobalcompact.org/docs/news_events/8.1/2011_Global_Compact_Implementation_Survey.pdf>.

Goldberg, John C. P., and Benjamin C. Zipursky. 'Torts as Wrongs'. *Texas Law Review* 88, no. 5 (2010): 917–86.

Goodin, Robert E. *Protecting the Vulnerable: A Reanalysis of our Social Responsibilities*. Chicago: University of Chicago Press, 1985.

Gosselin, Abigail. 'Global Poverty and Responsibility: Identifying the Duty-Bearers of Human Rights'. *Human Rights Review* October–December (2006): 35–52.

Gregor, Mary. 'Kant's Theory of Property'. *Review of Metaphysics* 41, no. 4 (1988): 757.

Griffin, James. *On Human Rights*, Oxford: Oxford University Press, 2008.

Hathaway, Oona A. 'Do Human Rights Treaties Make a Difference?'. *The Yale Law Journal* 111 (2002): 1870.

Hathaway, Oona A. 'Making Human Rights Treaties Work: Global Legal Information & Human Rights in the 21st Century'. *International Journal of Legal Information* 31 (2003): 312.

Hathaway, Oona A. 'Why Do Countries Commit to Human Rights Treaties?' *The Journal of Conflict Resolution* 51 (2007): 588–621.

Hart, H. L. A. *The Concept of Law*. Oxford: Clarendon Press, 1975.

Hart, H. L. A. *Essays on Bentham*. Oxford: Oxford University Press, 1982.

Hirshberg, Gur. 'Situating Friendship: An Aristotelian Treatment of Personal Relations and Moral Choice'. *Philosophical Writings* 10 (1999): 23–36.

Hobbes, Thomas, and Edwin Curley, ed. *Leviathan*. Indianapolis: Hackett Publishing Company, Inc, 1994.

Hohfeld, Wesley Newcomb. *Fundamental Legal Conceptions as Applied in Judicial Reasoning*. Westport, Connecticut: Greenwood Press, 1978.

Holmes, Stephen. *The Cost of Rights: Why Liberty Depends on Taxes*. 1st ed. New York: W. W. Norton, 1999.

Human Rights Council of the United Nations. 2011 report. Seventeenth Session, 21 March 2011, A/HRC/17/31 <http://www.business-humanrights.org/media/documents/ruggie/ruggie-guiding-principles-21-mar-2011.pdf>.

Human Rights Watch. 'The Price of Oil'. HRW Index No. 1-56432-225-4, January 1999, 7, 53–74.

Human Rights Watch. 'Fingers to the Bone: United States Failure to Protect Child Farmworkers'. New York: Human Rights Watch, 2000, 52 <http://www.hrw.org/reports/2000/frmwrkr/>.

Human Rights Watch. 'Underage and Unprotected: Child Labor in Egypt's Cotton Fields', vol. 13, no. 1 (E), January 2001, 14–15 <http://www.hrw.org/reports/2001/egypt>.

Human Rights Watch. 'Hidden in the Home: Abuse of Domestic Workers with Special Visas in the United States'. vol. 13, no. 2 (G), June 2001, 12–15 <http://www.hrw.org/reports/2001/usadom/usadom0501.pdf>.

Human Rights Watch. 'Without Remedy'. vol. 15, no. 1 (C), January 2003, 33–46. <http://www.hrw.org/reports/2003/01/06/without-remedy>.

Human Rights Watch. 'Bad Dreams'. vol. 16, no. 5 (E), July 2004, 48–53, 58, 62, 76, 78 <http://www.hrw.org/sites/default/files/reports/saudi0704.pdf>.

Human Rights Watch. 'Help Wanted'. vol. 16, no. 9 (B), July 2004, 5, 26, 32–3, 40–2 http://www.hrw.org/sites/default/files/reports/indonesia0704full.pdf>.

Human Rights Watch. 'Maid to Order: Ending Abuses against Migrant Domestic Workers in Singapore'. vol. 17, no. 10 (C), December 2005, 42–8 <http://www.hrw.org/reports/2005/singapore1205/singapore1205web.pdf>.

Human Rights Watch. 'Swept Under the Rug'. vol. 18, no. 7 (C), July 2006, 73–6. <http://www.hrw.org/sites/default/files/reports/wrd0706webwcover.pdf>

Human Rights Watch. 'A High Price to Pay: Detention of Poor Patients in Burundian Hospitals', vol. 18, no. 8 (A), September 2006, 31–4 <http://hrw.org/reports/2006/burundi0906/burundi0906webwcover.pdf>.

Human Rights Watch. 'Building Towers, Cheating Workers'. vol. 18, no. 8 (E), November 2006, 38–9 <http://www.hrw.org/sites/default/files/reports/uae1106webwcover.pdf>.

Human Rights Watch.'Small Change: Bonded Child Labor in India's Silk Industry', vol. 15, no. 2 (C), January 2003, 27–8, 34–5 <http://www.hrw.org/reports/2003/india/>.

Human Rights Watch. 'The Enron Corporation', January 1999 45–6. <http://www.hrw.org/reports/1999/enron/>.

Human Rights Watch Children's Rights Project and Human Rights Watch/Asia. 'The Small Hands of Slavery: Bonded Child Labor in India'. New York: Human Rights Watch, 1996, 28–9 <http://hrw.org/reports/1996/India3.htm>.

Hume, David. *A Treatise of Human Nature.* Edited by L. A. Selby-Bigge, 2nd ed. Oxford: Clarendon, 1978.

Hunter-Henin, Myriam. 'France: Horizontal Application and the Triumph of the European Convention on Human Rights'. In Dawn Oliver and Jorg Fedtke, eds, *Human Rights and the Private Sphere: A Comparative Study.* New York: Routledge-Cavendish, 2007.

Igneski, Violetta. 'Distance, Determinacy and the Duty to Aid: A Reply to Kamm'. *Law and Philosophy* 20, no. 6 (November 2001): 605–16.

Jeske, Diane. 'Friendship, Virtue, and Impartiality'. *Philosophy and Phenomenological Research* 57, no. 1 (March 1997): 51–72.

Jeske, Diane. 'Special Relationships and the Problem of Political Obligations'. *Social Theory and Practice* 27, no. 1 (January 2001): 19.

Kagan, Shelley. *Normative Ethics.* Colorado: Westview Press, 1998.

Kamm, F. M. 'Does Distance Matter Morally to the Duty to Rescue?' *Law and Philosophy* 19, no. 6 (November 2000): 655–81.

Kamm, F. M. *Intricate Ethics: Rights, Responsibilities and Permissible Harm.* Oxford: Oxford University Press, 2007.

Kant, Immanuel. *The Metaphysics of Morals.* Mary Gregor, ed. Cambridge: Cambridge University Press, 1996.

Keller, Simon. 'Four Theories of Filial Duty'. In *The Philosophical Quarterly* 56 (2006): 254.

Klein, Naomi. *No Logo.* New York: Picador, 2000.

Klinenberg, Eric. *Fighting for Air: the Battle to Control America's Media.* 1st ed. New York: Metropolitan Books, 2007.

Kolodny, Niko. 'Which Relationships Justify Partiality: The Case of Parents and Children'. *Philosophy and Public Affairs* 38 (2010): 37.

Kolstad, Ivar. 'Human Rights and Assigned Duties: Implications for Corporations'. *Human Rights Review* 10 (2009): 569–82.

Kommers, Donald P. *The Constitutional Jurisprudence of the Federal Republic of Germany.* 3rd ed. Durham: Duke University Press, 2012.

Korsgaard, Christine. 'Creating the Kingdom of Ends: Reciprocity and Responsibility in Personal Relations'. *Philosophical Perspectives* 6 (1992): 305–32.

Korsgaard, Christine. 'The Reasons We Can Share: An Attack on the Distinction between Agent-Relative and Agent-Neutral Values'. *Social Philosophy and Policy* 10, no. 1 (1993): 24–51.

Kramer, Matthew H. 'Rights Without Trimmings'. In *A Debate Over Rights: Philosophical Enquiries.* Oxford: Clarendon Press, 1999.

Kramer, Matthew H., and Hillel Steiner, 'Theories of Rights: Is There a Third Way?' *Oxford Journal of Legal Studies* 27 (2007): 281–310

Kumm, Mattias. 'Who is Afraid of the Total Constitution? Constitutional Rights as Principles and the Constitutionalization of Private Law'. *German Law Journal* 7, no. 4 (2006): 341.

Kuper, Andrew, ed. *Global Responsibilities: Who Must Deliver On Human Rights?* New York: Routledge, 2005.

Lee, Youngjae. 'International Consensus as Persuasive Authority in the Eighth Amendment'. *University of Pennsylvania Law Review* 156 (2007): 67.

Lewan, Kenneth M. 'The Significance of Constitutional Rights for Private Law: Theory and Practice in West Germany'. 17 *International & Comparative Law Quarterly.* (1968): 571.

Locke, John. *Second Treatise of Government (1690).* Edited by C. B. Macpherson. Indianapolis: Hackett Publishing Company, Inc, 1980.

MacCormick, D. N. 'Rights in Legislation'. In P. M. S. Hacker and J. Raz, eds, *Law, Morality and Society: Essays in Honour of H. L. A. Hart.* Oxford: Oxford University Press, 1977.

McBeth, Adam. 'Crushed by an Anvil: A Case Study on Responsibility for Human Rights in the Extractive Sector'. *Yale Human Rights & Development Law Journal* 11 (2008): 127.

McCaffrey, Stephen C. 'A Human Right to Water: Domestic and International Implications'. *Georgetown International Environmental Law Review* 5 (1992): 1.

McCrudden, Christopher. 'A Common Law of Human Rights?: Transnational Judicial Conversations on Constitutional Rights'. *Oxford Journal of Legal Studies* 20 (2000): 499.

McMahon, Bryan, and William Binchy. *Law of Torts.* 3rd ed. Dublin: Butterworths, 2000.

Mill, John Stuart. *Utilitarianism.* Edited by Colin Heydt. Peterborough, Ontario: Broadview Press, 2011.

Miller, David. 'Reasonable Partiality towards Compatriots'. *Ethical Theory and Moral Practice: An International Forum* 8, no. 1–2 (April 2005): 63–81.

Montero, Julio. 'Global Poverty, Human Rights and Correlative Duties'. *Canadian Journal of Law and Jurisprudence* 22, no. 1 (2009): 79–92.

Moravcsik, Andrew. 'The Origins of Human Rights Regimes: Democratic Delegation in Postwar Europe'. 54 *International Organization* (2000).

Nagel, Thomas. *The View From Nowhere.* New York: Oxford University Press, 1986.

Nolan, Aoife. 'Addressing Economic and Social Rights Violations by Non-State Actors through the Role of the State: A Comparison of Regional Approaches to the Obligation to Protect'. *Human Rights Law Review* 9 (2009): 2.

Nozick, Robert. *Anarchy, State, and Utopia.* New York: Basic Books, 1974.

O'Cinneide, Colm. 'Ireland: Irish Constitutional Law and Direct Horizontal Effect—A Successful Experiment?'. In Dawn Oliver and Jorg Fedtke, eds, *Human Rights and the Private Sphere: A Comparative Study.* New York: Routledge-Cavendish, 2007.

Oliver, Dawn. *Common Values and the Public–Private Divide.* London: Butterworths, 1999.

Oliver, Dawn, and Jorg Fedtke, eds. *Human Rights and the Private Sphere: A Comparative Study.* New York: Routledge-Cavendish, 2007.

'On the Margins of Profit'. Human Rights Watch, February 18, 2008. <http://www.hrw.org/en/reports/2008/02/18/margins-profit-0>.

O'Neill, Onora. 'Review: In a Starving World, What's the Moral Minimum?'. *The Hastings Center Report* 11, no. 6 (December 1981): 42–4.

O'Neill, Onora. *Towards Justice and Virtue: A Constructive Account of Practical Reasoning.* Cambridge: Cambridge University Press, 1996.

O'Neill, Onora. *Bounds of Justice.* Cambridge: Cambridge University Press, 2000.

O'Neill, Onora. 'The Dark Side of Human Rights'. *International Affairs* 81, no. 2 (2005): 427–39.

Parfit, Derek. *Reasons and Persons.* Oxford: Clarendon Press, 1984.

Paul, Jeffrey, ed. *Reading Nozick: Essays on Anarchy, State, and Utopia.* Totowa, New Jersey: Rowman & Littlefield, 1981.

Perry, Stephen R. 'Protected Interests and Undertakings in the Law of Negligence'. *The University of Toronto Law Journal* 42, no. 3 (Summer 1992): 247–317.

Perry, Stephen R. 'Two Models of Legal Principles'. 82 *Iowa Law Review* (1996–7): 801.
Pildes, Richard. 'Two Conceptions of Rights in Cases Involving Political "Rights"'. *Houston Law Review* 34 (1997): 323.
Pildes, Richard. 'Why Rights Are Not Trumps: Social Meanings, Expressive Harms, and Constitutionalism'. *Journal of Legal Studies* 27 (1998): 725.
Pildes, Richard. 'Dworkin's Two Conceptions of Rights'. *Journal of Legal Studies* 24 (January 2000): 309–16.
Pitts, Chip. 'The Drivers of CSR'. In *Corporate Social Responsibility: A Legal Analysis*. Lexisnexis, 2009, 33–52.
Pogge, Thomas Winfried Menko. *World Poverty and Human Rights: Cosmopolitan Responsibilities and Reforms*. Oxford: Polity, 2002.
Poole, Thomas. 'Dogmatic Liberalism? T. R. S. Allen and the Common Law Constitution,'. *The Modern Law Review* 65, no. 3 (2002): 463–75.
Poole, Thomas. 'Back to the Future? Unearthing the Theory of Common Law Constitutionalism'. *Oxford Journal of Legal Studies* 23, no. 3 (2003): 435–54.
Postema, G. J. 'Classical Common Law Jurisprudence (Part 1)'. *Oxford University Commonwealth Law Journal* 2 (2002): 155.
Postema, G. J. 'Classical Common Law Jurisprudence (Part 2)'. *Oxford University Commonwealth Law Journal* 3 (2002): 1.
Postow, B. C. 'Care Ethics and Impartial Reasons'. *Hypatia* 23, no. 1 (2008): 1–8.
Rainbolt, George W. *The Concept of Rights*. Dordrecht, The Netherlands: Springer, 2006.
Ratner, Steven R. 'Corporations and Human Rights: A Theory of Legal Responsibility'. *The Yale Law Journal* 111, no. 3 (2001): 443–545.
Rawls, John. 'The Idea of an Overlapping Consensus'. *Oxford Journal of Legal Studies* 7 (1987): 1.
Rawls, John. *The Law of Peoples, with 'The Idea of Public Reason Revisited'*. Cambridge, Massachusetts: Harvard University Press, 1999.
Rawls, John. *Justice as Fairness: A Restatement*. Cambridge, Massachusetts: The Belknap Press of Harvard University Press, 2001.
Raz, Joseph. 'The Rule of Law and its Virtue'. In *The Authority of Law: Essays on Law and Morality*. New York: Oxford University Press, 1979.
Raz, Joseph. 'On the Nature of Rights'. *Mind*, 93 (Apr. 1984): 194–214.
Raz, Joseph. *The Morality of Freedom*. Oxford: Clarendon Press, 1986.
Raz, Joseph. 'Human Rights without Foundations'. In Samantha Besson and John Tasioulas, eds, *The Philosophy of International Law*. Oxford: Oxford University Press, 2010, 321–37.
Reader, Soran. 'Distance, Relationship and Moral Obligation'. *Monist: An International Quarterly Journal of General Philosophical Inquiry* 86, no. 3 (July 2003): 367–81.
Réaume, Denise. 'Individuals, Groups, and Rights to Public Goods'. *University of Toronto Law Journal* 38 (1988): 1–27.
Reichman, Amnon. 'Property Rights, Public Policy, and the Limits of the Legal Power to Discriminate'. In *Human Rights in Private Law*. Portland, Oregon: Hart Publishing, 2001, 245–83.
Reichman, Amnon. 'A Charter-free Domain: in Defence of Dolphin Delivery'. *University of British Columbia Law Rev*iew 35 (2002): 329.
RIGHTNETWORK: All That's Right With the World, 'Company Overview' 8. <http://www.drumsandwhistles.com>.

Rishworth, P. 'Common law Rights and Navigation Lights: Judicial review and the New Zealand Bill of Rights'. *Public Law Review* 15 (2004): 103.

Ross, W. D. *The Right and the Good*. Oxford: Clarendon Press, 1930.

Rousseau, Jean-Jacques. *The Social Contract and the Discourses*. New York: A.A. Knopf, 1993.

Sajo, Andras, and Renata Uitz. *The Constitution in Private Relations: Expanding Constitutionalism*. Utrecht, The Netherlands: Eleven International Publishing, 2005.

Sassen, Saskia. *Losing Control? Sovereignty in an Age of Globalization*. New York: Columbia University Press, 1996.

Scanlon, John, Angela Cassar, and Noémi Nemes. *Water as a Human Right?* Gland, Switzerland: IUCN Publications, 2006.

Scheffler, Samuel. 'Relationships and Responsibilities'. *Philosophy and Public Affairs* 26 (1997): 189–209.

Sen, Amartya. 'The Right Not to Be Hungry'. In *The Right to Food*. International Studies in Human Rights. Netherlands: Martinus Nijhoff Publishers, 1984.

Sen, Amartya. 'Elements of a Theory of Human Rights'. *Philosophy and Public Affairs* 32, no. 4 (2004): 315–51.

Sen, Amartya Kumar, and Bernard Williams. *Utilitarianism and Beyond*. Cambridge UK; New York: Cambridge University Press, 1982.

Shiffrin, Seana Valentine. 'Are Credit Card Late Fees Unconstitutional?' *William and Mary Bill of Rights Journal* 15 (2006): 457.

Shue, Henry. *Basic Rights: Subsistence, Affluence, and U.S. Foreign Policy*. Princeton, New Jersey: Princeton University Press, 1980.

Shue, Henry. 'The Interdependence of Duties'. In *The Right to Food*. International Studies in Human Rights. Netherlands: Martinus Nijhoff Publishers, 1984.

Shue, Henry. 'Mediating Duties'. *Ethics* 98, no. 4 (1988): 687–704.

Sidgwick, Henry. *The Methods of Ethics*. 7th ed. Chicago: University of Chicago Press, 1962.

Singer, Joseph. 'The Legal Rights Debate in Analytic Jurisprudence from Bentham to Hohfeld'. *Wisconsin Law Review* 6 (1983): 975.

Singer, Peter. 'Famine, Affluence and Morality'. 1 *Philosophy and Public Affairs* 3 (Spring 1972): 229–42.

Simmonds, N. E. 'Rights at the Cutting Edge'. In *A Debate Over Rights: Philosophical Enquiries*. Oxford: Clarendon Press, 1998.

Sreenivasan, G. 'A Hybrid Theory of Claim-Rights,' 25 *Oxford Journal of Legal Studies* (2005): 257.

Starck, Christian. 'Human Rights and Private Law in German Constitutional Development and in the Jurisdiction of the Federal Constitutional Court'. In Daniel Friemann and Daphne Barak-Erez, eds, *Human Rights in Private Law*. Portland, Oregon: Hart Publishing, 2001.

Steiner, Hillel. *An Essay on Rights*. Oxford: Blackwell Publishing, 1994.

Steiner, Hillel. 'Working Rights'. In *A Debate Over Rights: Philosophical Enquiries*. Oxford: Clarendon Press, 1998.

Sumner, L. W. *The Moral Foundations of Rights*. Oxford: Clarendon Press, 1987.

Sunstein, Cass. *The Partial Constitution*. Cambridge: Harvard University Press, 1993.

Talbott, William. *Which Rights Should be Universal?* Oxford: Oxford University Press, 2005.

Tasioulas, John. 'Taking Rights out of Human Rights'. *Ethics* 120, no. 4 (2010): 647–78.

Taylor, Charles. 'The Conditions of an Unforced Consensus on Human Rights'. In *The Politics of Human Rights*. London: Verso, 1999.
Thomas, Alan. 'Reasonable Partiality and the Agent's Point of View'. *Ethical Theory and Moral Practice: An International Forum* 8, no. 1–2 (April 2005): 25–43.
Thomas, Jean. 'Which Interests Should Tort Protect?'. *Buffalo Law Review* 61 (2013): 1.
Thomson, Judith Jarvis. *The Realm of Rights*. Cambridge, Massachusetts: Harvard University Press, 1990.
Tushnet, Mark. 'An Essay on Rights'. *Texas Law Review* 62 (1984): 1363.
Tushnet, Mark. 'The Issue of State Action/Horizontal Effect in Comparative Constitutional Law'. *International Journal of Constitutional Law* 1 (2003): 79.
Tzeutschler. 'Corporate Violator: The Alien Tort Liability of Transnational Corporations for Human Rights Abuses Abroad'. *Columbia Human Rights Law Review* 30 (1999): 359.
UNCTAD, *World Investment Report 2007: Transnational Corporations, Extractive Industries and Development*. New York: United Nations, 2007 <http://www.unctad.org/en/docs/wir2007_en.pdf>.
Unger, Peter. *Living High and Letting Die: Our Illusion of Innocence*. Oxford: Oxford University Press, 1996.
Waldron, Jeremy. *Theories of Rights*. Oxford: Oxford University Press, 1984.
Waldron, Jeremy. *The Right to Private Property*. Oxford: Clarendon Press, 1988.
Waldron, Jeremy. 'When Justice Replaces Affection: the Need for Rights'. *Harvard Journal of Law and Public Policy* 11, no. Summer (1988): 625–47.
Waldron, Jeremy. 'Rights in Conflict'. In *Liberal Rights: Collected Papers, 1981–1991*. Cambridge: Cambridge University Press, 1993 .
Waldron, Jeremy. 'Pildes on Dworkin's Theory of Rights'. *The Journal of Legal Studies* 29, no. 1 (January 2000): 301–7.
Waldron, Jeremy. 'Who is My Neighbour: Humanity and Proximity'. *The Monist* 86, no. 3 (2003): 333–54.
Waldron, Jeremy. 'Nozick and Locke: Filling the Space of Rights'. *Social Philosophy and Policy* 25 (2005): 81–111.
Waldron, Jeremy. 'Foreign Law and the Modern *Ius Gentium*'. *Harvard Law Review* 119 (2005): 129.
Walters, M. D. 'The Common Law Constitution and Legal Cosmopolitanism'. In *The Unity of Public Law*. Oxford: Hart Publishing, 2004.
Webber, Grégoire. 'On the Loss of Rights.' In Grant Huscroft, Bradley W. Miller, and Grégroire Webber, eds, *Proportionality and the Rule of Law: Rights, Justification, Reasoning*. Cambridge: Cambridge University Press, 2014.
Weber, Max. *Sociological writings*. New York: Continuum, 1994.
Weinrib, Ernest J. *The Idea of Private Law*. Cambridge, Massachusetts: Harvard University Press, 1995.
Weissbrodt, David, and Maria Kruger. 'Norms on the Responsibilities of Transnational Corporations and other Business Enterprises with Regard to Human Rights'. *American Journal of International Law* 97 (2003): 901–22.
Wellman, Carl. *Real Rights*. New York: Oxford University Press, 1995.
Wellman, Carl. *The Proliferation of Rights: Moral Progress or Empty Rhetoric?* Boulder, Colorado: Westview Press, 1999.
Wenar, Leif. 'The Nature of Rights'. *Philosophy and Public Affairs* 33 (2005): 223.
Williams, Bernard. 'A Critique of Utilitarianism'. In *Utilitarianism: For and Against*. New York: Cambridge University Press, 1973.

Williams, Bernard. 'Persons, Character and Morality'. In *Moral Luck*. Cambridge: Cambridge University Press, 1981.

Wolf, Susan. 'Morality and Partiality'. *Philosophical Perspectives* 6, no. Ethics (1992): 243–59.

Wood, Stephen G., and Brett G. Scharffs. 'Applicability of Human Rights Standards to Private Corporations: An American Perspective'. *The American Journal of Comparative Law* 50 (2002): 531–66.

World Health Organization. *The Right To Water.* Health and Human Rights Publications, Series 3, 2003,<http://www.who.int/water_sanitation_health/en/righttowater.pdf>.

Index

www.ingramcontent.com/pod-product-compliance
Lightning Source LLC
LaVergne TN
LVHW011751200926
848484LV00003B/677
* 9 7 8 0 1 9 9 6 7 7 7 3 3 *